THE DISMAL SCIENCE

Stephen A. Marglin

The Dismal Science

How Thinking Like an Economist
Undermines Community

HARVARD UNIVERSITY PRESS

Cambridge, Massachusetts, and London, England   2008

Library of Congress Cataloging-in-Publication Data

Marglin, Stephen A.
   The dismal science : how thinking like an economist undermines community /
Stephen A. Marglin.
     p. cm.
   Includes bibliographical references and index.
   ISBN-13: 978-0-674-02654-4 (alk. paper)
   ISBN-10: 0-674-02654-3 (alk. paper)
   1. Economics—Sociological aspects. 2. Markets—Social aspects. 3. Economic
development—Social aspects. 4. Communities. 5. Social structure—Economic
aspects. I. Title. II. Title: Thinking like an economist undermines community.
HB724.M37   2007
306.3—dc22   2007020882

Lines from "The Capital," copyright 1938 by W. H. Auden, from *Collected Poems* by W. H. Auden.
Used by permission of Random House, Inc., and Faber and Faber Ltd.

Excerpt from *The Rock: A Pageant Play Book* by T. S. Eliot, copyright 1934 by Harcourt, Inc.,
and renewed 1962 by T. S. Eliot, reprinted by permission of Harcourt and Faber and Faber Ltd.

This book is for Jessie, with love

Contents

Preface

Although the word *development* does not figure very prominently, this book is my distillation of a quarter century of attempts to understand what is lost as economic development proceeds. Along the way that question became bound up with another one: what role does economics play in this loss? My answer is that what is lost is community. Many would agree but would blame—or credit—the modern state, which—starting with the French state that emerged from the 1789 Revolution—has been hostile to communities other than the imagined community of the nation (the phrase "imagined community" is Benedict Anderson's). I agree that the state must shoulder a good deal of the responsibility for the demise of community, but there is another cause. Markets subject to community discipline and control are one thing, but when markets become a sphere unto themselves, an autonomous system that regulates our lives, they join the state as the proximate cause of the community's demise.

Economics is the enabler; economics provides the justification for building a world based on markets. This world, our "developed world," has no place for community, except for national communities, and as globalization proceeds, less and less place for national communities as well.

I am the last of an anomalous generation of economists who came into the field between 1930 and 1960. Before that time, economics had been, to say the least, a market-friendly discipline, Marx and a few others being exceptions. The Great Depression temporarily changed matters by exposing the falsehood of a major tenet of received doctrine—that normally markets would work so as to provide a job for every willing worker. As a result, economic dogma became open to challenge as never before or since. A new kind of economist, sympathetic to the idea that markets have limits and that government can play a role in transcending those limits, was attracted to the discipline. Economics might further an agenda other than the agenda of unqualified endorsement of the market system. For some time after that, young people were attracted to economics by large questions, including the relationship between efficiency and equity, the poverty of some and the wealth of others, socialism versus capitalism.

Economics has since reverted to its market-friendly form with a vengeance. Since my own student days, graduate study in economics has focused more narrowly on technique, on making students ever more sophisticated in terms of mathematical ability. In the process, students are taught to put aside large questions, which inevitably take them beyond mathematics, in favor of smaller, more manageable problems. The narrowing of the economic mind has approached its inevitable limit: the present generation of economics students, I fear, doesn't even begin with large questions. Students' eyes are focused on the prize of career advancement from the get-go, and large questions would only get in the way.

If I was excited by a field of social inquiry that seemed to combine the possibility of practical relevance and rigorous theorizing, the scope for applying economics seemed diminished by its very successes. By 1959, the year I graduated from college, economic depression, the great laboratory for Franklin Roosevelt's economists and planners, was ancient history. The United States had solved its economic problems, or so my teachers told me: John Maynard Keynes's *General Theory of Employment, Interest and Money* had unlocked the secret to ever-expanding prosperity, and in the United States all that stood in the way of economic utopia were a few Republican politicians who still slept with pictures of Calvin Coolidge under their pillows. Europe was not far behind—though maybe the pictures under the pillows were different.

Development was the last frontier. I went to India to put the gospel of economic development into practice. My fellow missionaries and I lacked the religious temperament, but missionaries we were, bringing the promise of what Ashis Nandy has called secular salvation to the "Third World," a world as yet neither capitalist nor socialist but a battleground between the two economic systems. Indeed what attracted me to India in particular was its mix of commitments to both growth and an equitable distribution of income, which were to be achieved through governmental planning and control of the "commanding heights" of the economy, coupled with an equally strong commitment to democratic political institutions.

I arrived in Delhi in the spring of 1963 to join a team of advisors to the Planning Commission. I was puzzled by a debate that had engaged development experts from many disciplines: how to induce the peasants to adopt fertilizers, pesticides, and other technologies that, even before the Green Revolution reached the Indian subcontinent, promised dramatic increases in production and income. My question was rather: Why would the peasants *not* adopt these techniques? Were Indian peasants an affront to the logic of *homo economicus,* always on the lookout for ways to make himself better off? With the help of Raja Ram, a Delhi University graduate student from a farming family in Dhabi Kalan, a village about 150 miles northwest of Delhi, I arranged to visit Dhabi to see for myself whether the charge of economic irrationality was true. Were fertilizers and pesticides known to farmers? Were there profit opportunities that were ignored or resisted?

Serendipitously, the village provided a good setting for examining change—or the lack of change. Dhabi was situated at the end of the area serviced by the new Bhakra Dam, a multipurpose water-resources project designed to harness the irrigation and energy potential of one of the great rivers that flowed down from the Himalayas to the plains of Punjab. Irrigation allowed farmers to grow crops for which rainfall was inadequate: wheat and mustard in the winter season, long-staple cotton in the summer. But in and around Dhabi, the farmers' methods were no different from those used in rain-fed agriculture, where water was the limiting factor and chemicals irrelevant. Chemical fertilizer was known to local farmers (as "English manure") but was widely suspected of damaging the land; crop pesticides were unknown.

After some discussion, a small coterie of relatively educated and worldly landowners, centered around Raja Ram's family, was willing to try something new, and we agreed to experiment with new ways of growing winter wheat the next season. I would visit periodically to make sure that the farmers got accurate information and, more important, that they obtained the chemical inputs in a timely manner. Our interests were complementary. The farmers wanted to see whether the new agricultural techniques would increase production and income. I simply wanted to see what would happen: would they find the innovations easy to carry out? If successful—as I was confident they would be—would the new methods spread throughout the village and beyond?

But experiment with just how much and what kinds of fertilizer and pesticide? I didn't know, but I had access to the resources of the Ford Foundation, then in the midst of a program of technical and organizational assistance to farmers based on the American model of agricultural extension services. After some initial hesitation, based no doubt on an accurate assessment of the depths of my ignorance and inexperience, one of the Ford Foundation advisors agreed to give me a set of basic and foolproof recommendations to pass on to the Dhabi cultivators. I dutifully took note of a recommendation like "20-20-10," with no sense of what the numbers meant. Only later did I manage to figure out that this was standard terminology for fertilizer composition in terms of nitrogen, phosphorous, and potassium.

Somehow it all came out right. The recommendations improved wheat production markedly on the experimental plots, and other farmers became interested in what we were doing. There was even some diffusion of the technology, though it was not as rapid as I anticipated.

The farmers learned a profitable new technology, and I learned two ingredients for successful innovation, which, obvious as they might be, had escaped my understanding: first, that new ideas needed to come from a trustworthy source; and second, that some prior exposure to the larger world—service in the military or a stint in a high school some distance from home—predisposed the original innovators to different ways of believing, being, and acting in the world. In short, a partial restoration of my faith in economic logic: economic motives were part of the story but hardly the whole story.

Beyond answers to the question that had brought me to Dhabi, I learned something infinitely more valuable: an entirely different way of knowing and being in the world from anything I had ever imagined. Like all of us, I was a product of my culture; I had never questioned the idea that society was composed of self-interested individuals who rationally calculated their way to more and more. In Dhabi, I experienced something very different: not that people lacked all sense of self or of individual interests, not that people acted without rational deliberation, but that people lived their lives in deep connection with others—in short, in community. A human life was not conceived of as beginning at birth and ending with death, but as a link in a chain that extended backward to time immemorial and forward as far as the imagination might reach, as a link in a chain that existed in space as well as in time, connecting family, clan, and village.

The encounter with Dhabi Kalan had a profound impact on me and started me along a different path from the one to which my own upbringing, education, and culture, not to mention my chosen profession, had guided me. Although I didn't know it at the time, I was at the beginning of a long quest, of which this book is a product.

My awakening to cultural difference unfolded gradually. In my last stint as a missionary in 1967–1968, I served as visiting professor in a section of the Indian Statistical Institute attached to the Planning Commission in New Delhi. As part of my duties, I shared the teaching of an introductory graduate economics course for the eight or ten advanced statistics students who received part of their training at the Planning Commission unit. Sitting in on the course before my own part began, I was gratified by the high level of mathematical proficiency my co-instructor assumed of the students, well beyond the norm I was used to at my own institution back in the States. I prepared a very mathematical presentation.

As I got into the rhythm of teaching, I was pleased by how quickly and easily the students absorbed the math. It all seemed too good to be true. One day, perhaps inspired by John Kenneth Galbraith's *The New Industrial State*, with its incisive analysis of the disjuncture between economic theory and lived reality, I ventured beyond mathematics and asked my students questions designed to elicit how well they were absorbing the economics behind the math. The issue was how people make choices between consuming more now and consuming more later, dressed up in the form of intertemporal indifference maps. It quickly became apparent that the students hadn't a clue.

After getting over my anger and disappointment—first at the students and then at myself—I realized that for these students economics was just part of the game of graduate studies: those who did well went on to secure jobs and livelihoods, while those who did badly might have to settle for driving a cab. To do well meant mastering the mathematical formalism, not necessarily comprehending the underlying economics.

And then another thought dawned on me: there was no reason for these young Indians, bright as they were, to grasp a concept as alien to their own lives as the theory of intertemporal consumption choice. Chapter 7 of this book argues that even in the modern West, where standard economics at least resonates even if it does not adequately describe, people do not ordinarily use the economist's paradigm of choice to make intertemporal consumption decisions. Even less could it be expected that people steeped in a very different way of being and thinking would use the kind of apparatus imagined by the economist.

This teaching experience made me think about the cultural specificity of economic theory for the first time. I'm sure the political context heightened my awareness of the need to question received doctrine. We were at the height of the Vietnam War and the antiwar movement. And then came the assassination of Martin Luther King Jr. and, most important of all perhaps, May 1968, when the streets of Paris seemed—from the distance of Delhi at least—to offer one more chance to realize the potential that had first surfaced in 1789 and resurfaced in 1871. For a moment, France, and maybe the whole world, seemed poised on the brink of revolution. I began to reconsider various certainties, including the certainty that my fellow missionaries and I had something to offer despite our abysmal ignorance of the history and culture of the country we were proposing to transform, and our immunity, as birds of passage, to bearing the consequences of our advice.

I became an ex-missionary. As the 1960s came to an end, it was gradually emerging that there was more to the story of the United States and Western European economies than my teachers had fathomed. Maybe the modern West had not found in Keynesian economics a key to permanent prosperity, a key that would open the door to social and political stability. Maybe Neanderthal Republican politicians were not the only obstacle to permanent prosperity.

For the next decade, my research and teaching focused on issues that came out of the historical experience of the West, but in the late 1970s, the appointment of a free-market economist to the post of director of the Harvard Institute of International Development (HIID), an organization that advised Third World governments on development policy, became the occasion for a university-wide protest. The grounds for dissent varied: many, particularly students, opposed the man because of his prominent association with the government of Augusto Pinochet, the dictator of Chile; others, including many professionals within the HIID, objected to the narrow vision of development that the appointee would have brought to the organization, which had in recent years broadened its base to include sociologists and anthropologists. My own objections were closer to those of the HIID dissidents than to those of the students, but closeness to Pinochet and narrowness of vision were not unrelated.

In the course of the protest, I was asked on more than one occasion to state my own views on development. "It is well and good to be against Professor X, but what are you *for?*" That question abruptly brought me back into the development arena. It was easy enough to argue the necessity of going beyond efficiency, of doing something more than "getting prices right," of paying attention to the distribution of income. "Trickle down" was never going to do enough for the people at the bottom. But what else? I had an intuitive sense that economic development dissolved the glue that held families like Raja Ram's together, not to mention the glue that kept a village like Dhabi together. But what was that glue? And, more important, was there inevitably a tradeoff between material prosperity and maintaining the cultural integrity of the family or village? And is cultural integrity necessarily a good thing if this involves, as it did in Dhabi, the subordination of women (particularly of young women), untouchability, and large disparities in income and wealth? Does cultural integrity require that every custom, every tradition, be maintained? How much can a culture change without losing its identity? And how and why does that identity matter? I have been searching for answers to these questions for more than twenty-five years.

In this search, the perspective of Frédérique Apffel-Marglin, a cultural anthropologist, has been an important counterweight to my own perspective as an economist. (In addition, we share a common interest in four children, an expanding number of grandchildren, three horses, one dog, and a variable number of cats, not to mention a large garden and a small orchard.) During the 1980s, the two of us organized an interdisciplinary group under the auspices of the World Institute of Development Economics Research (WIDER), a training and research arm of the United Nations University located in Helsinki. The WIDER group sought to understand the connection between Westernization and modernization, the better to open up space for those who were looking for alternatives. Many people participated in our deliberations and in the various books that came out of our seminars and research (including Apffel-Marglin and Marglin 1990, 1996; Banuri and Apffel-Marglin 1993).

In addition to Apffel-Marglin, Tariq Banuri and Ashis Nandy have had a disproportionate impact on my intellectual growth. I should also recognize the benefits of arguing at great length with Amartya Sen, whose views were and remain strongly opposed to my own but whose force of intellect and conviction on these matters sharpened my thinking considerably.

My next most important debt is to my students, both graduate students and students in an undergraduate social studies seminar on development and modernization. Franck Amalric, David Grewal, Sanjay Reddy, and Patrick Toomey were particularly helpful, but many others, too many to list, shaped my thinking with their questions and observations. My colleagues in the Harvard Economics Department, Ben Friedman and Jerry Green, read parts of the manuscript and provided helpful comments. So did Blair Hoxby of the

Stanford English Department. David Colander of the Economics Department of Middlebury College and David Ruccio of the Economics Department of Notre Dame alerted me to the centrifugal forces at play in an early draft of this book, and Colander was particularly helpful on how to sharpen the focus. Jay Garfield of the Philosophy Department of Smith College helped me to sort out agency and obligation in tragic choices. Bruce Ecker gave me the perspective of an intelligent and interested layperson, which led me to revise the argument to make it more intelligible to those with little or no background in economics. Ira Raja, daughter of Raja Ram, has gently prodded me on the negatives of community. Gilles Raveaud, fellow-traveler on the path to a new economics, has made me acutely aware of how even within the West, differences in culture and history inform the meaning and moral valence of community. Mike Aronson, senior editor for social sciences at Harvard University Press, has been an extremely supportive advocate and at the same time a perceptive critic. This is a better book because of him. Jane Trahan assisted in the preparation of the manuscript, not only in the sometimes dreary if not dismal mechanics, but also in suggestions for clarifying the argument.

My younger daughter, Jessica Marglin, read large parts of the manuscript not once, but twice, and made valuable comments, including—at a point when I naively imagined that I was almost done—a tactful warning that the book needed substantial revision if I was serious in my intention to connect with an audience beyond the academy. Time will tell whether I responded sufficiently to reach that larger audience. In addition, Jessie endured the not-ready-for-prime-time first version of an introductory course in economics that incorporated my critique of the foundational assumptions of the discipline. She (and other students in the first and successive versions of that course) have without any doubt improved the argument.

My thanks to all these people. We may not be a community in any meaningful sense of the word, except for the affinity I feel for them and their necessity to my project.

CHAPTER 1

Economics, the Market, and Community

The first-century Jewish sage Hillel asked, "If I am not for myself, who will be? And if I am only for myself, what am I? And if not now, when?" (*Pirkei Avot* [Ethics of the Fathers] 1:14, in Harlow 1989, 607). The claims of the individual and the claims of the community conflict. And not a bad thing: this tension is normal, healthy, and even creative. It should not be resolved once and for all in favor of either the individual or the community. But over the past four hundred years, the ideology of economics has fostered both the self-interested individual and the market system, and has undermined, and continues to undermine, the community. This book analyzes how this has happened.

In 1990, a boy with adenosine deaminase (ADA) deficiency was born into an Amish community. ADA deficiency compromises the body's immune system so drastically that survival beyond the age of three used to be quite rare. A related immune deficiency compelled another boy, David Vetter, born almost twenty years earlier, to spend the entire twelve years of his life in a confined environment specially designed to keep out chance infections. David, the subject of the John Travolta movie *The Boy in the Plastic Bubble*, succumbed when a bone-marrow transplant designed to supply the missing enzyme went awry, but for the Amish boy a drug was available to compensate for his body's immune deficiency. Taking this drug, he could hope for a fairly normal life, not unlike the life led by diabetics on insulin. And because the family income was sufficiently low, Medicaid would pay the costs, staggering though these were. The drug alone cost $114,000 per year, and additional costs would bring the annual total up to $190,000.

Happy ending? Not so fast. On principle, most Amish do not participate in government programs like Medicaid. If this money was to be spent on the boy, it would have to come from the community. But medication was not a short-term fix. The expenditure would go on indefinitely, and there was too little experience with the drug to predict its long-term consequences. Even with the drug, the boy might or might not make it into adulthood.

Anguished, his parents consulted the bishop and elders of their congregation. The newspaper reports (Drake 1991a, b) are ambiguous, but my reading is that the congregation would provide counsel, and, having done so, would leave the decision to the parents. The alternatives were clear: once Medicaid was eliminated from the menu of options, the choice boiled down to almost certain death for the child or economic stress, maybe even disaster, for the community.

The couple did not treat their baby. Three months later he was dead.

A local (non-Amish) physician who was asked by the congregation to evaluate treatment options offered this commentary: "What is at stake is the ability to maintain an independent culture." When asked why he would not accept Medicaid, the boy's father put it like this: "If we take money from the government, then we are not Amish."

What Does This Have to Do with Economics?

Community is evidently so important for the Amish that its members would allow a child to die for its sake. This book argues that the market bears a large share of the responsibility for eroding this kind of community, for undermining the centrality of community in our lives. By "the market" I mean something different from the variety of markets that have been with us since time out of mind and exist in virtually all societies, certainly including the Amish. I mean, with Karl Polanyi (1944), a self-regulating market *system*, a world in which markets collectively allocate resources, set prices, determine the distribution of income—in short, a system in which markets provide for our needs and wants and from which we derive our sustenance. And something more: a system that not only regulates itself but also regulates ourselves, a process that shapes and forms people whose relationships with one another are circumscribed and reduced by the market.

Even granting provisionally—stipulating, as the lawyers say—that *markets* are somehow destructive of community, does it not confuse the messenger with the message to lay the blame on *economists?* Economists may not grasp the way the Amish—or others at odds with the self-interested, calculating individual—approach life, but this lack of comprehension is a far cry from actively undermining community. The charge is especially hard to square with the self-image of economists as possessing a discipline primarily concerned with telling it like it is. In the economists' view, "positive economics" is a purely descriptive endeavor logically distinct from its normative adjunct, "welfare economics," the part of economics that is concerned with evaluation as a preliminary to making policy prescriptions.

I am not confusing the messenger with the message: economics is an accessory, both before and after the fact. Surveys conducted by sociologists Gerald Marwell and Ruth Ames (1981) and experiments undertaken by economist Robert Frank in collaboration with psychologists Thomas Gilovich and Dennis Regan (1993) support the idea that studying economics is associated with less cooperative, less other-regarding behavior (but see Yezer et al. 1996 for evidence and argument to the contrary). It is not difficult to see why: economics celebrates the self-interested, calculating individual and the market as a means of realizing individual satisfactions, and this celebration is important in overcoming opposition to extending the sway of the market and, by the same token, undermining community. Economics is not only descriptive; it is not only evaluative; it is at the same time constructive—economists seek to fashion a world in the image of economic theory.

The problem with the idea that economics is purely, or even primarily, a descriptive undertaking is that the apparatus of economics has been shaped by an agenda focused on showing that markets are good for people rather than on discovering how markets actually work. And from this normative perspective has come the constructive agenda. If you believe that economics is or should be about describing the world, then it is a case of the tail wagging the dog. If you believe, as I do, that the normative agenda has been central to economics from well before Adam Smith's time, then it is more understandable why the apparatus of economics is built on foundations that undermine community. Undermining community is the logical and practical consequence of promoting the market system.

This much is certain: if all we economists cared about was describing the world, we could easily forgo much of the framework that I find problematic. Take one of the most basic tools of economic analysis, demand. If we did not care about drawing conclusions about how well markets work, as distinct from how markets actually work, we could start directly from the demand curve rather than basing demand on choices made by rational, calculating, self-interested individuals. We do not take demand as the starting point because it would then be impossible to argue that—subject to some fine and not so fine print—a system of markets maximizes welfare.

In making this argument, economics relies on value judgments implicit in foundational assumptions about the self-interested individual, about rational calculation, about unlimited wants, and about the nation-state, and it is these assumptions that make community invisible. In arguing for the market, economics legitimizes the destruction of community and thus helps to construct a world in which community struggles for survival.

To be sure, on the other side of the ledger, markets can be credited with promoting economic growth, and it is undeniable that much good has come with growth (longer lives, less physical discomfort and even less pain, better nutrition, less hard physical toil, to mention only a few of the positives of growth). My argument with my fellow economists is not that they strike a different balance with respect to the gains and the losses of extending the sway of markets; it is that they do not recognize the losses at all. If communities are once again to flourish, then we will have to address the failures of a social order based on markets, and not just applaud its successes. Poverty makes growth necessary for much of the world—Mohandas Karamchand Gandhi, the Mahatma, once wrote that if God wanted a warm reception from the Indian masses, He would be well advised to appear in the form of a loaf of bread (Gandhi 1931). By contrast, we who live in rich countries, awash in goods and services, have no such compelling argument. Indeed, we may have good reason to dismantle the engine of growth—not because growth is a threat to our relationship with nature,[1] but because it is a threat to our relationships with one another.

Economists may respond by disclaiming interest in, along with responsibility for, community, leaving the inquiry to sociologists, anthropologists, and historians. The problem is that the foundational assumptions of economics not only make community invisible; these assumptions also limit the ability of economists to understand the parts of the world in which we must perforce take an interest. An economist need not care about community, but it is harder to avoid such issues as the determinants of saving and investment, or the role of the distribution of income in assessing economic outcomes, or even in addressing the question of why markets are good for people. In all of these areas, the foundations of the discipline not only undermine community; they undermine economic analysis.

I will be accused of setting up a straw man, an "economics" so drastically simplified and out of date that it caricatures the breadth and depth of the intellectual enterprise of contemporary economics. I have two responses. The first is that the enterprise of economics is better characterized by the content of elementary texts than by what goes on at the frontiers of economic theory. A perusal of leading texts leaves no doubt as to the core message: markets are good for people. This is a message found not only in what might be termed a conservative text, Gregory Mankiw's *Principles of Economics*—which it may be noted is the largest selling text—but also in more nuanced form in texts written by leading liberal economists (Baumol and Blinder 2003; Krugman and Wells 2005).

Second, even at the frontiers, there is little questioning of the foundational assumptions of economics; for the most part, criticism focuses on issues outlined in Appendix A, issues of the structure of markets, goods, and information. The exception is the recent flurry of research activity in so-called behavioral economics. If the research agenda of behavioral economics were to be carried through unflinchingly, the results might well be devastating for the self-interested, utility-maximizing individual who has had the leading role in economics since its emergence as a separate discipline from more general inquiry in ethics, statecraft, political philosophy, and the like. But so far, as is made clear in the introduction to *Advances in Behavioral Economics* (Camerer et al. 2004), behavioral economists typically do no more than "modify one or two assumptions in standard theory in the direction of greater psychological realism" (Camerer and Lowenstein 2004, 3). Clearly the goal is not to provide an alternative normative and constructive agenda, or behavioral economists would not show so much deference to the need to save the appearances of mainstream theory. Judging from *Advances in Behavioral Economics*, which brings together some of the most important contributions to this field, behavioral economists seem almost desperate to fit their subversive conclusions into a utility-maximizing framework of calculation, the sine qua non of professional respectability, even while recognizing nonrational elements in the calculations.[2]

While there is in my view a well-established church of economics, there is no high priest, no final arbiter of what constitutes economics, much less a final arbiter of what constitute the assumptions of economics. My characterization necessarily involves a subjective element; it is my reading of the center of gravity of a field with a gamut of practitioners and practices. The characterization of the foundational assumptions in this book is my attempt to infer a coherent basis for this center or core. I have been urged to recognize the variety within economics by some qualification such as "mainstream" or "standard" or "neoclassical." I generally resist the advice not only because it is tedious always to qualify, but because, notwithstanding the variety, the mainstream, in my view, is so dominant that the other streams have become mere trickles. If we focus on what is taught in the typical principles course, or on the entire undergraduate curriculum, or even on the content of graduate theory courses, I think there is a consensus, and it is this consensus to which the term *economics* refers in this book. It is this consensus that makes the community disappear from economic analysis and that aids and abets the market as it undermines community.

Two books, one written a half century ago, the other just a few years old, deserve attention in thinking about the relationship between the market and community—not for what they say about this relationship, but for the glaring omission from what are otherwise probing accounts of, on the one hand, the demise of community and, on the other, the limits, as well as the strengths, of the market.

The first is Robert Nisbet's *The Quest for Community*. Nisbet, writing in the dark mid-twentieth-century days after the defeat of one form of totalitarian government and the beginning of a long Cold War against another, was particularly concerned with how Nazi Germany and Communist Russia manipulated people's yearning for community to institute the most repressive societies that Europe had ever known. His argument is that individualism destroys community, but the search for community remains unabated. The modern state rushes in to fill the gap, not only providing the material succor that community previously did, but offering meaning and purpose to individuals as members of a national community. This, for Nisbet, is a generic process of modernity; it is simply taken to an extreme by the totalitarian Right and Left.

This is a striking account, and I believe it offers an important perspective on the demise of community. But the most surprising aspect of Nisbet's argument in the lens of this book is how little attention is paid to the market. For Nisbet, a market system is not part of the problem because markets work only with the support of community-based institutions:

> There has never been a time when a successful economic system has rested upon purely individualistic drives or upon the impersonal relationships so prized by the rationalists [by "rationalists" Nisbet means the disciples of the Enlightenment]. There are always, in fact, associations and incentives nourished by the non-economic processes of kinship, religion, and various other forms of social relationships. (Nisbet 1990 [1953], 212–213)

The failure of the market to accommodate the needs of community provides just one more excuse for state intrusion (Nisbet 1990 [1953], 215).

Nisbet is surely right that, from its own point of view, the modern nation-state has reasons for eyeing local communities with suspicion and acting accordingly (see Chapter 10). But the state is not the only culprit. The market, too, this book argues, bears responsibility for the destruction of community. Indeed, state and market often work hand in glove, as the example of the North American Free Trade Agreement (NAFTA), which we shall examine momentarily, makes abundantly clear. There is no reason to choose between Nisbet's emphasis on the state and this book's emphasis on the market.

John McMillan's *Reinventing the Bazaar* is the second book that provides a window on the relationship between market and community. McMillan is an enthusiast of the market, but he is scrupulously attentive to various causes of market failure. Missing—even as markets are missing from Nisbet's study—is any attention to community and, in particular, to the corrosive effect of markets on communities. Not surprising, since McMillan operates strictly within mainstream economics. Even within this relatively narrow framework, there are many possible reasons why there might be losses that outweigh the mutual gains of economic agents operating in markets; McMillan explores these reasons with clarity and wit.

In Appendix A, I set out my own version of these reasons in a critique of what I call the structural assumptions of economics. This critique looks, for example, to what in the jargon are called "externalities," unintended by-products of an exchange that fall on third parties. If Mr. A gives Ms. B heroin in exchange for sex, the economist will have a relatively easy time showing why this trade might be undesirable despite the wishes of the two participants. Providing heroin to Ms. B contributes to an addiction, and Ms. B might in the future rob or kill in order to satisfy her craving. The effects on Ms. B's victims, externalities of the original transaction, would swamp the benefits that Mr. A and Ms. B derived from the original exchange.

The structural critique is not limited to externalities. Welfare economics recognizes that the normative claim for the market requires not just any system of markets, but a system of *competitive* markets, a system of markets in which there are so many players that no single agent has any economic power. Prostitution, especially where it is illegal, hardly fits the model of the competitive market, but then neither do most markets, as we shall see in Appendix A.

The normative claims for the market also preclude information asymmetries. It is not that agents have to be fully informed, but, even on the narrowest efficiency grounds, the market can be improved upon in situations where some agents know more about the goods and services on offer than do other agents. Presumably both prostitutes and their clients know much more about their own health, and specifically whether they are carriers of sexually transmitted diseases, than they know about each other's health. But again, information asymmetries are hardly peculiar to sex markets.

There are thus many arguments against a market in sexual services based on a critique purely internal to economics. And in this respect, the only peculiarity of prostitution is that the externalities may be more important, the monopoly element more pronounced, and the consequences of asymmetric information more serious than in other markets.

So why do we need to look for other critiques? My answer is that the structural critique does not question the logic of markets. It looks instead to making markets work better. Externalities? Internalize the externalities by creating new rights and claims and new markets in which these rights and claims are traded. If the problem is heroin addiction, legalize this and other hard drugs to bring street prices down to a level that eliminates the incentive to crime. Too few sellers? Open up the market by legalizing prostitution and perhaps by propaganda to reduce the stigma associated with the sex trade. Information asymmetries? Introduce regulations to insure full disclosure of all relevant information about one's health status, at least with respect to potentially lethal infections like HIV. In short, create new markets to solve the problems of markets.

This is the fundamental difference between the foundational and the structural critiques. The economist's faith in the market relies not only on a belief that market imperfections do not matter, either because they are small and intrinsically unimportant, or because they can be overcome by new and improved markets. The economist also relies, explicitly or, more usually, implicitly, on foundational assumptions about economic agents themselves: that agents rationally calculate their individual self-interest in ever more consumption, free of ties to any community save the community of the nation. Drop these foundational assumptions and willing buyer and willing seller carry much less weight, and the damage to human relationships from markets cannot be repaired by more markets.

The point is not that there is no case to be made for the market, even a market in sexual services. It is rather that the foundational assumptions of economics preclude a searching investigation of the limits of markets. Markets for sexual services, or for body parts, surrogate motherhood, and the like, dramatize the problem, but the corrosive effects of markets are not limited to these extreme cases. What limits should be placed on markets for the sake of community? In place of such an investigation, economics substitutes a mantra of market freedom based on assumptions of dubious merit, whether considered as facts about people or ethical norms.

In adopting a particularly extreme form of individualism, in abstracting knowledge from context, in limiting community to the nation, and in positing boundless consumption as the goal of life, economics offers us no way of thinking about the human relationships that are the heart and soul of community other than as instrumental to the individual pursuit of happiness. Economics takes very much to heart the famous dictum of the nineteenth-century physicist Lord Kelvin that we know only what we can measure.[3] Indeed, economics takes the dictum a step further, from epistemology to ontology: what we can't measure—entities like community—doesn't exist.

How the Market Undermines Community

If economics is an accomplice of the market, how does the market undermine community? NAFTA provides examples. NAFTA is in the news off and on, but around the occasion of its tenth anniversary on January 1, 2004, there was an understandable spike in media attention. The first story I heard was one on public radio about how consumers on both sides of the border benefit from the expansion of trade between the United States and Mexico.

Tom Fullerton, an economics professor at the University of Texas at El Paso, literally walks the reporter through the benefits of trade, taking him through supermarkets on both sides of the border. Consumers in El Paso, on the Texas side, benefit from being able to buy "a Mexican soft drink that comes in pineapple, lime, tutti-frutti and tangerine . . . flavors that are not typically available from U.S. manufacturers" (Marketplace Morning Report 2003). There are also "tortilla chips imported from Nuevo Leon, Mexico."

But the benefits of trade are not limited to the U.S. side of the border; trade, after all, works both ways. In Ciudad Juarez, on the other side, the reporter is shown "four different varieties of Minute Maid orange juice . . . comparable to what's observed in the United States." And in the deli section, "the imported Oscar Mayer sliced ham cost about $3."

"A similar Mexican product sells for half as much," the reporter observes, "so how can the expensive import compete?" The professor has a quick response: "U.S. products enjoy an excellent quality reputation south of the border. Mexican consumers flock to U.S.-produced goods because of the reputation for consistent quality." Or is it that in a world of relative wants, Oscar Mayer ham has a cachet that Mexican products cannot match? I remember years ago in India seeing whole peppercorns for sale in the small jars we see in this country at supermarkets—an American brand at an exorbitant price. In India, pepper and other spices and condiments were and still are sold out of bins that fill the shop with an array of smells and colors. I asked the shopkeeper how he could hope to sell these jars, seeing that the pepper was most likely produced in India, exported to the United States, packaged there, and reimported for embassy personnel or other foreign nationals. His response was revealing: "no problem, sir; as long as it has a foreign label, we can sell anything—even Indian pepper."[4]

Benefits to consumers are only part of the deal. NAFTA and other trade liberalization projects are touted—and attacked—for what they do for jobs. NAFTA did create jobs, but it also destroyed jobs. And when these jobs were in plants on which whole communities depended, the results could be devastating. In theory, the beneficiaries, consumers who now can drink tutti-frutti soda as well as workers who find better jobs, should be able to compensate the losers. But in practice, compensation is not forthcoming. And how, anyway, do you compensate somebody for the destruction of the community in which she grew up, is raising a family, and hopes one day to retire and look after her grandchildren?

Think Illinois and Ohio; think Indiana. Think manufacturing companies in small towns. An article published at the end of 2003 (Weiner 2003, originally published in *The New York Times*) described the effects of trade liberalization and outsourcing in these terms:

> "We're the losers," said Bonnie Long, one of at least half a million American manufacturing workers who lost their jobs due to Nafta, despite the surge in trade. "We lost our health care, our living wages. The winners are the corporate executives who don't even live here and can locate their factories wherever they find the cheapest labor." . . . Thousands of towns across the nation . . . have seen jobs and health benefits disappear with the accord.

What is also disappearing is a way of life in Goshen, home to 30,000 people [including Bonnie Long] and the seat of Elkhart County in northern Indiana. The town once lived by making things. . . .

Half of Elkhart County depends on manufacturing. Once dozens of locally owned factories across the state churned out parts for all sorts of products, electronics, pharmaceuticals, furniture, pianos and especially for the automotive industry.

Even before Nafta those jobs were facing growing pressure from emerging low-wage competitors abroad. Since Nafta took hold, hundreds more jobs have gone south to Mexico, transplanted by big corporations that bought out local firms. Chinese competition is intensifying the losses.

"We've traded high-skill jobs for low-skill jobs, and the trend has worsened over the last four years," said Bill Johnson. He sold his family's business, Goshen Rubber Company to a multinational corporation, Parker Hannifin, in 2000.

Compare Goshen Rubber Company, a division of a multinational, with a firm owned by a local family:

Gerald A. Trolz [is] a local hero because he would not sell or relocate Goshen Stamping, his small hardware manufacturing firm, even after his main customer moved to Mexico and half his sales went with it.

He said the only reason he has been able to keep his firm in Goshen is that he owns it: he does not answer to stockholders. "The experts don't see what's happening here, on the shop floor, so it's easy for them to say that Nafta was good or bad," Mr. Trolz said. "Until this levels out, it is just plain havoc." (Weiner 2003, originally published in *The New York Times*)

This echoes a piece that ran in the *Wall Street Journal* a few years earlier about the difference between local and absentee businesses. The article focused on the relationship between a family meatpacking business, Dewig Meats, and the hog farmers in an Indiana community (Quintanilla, 1999). Here's the takeaway:

"It was difficult," says Mr. Dewig, as he recalls the family's deliberations over how to deal with local farmers when the hog business first fell out of bed. "Prices were an absolute bargain, but we also had to know in the back of our head that if we weren't fair, we'd end up paying for it."

This isn't the kind of thing that much troubles a big, publicly held company. It is different when, as Mr. Dewig says, "I've got to live with these people."

You will note that Mr. Dewig explains his actions in terms of self-interest, not benevolence. Adam Smith may have been on to something when he pointed out that it is not to the benevolence of the butcher that we look for our meat to be provided—we appeal to his interest rather than to the goodness of his heart. All the more reason why we have to be careful how we structure our institutions, our economic institutions in particular, so that they serve, not undermine, our basic values. (Of course, you can read Mr. Dewig as justifying his actions in the only idiom acceptable to modernity, even though benevolence is as much a factor as self-interest.)

The real devastation of NAFTA has occurred not in the United States, but in Mexico. Don't take my word for it: here is what *BusinessWeek* said in its (mostly positive) evaluation of the effects of ten years of NAFTA on the Mexican economy:

> The agriculture sector is still reeling from the competitive shock of NAFTA. One consequence was the virtual wipeout of Mexico's small farmers by a flood of subsidized U.S. food imports. Some 1.3 million farm jobs have disappeared since 1993, according to a new report by the Carnegie Endowment for International Peace, a Washington think tank. [1.3 million jobs, I might add, swamps the creation of manufacturing jobs in Mexico over the same period.] "NAFTA has been a disaster for us," complains Julián Aguilera, a pig farmer from the northern state of Sonora. He and 800 of his peers have staged several big demonstrations to protest a 726% increase in U.S. pork imports since the agreement took effect. "Mexico was never prepared for this," says Aguilera, who has been raising pigs for 28 years, just like his father before him.
>
> Nor was the U.S. As the *campesinos* lost their livelihood, they headed to the border. By most estimates the number of Mexicans working illegally in the U.S. more than doubled, to 4.8 million between 1990 and 2000. Despite tightened security along the 3,200-km border in the wake of September 11, hundreds of thousands of Mexicans continue to risk life and limb each year to reach America. The money they send back to their families will total $14 billion this year, more than the $10 billion or so in foreign direct investment Mexico expects to receive in 2003.

The mass migration has turned rural hamlets into ghost towns. Tiny farm plots lie fallow, their modest adobe farmhouses shuttered. The owners have gone to "el otro lado," the other side [emphasis added]. Panindícuaro in Michoacán, one of Mexico's poorest states, has one [of] the highest incidences of migration: State officials figure that one out [of] every seven people leaves for the U.S. Panindícuaro's parish priest, Melesio Farías, recently held a funeral mass for a father in his mid-thirties who died trying to cross the Arizona desert. "I tell them to forget the U.S. and to work at home," says Farías. "But if Mexico can't offer them jobs, why should they stay here and live in poverty?" (Smith and Linblad 2003)

All this was predictable. Indeed, it was predicted. In the days leading up to the Senate vote on NAFTA, I tried to get an op-ed piece published on the likely effects of the treaty on Mexican peasant communities. Not one newspaper was interested in publishing the piece, and I'm not speaking here of the *New York Times* and the *Wall Street Journal,* but of regional papers, many of them in agricultural states where one might have expected at least some interest in the plight of fellow farmers on the other side of the border.

But, again, don't take my word for it. Here's what a *New York Times* reporter had to say early in 2003: "Mexican officials say openly that they long ago concluded that small agriculture was inefficient, and that the solution for farmers was to find other work. 'The government's solution for the problems of the countryside is to get *campesinos* to stop being *campesinos,*' says Victor Suárez, a leader of a coalition of small farmers" (Rosenberg 2003).

So the devastation of Mexican villages didn't just happen; it wasn't just collateral damage of the market system. It was a deliberate strategy for what might be described as bringing the Mexican peasant into the twenty-first century—kicking and screaming if necessary. It was a clear case of the state using the market for political and social as well as economic ends—in this case, the ends of an urban elite sure in its conviction that it knew best about what was good for the millions living in the Mexican countryside. How's that for the winners compensating the losers?

Even if somehow everybody were to gain as an individual, markets still undermine communities. The paradox is that people gain in one dimension, the economic, but lose in others. Only economists insist that the gains and losses can be tallied on a single scale (E. Anderson 1993, 141–167).

In a word, markets are the cutting edge of the loss of human connection. Economists see this as a virtue. Impersonal markets accomplish more efficiently what the connections of social solidarity, reciprocity, and other redistributive institutions do in nonmarket societies. Take fire insurance. I pay a premium of, say, $200 per year, and if my barn burns down, the insurance company pays me $60,000 to rebuild it. A simple market transaction has replaced the more cumbersome process of gathering my neighbors for a barn raising. In terms of building barns with a minimal expenditure of resources, insurance may indeed be more efficient than gathering the community each time somebody's barn burns down. But in terms of maintaining the community, insurance is woefully lacking. Barn raisings fostered mutual interdependence: in earlier times, I would have had to rely on my neighbors economically as well as in other ways, and they on me.

Fire insurance originated in England in the wake of the Great London fire of 1666 (Richard 1956, 13) and spread to the Continent and North America over the course of the next century. Before then, what the historian Michèle Ruffat notes for France was undoubtedly true elsewhere: fire and its consequences were the province of mutual assistance based in the local community. Like other community-based institutions, these mutual assistance organizations relied on the individual's regard for both self and others, with the monitoring available to community-based organizations an important antidote to the moral hazard inherent in providing relief for the consequences of a (partially) controllable event such as fire (Ruffat 2003, 187–188).

Like fire insurance, life insurance and health insurance were originally embedded in community, and the evolution of insuring human beings is particularly instructive. In medieval and early modern Europe, guilds provided assistance to members who had fallen on hard times as well as to widows and children of members who had died. Confraternities were religious devotional societies but also much more: they provided care in sickness and death, and indeed beyond the grave, providing funds to say masses that would ease the passage of the departed through purgatory (Flynn 1989; Black 1989).

Insurance, particularly for the confraternities, was closely allied to charity. Members' claims took precedence, but most confraternities extended material as well as spiritual support to the poor of their communities as well as to their own members. Although looking back we can easily identify mutual insurance as a separate and distinct reason for confraternities, in the premodern European setting, insurance, charity, and spiritual consolation were all of

a piece. And though it might strike the modern mind as odd that death benefits would include insuring the progress of the soul out of purgatory, it would
have struck the medieval mind as odd to separate insurance for the here-and-
now from insurance for the hereafter.

The first commercial life-insurance policy issued in England, at least the
first for which a record survives, dates from 1583 (Clark 1999, 18). But for
both technical and moral reasons, it took a long time for this market to
take hold. The technical problems concerned both the statistical inade-
quacy of mortality data and the limited understanding of actuarial risk.
The moral problem was precisely the substitution of commerce for the community's compassion. The moral point was put succinctly by the Count of
Mirabeau, one of the leaders to emerge from the cauldron of revolution in
France and, for a short period in 1791, president of the National Assembly,
a body not noteworthy for a preoccupation either with community or
with compassion: "Insurance," according to Mirabeau, "substitutes the
service of calculation for the service of humanity and causes the disap-
pearance of a general sensitivity, which is one of the bases of society."[5]
Shortly thereafter, in 1793, the Convention, successor to the National
Assembly, ended the short-lived experiment with commercial life insurance that had begun in the last days of the ancien régime. (When mari-
time insurance was legalized in France in 1681, other forms of insurance,
especially life insurance, were prohibited for both moral and practical
reasons.)

In the nineteenth century, so-called friendly societies competed with the
nascent life-insurance industry for the pennies and shillings of the English
workingman. The friendly societies could not offer the same actuarial security as large insurance companies, like the Prudential, founded in 1853, but
the friendly societies offered something else, a sense of belonging that
counteracted the progressive loss of community characteristic of the age.
Meetings, feasts, ritual—all combined to recreate something of what the
confraternity had provided in an earlier age.

Over time, this approach lost out decisively to the insurance companies, and
eventually to governmental provision of social security, both in Great Britain
and in the United States. The story is a complicated one, but a chief reason was
the inability of the friendly societies to regenerate themselves. Once cut loose
from moral ties to their communities, it became increasingly difficult for societies with large numbers of older members to recruit from among the younger

generation. When the moral calculus of cross-generational redistribution was replaced by a calculus of individual self-interest, it no longer made sense for a young man to take on the financial burden of sustaining the elderly (Gosden 1973, 17).

As the nineteenth century unfolded, lodges affiliated with national fraternal orders replaced independent local organizations. These fraternal orders continued to offer a combination of fellowship, ritual, and insurance, but were in practice even less embedded in community than the local friendly societies they replaced.

In Britain, the enactment of compulsory health insurance in 1911 changed the playing field dramatically. It brought the fraternal orders and the insurance companies into direct competition. Until then, the fraternal orders had specialized in health insurance, while the insurance companies had provided a rudimentary life insurance, generally enough to provide a decent burial, which is to say, enough both to avoid a pauper's grave and to permit some degree of display by the bereaved widow or widower (or, for that matter, parents: it was common practice to insure the lives of one's offspring so that a child's death would not be a financial as well as an emotional burden). To maintain their ranks against this new competition, the fraternal orders felt it necessary to adapt to the ways of commercial insurers, including the use of paid canvassers and centralized record keeping, and to minimize the practices, such as rituals, that had set them apart (Alborn 2001, especially 584, 593–594). It did not require tremendous powers of clairvoyance to predict where this would lead. Soon after the National Insurance Act came into force, a member of the largest fraternal order in Britain, the Oddfellows, echoing Mirabeau, warned the brothers against becoming "actuarial friendly society men rather than actual friendly society men [with] souls . . . in pawn to the devil of arithmetic" (*Oddfellows' Magazine* [1915] 46:639–640; quoted in Alborn 2001, 594). On the other side of the Atlantic, fraternal orders also became, in the words of one historian, "entrepreneurial organizations that operated so as to maximize membership growth and financial profit or stability" (Clawson 1989, 17).

As commercial enterprises, the fraternal orders, like the independent friendly societies, were at a disadvantage with respect to the commercial insurers, and were over the course of the next few decades swept from the field. But commercial insurance was in the end no more adequate to the task of providing adequate safeguards against the financial hazards of death, old age, and sickness than the fraternal orders had been. Government provision for social security became the norm in rich countries during the twentieth century, and if the boundaries between governmental and private insurance are still contested in the twenty-first century, it is certainly not the case that an unfettered market in health insurance is on anyone's policy agenda. But, then, neither is embedding insurance in community—except at the fringes of society.

Trade liberalization and insurance are hardly the only examples of how markets undermine community. A *Wall Street Journal* reporter, Robert Tomsho, has written eloquently of farmer Ron Ashermann's decision to sell his water rights to the city of Aurora, Colorado (a suburb of Denver), because the price Aurora was willing to pay "means deliverance from a debt-ridden way of life" (Tomsho 2000). But the irrigation ditches will dry up if Mr. Ashermann's example is followed by his neighbors, and along with the ditches the community of Rocky Ford, where four generations of Ashermanns have tilled the land. The death of the community is an external effect, a mainstream economist would say, of selling water rights. However, naming the devil does not exorcise it.

Tomsho notes that some of Ashermann's neighbors consider such sales to be unethical, but there are no individual villains in this piece. The problem lies rather in a system in which "water rights are treated as private property, [so that] preventing a sale is as unlikely as stopping a city dweller from selling his house" (Tomsho 2000). In short, the problem is the market.

You may wonder whether Mr. Ashermann's decision doesn't undermine the contention that locally owned businesses will be more sensitive to the survival of the community than large corporations whose only stake in the community is as a source of labor. To be sure, in this case the decision might have been the same, but there is still an important difference: at least in Rocky Ford the ethical issues were sufficiently alive to be the occasion for a front-page *Wall Street Journal* story. If Ashermann were a multinational, the decision to transfer water rights from agriculture to a "higher value" use like urban consumption would be business as usual.

The takeaway is this: commodification may make for greater efficiency, but every time a good or service is turned into something that is bought and sold, the result is to substitute impersonal market relationships for personal relationships of reciprocity and the like. Eventually economic ties wither altogether, and the community is put at risk.

The Economist's Response: Economizing on Love

The English monetary economist Dennis Robertson once suggested the opposite: that using the market to accomplish the basic tasks of life frees up energy for other ways of connecting. "What does the economist economize?" Sir Dennis asked rhetorically (1956, 154). His answer: "That scarce resource Love, which *we* know, just as well as anybody else, to be the most precious thing in the world." By using the impersonal relationships of markets to do the work of fulfilling our material needs, we economize on our higher faculties of affection, reciprocity, personal obligation—love, in Robertsonian shorthand—which can then be devoted to higher ends.[6]

In the end, his protests to the contrary notwithstanding, Sir Dennis knew more about banking than about love. Robertson made the mistake of thinking that love, like a loaf of bread, gets used up as it is used. Not all goods are "private" goods like bread. There are also "public" or "collective" goods, which are not used up by being used by one person. A lighthouse is the canonical example: my use of the light does not diminish its availability to you. Love is a hyper public good: it actually increases by being used and indeed may shrink to nothing if left unused for any length of time. I tried once to sum this up in a ditty:

> Love is a very special commodity,
> An irregular economical oddity.
> Bread, when you take it, there's less on the shelf.
> Love, when you make it, it grows of itself.

If love is not scarce in the way that bread is, it makes little sense to design social institutions to economize on it.[7] On the contrary. The sensible thing to do is to create institutions to draw out and develop the stock of love—institutions like barn raisings. It is only when we focus on barns rather than on the people raising barns that insurance appears to be a more effective way of coping with disaster.

The example of insurance may appear to be somewhat random, but it is in fact not. The Amish, perhaps unique in twenty-first century America in their attention to fostering community, forbid insurance precisely because they understand that the market relationship between an individual and the insurance company undermines the mutual dependence of the individuals. For the Amish, barn raisings are not exercises in nostalgia, but the cement that binds the community together.

But why is it of concern whether communities hold together or not? What is so special about community, of all forms of social organization, that justifies swimming against the tide of modernity to preserve or, indeed, to re-create it?

CHAPTER 2

What Is Community?
And Is It Worth the Cost?

"Community" is a plastic word, with meanings that range from chat rooms to professional associations to political federations. For me, the distinctive feature of community is that it provides a kind of social glue, binding people together in relationships that give form and flavor to life. By the same token, community depends on constraints and obligations that transcend the calculation of individual utility. Whether people who sense the need for community are also willing to respect these commitments and obligations is an open question, as is whether it is feasible to build communities that provide deep human connection while preserving an adequate space for individual diversity. This much is sure: we will never find the answer to this question as long as we are blinded by an ideology, the ideology of the market, which makes community invisible.

Community should be distinguished from association. The distinction is fundamentally one of commitment and identity. Associations, even while they provide their own form of social glue, make little claim on our loyalties and at best make minor contributions to our identities. We may be members of a bowling league, the Polish American Society, or a Thursday night poker game, but none of these affiliations defines our being. The reason is that we can shed affiliations—piecemeal or all at once—like so many snake skins. If any association asks too much of us, or if we don't agree with its direction, we always have the option of choosing exit over voice, flight over fight.[1] The result is that associations are vulnerable to centrifugal forces that often are irresistible.

Community, by contrast, is central to who we are. We are not determined once and for all by, nor chained to, our communities, but neither can we simply resign as we can from a bowling league. A thirteenth-century Jew living in a village in Germany wondered whether he could leave the village, perhaps to pursue better opportunities elsewhere. The problem was that his departure would leave his fellow Jews without the ten adult men necessary for reciting certain prayers. When the question reached Rabbi Meir of Rothenburg, the great Talmudic authority of European Jewry in his day, known as the Maharam, the rabbi responded that the man could not abandon his community unless he found a replacement (Finkel 1990, 18).[2] The constraint need not be as extreme as this: the point is that leaving a community involves costs—moral, legal, psychological, or economic—that are not part of the calculus of whether one abandons one's fellow bowlers.

Granted that association is distinct from community, might it not be the case that a sufficient density of associations creates community through the overlapping networks that these associations create? Possible, but doubtful. To borrow an analogy from the twentieth-century economist Joseph Schumpeter (1934 [1911], 64), a web of associations is as different from community as twenty stagecoaches strung together are different from a train of railroad cars.[3]

In the past, community bonds, like community identities, have rarely been freely chosen. It may indeed be essential to community that we choose neither the ties that bind us to one another in communities nor the identities that communities give us. For once we can choose to belong, does it not follow that we can choose not to belong? Once opting out becomes easy, communities become subject to the same centrifugal forces as associations. This is the idea behind my contention that if communities are to survive the test of time, the relationships, commitments, and obligations binding us together must not be easily shed, not dissolvable except at some significant cost.

In this respect, the family is a primordial community. Children do not choose their parents, and, adoption and designer babies apart, parents do not choose their children (even though most modern people choose whether to have children and how many to have). We also create families, through marriage or domestic partnerships. But unless these families involve substantial barriers to exit, there is unlikely to be community in these relationships, any more than in other groups we create to facilitate individual ends.

Communities of Necessity and Communities of Affinity

It may be useful to distinguish two kinds of community, communities of *necessity* and communities of *affinity*. Precapitalist economic, social, and political arrangements offer abundant examples of communities of necessity. In the

Middle Ages, the manor, which will be examined in Chapter 5 (and in greater detail in Appendix B), brought men and women of varying degrees of freedom and unfreedom together in a common enterprise of agricultural production, bound to each other, as we shall see, by social and political as well as economic ties. In early modern European cities and towns, small workshops brought workmen into the extended families of the master manufacturer; household discipline extended beyond the workday to virtually every facet of the workman's life.

We hardly have to go back to medieval or early modern Europe for examples of communities of necessity. American history is replete with examples. Agricultural production, to be sure, was very early organized along individualistic, if not capitalistic, lines. In New England at the time of the Revolution, the family farm was the archetypical productive unit. But the isolated farm was the exception, not the rule. Villages tied families together through social, political, and economic relationships. In these villages, health-care delivery relied not only on doctors and other medical practitioners who were normally paid a fee for service and functioned in as individualistic a way as other professionals, artisans, and craftsmen; it also relied on people who saw to the physical and psychological needs of the sick and dying on the basis of neighborly reciprocity instead of fee for service.

Martha Ballard was the "midwife" (in quotes because she was a general practitioner who treated a wide variety of medical conditions as well as facilitating births) of Laurel Thatcher Ulrich's splendidly evocative account of medicine on the Maine frontier. Ballard repeatedly visited a small boy, James Howard, in August 1787 to treat him for scarlet fever. Her diary entry for August 10 notes, "At Mrs Howards. Her son very sick." Martha's diary meticulously records the fees she received for her services.

But Martha was not the only visitor on that day. Her diary also records the presence of "Capt Sewall & Lady" (Ulrich 1991, 37). The Sewalls were not paid for their efforts, but rather were

fulfilling basic obligations of neighborliness. . . . In watching little James Howard, they were returning the help they had received earlier that month when their own child was dying of [scarlet fever]. Their obligation wasn't to Mrs. Howard in particular—she had been too busy nursing [her daughter] Isabella to have helped with the care of [Mrs. Sewall's son] Billy—but to the common fund of neighborliness that sustained families in illness. (Ulrich 1991, 63)

These obligations were not limited to frontier communities such as Martha Ballard's. In the midst of a dysentery epidemic, Abigail reported from the Adams family home in Braintree, to her husband John, away in Philadelphia at the First Continental Congress, "Such is the distress of the neighborhood that I can scarcely find a well person to assist me in looking after the sick" (quoted in McCullough 2001, 25).

In the twentieth century, what neighbors once did for the incapacitated has become the job of practical nurses, and is no longer an activity that binds the community together—except where poverty puts professional nursing out of economic range. In her description of reciprocity in a poor black urban neighborhood ("The Flats") in Illinois, anthropologist Carol Stack relates that Magnolia Waters, one of her informants (I suppose Stack would say teachers), unexpectedly came into some money after the death of an uncle. "Money," Stack notes, did not change the community obligations of Magnolia and her husband, "but their ability to meet these needs had temporarily changed," giving her the wherewithal to pack up her family for a train ride and extended stay in the South to sit at the bedside of another uncle who had fallen ill (Stack 1975, 106).

This event is emblematic of the larger story that Stack tells. The community she describes, defined by kinship networks both biological and psychological, was held together by the obligation to share, the needs of the temporarily fortunate subordinated to the needs of the less fortunate. If someone in the Flats wins the lottery, figuratively or literally, he or she cannot turn down kin for whom a portion of the winnings could pay a landlord his overdue rent, put food on the table, or buy winter clothing for the kids—not without risking ostracism and being cut off from the community's resources in his or her own time of need.

The problem with communities of necessity is that, absent legal compulsion, they are vulnerable to prosperity or, rather, the prospect of prosperity. Marshall Berman sums up the problem very well in a gripping story with protagonists of epic proportions. On one side of the battle was Jane Jacobs, the apostle of coherent, vibrant, urban neighborhoods (Jacobs 1961), and on the other was Robert Moses, the champion of urban planning whose Lower Manhattan Expressway was to be the culmination of a career that would change the landscape of New York forever even while it fragmented Jacobs's neighborhood (see Caro 1974 for a biography of Moses). Jacobs won that round: the Lower Manhattan Expressway was never built.

Alas, Jacobs's victory in Manhattan came too late for Berman's old neighborhood in the Bronx. The Cross-Bronx Expressway cut the Bronx in two, literally. It uprooted 60,000 people and destroyed the organic coherence of the neighborhood for those who remained (Berman 1988, 292).

But, Berman asks, was the Expressway the real cause of his neighborhood's demise, or only a precipitating factor? "What," he wonders, "if, like Jacobs' lower Manhattan neighbors a few years later, we had managed to keep the dread road from being built? How many of us would still be in the Bronx today, caring for it and fighting for it as our own? Some of us, no doubt, but I suspect not so many, and in any case—it hurts to say it—not me" (Berman 1988, 326).

The underlying cause of the neighborhood's collapse, according to Berman, was the very meaning of the American Dream: "The Bronx of my youth was possessed, inspired, by the great modern dream of mobility. To live well meant to move up socially, and this in turn meant to move out physically; to live one's life close to home was not to be alive at all" (Berman 1988, 326). In other words, once Berman's neighborhood was no longer a community of necessity, it became subject to the same centrifugal forces as are associations: exit dominates voice; flight wins out over fight.

This oversimplifies. The grass may be greener in suburbia, but the intensity of attraction depends on many variables. For the young, the grass has always been greener somewhere else. Communities have always had to cope with the lure of "out there" for the young, especially for young men who reach the age of emancipation from family control but have not entered into the responsibilities of householding. W. H. Auden conjures up the allure of the big city in the concluding stanza of his poem "The Capital":

> But the sky you illumine, your glow is visible far
> Into the dark countryside, enormous and frozen,
> Where, hinting at the forbidden like a wicked uncle,
> Night after night to the farmer's children you beckon.
>   (Auden 1991, 178)

The bright lights of the capital may offer riches or fame, but moving up is only one reason for moving out. "The farmer's children" may also be searching to escape a narrow oppressiveness that forbids any kind of self-development or self-expression.

It is hardly surprising that successful communities have had to develop strategies for allowing young men to satisfy their wanderlust. (In contrast with young men, young women used to move seamlessly from parental to spousal control without ever enjoying the liminal space accorded men.) Many hundreds of years ago, when guilds flourished and even dominated some sectors of manufacturing in Germany and other parts of Europe, an accepted stage of life between apprenticeship and journeyman status was the *Wanderjahr,* a year in which young men went from town to town, working (and playing) in a variety of environments. This was a time to explore the world in relative freedom from the commitments that characterized the lives not only of apprentices but also of journeymen settled on a career ladder leading to master status, with all its privileges and responsibilities. In our own time, the Amish still grant such leaves of absence, which they call *Rumspringa* ("running around"), to adolescents and young adults. From the time an Amish teen turns 16, when he (or she) is no longer subject to parental moral authority, to the time of baptism and acceptance of church rules (the *Ordnung*), the constraints that circumscribe social behavior are suspended.[4]

The trick has been to allow the young to explore the wider world in a way that does not jeopardize returning to the community and embracing the commitments and responsibilities of community membership. Neighborhoods that are founded on the principle of, as an interlocutor of Berman put it succinctly if inelegantly, " 'Get out shmuck, get out!' " (Berman 1988, 327) can hardly be expected to celebrate, or even countenance, a return to the fold after a Wanderjahr or Rumspringa. In Berman's Bronx, returning to the fold would have been an advertisement of failure.

To the extent that exit becomes an option, necessity is attenuated. Communities of *affinity* are another matter. Shared affections, common goals, a unity of vision and ideology, and mutual responsibilities—not adversity— are what hold communities of affinity together. T. S. Eliot may have exaggerated both the importance of community to a good and fulfilling life and the importance of religion in defining community, but his pageant play *The Rock* was certainly onto something important in emphasizing the spiritual dimension of communities of affinity:

> What life have you if you have not life together?
> There is no life that is not in community,
> And no community not lived in praise of God.
> Even the anchorite who meditates alone,
> For whom the days and nights repeat the praise of God,

Prays for the Church, the Body of Christ incarnate.
And now you live dispersed on ribboned roads,
And no one knows or cares who is his neighbour
Unless his neighbor makes too much disturbance,
But all dash to and fro in motor cars,
Familiar with the roads and settled nowhere.
Nor does the family even move about together,
But every son would have his motor cycle
And daughters ride away on casual pillions.

Much to cast down, much to build, much to restore. . . .

Religious communities are a prime contemporary example of communities of affinity, but this is not to say that communities of affinity must be based in religion. Intentional communities—a particular sort of community of affinity in which there are a variety of kinds and degrees of sharing, including some sharing of goods if not total communal ownership—have waxed and waned; some intentional communities are religious in inspiration and practice, but hardly all. And over the course of the twentieth century, the families that Americans and Europeans created through marriage and domestic partnerships increasingly became communities of affinity rather than necessity, as women's opportunities for paid work and property ownership increased.

Observe that, like communities of necessity, communities of affinity may or may not be freely chosen. The families we create by marriage, not to mention intentional communities, are; birth families are not; religious communities may or may not be. But as long as leaving one or the other community involves a significant cost, neither religious affiliation nor marriage nor an intentional community can be thought of as simply one association among others.

If communities of necessity are put at risk by the temptations of prosperity, communities of affinity run an inherent risk of dissolving into associations. It is certainly possible for these communities to survive, and some communities not only survive but thrive, on the basis of affinity alone. Yet there is no question in my mind that necessity enhances the chances of survival. A four-legged stool can remain upright with only three legs, but it is more likely to tip over. The Amish have successfully maintained group cohesion over a long period because they are bound together by ties, such as the prohibition on insurance, that both foster mutual dependence and bolster ties of affinity. Consciously or not, the Amish insistence on economic ties represents a recognition of the limits of affinity alone as a unifying force.

The experience of a variety of religious communities illustrates the problem of trying to maintain community on the basis of affinity alone. In the United States, assimilation has undermined Jewish communities for a century. Protestants who move from one place to another may find that the proximity of the Methodist Church in their new neighborhood is a more important consideration that their commitment to Presbyterianism—or vice versa. The Catholic Church has fared no better: attendance at mass has fallen dramatically over the past half century, and most U.S. Catholics appear to honor the Church's teachings on birth control in the breach.

With regard to marriage as the basis of the family community, it is a commonplace that half of U.S. marriages end in divorce, so that it is not clear where marriage as community ends and marriage as association begins.[5] I have no precise statistics on intentional communities, but it is clear that affinity has not been sufficient to maintain most intentional communities over the long haul.

It is the importance of ties of necessity that puts community at odds with the foundational assumptions of economics. Markets, based on voluntary, instrumental, opportunistic relationships, are diametrically opposed to the long-term commitments and obligations that characterize community. By promoting market relationships, economics undermines reciprocity, altruism, and mutual obligation, and therewith the necessity of community. The very foundations of economics, by justifying the expansion of markets, lead inexorably to the weakening of community.

The Many Ties That Bind

Communities, to be sure, are in practice bound together by much more than economics. And different kinds of relationships combine necessity and affinity in varying proportions. First, all communities have a political structure, a system of rules and regulations and a means of enforcing those regulations on its members. These rules need not be codified in formal legislation and may be largely unspoken as well as unwritten.

Rules and regulations cover a variety of behaviors and demarcate the private from the public spheres. Of great importance are the rules governing exit and entry, and as we have seen, successful communities have developed relatively tolerant policies for "leaves of absence" for young men on the cusp of adulthood. It has always been important, except perhaps for communities that are physically isolated, to provide their young men with opportunities to check whether the grass on the other side of the fence really is greener.

Communities are not just about economics and politics, but about sociality as well. Members of a community celebrate together and grieve together, rejoice with one another and console one another.

Communities create a common future for their members and remember a common past. A vision of the future as well as a common memory are central elements in regenerating the community, in providing continuity and connection between the generations. Perhaps more than any other dimension of community, the emphasis on regeneration is what distinguishes community most clearly from what I have called *association*.

Regeneration requires a basic consensus about values. Michael Sandel (especially in Sandel 1996; see also 1998 [1982]) has been a leading critic of the "procedural republic," in which the only agreed-upon value is that every individual be free to pursue his or her own notion of the good, subject only to the Rawlsian constraint of equal liberty for all. For Sandel, the procedural republic is a figment of the liberal imagination rather than a basis for imagining a social reality. I agree. Only the most committed libertarians can believe in the possibility of social cohesion without some consensus beyond the virtue of pursuing one's own conception of the good. The consensus can evolve over time, but consensus there must be. Toleration is not a sufficient basis for any kind of society, not to mention community.

Does this make intolerance a necessary ingredient of community? At what point does toleration break down the consensus on other values, and thus the social cohesion that is necessary to community? Is community necessarily antithetical to values of tolerance—or, for that matter, antithetical to equality, diversity, openness?

I have no good answer to the question of whether it is possible to build communities that are egalitarian, diverse, open, and tolerant. But I can at least make clear that it is not part of my ambition to re-create the hierarchical, narrow, closed, oppressive communities of a bygone era or to fashion new cultlike social organizations. The past—and present-day communities like the Amish—give only very partial guidance; neither provides a model or template.

Indeed, the nineteenth-century British historian and author Thomas Carlyle—to whose essay "Occasional Discourse on the Negro Question" we owe the characterization of economics as the "dismal science" (Persky 1990; Levy 2001)—proposed what I would regard as a model of everything that is objectionable in community. Economics is a dismal science—but not because it prefers the market outcome of wage bargaining between plantation owners and freedmen to the outcome of a community in which white masters control the labor of black serfs, which was Carlyle's proposal for addressing the upheaval of the West Indian sugar economy that came in the wake of abolition of slavery in the British Empire in 1833 (Carlyle 1850 [1849]).

The problem for Carlyle was the indolence of the freedmen: the result of their low level of material desires—conflated to a single good, pumpkins, in Carlyle's telling—and the ease with which their desires could be satisfied. These two factors combined to reduce the supply of labor to the plantations to the point that very little labor was forthcoming at wages consistent with the planters' making a profit. (Indeed, there was no guarantee that higher wages would coax out more labor: higher wages make it possible to satisfy the worker's money needs with less labor—or, as the economist would say, income effects may swamp substitution effects.) Carlyle coined the term "dismal science" to characterize a way of viewing the world that would condone an unholy idleness in the name of the law of supply and demand—though rejecting traditional Christianity, he never got over his Calvinist upbringing and could see nothing positive in leisure, at least not in the leisure of black Jamaicans. Carlyle was, to be sure, no more attracted by a policy of working within the framework of supply and demand to solve the planters' labor problem. He rejected the idea of importing enough free black workers to drive wages down because he was all too familiar with the example of Ireland, still reeling from the potato famine, where a labor surplus kept wages down but did so at the price of untold misery to the population. At the same time, Carlyle recognized the injustice of chattel slavery, noting that the cruelties of the system were a large part of the reason for its demise.

So what was to be done? Carlyle's solution was an enlightened serfdom: "You," he says to the blacks, "will have to be servants to those that are born *wiser* than you—servants to the whites, if they are (as what mortal can doubt they are?) born wiser than you" (Carlyle 1850 [1849], 536). Just as the economist has no problem resolving the conflict between the individual and community by throwing out the community, Carlyle had no problem throwing out the individual. Worse: reflecting the endemic racism of his time and place, which divided the world between natural-born rulers and natural-born servants, Carlyle saw the manorial community that had once been the organizing principle of European agriculture not as a system founded on oppression, but as the model of a contractual system that would allow everybody his or her rightful place in a world dedicated to "commerces, arts, politics, and social developments, which, alone, are the noble product, where men (and not pigs with pumpkins) are the parties concerned" (Carlyle 1850 [1849], 532).

To the everlasting credit of the dismal science, John Stuart Mill responded (in "The Negro Question") with a firm rejection of the basic principle of a natural hierarchy of races that underlay Carlyle's conception of community (Mill 1850, 467–468). Alas, the rejection of a natural hierarchy all too easily leads to a false syllogism—everybody is the same; thus, you are like me. . . . And my Truth is your Truth—which we shall see (in Chapter 13) can be as devastating to diversity and tolerance as is the idea of a hierarchy of races.

One Community or Many?

There is no contradiction between being a member of a neighborhood improvement association and a member of the Knights of Columbus, between being a member of the PTA and a member of the Rotary Club. But can the same be said for communities? As the term is sometimes used, community is an all-encompassing, absolute identification: one can no more belong to multiple communities than one can have multiple identities. In his recent book *Identity and Violence*, Nobel Laureate Amartya Sen takes issue—rightly in my judgment—with this view of identity and community. But Sen goes much further: for him there is no difference, or, at least, there ought not to be a difference, between the claims made on the individual by community and the claims made by association. In my view, the distinction is key, so the question of whether I can be a member of more than one community is more difficult for me than it is for Sen.

The central issue is the nature of the claims that community makes on my loyalties. If the claim is absolute, then I can hardly be a member of two communities at once. Considering marriage as a community is instructive. Western traditions, going back well before modernity, make the community of husband and wife absolute; there is no room for plural wives (or plural husbands for that matter) to divide one's loyalties. But this is not the only way to conceive of marriage: other traditions allow for multiple wives and, less frequently, multiple husbands. If the multiple wives of a polygamous marriage each maintain a separate household, among which their husband-in-common splits his time, he can be understood as belonging to multiple communities. Legal aspects of divorce apart, it is unlikely that the ties that bind him to each of these households are as easily dissolvable—economically, morally, or emotionally—as the connections to a PTA or to the local Rotary Club.

With or without polygamy and polyandry, one may simultaneously be part of a nuclear family, belong to an extended family, adhere to a religious organization, and be a citizen of a nation-state—all of these connections can be severed, but only at considerable cost. Each of these groups is a community; each makes strong claims on our loyalties.

What happens if these claims come into conflict? On the eve of World War II, the English author E. M. Forster may have shocked readers of *The Nation* by asserting, "If I had to choose between betraying my country and betraying my friend I hope I should have the guts to betray my country" (1938, 66). But Forster, as he himself notes (ibid., 66), shocks only the modern sensibility: it is very much a modern idea that one claim—the claim of the nation-state—necessarily trumps all others.[6]

Outside the conceptual framework of the modern West, the adjudication of these claims is more difficult. Even the harshest critic of the ideology of the nation-state would probably be less absolute than Forster: choosing between friend and country would likely depend very much on context—as would choosing among family, religion, and nation. The nation-state, of course, has the means to assert the primacy of its claims vis-à-vis the claims of other communities. But it does not always do so. To its credit, the United States has in recent years taken a relatively tolerant position when the claims of citizenship and the claims of religion have come into conflict. The Amish, for example, are exempted from military service as conscientious objectors, and—as was noted in the previous chapter—from participation in social security programs that they believe undermine the solidarity of their religious community.[7]

Why Not Leave It to the Market?

This book argues that to take community seriously is to go beyond the utility-maximizing framework that characterizes economics. We will by the same token go beyond the idea that a society's choices are, or at least ought to be, the outcome of individuals' rational calculation of their separate self-interest.

But need we go so far? Doesn't the role of community instead come down to what goes into people's utility functions? In a world where people are, in Milton and Rose Friedman's phrase, "free to choose" (Friedman and Friedman 1980), or where, in Amartya Sen's view, one "celebrates cultural diversity to the extent it is as freely chosen as possible by the persons involved" (2005, 150), should not community be a matter of personal choice, no less than which flavor of ice cream one consumes? If people want community, they will have it; if not, they won't.

There is an important point at stake here, perhaps the central point of this book: to the extent that the issue of community is one of preferences, and preferences are, as economists are accustomed to insist, grounded in human nature, a concern for community does not lead to criticism of economics. It would truly be blaming the messenger for the message to fault economics for the content of immutable preferences. If, however, as this book argues, preferences are not immutable, and the apparatus of economics itself influences the kinds of choice both individuals and societies make, then economics, at least as presently constituted, is part of the problem and is unlikely to be part of the solution.

With regard to associations, we can imagine "leaving it to the market"— that is, leaving it to the collective self-interest of individual agents. Indeed, associations can be thought of as organizations created by individuals to achieve certain limited purposes. Associations may take on a life of their own, but it is hard to argue against the freedom of individuals to enter and exit at will, more or less costlessly, or against subjecting the life of the association to a referendum of individual preferences.

Community, I have suggested, is unlikely to survive if it is subject to this kind of test, especially if community is stripped of elements of necessity. If community is treated as just another good, subject to the dynamics of supply and demand, something that people can choose or not as they please, according to the same market test that applies to different brands of cola or flavors of ice cream, it is at risk of being undone by a combination of problems, one congenial to the framework of economics, one outside that framework.

The first is the "free rider" problem. My decision to purchase fire insurance rather than participate in the give and take of barn raisings with my neighbors has the side effect—the "externality" in economics jargon—of lessening my involvement with the community. This effect may be small, no harm done, if I am the only one to act this way. But when all of us opt for insurance, and we all leave caring for the community to others, there will be no others to care, and the community will disintegrate. I buy insurance because it is more convenient, and—acting in isolation—I can reasonably say to myself that my action hardly undermines the community. When we all do so, the cement of mutual obligation is weakened to the point that it no longer supports the community.

The economist may respond that the free rider problem complicates the utility-maximization framework and rightly injects a note of caution into the general enthusiasm for the market. It does not require us to abandon the utility-maximizing framework.

At this point, it may be useful to recall the story about the Amish boy that began the last chapter: Is it reasonable to argue that a decision to allow a child to die for the sake of community can be understood in terms of an individualistic calculus of utilities? Is the difference between an Amish decision and the decision of a non-Amish family reducible to a difference in the particular goals the individual is pursuing?

There are many issues to sort out in trying to fit the square peg of a decision to let a child die into the round hole of individualistic utility maximization. But I shall focus on just one, the issue at the heart of the foundational critique of economics: Can we understand this choice as affirming the universality of utility maximization? As affirming that when people want community enough, they will have it? Does the choice faced by the Amish parents differ from other choices only because their utility function is somewhat unconventional?[8]

Looking at the problem in terms of utility maximization, the boy's death occurred not because the Amish think less individualistically but because Amish individuals have different "preferences." Valuing community, the Amish parents had a different "objective function": instead of self-centered utility, their goal was to maximize some combination of hedonistic satisfactions and community survival chances. Parents who strongly value community would take into account the effects on the community of a decision to use the community's resources to keep their child alive, or to accept Medicaid for their immune-deficient child. By choosing to let their child die, the Amish couple simply reveals a high weight for the community in their preferences. There is no need to transcend individual preferences.

Community thus becomes one more variable, alongside other inputs into a pleasure–pain calculus. In this way of looking at things, the stumbling block to community is not the individualistic map but people's preferences—and for the economist, these are sacrosanct. If people value community, they will have community. If not, they won't.

This way of framing the problem makes sense if our goal is to preserve the appearances of utility maximization, but not if we are really trying to understand how parents could sacrifice their child. Why not? Simply put, because it takes an implausibly strong "preference for community" for a rational calculation of utilities to lead to the action the Amish couple actually took. In the framework of utility maximization, the Amish parents of an immune-deficient child would rather, I believe, have decided that the consequences for the community of their accepting Medicaid, or even the burden on the community of paying for the baby's medicines, were small in comparison with the immediate consequences of doing neither—just as most non-Amish would have decided.

In short, it simply is not credible that a decision to put the community ahead of one's individual interest can be understood in the language of utility maximization. It seems infinitely more likely that a sense of identification with, and obligation to, the community, not a utility calculus, drove the couple's fateful decision not to treat their baby.

Moreover, while the balancing of a child's life and the needs of the community can be fitted into the language of economics, the limits of standard economics are severely tested by choices that involve changes in individual "preferences." If the individual preferences registered in market transactions are to provide a reliable indication of what is good for people, these preferences must at the very least be unchanging. But a decision to accept Medicaid, like the purchase of fire insurance, not only makes the individual less dependent on the community; it subverts the beliefs that sustain mutual dependence. And the process of undermining interdependence becomes self-validating.

As is behavior that reinforces community ties. The decision to reject Medicaid—even if it has the awful consequence of a baby's death—reinforces community interdependence and strengthens the beliefs that support this interdependence. When belief systems change according to the choices we make, we cannot compare outcomes as we do when beliefs are fixed. It becomes impossible to conclude that because individuals do not take actions that maintain and sustain community, they do not value community, or at least would not value community under another set of behavioral norms.

Refusing to participate in programs like Medicaid may strike outsiders as taking principle too far, but it is clear that the principle makes sense in the context of the Amish worldview. The Amish treat long life like marital happiness or a sunny disposition, as blessings for which one might pray, hope, and even work—but not as a commodity to be purchased in the marketplace.

We all can learn from Amish society. We may not be ready to swap our world of commodities for a world of blessings, but we may come to understand what we lose when we commodify blessings. Above all, the Amish show us, warts and all, another way of being in the world, another way of navigating social space, one in which the market is subordinated to community rather than ruling the roost.

But do the Amish show us anything about economics? The answer is yes: the Amish show us the limits of thinking of human behavior in terms of individuals calculating their self-interest—in short, the limits of thinking like an economist.

CHAPTER 3

The Cutting Edge of Modernity

Economists often act as though the discipline came out of nowhere—or everywhere. Once a thriving subject and an integral part of economics, the history of economic thought now exists in a limbo, the field of antiquarians. For "real" economists, historians of economics have as little to do with economics as, in their minds, historians of physics or chemistry have to do with discovery and advances in the natural sciences. This book is not a history of economic thought, but it engages one of the main questions that underlies the history of thought: it explores the connection between economics and the modern culture that grew up in Western Europe and North America over the last four hundred years.

To be sure, in the twenty-first century, modernity has spread well beyond the Atlantic heartland. The elites of Lima and New Delhi are as Western in their culture as the elites of New York and Paris and as far from the non-modern cultures of the pueblos of the Peruvian *Altiplano* or the villages of rural India as are the Americans or the French. The modern West is no longer only a place; it is also a frame of mind.

Economics is intimately connected to modernity; the foundational assumptions of economics are in my view simply the tacit assumptions of modernity. The centerpiece in both is the rational, calculating, self-interested individual with unlimited wants for whom society is the nation-state. But as the following story suggests, people are at best (or at worst—it all depends on your point of view) half-modern.

Pollution for Sale?

Some years ago, Lawrence Summers, in turn a distinguished economist, government official, and university president, who was then the Chief Economist of the World Bank, sent a memo to one of his subordinates. This memo said in part:

> Just between you and me shouldn't the World Bank be encouraging more migration of the dirty industries to the LDCs [less developed countries]? . . .
>
> A given amount of health-impairing pollution should be done in the country with the lowest cost, which will be the country with the lowest wages. I think the economic logic behind dumping a load of toxic waste in the lowest-wage country is impeccable and we should face up to that. . . .
>
> Only the lamentable facts that so much pollution is generated by non-tradable industries (transport, electrical generation) and the unit transport costs of solid waste are so high prevent world-welfare-enhancing trade in air pollution and waste.

The Economist (February 8, 1992, 66), to which the memo was leaked, found the language "crass, even for an internal memo," but "on the economics his points are hard to answer."

In my experience, people who have not been exposed to a college course in economics are likely to be outraged by the memo—if "the economic logic behind dumping a load of toxic waste in the lowest-wage country is impeccable," so much the worse for economic logic. But what a difference a year makes. After a freshman course in economics, college students begin to think like economists—that is the point of freshman economics after all—and will explain why and how both the low-wage and the high-wage countries benefit from the relocation of toxic wastes.

Make a list of all the things that you feel should not be traded in markets, even if there are willing buyers and sellers. If you are an economist, or even if you have had a year of freshman economics, your list is likely to be a short one, maybe limited to addictive drugs and one or two other things. But if you are among the uninitiated you might include anything from sexual relations to votes in public elections, not to mention toxic wastes. It might include body parts, pornography (perhaps only child pornography). A smaller number of lists will include medical care, education, or military service, or possibly all three. On the fringes of American society are groups that would put insurance on the list. And in the forests of Thailand are groups that would put the land itself on the list (see Chapter 13).

My concern, however, is not about the specifics of one list or another, but about the difference in the criteria for inclusion used by economists and noneconomists. This book traces those differences to the assumptions about people that form the core of economics and which are at odds with the way noneconomists (that is, most of us) think about people. From the economist's perspective, most of us are not sufficiently modern.

Economics as Myth

The assumptions of economics are only half-truths about people, even in the culture that gave birth to economics. None of us, even the most sophisticated economist, is completely modern. Modernity—economics—contends with the pre- or nonmodern in all of us, which is why the conclusions of economics are contestable even within the modern West.

Economics encapsulates the myths of modernity. My *American Heritage Dictionary* (1991, 827) defines myths in various ways. It begins with myth as a "traditional story dealing with supernatural beings . . . that serve as primordial types in a primitive view of the world." The dictionary's second meaning is even more on the money: "a real or fictional story . . . that appeals to the consciousness of a people by embodying its cultural ideals or by giving expression to deep, commonly felt emotions." The third meaning hits the jackpot: "a fiction or half-truth, esp[ecially] one that forms part of the ideology of a society."

I do not oppose myth to truth. Even in the last sense of the word, myth as ideology, we are not in the realm of true and false, but rather in the realm of what is beyond our powers to confirm or deny. Thus ideology is not for me "a disparaging term used to describe someone else's political views which one regards as unsound" (*Cambridge Dictionary of Philosophy* 1999, 406). Acting on myth or ideology is not a failing or disease of the Other against which you and I have immunity. We all operate on the basis of assumptions that cannot be proved or disproved. This does not mean there is nothing to discuss, nothing to learn. To the contrary, this essay reflects many years of trying to understand the myths of modernity, especially as these are refracted through the lens of economics. But the first precondition of transcending the limits of our myths and ideologies is to recognize them for what they are, rather than seeing them as truths about people at all times and all places. Indeed, I would strongly caution against putting too much faith in any assumption about human nature. What we know about human nature relative to the claims that are made about human nature is about the same as the relative weight of your little finger and the weight of your body.

That the foundational assumptions of economics are cultural myths rather than universal truths was brought home to me forcefully some years ago in Moscow. Shortly after the fall of the Soviet Union, a Finnish colleague and I had gone there to recruit Russians for a collaborative intellectual enterprise on the scope and limits of economics in addressing ecological problems. One afternoon, we had a particularly lively discussion, and there was a general interest in continuing into the evening. The Russians proposed supper at the apartment of Sergei and Lena. Sergei was associated with the School of Cultural Politics, where the afternoon meeting had taken place, but in fact we knew Lena much better because she had been our interpreter since our arrival. Lena had already given us a warm welcome and excellent dinner the evening before, so it took considerable reassurance from her to convince us that six or eight people descending on her would not be a major inconvenience. Her only concession was to allow us to purchase some food and drink for the occasion. We went to a *gastronom,* a delicatessen–grocery store, which despite being a state enterprise was reasonably well stocked. Both because of the long lines and the clumsy system (customers got a ticket specifying their purchase, went to a cashier to pay, and then back to the salesperson for the goods), the process took a while, but for me the chance to see what more or less ordinary Muscovites could purchase in early 1993 outweighed any inconvenience. At last we were done: a lot of smoked fish, some wine and vodka, and enough other things to make a reasonable supper.

As we emerged from the gastronom, Lena, quite out of the blue, said: "Terrible, terrible." Earlier remarks had prepared me for some cryptic if not apocalyptic comment, but nothing seemed particularly terrible to my untrained eye. "What's terrible?" I asked.

"Milk."

"Milk?"

"Yes, milk. It's terrible. Here they sell milk for 54 rubles per liter [approximately $0.09 at the then current rate of exchange] and at the kiosk in front of our apartment house it costs 92 rubles."

Jokingly, I responded: "That's not terrible; it's a great opportunity."

Now it was Lena's turn to be surprised: "Great opportunity? What do you mean?"

"Simple. You buy milk here for 54 rubles and sell it in front of your house for, say, 75. You make a lot of money and the folks in your apartment get their milk cheaper." Once an economist, always an economist.

Lena thought about this for a moment and then said, "It won't work. You can't get the milk there. You can't buy gas."

"Listen," I said. "If you can make money from buying milk cheap, you can find gas."

Lena was silent for another moment and then shook her head, her exasperation with this uncomprehending foreigner showing through: "No, it still won't work. Even if you could find gas, there is no transport."

Now I began to feel a challenge. Here was first-year economics. Here was freedom for Lena's apartment house from the bondage of 92-ruble milk and a tidy profit in the bargain. "Look, if there is enough money in it, all these obstacles can be overcome."

After some more back and forth, a lightbulb went on just above my head: all this talk about "is" was really a cover for Lena's misgivings about "ought." The difficulties were not logistical but moral. As a matter of right, milk ought to sell for the same price in front of her apartment house as at the central gastronom. And it was immoral to bring this about through the mechanism of the market and the incentive of profit.

I realized that what was second nature to me was totally alien to Lena. Doubtless the quickness and sureness of my responses owed something to my professional training, but my profession was only frosting on the cake of market culture. Most people reared in a market culture, economists or not, would have no trouble understanding rudimentary arbitrage, even if they could not define this term.

I realized two other things. First, although it was certain that more than seventy years of communism were part of this story of cultural difference, Lena's resistance to the logic of the market ran much deeper, the product more likely of centuries of wariness than of decades of communist propaganda.

Second, however ingrained market logic might be for the present generation of Germans, French, and Americans, hardly a century ago Lena's suspicions could have been found all over Western Europe and the United States. It oversimplifies to identify the populism that swept the American prairies in the 1890s with wholesale condemnation of the logic of the market, but I do believe that many populists would have taken Lena's side of our exchange rather than mine.

But we don't have to go to Russia or back to nineteenth-century Kansas to see resistance and acclimatization to the logic of economics. Every year thousands of undergraduates all over the United States take courses in the principles of economics, partly, perhaps, because they are persuaded it is useful preparation for business or law school, but partly, I am sure, for enlightenment. Many ask (with Adam Smith) how to morally justify a world based on self-interest. Parents may have urged the importance of looking out for number one, but Smith's idea of an invisible hand propelling self-interest to serve the general interest sounds too much like other forms of adult hypocrisy of which the young become, as they grow up, increasingly aware. Imagine the relief, not to say exhilaration, to learn sophisticated arguments of why looking out for number one is a social virtue. And if there remain any doubts, students can always draw sustenance from the source of the wisdom of Economics 101: the arguments come from professors of economic science—objective, unbiased professors who have no other ax to grind than that of Universal Truth itself. (There remains an unconvinced minority. No matter how hard they try, they just don't get it. Needless to say, these students tend to limit their further exposure to economics. Given this selection bias, it is no wonder that economics is not a hotbed of introspection about its premises.)

The spread of the market was hardly automatic. It needed reinforcement and legitimization. It needed the economics profession's help in the very construction of the market economy. Long before Adam Smith, economists began breaking down the resistance of the Lenas of the world to the logic of the market. The centuries it has taken to convince (or marginalize) the resisters even in the most market-friendly societies on earth is a measure of how deep the resistance runs.

Adam Smith's contemporary, the philosopher and politician Edmund Burke, may have been speaking prematurely when he opined that the age of economists (and sophisters and calculators, perhaps the same thing for Burke) had arrived, but at the dawn of a new millennium, the economist's voice threatens to drown out all others. This does not mean that there is no longer resistance. There are still many Lenas out there, and one of the purposes of this book is to strengthen their voices. In my view, all of us, even the most die-hard economist, has something of Lena inside. Indeed, I would argue that a society based solely on the principles of economics couldn't last four minutes, not to mention the four hundred years that modernity has been in the ascendant.

This does not mean that I am unaware of the many achievements of modernity. Even if we focus only on the material side, there is no denying that economic abundance, improved nutrition, and longer life spans are among the salient features of the modern West that account for its powerful attraction all over the world. Most impressive are the remarkable improvements in infant and child survival rates over the last century and the accompanying increases in life spans. In the United States, infant mortality fell from over 150 per 1,000 live births to under 7 between the years 1900 and 2000 (for 1900 statistics, see *Historical Statistics of the United States* 1975, Series B, 182; for 1999, see Miniño et al., 2001, table 11), and life expectancy at birth rose correspondingly from under 50 to over 75 (*Historical Statistics of the United States* 1975, Series B, 107; Anderson and DeTurk 2002, table 7). A similar story has unfolded more recently in countries to which the benefits of modern health care have come only in the post–World War II period. In Portugal, to take one example, infant mortality fell from 53 to 6 in just the last three decades of the twentieth century; and in Saudi Arabia, to take another, from 118 to 24; correspondingly, life expectancies increased from 68 to 75.2 in Portugal, and from 53.9 to 70.9 in Saudi Arabia (United Nations Development Programme 2002, indicator table 8, 174–175).

The reduction in physical drudgery is also impressive. If you need convincing, read the poignant chapter from the first volume of Robert Caro's biography of President Lyndon Johnson titled "The Sad Irons" (Caro 1982, 502–515). Here Caro sets the stage for Johnson's struggle to bring rural electrification to the Texas hill country after he was first elected to Congress in the late 1930s. The sad irons were the irons that hill-country women used to press their families' clothes, emblematic of the backbreaking labor that farm women had to do before electricity. Ironing was the last step in doing the family wash, a weekly ritual that traditionally took place on Mondays and Tuesdays. On Mondays, water was carried from the well, often over a distance of more than a hundred yards. Then the water was heated on a wood stove. Only after these preliminaries could the actual washing and rinsing be done, in open tubs, with only the physical strength of the women to operate the paddles for beating the dirt out and the mangles and rollers for squeezing the water out. Tuesdays were reserved for ironing. The irons, six or seven pounds, not the lightweight "irons" of aluminum or steel alloy in use today, were heated on wood stoves (the same stoves that heated water and cooked food), then passed over the clothes that had been washed and dried the day before. A monumental chore at best, a hellish one when carried out in the 90- or 100-degree Texas summer.

All this took place in the United States within living memory but is unimaginable for almost all Americans today, for whom wash-and-wear is the rule. That in itself is a measure of how far we have come in terms of reducing the physical hardships of life.

But not all of us—and the exceptions tell us something about how modernity closes off thinking of hard work as something other than drudgery. The Amish came to the United States in search of religious freedom in the eighteenth century and have spread out from their original settlements in Pennsylvania across the Midwest and Canada. To the larger North American world, the Amish are quaint folk who shun much of the apparatus that modernity provides for reducing drudgery and increasing entertainment. Most Amish use only stationary sources of power—no automobiles, tractors, or other moving engines. Most use canisters of liquid propane gas for cooking and other chores, but not electricity, at least not from the grid. No electric appliances, radios, television, videos, or movies. They dress so simply, the women in pastels, the men in American Gothic, that they are sometimes called the plain folk. But for our present purposes, it is not the quaintness of the Amish that is noteworthy.

Alongside Caro, read a book by Sue Bender (1989), which recounts the time she spent living with an Amish family in the 1980s. As might be expected in a society in which work is gendered, Bender spent most of her time with other women, and much of her book is given over to a description of Amish women at work. In physical terms, there is little to distinguish the work that these women do today from what the hill-country women did in the 1930s, before electricity wrought its miracles. The Amish typically have indoor plumbing, so women do not need to carry water from a distant well, and hot water flows from the tap, but these innovations apart, washing and ironing are closer to the technology that made this labor so oppressive in the Texas hills two-thirds of a century ago than to the technology that mainstream America now utilizes.

Nevertheless, drudgery is not one of the words that come to mind in describing the Amish—women or men—at work. Why not? For one thing, Amish women, like Amish men, see themselves as doing God's work. They value not only the product but the process. They value themselves through their work. For another, Amish women do their washing and ironing, and much other work, together, communally. Work is a social occasion.[1] The contrast with the hill-country women could not be starker. A hill-country woman might have got satisfaction from seeing her family dressed in clean, well-pressed clothes, but the ironing and washing themselves brought her nothing but pain. And these women worked as they lived—in virtual isolation, each on her own farm, often meeting nobody outside the immediate family except for the occasional hired help that would show up for the harvest.

Both these differences are connected to modernity. Work in the West has long been instrumental to the acquisition of goods, arguably since Adam and Eve were expelled from the Garden and work was imposed as punishment in the matter of the forbidden fruit. It is true that for Martin Luther and some of the Protestant sects influenced by Luther's ideas, work became a calling, firmly embedded in the divine plan for human salvation. But apart from the Amish (and other fringe groups like the Old Order Mennonites), virtually all that survives of the idea of a calling in North America is that the nonacademic, blue-collar branch of secondary education often goes under the name of "vocational"—from the Latin for calling.

Economics reflects the negative valence attached to work by treating labor as simply the absence of leisure, unless it be particularly irksome, tedious, unhealthy, or physically exhausting, in which case it is assigned a penalty in the pleasure–pain calculus that is assumed to underlie the choices we make. Work is certainly not associated in the economist's mind with community.

Other losses have come with the growing importance of the ideology of economics. Economics teaches us to calculate everything from the relative benefits of vanilla and strawberry ice cream to the value of a human life. It teaches us to calculate what we can reasonably calculate but also to calculate the incalculable. It shouldn't surprise anyone that when the economist calculates the value of human life, the average inhabitant of Puerto Rico is found to be worth something like one-third the value of a resident of the mainland United States—the ratio of average earnings in the two places. The value of a sub-Saharan African drops off the chart. (Any wonder why it would be desirable to ship pollution from Los Angeles to Mombasa?)

The economist may in turn open the door, grudgingly or willingly, to the incommensurable, if not the incalculable. At the very least, he or she will say, economics teaches us the importance of achieving whatever goals we might set at least cost—the importance of efficiency. And economics offers a criterion for measuring efficiency even in cases where we might set goals in one dimension that are incommensurate with others. And a means: the market.

For instance, suppose the goal is to achieve a certain target in the realm of biodiversity, say species preservation, for reasons that are not reducible to economic terms. Economists would argue that, despite the noneconomic nature of the goal, there is still an economic dimension to the problem, namely, minimizing the cost of reaching whatever specific target of species preservation might be set. The measure of efficiency might be how many board-feet of tropical hardwoods must be sacrificed per species saved from extinction, and the economist would argue that the best way to achieve efficiency is to set up a market in tradable "rights" to kill off one of several endangered species. The language, as *The Economist* said of Summers, may be crude, but the benefits very real. The ability to buy and sell these rights would ensure that loggers using techniques or operating in particular locations where their operations would endanger relatively more species per board-foot of harvested lumber would find it profitable to sell their rights to loggers operating under more favorable conditions.

The logic is the same as the logic for markets in pollution that we encountered at the beginning of this chapter, or for the market in sexual services that we discussed in Chapter 1. The problem with this logic is that minimizing the costs of achieving given goals presupposes an unambiguous notion of what counts as costs. Economists count only what can be brought under the measuring rod of calculating self-interested individuals. That which affects the values, attitudes, behaviors, and ways of interacting with other people lies outside the economist's ken.

The Assumptions of Economics: A First Pass

Successive chapters in this book examine the founding myths of economics: individualism, knowledge as algorithm, the nation as the sole legitimate community, and unlimited wants. The basic idea of individualism is that society can and should be understood as a collection of autonomous individuals, that groups—with the exception of the nation—have no normative significance as groups, that all behavior, policy, and even ethical judgment should be reduced to their effects on individuals. Economics goes further. The economist's individual is fixed and unchanging; he is a responsible actor at all times and places; his preferences are not up for discussion, evaluation, or analysis; finally, he is self-interested in a particularly narrow way.

That individuals are fixed and unchanging means preferences are given once and for all. Responsibility means that individuals have agency: their preferences—subject to constraints (like income) but not to coercion (like physical force)—determine their choices, actions, and behavior. The idea that preferences are beyond discussion implies a radical subjectivism; one set of preferences is as worthy as another. Self-interest precludes acting for the sake of others, particularly acting for others out of a sense of duty or obligation.

A second founding myth is the modern ideology of knowledge, an ideology that privileges the algorithmic over the experiential, an ideology that elevates knowledge that can be logically deduced from what are regarded as self-evident first principles over what is learned from intuition and authority, from touch and feel. In the stronger form of this ideology, not only is algorithm privileged; it is the sole legitimate form of knowledge. Other knowledge is mere belief, becoming legitimate knowledge only when verified by algorithmic methods. This conception of knowledge comes out of a misplaced zeal for certainty, even where it is plain that we must make do with knowledge that will allow us to cope with the radical uncertainty that is our lot.

Third, the nation—at least when it speaks through a state—is the only legitimate social grouping. Since Adam Smith, economists have conceived of society as the nation. It is legitimate to ask whether the nation will be made better off by free trade, but it is parochial to ask whether workers, old folks, or farmers will fare better or worse. If readers had any doubt what was meant by society when Adam Smith wrote of the wonders of the invisible hand in promoting the social good, they had to look no further than to the title of his magnum opus: his was an enquiry not into the conditions under which the sick, the maimed, the widow, or the orphan might thrive economically, but into the conditions that determined "the wealth of nations."

Why this focus on the nation? In part, it is simply that the nation is shorthand for the state, and states are the entities that make economic policy. Economists carry on many conversations, but not least among these is the conversation with power. The economist might well respond to the question "Why focus on the state?" the same way, mutatis mutandis, the twentieth-century bank robber Willie Sutton supposedly answered the question "Why do you rob banks?" "Because that's where the money is," said Sutton. But there is more to the story: the state represents not just power, but legitimate power, and it is the attribute of representing a nation that confers legitimacy on the state's exercise of power. The abstraction "society" becomes the nation-state because nations can be assumed to resolve the problem of cutting up the economic pie in a morally acceptable manner, freeing economics to focus, as it has done since the days of Smith, on the size of the pie. In other words, the conception of the nation-state as the legitimate arbiter of distributional issues is critical to the economist's focus on efficiency.

The fourth myth is that wants are unlimited. It is human nature that we always want more than we have and that there is consequently never enough. The idea of unlimited wants, and its corollary of universal scarcity, is fundamental to economics. Indeed, every mainstream text with which I am acquainted defines economics as the study of how scarce resources are allocated to unlimited ends.[2] But the real issue of unlimited wants is not whether people want more, other things being equal; it is instead whether this desire for more is allowed free play in the economy. My contention is that the modern West is unique in the extent to which we allow rivalry— keeping up with the Joneses and the like—to be expressed in the acquisition and display of wealth. Other societies, with a keener understanding of the destructive potential of rivalry, have erected elaborate barriers and controls over how people can compete for prestige. As a general rule, the economy is out of bounds, or at the very least strictly regulated, as a domain for one-upmanship.

A couple of disclaimers are in order. Let me begin with an obvious one. I am not a neutral observer, and this book does not take a neutral position between modernity and its critics, or between economics and its critics. This is not an "on the one hand, on the other hand" book. I am not oblivious to the virtues of modernity or the strengths of economics. It is rather that the virtues and strengths, particularly of markets, are internalized by most of us and constantly trumpeted to the rest, whereas the vices and weaknesses are generally passed over in silence. I see this book as helping to right the balance.

A second disclaimer has to do with my use of the term *economics.* I indicated in Chapter 1 that I use economics as a shorthand for the mainstream consensus I believe exists at the core of the normative agenda—namely, the proposition that a system of unfettered markets is, subject to the qualifications discussed in Appendix A, good for people. Having said that, I should recognize the limits of the consensus. There are several perspectives alternative to mine from which this proposition has been criticized, and it is natural to ask, at the very least, how the present critique relates to two of the more prominent of these alternatives, a Marxian perspective on economics and an ecological perspective.

Is Marx an Alternative?

I am critical of capitalism and markets, but my critique is not from a socialist perspective, certainly not from a Marxist perspective. Maybe I should equivocate: Marxian economics, like non-Marxian economics, can be and is formulated in many different ways, and there is without doubt a formulation that is congenial to the perspective of this book. But taking the most straightforward reading of Marx, there is not much to choose between Marxist critics and mainstream defenders of the capitalist order, at least not with respect to the main concerns of this book. Both sides are committed to a self-interested individualism (though Marx is appropriately skeptical about the degree to which the majority of individuals can flourish in a capitalist society), and both are committed to the modern ideology of knowledge.[3] As for unlimited wants, Marxists see the historical role of capitalism as producing the material conditions for an end to scarcity—in the fullness of time, the productive apparatus will be sufficient to meet everybody's material needs. It is only with the "development of the productive forces" (to use a favorite phrase of Marx and his followers) that abundance can conquer scarcity. Chapter 11 challenges this view of scarcity.

The only issue on which Marx and his followers have a clear disagreement with the mainstream is over the role of the nation-state. And here Marxists clearly went wrong in underestimating the pull of nationalism on the working class during World War I, in which German, Austrian, and Hungarian workers slaughtered Russian, British, French, Italian, and (toward the end) American workers—and vice versa. In any case, official Marxism in Russia and, later, in China abandoned Marx's internationalism in favor of a rather crude nationalism when faced with the need to mobilize mass support. And nationalism is no less potent in the first decade of the twenty-first century.

In short, mainstream economists and Marxists largely agree on the assumptions of modernity even though they disagree totally on the issue of how well capitalism fulfills the promise of a society based on the rational, calculating self-interested individual. The fight to the death is not about goals but means: Marx's utopia, in which I am free "to do one thing today and another tomorrow, to hunt in the morning, fish in the afternoon, rear cattle in the evening, criticize after dinner, just as I have a mind" (Marx and Engels 1959 [1845], 254), is an individualistic utopia, just as Marx's argument for the superiority of socialism over capitalism rests on an ideology of knowledge that favors planning and calculation over impulse and intuition. Marx's problem with bourgeois society is not its promise of the reign of the calculating, maximizing individual who acts in terms of self interest, but the failure of capitalism to deliver on its promise. The problem with "Freedom,

Equality, Property and Bentham" (K. Marx 1959 [1867], 176) is that the working class gets so little of any of them, not that these goals are problematic in themselves.

What about Ecology?

Though my critique is not red, it has more than a little green in it. In the first place, for many ecologists and some communitarians, community includes ecology. In *A Sand County Almanac,* one of the basic texts of the contemporary ecology movement, Aldo Leopold expresses a philosophy of caring based on the idea that we humans are members of a larger community and are bound to this community by ethical ties:

> We abuse land because we regard it as a commodity belonging to us. When we see land as a community to which we belong, we may begin to use it with love and respect. . . .
>
> That land is a community is the basic concept of ecology, but that land is to be loved and respected is an extension of ethics. . . .
>
> All ethics so far evolved rest upon a single premise: that the individual is a member of a community of interdependent parts. . . . The land ethic simply enlarges the boundaries of the community to include soils, waters, plants, and animals, or collectively: the land. . . . A land ethic changes the role of Homo sapiens from conqueror of the land-community to plain member and citizen of it. It implies respect for his fellow-members, and also respect for the community as such. (Leopold 1968 [1949], viii–ix, 203–204)

In the United States, Leopold's ideas have hardly become mainstream in the six decades since the publication of *A Sand County Almanac.* But outside the modern West, some people actually live what Leopold preached. Andean culture, for example, is predicated on a community that includes humans, gods, and nature, all of which exist, interact, and converse on a basis of mutuality and reciprocity:

> In the Andean mode of thinking, *Ayllu* [community] refers not only to relationships between human beings but to the relationship between all the members of the *Pacha*—the stars, the sun, the moon, the hills, lakes, rivers, mountains, meadows, the plants and the animals of the *sallqa* (wild) and of the *chacra* [the cultivated field and orchard], along with the rocks and the human beings or *runas*, all are relatives and are at once children, parents and siblings. (Valladolid Rivera 1998, 58–59)

It is hard to exaggerate the difference between regarding nature as part of one's community and regarding nature as an input into a calculus of the self-interested individual's utility. A community extending to animals and plants, fields and rocks, rivers and mountains, a community extending backward in time to the ancestors and forward to generations yet unborn, will find the language of trade-offs and opportunity costs as alien as the calculating self-interested individual will find the idea of responsibility and ethical obligation.

Even when the point of departure for an ecological critique is the individual, this critique retains much common ground with the communitarian critique. An individualistic ecological critique also has two prongs: first, markets undermine the prospects for sustainability; second, economics facilitates the market.

How does the market, in the sense of a self-regulating system for allocating resources and distributing income and wealth, undermine ecology? Economists have got one thing right: markets promote production of goods and services.[4] If you see the world from an ecological perspective, stimulating production is itself problematic: economic growth and perhaps even present levels of production and consumption are not sustainable indefinitely. The question becomes how to limit production and consumption.

Some ecologists—the late Garrett Hardin comes to mind—see the problem primarily in terms of population growth and propose a lifeboat ethic of every man for himself. Poor countries with high population densities, particularly countries whose populations are growing rapidly, are to be left to their own devices, to sink or swim (Hardin 1968). Any assistance that might be offered would only exacerbate the problem.

In the global perspective urged by the Bruntland Commission, which first gave currency to the term *sustainable development* (World Commission on Environment and Development 1987), focusing blame on the poor seems misplaced. The major contributors both to environmental degradation and to resource depletion are the rich countries, not the poor countries. And the leader in both departments, not surprisingly, is the United States, which with 5 percent of the world's population accounts for approximately 25 percent of the world's carbon dioxide emissions, an indicator of the disproportionate U.S. contribution both to global warming and to the depletion of the planet's nonrenewable energy sources (American Museum of Natural History, 2007).

The relevant question for our purposes, however, is not whether to blame the poor or the rich, but whether markets properly take into account the degradation of the environment or the depletion of natural resources. And if not, why not?

Degradation and depletion in fact pose different problems. Environmental degradation turns on effects of production and consumption that are not mediated through markets, the economist's "externalities." Pollution—such as the sulfur oxides emitted in the process of generating electricity from high-sulfur coal and oil (the main cause of acid rain) or the carbon dioxide emitted as a by-product of the combustion of carbon-based fuels (the principal cause of global warming)—is a textbook example of an externality, and even the truest of the true believers recognize that externalities undermine the ability of markets to deliver on the promise of providing the biggest possible pie. Faced with externalities, the issue for most economists is how to invent the missing markets or, failing actual markets, how to imitate the market mechanism. Hence, the economist speaks of trade-offs between the environment and other goods, just as he or she speaks of exchanges between any two goods in the marketplace.

Resource depletion, in the view of ecological critics, overloads the capacity of the market to process information. Markets are not sufficiently forward-looking to reflect the true scarcity of natural resources relative to the demands that will be placed on them in the future. The defenders of markets are not impressed by this argument: in the economist's view, markets assemble all the available information, including the information of those preoccupied with resource depletion. Prices today reflect expected prices tomorrow and as far into as distant a future as one cares to imagine. A Mr. X who expects petroleum reserves, say, to run out in fifty years will project a much higher price than a Ms. Y who expects that new reserves will be discovered faster than the old reserves are played out. If there are enough Xs in the market, then not only the future price but the present price will be higher than in a market dominated by Ys. And this in itself will encourage conservation. Markets have the virtue of making people put their money where their mouths are, and the market price reflects a consensus of knowledge and information.[5]

My position is very simple. Whatever the theoretical possibilities for markets to process information, market prices tell us very little about the future: there are very limited opportunities for people to put their money where their mouths are. The requisite market for, say, delivery of crude oil even in a relatively nearby year like 2020—not to mention for fifty or a hundred years hence—doesn't exist. In the absence of these "futures" markets, Mr. X can put his intuition to the test only by continually rolling over relatively short-dated futures contracts or by holding physical inventories of oil. But the world doesn't always follow the theory. Even if Mr. X is right that the price of oil will increase, say, tenfold in fifty years, in the interim the price may fall so low that Mr. X's collateral is wiped away. Just ask the hedge-fund wizards who flamed out in 1998 when prices "temporarily" departed from the trajectories that their models guaranteed would make them millionaires many times over (Lowenstein 2000).

Additionally, there is little reason to think that the people with money have better mouths, not to mention brains, than others. This is not a problem of asymmetric information, the informational problem on which the economist's own critique focuses (see Appendix A), but a problem of *no*, or at most, very little and very uncertain, information, the kind of problem addressed in Chapters 7, 8, and 9.

All this may severely limit the role of the market, but as in the case of the communitarian critique, we must ask what this has to do with economics. My answer is that the ecological critique is, if anything, more damning of the economist's way of thinking than is the communitarian critique.

Given the recognized importance of externalities, even the most market-friendly economists are likely to recognize a role for government or other collective intervention in the allocation of resources. But what kind of intervention? Even when recognizing the limits of markets, economists generally think in terms of interventions based on the market itself, such as taxes and subsidies that modify the prices that agents face, and almost always formulate their analysis in terms of market-like calculations of benefits and costs. The ecological critique challenges the very idea that we can calculate the benefits and costs of measures to arrest deterioration or enhance sustainability. Many, if not all, critics of economics from an ecological perspective would have us understand ecology as John Maynard Keynes and Joseph Schumpeter understood investment and entrepreneurship—as beyond the scope of calculation and therefore lying squarely in the realm of experiential knowledge, in Keynes's terms the realm of animal spirits (Keynes 1936, 161–162). And for the same reason that led Keynes and Schumpeter to downplay the role of calculation: the overwhelming uncertainty and ignorance in which we must act. The ecologist's suspicion of attempts to calculate benefits and costs of global warming or depletion of oil reserves reflects the same perspective as the argument that markets cannot effectively allocate resources when agents are for relevant intents and purposes clueless about the future.

Of course, there is an important difference between the implications of relying on experiential knowledge in the two settings. Where Keynes and Schumpeter saw the needs of their day as requiring entrepreneurs whose animal spirits would make them willing to take chances and damn the consequences (see Chapter 7), our present ecological situation requires caution and prudence, a disposition not to take chances where there are safer alternatives available.

This approach is not without its own problems, but it may be the most effective antidote to the willingness of too many economists to rely on simple (and simplistic) models to foster the myth that ecological issues—global warming for starters—are at worst minor nuisances that can be dealt with by tinkering with taxes and markets. These economists will have a lot to answer for if the cataclysmic outliers in the set of possible outcomes materialize (Goggin 2004, chap. 3).

Two economists, Herman Daly and the late Kenneth Boulding, pioneered the argument that mainstream economics fails to take adequate account of the ecological constraints under which the economy operates. Boulding (1966) made a distinction between "cowboy" economics appropriate to an open system, which can draw on virtually unlimited stocks of resources and has equally unlimited sinks in which to throw the garbage, and "spaceman" economics, appropriate to a closed system, which, with no stocks and no sinks, must recycle its materials and limit energy consumption to the inflows from the sun. Daly similarly distinguishes between an economics that has to deal with localized externalities from an economics that must address pervasive externalities (Daly and Cobb 1989). In short, the message of Daly and Boulding is that mainstream economics is all well and good when the impact of the economy on the environment and the resource base is small, but that this same economics becomes irrelevant when we are up against ecological constraints.

It is true that neither the problem of externalities nor the problem of resource depletion is predicated on economic growth. A stationary, nongrowing economy also pollutes and draws on fixed resources. The key point is that economic growth transforms the economy to the point that mainstream economics is no longer adequate to diagnose problems or prescribe solutions. With growth, externalities that might be marginal annoyances can become threats to survival. My neighbor's chimney pollutes, but if I have only one neighbor in a quarter-mile radius, I can probably live with the externality of the smoke from his hearth fire. Not so if I live cheek to jowl with many neighbors. Similarly with a natural resource like oil: with or without growth, the oil we use today is not available tomorrow or the day after, but the problem becomes more severe on Wednesday if Tuesday's oil consumption is double Monday's.

Moreover, exponential growth can burst on our consciousness with explosive force. The problem is captured in a parable critics tell about the pond lilies that double in area every day. If the pond is going to be full of lilies on the thirtieth day, on which day will the pond be half full? The answer, surprising to some, is the twenty-ninth day.

Boulding and Daly illuminate the problem of calculating how best to comply with resource and environmental constraints, but both beg the question of when the environment and the resource base will become binding constraints. If the day when the lily pond becomes full is December 31, 2049, or even December 31, 2099, most of us would agree that responsible people cannot escape the need to do something now. But if the day of reckoning is December 31, 2999, most of us would feel that we needn't be in too much of a hurry. If the day of reckoning is far enough in the future, ecological problems may be manageable; if it is close at hand, we will have to go beyond the market, and well beyond economics, in searching for ways to reduce the quantity of resources we use and the volume of garbage we spew out.

So which is it: one hundred or one thousand years? With respect to some issues—global warming for example—there is a broad scientific consensus that the day of reckoning is close at hand. For other issues—like reserves of fossil fuels—the crystal ball is murkier. More to the point, we have only a poor idea of the cost of mitigating global warming or the cost and availability of substitutes for fossil fuels. In any case, whether we make much or little of ecological constraints, especially resource constraints, depends, in my view, more on psychology than on science; "animal spirits" count for more than does assessment of the ecological consequences of a continuation (not to mention acceleration) of historical patterns of growth, or for that matter on different evaluations of an agreed-upon assessment of the ecological prospect.

Optimists believe that there is always a technological fix around the corner—whether the problem is the ozone layer, global warming, or oil depletion.[6] They point to a history of human ingenuity that has averted crisis. For instance, limits on the availability of wood and coal for heat and transport, or whale oil for light, were recognized in the nineteenth century, and it was hardly unreasonable to worry about a future without adequate forests, coal reserves, and whales. The discovery of petroleum removed these concerns. So will it be in the future: technology will provide another source of energy when we have depleted existing sources of petroleum.

Or does technology merely postpone the day of reckoning for a little while?

Pessimists see the future as a game of Russian roulette—just because the bullet doesn't end up in front of the firing pin the first few times you spin the barrel of your revolver, you have no guarantee that it won't be there the next time. And if you keep playing long enough, you can be confident that sooner or later you'll run out of luck.

Who is right? I have no answer to that question, but for reasons that this book will make clear, it is easier for me to resolve the dilemma than it is for someone caught between a congenitally optimistic mainstream economist and a congenitally pessimistic ecological critic. Consider the problem in terms of game theory, as one of choosing whether to act on the assumption that the pessimists are right or on the assumption that the optimists are right. At first glance, this is not terribly helpful because there is no compelling way of choosing whom to believe, no "dominant strategy." We will be better off believing the pessimists if they turn out to have the better crystal ball, and believing the optimists if their guess is correct.

The ecological way of solving the problem is the so-called precautionary principle, which would have us follow a "minimax" strategy—maximize our well-being in the worst-case scenario. We would side with the pessimists to minimize the possibility of unpleasant surprises down the pike.

I come to the same conclusion as the pessimists, but not in order to minimize the possibility of unpleasant surprises. What if most, or even a good deal, of our consumption is devoted to fulfilling relative wants, wants that come out of our desire for respectability, or status, wants whose fulfillment allows us to "keep up with the Joneses"? Then my consumption creates externalities for you: the more I consume, the worse off you are. And vice versa. In this case, we might all benefit from limits on consumption—independently of the ecological benefits of these limits. In this case, there may indeed be a dominant strategy: we all may be better off if we assume the pessimists are right and act accordingly, even if in the end it turns out that the optimists were right all along. In this view, we all would benefit from stepping back from the rat race of work and spend, even if the ecological argument for simple living were to turn out to be wrong.

In this way of posing the problem, we would still describe the payoffs in a matrix with four entries, depending both on the developmental strategy we follow, which is to say whether we heed the pessimists or the optimists, and on who turns out to be right. Even without going through the numbers, it is easy to see that this is a different game from the last one: if we believe the optimists and indulge our tastes for consumption goods, we reduce our satisfactions all around, compared with what is attainable with modest living, because of the negative externality that your consumption has on my well-being (and mine on yours). We do better if the optimists are right than if they are wrong, but not as well as we would have done if we had listened to the pessimists and limited our consumption. Conversely, if we follow the lead of the optimists but the pessimists turn out to be right, we get a double whammy of negative consumption externalities and the ecological damage of high living in a fragile ecology. In both cases, we would do better by living modestly in accordance with the pessimistic counsel. Conclusion: whoever is right, we increase our well-being by living modestly. We might be doing the right thing for the wrong reason, but we would at least be doing the right thing.

The Argument So Far

Here are the themes we have developed:

1. Community is important to a good and meaningful life.
2. The market undermines community because it replaces personal ties of economic necessity by impersonal market transactions.
3. Economics aids and abets the market; its very foundations make community and its virtues invisible and legitimize the focus on efficiency as the normative standard by which to judge economic outcomes.
4. These foundational assumptions must be distinguished from assumptions about the structure of markets, goods, and information. "Structural" critiques are the stuff of economics, and the discipline changes by responding to one or another structural critique. A critique based on foundational assumptions, by contrast, is deeply subversive of the discipline as presently constituted. If one takes the foundational critique seriously, it is hard to ignore community.
5. The foundations of economics are not universal truths about human nature, but implicit assumptions of modernity. The ambivalent relationship between noneconomists and economics reflects the ambivalence with which modernity is regarded. Even in Europe and North

America, the cradle of modernity, we are only half-modern (and a good thing, too).

The next eight chapters explore these foundations, and the last two chapters apply the argument to issues of economic development. We begin with individualism.

CHAPTER 4

Individualism

Individualism is one way of being in the world rather than the only way. I begin with this obvious point because individualism is such an important piece of the ideology of modernity and so central to economics that it is easy to lose sight of the obvious. Let me be clear: by individualism I do not mean the idea that you and I are separate biological entities. "Biological individualism" is a perfectly reasonable idea, particularly if you aim to argue that individualism is universal, but it is useless for our purposes precisely because it makes no distinction between the modern worldview—the worldview of economics—and any other worldview. Raja Ram and Jagat Pal are recognized as separate biological individuals in their Indian village no less than Tom and Bill are recognized as separate on Wall Street or Main Street.

Even if we put aside biological individualism, we quickly run up against the fact that we are dealing with one of those plastic words which mean very different things to different people; even for the same person, its meaning varies according to context. Indeed, I would attribute much of the hold that individualism has on the modern mind to a confusion of meanings. It is easy to see the attraction of individualism in the context of an oppressive regime based on hereditary or ascriptive privilege. In this context, individualism can only appear as liberating. But outside this specific context, it is harder to disentangle those elements of individualism that are truly liberating from those that offer a new form of oppression in place of the old.[1]

There are, to be sure, some common denominators among the different meanings of individualism.[2] First is the *dignity* of each and every human being as something intrinsic to human nature. We are all children of the same God, or we each possess a rational will, or some such universal. Next, *autonomy.* We each have the capacity for rational self-direction, and social conditions are, or should be, such that we can exercise this capacity. Then, *privacy*. There exists a realm of behavior that is, or ought to be, free from outside scrutiny. Finally, *self-development*. There is a normative value in the flowering of each member of society, which is to say that what is unique in each of us should be given expression—at least to the extent that one flower does not crush another.

We can distinguish three spheres to which individualism has been applied, all of which bring out the central role of individualism in the attack on social structures that constrain people's liberty. One is *religious individualism*, the idea—which took hold in Europe with the Reformation (but is hardly unique to Protestantism)—that there is a direct connection between the individual and the divine. In contrast with Catholic doctrine, Protestant individualism has no need for priest or other intermediary. *Political individualism* similarly has no role for intermediate structures between the state and the citizen. No role for religious sect, guild, union, trade association, civic organization, or the myriad other structures that constitute civil society, certainly not if these institutions have a hold on individuals that trumps the individual's autonomy—or loyalty to the state. *Economic individualism* translates the same basic idea to the sphere of production and exchange. The economy ought to be organized on the basis of activity undertaken by property-owning agents who interact in competitive markets, markets in which monopolies or other concentrations of power play no role.[3]

The Economist's Individualism

All of these ideas emerged in the early modern period. But none fully captures the meaning of individualism in the economist's conception of the world. The closest evidently is economic individualism, but our concern here is the individual in the economic imagination, and this is at one remove from, one layer behind, economic individualism. It does not directly concern, as does economic individualism, a set of institutions; it is rather a characterization of people that makes us believe that a certain set of institutions—markets and private property[4]—are the most sensible way of organizing production and exchange.

If we take Adam Smith at face value, he started with a conception of human nature—the calculating, self-interested individual—and moved from that conception to the conclusion that markets are the best hope for channeling our basic drives into socially useful behaviors. My procedure is the opposite, a kind of reverse engineering. I start with markets and ask what we have to assume about human beings to justify the idea that the market system is a desirable way of organizing human action. Not surprisingly, even though Smith and I start at different ends of the argument, there is considerable overlap in our two accounts: here I focus on why the market requires the self-interested individual if it is to function well, but we return to the issue of rational calculation in later chapters.

There are many steps in the argument. First, we have to ask what we mean when we assert that markets are a desirable or sensible way of organizing production and exchange. The brief answer is that mainstream economists have focused on a single virtue: how well economic institutions deliver the goods. Literally. The best economic organization is the organization that provides the biggest pie, the greatest consumption. Efficiency, the minimization of waste, is the name of the game.

Of course, as Appendix A makes clear, economics has for a long time recognized that there is an inherent ambiguity in the idea of the size of the pie once we allow for multiple consumers with a multiplicity of tastes. To resolve this ambiguity, mainstream economics relies on the concept of *Pareto optimality*—outcomes that cannot be improved upon for everybody; the first and second welfare theorems establish reciprocal connections between competitive market outcomes and Pareto optimal outcomes.[5]

Observe that the concept of Pareto optimality already takes us some way toward a particular kind of individualism, *methodological individualism*, in that societal well-being is reduced to the well-being of separate individuals. The individual is the atom, the basic unit which has a logical and existential primacy. But the economist also presupposes the existence of at least one group of individuals, "society," the welfare of which is a legitimate concern. Economics does not require us to examine or justify the idea of society, but I will argue that it is not sheer accident that what is in principle an arbitrary collection of individuals in practice becomes identified with the nation-state (see Chapter 10).

This view of the individual in society should be contrasted with the libertarian view of the individual outside of society. Milton Friedman in particular has gone beyond the standard defense of capitalism on the grounds that this form of economic organization delivers the goods to make the libertarian case that capitalism directly enhances the freedom of the individual (1962). I shall return to this argument in the course of this chapter, but for now the point is that, however important in its own right, Friedman's libertarian argument for the market is not standard economics.

In the libertarian view, any group larger than the individual is the creation of individuals who come together to promote their separate interests. The state, for instance, can be justified only on the Hobbesian ground (see Chapter 6) that the gains to the individual of curtailing the liberty of others exceed the costs of limiting one's own freedom. Thus the libertarian view is not only that group behavior, policies, and even ethical judgments are to be reduced to their effects on individuals, that the actions undertaken by larger units have no legitimacy apart from their beneficial effects on their constituents; but also that these larger units exist at the sufferance of the individuals who comprise them.[6] The Enlightenment economist (as well as minister in the court of Louis XVI) Anne-Robert Jacques Turgot contributed such a formulation of the individual outside society to Denis Diderot's *Encyclopédie* (1752–1772, 7, 73, quoted in Lukes 1973, 77): "The citizens have rights, rights that are sacred for the very body of society: the citizens exist independently of society; they form its necessary elements; and they only enter it in order to put themselves, with all their rights, under the protection of those very laws to which they sacrifice their liberty."

From a libertarian point of view, it makes no sense to ask how to maximize the size of the economic pie for society as a whole—the central normative question of economics. No one is—or should be—concerned with anything more than his or her slice, and an individual will not agree to participate in society unless by doing so his or her slice is enlarged. And society's only legitimate role is to ensure that whatever rules of the game have been accepted by the players are in fact followed. In mainstream economics, by contrast, individualism plays an instrumental role: individuals are so constituted that, by their self-serving actions, they promote efficient production and distribution when their interactions are mediated by a market system.[7]

Methodological individualism provides a point of departure for understanding how the individual serves society, but only a beginning. There are four further assumptions that flesh out the basic idea of individualism in a way that Pareto optimality becomes a plausible criterion of sensible economic organization and the market a plausible means for realizing Pareto optimality. Without *given preferences*, Pareto optimality may not even be a coherent criterion of societal well-being, much less a plausible one. If the assumptions of *universal agency, radical subjectivism,* and *self-interest* do not hold, market outcomes can possibly be improved upon for everybody, which is to say that the market fails even the minimal test of Pareto optimality.

Given Preferences. This assumption is in some sense the hallmark of economics. Descriptive economics can get along very well without assuming that preferences are given once and for all, but the normative and constructive agenda of demonstrating the virtue of a market system requires given preferences. Without this assumption, we can't take preference satisfaction as a measure of well-being. If the grass is always greener on the other side of the fence, an individual's choices don't tell us much about his or her well-being because choices change every time the fence is crossed. Things are not any better if the grass is always greener on this side of the fence. In neither case can we build up a picture of societal well-being from the raw material of individual choice, as the Pareto criterion dictates.

Even more troubling is the very real possibility of path-dependent preferences: if I listen to Bach, I may come to prefer Bach; however, if I listen to the Beatles, I may end up preferring the Beatles. If musical preferences reflect an accident of the listening that one has done rather than some innate qualities of mind and heart, it is hard to vest these preferences with the authority over individual well-being that the Pareto criterion presupposes.

In extreme form—and economists in this respect tend to the extreme—preferences include not only tastes but values. There is no difference between one's view of the relative merits of chocolate and vanilla ice cream and one's view of the relative merits of prostitution, sex between friends, and sex within a committed relationship. In economics the individual is no more than a set of preferences, coupled with the capacity to act on them.

Universal Agency. Universal agency means that everybody has the capacity to deliberate and calculate alternative courses of action, to make rational choices, and to act on these choices; it means, so to speak, that everybody is a player. This does not mean that we are all endowed with the same resources of physical strength, intellectual capacity, or capital assets. But it does mean that we each have the minimal capacity to participate on the same terms as everybody else—and are not prevented from doing so by law, custom, or naked power.[8] Thus children, who have not yet attained full emotional and rational development, lack agency. In premodern times, serfs, whatever their stage of emotional and rational development, lacked agency. In the United States, only in the twentieth century did blacks and women come to be recognized as agents in their own right.

Universal agency also means that we all act without coercion. Coercion is of course not the same thing as constraint. Economics has been called, not totally accurately but not without reason, the study of choice under constraint, which is to say that constraint is the general rule: constraint is, after all, no more than the reflection of scarcity. But we recognize that the choice between giving up one's money or giving up one's life under the constraint of an armed robber is fundamentally different from the choice between taking a vacation in the mountains or taking a vacation by the sea. It is the your-money-or-your-life kind of constraint that is eliminated by the assumption that there is no coercion. (Choices where there are no good alternatives have been called tragic or desperate choices by Calabresi and Bobbit 1978, Walzer 1983, and Nussbaum 2001. Chapter 12 examines the tragic choice between working in sweatshops and worse.)

Agency rules out coercion, but what if intermittent bouts of ill health make it impossible to hold a job, or limited skills and long spells of unemployment mean that the upside is bare survival and the downside is economic disaster? Under these conditions, does the individual have agency to make such decisions as how much money to put aside for retirement or for a rainy day? People whose life experience continually impresses on them their impotence, their inability to carry out their plans, may have as little real agency as the man faced with the choice between his money or his life.

It is probably clear why universal agency is necessary for a market system to reach a Pareto optimal outcome. Lacking agency, individuals cannot act on, or even express, their desires. A slave's workday is not determined by a free exchange of labor power for the means to consume, and for the slave, markets are not vehicles for voluntary exchanges.

Radical Subjectivism. Radical subjectivism is the idea that there is no judge beyond the individual of his or her preferences. In Lawrence Summers's words, "One important thing that is distinctive about the way economists approach the world is their great emphasis on respect for individuals—and the needs, tastes, choices and judgment they make for themselves" (Summers 2003). Not only are preferences given; satisfaction of these preferences is the appropriate measure of the individual's well-being. *De gustibus non disputandum est:* "It is the basis of much economic analysis that the good is an aggregation of many individuals' assessments of their own well-being, and not something that can be assessed apart from individual judgments on the basis of some overarching or separate theory" (ibid.).

This is not such a radical idea when it comes to chocolate versus vanilla ice cream, but it is extremely radical when ethical and moral judgments are assimilated to tastes. In fact, this idea appeared at the dawn of modernity, in benign form in the sixteenth-century French humanist Michel de Montaigne's relativism (see Chapter 5) and more provocatively in the thinking of the seventeenth-century English philosopher Thomas Hobbes. Here is Hobbes's version (1968 [1651], 120):

> Whatsoever is the object of any mans Appetite or Desire; that is it, which he for his part calleth *Good:* And the object of his Hate, and Aversion, *Evill;* And of his Contempt, *Vile,* and *Inconsiderable.* For these words of Good, Evill, and Contemptible, are ever used with relation to the person who useth them: There being nothing simply and absolutely so; nor any common Rule of Good and Evill, to be taken from the nature of the objects themselves; but from the Person of the man.

Hobbes was clearly ahead of his time, for this was undoubtedly one of the ideas that made *Hobbesian* a term of abuse. It was only in the twentieth century that radical subjectivism came into its own and attained a respectability that makes it the conventional wisdom of our day rather than the subject of intense controversy.

Radical subjectivism is a necessary assumption in the argument for the market. If there are grounds for rejecting some preferences, values, and beliefs in favor of others, it cannot be argued that a system that facilitates the satisfaction of whatever preferences a person might happen to hold is promoting the well-being of that person, much less the well-being of society.

Self-Interest. First off, self-interest is not a necessary element of individualism, for individualism is compatible with other-regarding values and behavior. Indeed, Immanuel Kant, a contemporary of Adam Smith and perhaps the Enlightenment philosopher par excellence, made individualism the starting point of his philosophy, but Kant's individualism is hardly the economist's individualism. Kant's categorical imperative, the apex of his moral philosophy, enjoins us to treat our fellow human beings not as means to our own satisfaction, not in terms of our own self-interest, but as ends in themselves, as individuals whose goals and strivings are as worthy as our own. Yet Alexis de Tocqueville, the astute French observer of the nineteenth-century American scene, thought that individualism must eventually become self-interested (1969 [1835–1840, vol. 2, part 2, chap. 2], 506). And the economist's version of individualism is surely self-interested—in one sense or another.

Self-interest, like community, like individualism, indeed, like many of the concepts this book examines, means different things to different people. Economists often interpret self-interest so broadly that I am "self-interested" if I derive satisfaction from the happy face of a child eating ice cream and buy a kid an ice-cream cone in order to increase my own satisfaction. At this extreme, whatever I do must serve my self-interest—if it didn't, I would do something else.[9] Giving away all my worldly possessions to feed the poor is no less an expression of my self-interest than is spending my money on wine, women, and song.

The many problems with this notion of self-interest start with its imperviousness to contradiction. If all behavior is self-regarding, the proposition that people are self-interested becomes essentially definitional; we have no way of knowing whether this is an apt characterization or not. In addition to being unfalsifiable, identifying self-interest with actual behavior is circular. Behavior reveals self-interest. How do we know? Because self-interest guides behavior. In this broad interpretation, self-interest becomes just another way of saying that individuals maximize utility.

For normative purposes, the major problem of permitting other-regarding behavior in the tent of self-interest is that it allows a flood of externalities to enter into consumer choice. I not only rejoice in seeing smiling faces around me and mourn your losses as my own, but I may be buffeted by the winds of fashion and fad. My utility depends not only on my consumption but on yours—and everybody else's. If the externality is negative, so that I feel deprived when I see you consume, keeping up with the Joneses may become endemic. But we know that, in the presence of externalities, the identification of the competitive market with society's overall well-being breaks down, even in the limited sense of the first and second welfare theorems. If people consume to keep up with the Joneses, then the market will generally lead to greater production and consumption than is socially optimal on the basis of the Pareto criterion. Consuming becomes like standing up to get a better view at a football game. If I stand, the person behind me has to stand just to see as well as before. And the person behind her. Soon the whole stadium is standing and no one has a better view: we would all be better off if we sat down. Similarly, if you and I consume to keep up with the Joneses, we would all—you, me, and possibly

Mr. and Mrs. Jones as well—be better off if we took more time to smell the roses.

The idea that a market system is the most sensible way of organizing economic activity also fails to hold up if individuals are generally altruistic. The market is not an effective framework for registering the pleasure derived from someone else's being well fed, clothed, and housed. In the presence of altruism, the externalities are positive rather than negative, but the market system fares no better as a machine for efficiently allocating resources than when people are concerned with keeping up with the Joneses.

Thus normative considerations point toward a narrow definition of self-interest—one in which self-interest is a focus on one's own self, where my perception of how I ought to act, how I ought to be, is completely independent of what anybody else in society is consuming or doing. For the market to produce desirable outcomes, even in the limited sense of Pareto optimality, economic man must be an island unto himself.

A narrow definition of self-interest is a necessary element of the normative agenda of economics for two reasons: first, a focus on the self eliminates the web of interconnections associated with a broader notion of self-interest; that is, a narrow notion of self-interest eliminates a whole class of externalities that might rob markets of their Pareto optimal properties. There is an additional reason for taking a narrow view of self-interest: a broader view is inconsistent with the notion of given preferences. If one is other-regarding in the positive sense of feeling a neighbor's pain and joy, it is difficult to see how one's preferences would not respond to the other's notion of the good. Our Golden Rule should be to do unto others as they would have us do unto them; as self-regarding people, the most we might do is to treat others as we would have them treat us, a Golden Rule that does not require us to get out of our own skins. If I am other-regarding in the negative sense of keeping up with the Joneses, then my preferences will respond to the fads and fashions that move Mr. and Mrs. Jones.

The bottom line is that the normative agenda of economics severely constrains the meaning of self-interest. Each individual must be concerned only with his or her own consumption, eschewing both altruism and envy. Any concern with the consumption of others would jeopardize the ability of the market to make the most efficient use of existing resources—even if all the other foundational assumptions were fulfilled.

Whatever Happened to Self-Development?

The economist's individualism has a family resemblance to other meanings of individualism. Agency and self-interest are projections of autonomy; given preferences reflect privacy and perhaps also dignity; and radical subjectivism is the image of self-development. But the images are askew, like those in the fun-house mirror at the county fair. If individualism is a core assumption of modernity, economics is not only a stripped-down version of modernity; it is at the same time a distorted one.

It is the confusion of meanings that allows individualism to hold such sway both in the modern world and in modern economics. Individualism means one thing—dignity, privacy, autonomy, and self-development—in the general language, and it means another—given preferences, universal agency, radical subjectivism, and self-interest—in the economics that describes, judges, and molds the behavior of ordinary people. In a word, bait and switch.

Take self-development. Many observers of modernity, from John Stuart Mill (1947 [1859]) to C. B. Macpherson (1987) and Robert Bellah and his collaborators (1996), have been at pains to separate self-development from other aspects of individualism. Mill, living in the first bloom of Enlightenment freedom, is celebratory (Mill's term for self-development is *individuality*). Macpherson (who distinguishes *developmental individualism* from *possessive individualism*) is less effusive than Mill, and Bellah and his coauthors (who separate *expressive individualism* from *utilitarian individualism*) are even more guarded.

But however celebratory or critical we may be of the idea of self-development, we should have no doubt that self-development is opposed to the basic idea of individualism in economics. Self-development is the flowering of that which is special and unique within each of us, the process by which the acorn becomes the oak rather than the maple, by which the generic and the unique combine to form an individual who is ever in a state of becoming. Central to this process is change in preferences. Self-development is thus the opposite of given preferences. Alexandre Vinet, a Swiss literary historian and contemporary of Mill, went even further. For Vinet, self-development and individualism were enemies. In *Etudes sur Blaise Pascal* (4th ed.), Vinet stated that individualism was "an obstacle and negation of any society; [self development] a principle to which society owes all its savor, life, and reality" (quoted in Swart 1962, 84–85).

Of course, once we recognize that preferences change, we must also recognize that the process of change is a social process, a process that depends on social interactions of all sorts. It becomes difficult to conceive of the relationship between the individual and society as a one-way street leading from the individual to society. Individuals may or may not construct society. Society most assuredly constructs individuals.

Holism as Counterpoint

Individualism—more specifically, the economist's version of individualism—offers at best a one-sided picture. It doesn't, we have seen, give us much of a handle on the willingness of the Amish to allow a child to die in order to foster community (see Chapter 2), or the refusal of the Thai forest dweller to accept a division of the forest into separate lots (see Chapter 13). For the Amish as for the Thai forest dweller, the focus is on the relationships between people, and individual well-being is subordinated to promoting or at least maintaining these relationships.

This is to say that there is another side to people, a side diametrically opposed to notions of given preferences, universal agency, radical subjectivism, and self-interest. "Holism," to use Louis Dumont's (1977, 4) terminology for an organic conception of people and their relationships with one another, replaces the atomic metaphor with a subatomic view of the individual. We are like neutrinos, positrons, and other particles that have a transitory existence unless united with the complementary particles that make up a sustainable whole. Social relationships define individuals, and it is these relationships, not the individuals themselves, that are the primary matter of society. Individuals are like the points at the two ends of a line segment in a geometric construction. The line segment itself, the relationship between the points, is what provides structure, not the end points. In place of given preferences, universal agency, radical subjectivism, and self-interest, we have malleable preferences, mutual dependence, community standards, and obligation.

Malleable Preferences. As the individual is constructed by society, so are his or her preferences. If we insist, as economists are wont to do, on identifying people with their preferences, we must see people as human *becomings* rather than as human beings. For some, the idea that preferences are malleable conjures up images of Madison Avenue and persuasion for hire. Advertising is surely one aspect of malleable preferences, and nobody but an economist committed to the hypothesis of given preferences can fail to see persuasion as a primary role for advertising.

But that is not all there is to the story. A chief fault line between the economist's and the noneconomist's conception of politics lies precisely on the issue of the nature of preferences. Economists, who see (or at least take) preferences as given, analyze politics in terms of preference aggregation: how do we add up or otherwise aggregate preferences across people. Nobel Laureate Kenneth Arrow created a new subdiscipline of economics, "social choice," with his 1951 demonstration that without some limits on the variability of individual preferences, there was no way of aggregating individual preferences into an ordering for a whole group of people—at least not without violating some basic assumptions of consistency and the like—while taking account of the preferences of the various members of the group (Arrow 1963 [1951]). Much ink has been spilled since Arrow published his remarkable result, but no one, to my knowledge, has pointed out the obvious: the very process of socialization imposes limits on the variability of preferences, values, and beliefs. To be sure, different cultures impose different limits, but every culture imposes some limits. So the assumption of no restrictions on preferences besides consistency may be more demanding than is necessary once we understand the universality of cultural influences on preference formation.

In opposition to Arrow's view of social choice as solely an aggregation of preexisting individual preferences, I would argue that social choice is also about changing people's minds—which is, after all, a main point of political debate.[10] Once in a great while, the representative institutions of the U.S. government, conceived of by the Founding Fathers as institutions for transforming as well as for registering preferences, actually rise to the occasion—despite the baleful influence of money, media, and manipulation on the deliberative process.

Mutual Dependence. As an individual, one has partial and incomplete agency. Agency is a function of our relationships with other members of society rather than a given of the individual. In a holistic conception of the person, we never attain complete agency as separate persons. We cannot because interdependence is part of the human condition.

Nor is this necessarily for the worse. Granted, the limits on personal agency experienced by serfs or slaves were oppressive, but as parent or child, teacher or student, husband or wife, one also faces limits on agency because of the constraints of mutual dependence. In short, a holistic conception of people necessarily limits agency, but the limits run the gamut from oppressive to life-enhancing, with a large gray area of relationships that have the potential to be either—and sometimes both at the same time. Mutual dependence may be the source of tremendous problems, but it is also mutually nourishing.[11]

Lawrence Kushner, rabbi not only in the contemporary sense of leader of a Jewish congregation but also in the traditional meaning of teacher, summarized mutual dependence this way:

> No one has within themselves
> All the pieces to their puzzle.
> . . . . .
> Everyone carries with them at least one and probably
> Many pieces to someone else's puzzle.
> . . . . .
> And when you present your piece
> . . . . .
> To another, whether you know it or not,
> Whether they know it or not,
> You are a messenger from the Most High. (Kushner 2000 [1977], 70)

The distinction between coercion and constraint, if blurred in an individualistic perspective, dissolves in a holistic context. Under conditions of interdependence, we won't get far with a binary opposition, asking whether Sally or Bill is choosing "freely," which is to say that Sally or Bill is optimizing under constraint or is instead being obliged to behave in a certain way. Rather, each specific choice situation requires a separate analysis of the dynamic of interdependence and how this dynamic plays out in the realm of Sally's and Bill's behavior. In the context of community, we will never resolve the tension between constraint and coercion.[12]

Community Standards. Group standards override individual preferences. Actually, Hobbes understood this, for immediately following his bow in the direction of radical subjectivism, he bows to the judgment of the community: what we call good and evil depends on "the Person of the man," but this is true only in the state of nature:

> There being nothing simply and absolutely [good and evil]; nor any common
> Rule of Good and Evill, to be taken from the nature of the objects them-
> selves; but from the Person of the man (where there is no Common-wealth

[that is, in the state of nature]); or, (in a Common-wealth,) from the Person that representeth it; or from an Arbitrator or Judge, whom men disagreeing shall by consent set up, and make his sentence the Rule thereof. (Hobbes 1968 [1651], 120–121)

Obligation. Opposed to self-interest is the moral duty to act for the well-being of others—for individuals or for community. Recall the Amish parents who let their child die of a treatable immune deficiency because, one way or another, treatment would fray the bonds of community. In Chapter 2, I argued that we can make sense of the couple's action only in terms of a moral obligation to sustain the community.

It is important to distinguish obligation from externalities as an explanation for other-regarding behavior. In the case of these Amish parents, the alternative to understanding their action in terms of obligation would be to understand it in terms of a complex calculation by the couple of the pluses and minuses to their own utility from allowing their child to die versus treating the child. In this perspective, the direct loss of utility from the death of the baby is counterbalanced by the increase of utility that the couple gets from the positive effect of their sacrifice on their fellow Amish. What positive effect? The perceived well-being of their neighbors rises as a result of the greater sense of solidarity each one of them feels, which is in turn the result of the self-sacrificing action of the parents.

Arcane? Yes. Logically consistent? Yes. Plausible? Not unless you are an economist.

How could we ever sort out the two interpretations, externalities and obligation? And why should we concern ourselves with whether we take account of others because to do so positively affects our own happiness or because we feel morally obliged to do so?

In both cases, the normative agenda of economics is undermined because externalities and obligation create similar problems for the welfare-maximizing claims on behalf of the market. But obligation is much more subversive of the way economists approach the world than is other-regarding behavior framed in terms of externalities. Obligation puts the ethical issue between self- and other-regarding behavior front and center, whereas externalities blur the ethical issue by putting other-regarding behavior on the same plane as any experience that turns up the utility meter. Thinking like an economist survives externalities much better than obligation.

Important as it is for the purposes of this book, it is not easy to disentangle externalities from obligation, because externalities in an individual calculus of utilities and duty will often lead to the same kinds of actions, behaviors, and choices. But not always: the surprise ending of a short story by Jean-Paul Sartre ("Le Mur" [The Wall], in a collection of the same name, 1971 [1939], 9–35), provides important insight into the difference between externalities and obligation.

Sartre's hero, Pablo Ibbieta, captured by the Fascists during the Spanish Civil War, is offered a reprieve from the death sentence that otherwise will be carried out momentarily. The quid pro quo? Tell us, his interrogator demands, where a certain Ramon Gris is hiding. Ibbieta, knowing that Gris is safely hidden, thinks to have a bit of fun with his captors; he sends the Fascists on a wild goose chase to a nearby cemetery.

To Ibbieta's astonishment, he is reprieved: he learns from a fellow prisoner that Gris has been found more or less where Ibbieta sent the search party.

The real surprise is Ibbieta's reaction. We expect him to be horrified, or at least grief stricken, as would a man who has acted out of a calculus of utilities in which Gris's life and well-being entered into his own utility calculus with enough kick to make him willing to sacrifice his life to keep Gris alive. But no, Ibbieta is quite pleased with the outcome. He has acted not out of fellow feeling but out of obligation—not obligation to Gris so much as to a moral code:

> I would have liked to understand the reasons for my conduct. I preferred to die than to give up Gris. Why? My friendship for him had died a little before dawn [when Ibbieta was to be executed], at the same time as my love for Concha [Ibbieta's girlfriend], at the same time as my desire to live. Doubtless I still held him in high esteem; he was tough. But it wasn't for that reason that I accepted dying in his place: his life had no more value than mine; no life had any value. They were going to stick a man up against a wall and shoot him until he died: if it was me or Gris or somebody else, it was all the same. I well knew that he was more useful than me to the cause of Spain, but I didn't give a damn about Spain and anarchism: nothing mattered anymore. Yet I was there, I could have saved my skin by giving up Gris and I was refusing to do it. I found this funny: it was obstinacy. (32–33)

Gris's fateful move from a safe house to the cemetery was totally beyond the ken of Ibbieta.[13] Ibbieta has a clear conscience and delights in the existential

twist of fate that allows him to see another day.[14] He has fulfilled his obligation, and the externalities of Gris's fate are beside the point.

Individualism and Holism as Navigational Aids

Resist the inclination to think of individualism and holism as pictures
of different societies, a picture of the modern contrasted with the non-
modern.[15] These may be pictures of two different societies, but only as ideal
types; in reality, these two ways of conceptualizing ourselves in relationship
to others are maps used jointly to navigate social interactions—in every
society.

Society, after all, exists in the minds of its members, and how we imagine
society determines how we navigate it. In the European village of medieval
times or in the Andean village of today, just as in the cities of contemporary
North America, people use both maps, the individualistic and the holistic.

Seeing individualism and holism in terms of coexisting maps gives us a
new perspective on the old question of cultural progress. Once we move
from the material realm to the cultural realm, it is not exactly clear what the
yardstick of progress is, but in the modern West the temptation has been to
cut through all the ambiguities of progress by positing absolutes like freedom
and equality. Georg Wilhelm Friedrich Hegel famously saw human history in
terms of a struggle of the Absolute for total freedom. Karl Marx thought he
was just putting Hegel right side up when he posited the Forces of Production as the Absolute; he shared Hegel's view that the realization of human
potential lay in the expansion of human freedom. (In the Marxian view,
this realization could happen only on a general basis once humankind had
reached a level of material abundance adequate to solve the problem of
scarcity.)

The concern with freedom is no less prominent today. Indeed, three
economists, Nobel laureates all—W. Arthur Lewis, Milton Friedman, and
Amartya Sen—have written highly regarded books that take as a premise
that freedom is a universal value, a good of which there can never be too
much. The appendix to Lewis's *Theory of Economic Growth* poses the question
of growth to what end. Lewis answers that growth enlarges the array of
human choice and thus human freedom. Sen's *Development as Freedom* expands on Lewis's theme, arguing that, beyond the instrumentalist idea of
development as more goods and services, the expansion of choice is a virtue
in its own right. Friedman's *Capitalism and Freedom* takes an even stronger

position: that markets are not only vehicles for delivering goods and services, but are themselves an important component of freedom. Agency in economic matters is viewed not only instrumentally, not only as a means to a larger economic pie, but also in libertarian terms, as an end in itself—to truck, barter, and exchange are for Friedman existential goals.

The problem with such approaches is that they do not question the assumption that freedom, or agency in my terminology, is an unqualified good—the more, the better. To be sure, within the perspective of individualism, whether the economist's instrumental sort or the libertarian's absolute sort, more choice is always a good thing. But from a holistic perspective, it depends: the expansion of agency is desirable when set against oppressive relationships, but not in every case. In a holistic view of the world, agency is necessarily limited by a universal need for relationships with other human beings, and it would be throwing the baby out with the bathwater to oppose all mutual dependence in the name of freedom.

Outside the modern West, the individualistic and holistic maps have coexisted and continue to coexist openly, sometimes in tension, sometimes as complements. Even in contemporary Western society, where the individualistic map has come to dominate, the holistic map continues to play a role, for it is a necessary constituent of the glue that holds us together. The holistic map has gone underground, or, what amounts to the same thing, is considered the private and largely feminine map appropriate to the home, whereas the individualistic map—the public, masculine map—is appropriate to navigating public space. Community is one casualty of this imbalance. As the nineteenth-century sociologist Ferdinand Tönnies put it, "Community ways of life live on in Market society as the only real ways, even though they are decaying and even dying out" (Tönnies 2001 [1887], 252).

An economics that treats the whole person, the person animated by holistic as well as individualistic concerns, will necessarily take account of both maps and their interplay. We are a long way from such an economics, but it is at least a first step in the right direction to recognize what we lack.

Markets in Pollution Again

Chapter 3 began with a rhetorical question posed in a memo by Lawrence Summers when he was the World Bank's Chief Economist:[16] "Just between you and me, shouldn't the World Bank be encouraging more migration of the dirty industries to the LDCs [less developed countries]?" The memo justified moving dirty industries by rather standard economic arguments. If pollution could easily be transported from one country to another, both exporters and importers would be better off, assuming the exporters paid the importers to take a load of pollution: "I've always thought that under-populated countries in Africa are vastly *under*-polluted" (*Economist* 1992, 66).

Alas, dirty air cannot be packaged for shipping, and the transport of solid wastes is prohibitively expensive. The second-best option is to move dirty industries to the LDCs. Even though an exporter, say California, cannot pay Africa to take a load of dirty air off its hands, it can in effect pay to have polluting industries relocate from Los Angeles to Mombasa. And both sides will benefit, Los Angeles from a better environment and Mombasa from greater employment opportunities. Pollution may pose a problem for Africans as well as for Californians, but "the concern over an agent that causes a one-in-a-million change in the odds of prostate cancer is obviously going to be much higher in a country where people survive to get prostate cancer than in a country where under-5 mortality is 200 per thousand" (*Economist* 1992, 66).

The idea of trade in pollution highlights the role that individualism plays in the economist's love affair with the market, even a market that seems outlandish to noneconomists. A model will help us keep the main points at issue more sharply in focus. Suppose that it were possible to ship a load of, say, radioactive waste from the United States to Africa costlessly, and let us assume, to make things even simpler, that the trade is between individuals, Mr. C and Mr. A, rather than between governments. Let us suppose further that, in full knowledge of the potential harm from radioactivity, Mr. C and Mr. A enter into a voluntary agreement whereby Mr. A agrees to accept a ton of radioactive waste along with a payment of $200 from Mr. C.[17] Standard economics says that both Mr. A and Mr. C, and hence "society," are better off after the trade than before.

What's wrong with this conclusion? First, the assumption that preferences are given. If preferences are not given, then it becomes at the very least necessary to address the feedback from what Mr. C does to what he believes. If he can pay somebody to get rid of radioactive waste, it is easy for him to persuade himself that he has no further ethical responsibility for generating this waste. Out of sight, out of mind. Mr. C passes the ethical buck along with the 200 bucks he pays Mr. A. He does not face the ethical questions that pollution raises—for example, how does one relate to the land, to other people, to future generations?

Neither does Mr. A have any incentive to face the practical questions of how to modify technology and lifestyle to generate less pollution. "Out of sight, out of mind" applies at the pragmatic level as well as at the ethical. If necessity is the mother of invention, the division of labor that accompanies trade may be its wicked stepmother. Paying another to bear the burden of his pollution, Mr. C has no reason to interest himself in alternative ways of consuming and producing.[18] By contrast, if Mr. C has to live with his wastes, he may rethink both lifestyle and technology even if he is totally self-interested.

Then there is the issue of universal agency. Most likely Mr. A is acting out of dire necessity, maybe extreme hunger, in agreeing to the trade. The economist will insist—and it is not an easy argument to counter—that there is no reason to question such a trade. On the contrary.

Maybe, and maybe not. There is certainly good reason to argue that in a situation of dire necessity, Mr. A lacks agency. As has been noted, there is a difference between coercion and constraint, and the (often implicit) assumption of agency transforms all choices into decisions of constrained maximization.

What is the difference between coercion and choice under constraint? For one thing, the capacity to exercise the rational, deliberative faculty, which for many defenders of individualism is the basis of the equal dignity and respect owed all human beings. Faced with dire necessity, like hunger, people are presumably not in a position to weigh alternatives with the cool calculation that mainstream economic theory assumes.

Dire necessity does not inevitably rule out deliberation and calculation. It is possible to argue that the Amish couple who allowed their child to die lacked agency, but it would be difficult to argue that their lack of agency was because dire necessity precluded deliberation. The most that can be said is that dire necessity precludes the presumption of deliberation.

This is, however, an especially slippery slope: what if it were to turn out that the cool, calculating economic man (or woman) is yet another myth? To the extent that agency depends on calculation, a central tenet of individualism would be jeopardized. The line between coercion and choice under constraint would become blurred, just as the economists say it is. However, the blurring would not be because all choice reflects constraint in the way economists conceptualize choice, but rather because all choice is marked by the limits of rationality.

In addition to issues of given preferences and agency, trade in pollution brings us up against the assumption of radical subjectivism. Outsiders may think that neither Mr. C nor Mr. A is acting on an appropriate ethical plane, regardless of whether one or the other of them might modify his values, beliefs, and ultimately his actions if trade were forbidden. "None of your beeswax," says the economist.

Once again the noneconomist cringes. If Mr. C believes that there is nothing wrong with solving his problem by passing it on to Mr. A, do the rest of us have no recourse? If Mr. A enters the bargain not because he will otherwise go hungry, but because he aspires to the material lifestyle of a Californian, do his fellow citizens have no say?

Finally, there is the assumption of self-interest. If Mr. A is choosing to be a garbage can for Mr. C out of the necessity of hunger, his choice is an extreme version of desperate or tragic choice, a subject to which we will return near the end of this book (Chapter 12). But Mr. C's situation is different. An ethically sensitive Californian might see that one has an obligation to Mr. A to help him to avoid the Hobson's choice between going hungry and exposing himself to radioactive wastes.[19] Many would argue that it is incumbent on Mr. C not to allow the market to become a substitute for ethical action. Mr. A's lack of agency may be a signal to Mr. C to put his self-interest on hold.

Trade in hazardous wastes is hardly an isolated example. The logic of the market, as we have seen, is that the services of not only the butcher, the baker, and the brewer but also the prostitute should be available to the highest bidder. Once again, for the sake of clarity, let us replace the real world of transactions complicated by drugs, patriarchy, and sexually transmitted diseases—not to mention "imperfect" competition in the sex market—with a simple model designed to remove the structural issues that compromise markets from a normative point of view. Assume that the prostitute craves chocolate rather than heroin and is a man rather than a woman; and that there is full disclosure of STDs. We then can focus on the role of individualism in justifying transactions between a willing buyer A and a willing seller B.

Much of the argument hinges on the principle of given preferences, that people are formed once and for all. If people continually change as a function of their social interactions, including their interactions in the exchange of goods and services, selling sexual services may change both the buyer's and the seller's conception of self and others so fundamentally that the very idea of comparing A and B before and after their exchange is completely undermined. If we cannot identify B before the exchange with B after the exchange, we cannot speak meaningfully of B being better off after trading sex for chocolates—the fundamental virtue of the voluntary nature of trade. The commercialization of sexual relations may affect A's attitudes toward sexual partners, so that an A who hires a prostitute is not really comparable with an A whose sexual experience takes place in the context of loving or at least friendly relationships.

The individual who habitually hires a prostitute may be markedly less fit for the most elementary of communities—a long-term relationship with another human being—than the individual whose sexual experience is embedded in a richer fabric of relationship. Likewise for the individual on the other end of the bargain, though prostitutes may be more adept at compartmentalizing than are johns.

Like a market in pollution, a market in sexual services obliges us to look closely at the assumption of agency. One does not need an advanced degree in social work to realize that most prostitutes—men or women—do not normally choose to sell sexual services if they have alternatives. This severely compromises the characterization of the sex worker's choice as free of coercion, a characterization that is fundamental to the economist's justification of the market.

In the context of market for sexual services, radical subjectivism is equally contestable: a libertarian hard core apart, it is generally recognized that the very idea of society, certainly the idea of community, contradicts radical subjectivism. In the case in point, the consensus today, at least in the United States, is that sexual intercourse should not be embedded (as it were) in commercial intercourse, regardless of the benefits perceived by the As and Bs of the world. To allow trade in sexual intercourse undermines this consensus.

Finally, as in the case of trade in radioactive wastes, self-interest may meet its limit in a market for sexual services. The client cannot absolve himself of moral responsibility for what happens to the person on the other side of the transaction, especially if the prostitute enters into the transaction out of desperation.

The list of problematic markets could be multiplied—body parts, surrogate motherhood, and military service surface even when graduate students in economics discuss the limits of markets. But from the point of view of community, these markets only dramatize issues that inhere in a market system. Yes, many economists will admit that there are exceptions to the rule that willing buyers and willing sellers are proof of the desirability of trade and markets. But the exceptions are few, and to justify such markets as exceptions, appeal is made to structural "imperfections" in these markets, ignoring the foundational assumptions that are equally important to justifying market outcomes.

The reason is clear. Once you begin to doubt the foundations, the edifice begins to wobble. As Lawrence Summers put it (*Economist* 1992, 66), "The problem with the arguments against all of these proposals for more pollution in LDCs [is that these arguments][20] (intrinsic rights to certain goods, moral reasons, social concerns, lack of adequate markets, etc.) could be turned around and used more or less effectively against every Bank proposal for liberalization."

That is indeed the problem. Once the door is opened to doubt, who knows where the questioning might lead. Perhaps we are not hardwired to calculate individualistic self-interest; perhaps we should take account of other communities besides the nation; perhaps our reason for being is not the happiness of pursuing more and more and more.

CHAPTER 5

Some History

A central contention of this book is that the foundational assumptions of economics are not eternal truths about human nature but rather the distillation of complex myths—myths that emerged from cultural changes in Europe and North America over the last four hundred years. Myths these assumptions may be, but, as with all myth, there is at least a germ of truth in the way economics characterizes people and their interactions. This chapter explores that germ of truth: we examine the institutional changes that gave birth to the modern West, changes that made the economist's view of people, particularly the conception of the atomistic individual, plausible.

The problem that the English political philosopher Thomas Hobbes set himself was this: What holds society together? What prevents society from imploding as people struggle for survival and advantage? The answer Hobbes gives in *Leviathan* is that individuals themselves see the need for an all-powerful state to impose order on all. Each is willing to cede his or her inherent right to act for self-preservation and gain, on the condition that others cede their equal rights as well. People give up individual sovereignty as the price of social order.

We will have occasion to examine Hobbes in more detail in the next chapter; what is relevant here is the question, not the answer. A century or two earlier, nobody would have thought to pose the problem of human relations in Hobbes's terms. It never would have occurred to anyone to ask what binds people together, what keeps society from self-destructing. People were bound to each other by all sorts of ties: vertical ties, such as parent and child, master and apprentice, lord and vassal, lord and serf, priest and parishioner; and horizontal ties that bound members of a village or a clan or a religious faith to each other. In short, community was a central feature of people's lives. The tie between sovereign and subject, which would become for Hobbes the only tie that binds, was one tie among many, hardly the sole basis of social cohesion.

In other words, mutual dependence, power, affection and reciprocal obligation were taken for granted. But by Hobbes's day, all of these were under attack, and there was no longer an obvious basis for social order. For Hobbes, the questions were, What holds society together in the absence of mutual dependence, power, affection, and obligation? What holds together a society of equal individuals, each acting on the basis of a calculation of his own self-interest?

Hobbes's question marks the transition from the medieval conception of society to the modern. Our question is how mutual dependence, power, affection, and obligation—how community—bound people together, and how these ties declined to the point that a new basis of social order and social consciousness—modernity—came to define our very being. The assumptions of economics are the assumptions of modernity: economic man is a bare-bones, stripped-down version of modern man.

There is no single essence, but rather a complex web of changes that begat modernity. This said, we have to start somewhere, and in England, where change was early and rapid, a good point of departure is the transformation of institutional structures that governed the holding of land, particularly the "enclosure movement," which began in earnest in the late fifteenth century.

The Enclosure Movement

The first thing to be said is that the word "enclosure" mistakes form for substance. Enclosing the land (by hedgerows or other physical markers) was generally the last act of a long drama of transforming agriculture based in community to individualistic agriculture. Second, it must be understood that community-based agriculture did not mean a collectivism in which gangs of laborers plowed, harrowed, weeded, and harvested together. Much, perhaps most, of the actual work was done individually or in small groups. Third, land generally was not common property. Permanent "commons" constituted a small part of village lands and were generally inferior lands that were not cultivated at all. In short, preenclosure agriculture was based in the community not because it was a kind of primitive communism but because it required a large measure of cooperation and mutuality.

What was behind the enclosure movement? There are, broadly speaking, two views. One sees enclosure through the lens of the putative inefficiencies of an agriculture requiring coordination among the many members of the community holding parcels in a single field, a field that might be hundreds of acres in size. This view is of a piece with a view of economics that emphasizes efficiency as the normative goal of economic arrangements and sees history in terms of a teleology of a purposeful evolution of markets, property rights, and other institutions directed toward this goal.

In this, the conventional view, enclosure represents a triumph of efficiency: before enclosure, cultivators grew crops according to a community-wide discipline; after enclosure, the same land was more rationally cultivated by individuals pursuing their self-interest, often by converting the arable into permanent pasture for sheep, returning not only increased incomes for landlords, but also a greater contribution to national output and income. In this view, the local community stood in the way of economic progress and dissolved because the individual, calculating his self-interest, could do better—for himself and for the whole society—on his own.

This efficiency view is vulnerable both on the grounds of relatively narrow empirics and on the basis of the larger history of which enclosure was a part. At the level of narrow empirics, I think that Robert Allen, who has painstakingly studied enclosure in the Midlands of England, got it right. Allen concluded that only in heavy soils with a tendency to waterlogging was there a substantial productivity benefit from enclosure: enclosure allowed so-called hollow drains to be installed and maintained without necessitating the cooperation of the many landholders through whose parcels the drains would otherwise run (Allen 1992, 119–121). This special case apart, the chief effect of enclosure, according to Allen, was to redistribute income from tenants to landlords.

The alternative view takes the distribution of the pie as the central issue. It sees the enclosure movement through the lens of class struggle, specifically the struggle of peasants and lords. Like the efficiency view, the distributional view reflects a perspective on economics that goes beyond the specifics of enclosure, a view that emphasizes distribution as of equal importance in driving historical change as is the size of the pie.[1]

Each of these stories captures a piece of the truth: both efficiency and distribution played a role in enclosures. But the emphasis here, as well as in Appendix B, which fleshes out some of the details of the argument, is on distribution: in my judgment, enclosures were undertaken primarily because traditional community organization stymied the landlords in their attempt to get a larger share of the economic pie. The enclosure movement was important in itself—until the modern era, most people lived and worked on the land. But it was important as well as the emblem of larger changes: behind the enclosure movement was the breakdown of the feudal polity and the manorial economy. As feudalism and the manor disintegrated, rank counted for less and less compared with wealth, or rather, wealth came to determine rank. Changes in social relations based on landholding provided a template for the broader society.

This is not to say that enclosure was necessary or sufficient for the transition to modernity. Indeed, much of Europe made the transition without enclosures. But England's precocious embrace of modernity, particularly individualism, self-interest, and the nation-state, is, in my view, bound up closely with the changes wrought by enclosure—specifically, the metamorphosis of an agriculture based on a community of cultivators to an agriculture based on individual enterprise.

Before we get into the story of change, it might be helpful to have just a bit of background on how agriculture was organized before enclosure. In much of England—just how much is in dispute—and in large parts of continental Europe as well, premodern agriculture was based on manors consisting of several so-called open fields of up to several hundred acres each. Typically, the lord, free peasants, and unfree peasants (variously termed serfs, villeins, or just plain "natives") held parcels in several fields; diversification was necessary because fields would lie fallow at different times.

But it would be anachronistic to speak of ownership. The medieval vocabulary of landholding avoids the word altogether: everybody from the most powerful lord down to the meanest serf "held" land of somebody else, in a chain that went all the way up to a supreme territorial lord like the king of England. *Tenant* may mean *renter* in today's English, but it comes from a Latin root meaning "to hold," which is the meaning the corresponding word still has in modern French and Spanish. Instead of ownership, a product of modernity, different people had various rights to a single piece of land, rights that would overlap and even conflict and were certainly contested.

The "custom of the manor" bound all landholders—lords and peasants alike—to the communal discipline dictated by the prevailing agricultural technique. A given field of, say, two hundred acres might contain a dozen parcels, some the parcels of the lord *(demesne)*, some the parcels of the peasants. Within these two hundred acres, crops (mainly cereals: wheat and rye in the fall, oats and barley in the spring) were sown at the same time and harvested at the same time, and the entire field would lie fallow for a season.

The animals of lord and peasants grazed together on the fallow, stints being customarily allocated, usually according to the proportion of one's holding in the field. (Proportionality was often qualified by a minimum stint that every household had by right as a member of the community, no matter how poorly endowed with land. The loss of this right was a particular grievance of the poor when the open field was enclosed.) While fallow, the open field temporarily became the common field, managed collectively by the community of landholders.

But contrary to the claims of Garrett Hardin and myriad others who have followed Hardin's lead, the open field is neither apt metaphor nor early prototype for the disaster of unbridled consumption that Hardin and his ilk see as the fate of an overpopulated planet. For the good and simple reason that the open field was not governed by a regime of open access. Sensitive to the possibility of a "tragedy of the commons" (Hardin's terminology in his classic account [1968]), the village community was at great pains to regulate access to the open fields, even—especially—when fallow and managed as common property.

Members of the community were mutually dependent in many other ways than the discipline imposed by a common time for sowing, harvest, and fallow. In heavy soils, the better-off peasants would join their oxen together, the better to plow their own parcels or those parcels of the lord for which they bore responsibility. Every male over the age of thirteen was required to be in a pledge group, the members of which stood surety for each other for fines or other judgments in the manorial court. Sometimes collective punishments were imposed that the community had to meet together. And even on the most autocratic of manors, much of the administration and adjudication of disputes necessarily fell on the peasants themselves. Villagers not only lived in close proximity to each other but also needed each other. The survival of the community was the condition of individual survival. Woe to the man or woman with no community ties.

From the fifteenth century until the nineteenth, English landlords, sometimes in alliance with their more prosperous tenants, undid this community-based agriculture and replaced it with an agriculture based on individual enterprise. To what end? Why would the lords undertake such a monumental transformation?

I have already tipped my hand as between the two contending explanations, distribution and efficiency. But as history rather than social theory, enclosure—to use this term as shorthand for the whole drama rather than just the last act of erecting physical markers—is a story with multiple threads. One, lasting into the sixteenth century, was a long demographic contraction that reduced the population of England by 50 percent between 1300 and 1520 (Wrightson 2000, 99). In many places, depopulation left the lord without sufficient tenants to cultivate the land in the traditional manner. Enclosure, which facilitated conversion from arable to pasture, was the consequence.

A second element of enclosure was strategic: the attempt of landlords to increase their incomes at the expense of the peasants, and the counter-strategy of peasant resistance. The landlords' strategic Plan A was simply to raise money dues collected from peasant cultivators. Raising money dues—until the era of enclosures, it would be as anachronistic to speak of "rents" as to speak of tenants—was partly an act of greed, partly an attempt to recoup losses resulting from price inflation and to reap the benefits of productivity increases. But Plan A met with resistance, and resistance required a Plan B, which amounted to "if you can't beat 'em, get rid of 'em"—a very different kind of depopulation, one caused by the deliberate policy of the landlords.

The third element of enclosure was the changing relationship of landlords and peasants to the state. The decisive moment was the Glorious Revolution of 1688, which subordinated the interests of the monarchy to Parliament and thus to the interests of the landlords.

These three elements—demographic contraction, the struggle of landlords and peasants, and the changing relationship of these two classes to the state—intertwined, and their relative importance changed over time. In the early period, up to, say, 1520, gradual contraction of the population might have set the stage for a lord to eliminate the remaining peasants rather than acquiesce to their demands for more favorable terms, demands in which the peasants were encouraged by the relative scarcity of labor. In some instances, enclosure might have been no more than the coup de grâce to a system under demographic stress. In other cases, a fall in the number of peasant households was likely no more than a pretext.

In any case, in the early sixteenth century, if not sooner, population began once again to expand, and although there was a lull in enclosures, the pace picked up as the century wore on. Here the second element of the story—the struggle of landlords and peasants—came to the fore.

Plan A, the attempt to raise rents, fared differently according to the rapacity of the lord, the actual custom of the manor, and the tenacity of the peasants in defending that custom. But on two important points there is no doubt. First, the lords' project succeeded to the point of inflicting great hardship on the peasants: as the terms binding lord and tenant came up for renewal, the lord would attempt to impose higher annual dues or, more often, a higher "entry fine," the amount paid for the privilege (in the lord's eyes) or right (as the tenant saw it) to take up cultivation. The tenants likened this practice to the rack, a contemporary instrument of torture—hence the term "rack renting."

Second, even where the lord was able to impose his will, either because the custom of the manor permitted him to do so or because he was able to prevail against the custom of the manor, peasant resistance could prove very costly, especially because the sixteenth- and seventeenth-century English state lined up on the side of the peasants—not out of love but in accordance with the maxim that the more prosperous the peasantry relative to the lords, the greater the resources available to the state.[2] Or, as Francis Bacon put it, "the more gentlemen, ever the lower books of subsidies" (Bacon 1972 [1622], 123).[3] Ranging from passive resistance in the form of rent strikes to outright insurrection, peasant opposition inspired the lords to search for a new strategy, a solution that would end the conflict once and for all.

This solution, Plan B, was to dispossess the tenant, to extinguish his claims on the land. For good reason, "enclosing" was paired in the language of the sixteenth and seventeenth centuries with "engrossing," and both were linked with "depopulation." Engrossing, roughly the equivalent of monopolizing, was key, for this was the act of power and aggression. This was the act that created the modern concept of ownership by doing away with the complex of coexisting and overlapping claims, duties, and rights over the land that had bound all members of the manorial community together under the open field system. Enclosing the land—hedges and the like—simply put a physical seal on the new system.[4]

In the early modern period, enclosure was often (but not invariably) accompanied by the conversion of cropland to pasture. Fewer people are needed to take care of sheep than for cultivating cereals and other crops. The conversion of arable to pasture was a prototype of the use of technological change to solve labor problems, a prototype that has proven of great use to capitalists ever since: if the workers resist a change in the organization of work or a change in their standard of living, just get rid of the workers.

The changing relationship of landlords and peasants to the state came to dominate the story at the end of the seventeenth century: the Glorious Revolution of 1688 undid the alliance between the English state and the peasantry. The government in effect switched sides, facilitating rather than opposing enclosure. Indeed, the "parliamentary enclosures" of the eighteenth century provide a rare instance in which Marx's aphorism—that the executive (and, he might have added, the legislature as well) is little more than a committee for carrying out the political agenda of the dominant class (Marx and Engels 1955 [1848], 11–12)—holds true.

At the end of the drama, in the place of peasants and yeomen were large proprietors, sovereigns of their parcels, neither owing nor expecting the kind of cooperation that open-field agriculture required. Where there once had been community, there was more and more a collection of individuals pursuing their own interests as best they could. The seeds of modernity were sown in the villages of England.

The dispossessed tenant, the meaning of his existence eroded as his economic, political, and social ties to the land and to his fellows eroded, became the modern wage worker, remaining on the land at the sufferance of his master. From there it was a short social and psychological step—however long a geographical one—into the "reserve army" that constituted the labor force for England's industrialization (Lazonick 1974). By the eighteenth century, England was well into the era of classes, where the distinctions among people were economic, not social; or rather, where economic distinction had become the basis of social distinction.

The Transformation of the Nobility

The changes marking the transition from medieval to modern times were equally dramatic within the ranks of the powerful: vassalage fell into desuetude, and the nobility functioned within the royal government rather than as the local government. Although the nobility continued to be hereditary, by the dawn of modernity the noble had lost his feudal-manorial function as head of the local government with police, judiciary, and military powers all rolled into his economic power as landlord. There was nothing but his title to distinguish him from any other wealthy landowner. And within the government there was nothing to distinguish the noble from anybody else jockeying for position, power, and favor.

The political transformation actually started much before the dawn of modernity. The confrontation at Runnymede in 1215 from which emerged the Great Charter, *Magna Carta,* was the high watermark of the stand of the magnates against the Crown. Although the magnates prevailed in this battle, they lost the larger war of defending their collective power and privilege against royal power. By the mid-thirteenth century, the barons had learned that they had a better shot at power by dominating the king than by defending feudal privilege. But it took four hundred years of struggle before the barons, in alliance with a rising bourgeoisie, could claim victory. It took the Glorious Revolution to confirm parliamentary supremacy.

Taken together, these changes transformed the nature of social inequality. In place of barons, knights, merchants, free peasants, and serfs, society was legally homogeneous: for most practical purposes, all were equally subjects of the king, all in principle free to make of themselves what they might. A society of individuals.

Overseas Expansion and the Expansion of Mental Horizons

There were other factors at work in laying the foundations of modernity: for one thing, overseas exploration and the beginnings of empire in the New World. It is a commonplace that the influence of Europe in the world increased dramatically during the early modern period. But at the same time discovery and conquest opened Europe up to new ideas and other ways of being.

No one exemplifies the new spirit better than the essayist Michel de Montaigne. It is not that Montaigne and his humanist ilk were universally heeded—quite the contrary, Montaigne represents the road not taken—but rather, like the proverbial talking dog, that he had a voice at all. Montaigne's take on relativism is emblematic ("Of Cannibals," 1965, 152): "There is nothing barbarous and savage . . . except that each man calls barbarous whatever is not his own practice; for indeed it seems that we have no other test of truth and reason than the example and pattern of the opinions and customs of the country we live in. *There* is always the perfect religion, the perfect government, the perfect and accomplished manners in all things." New times, new ideas.

New Technologies

Technology, too, was changing. Without the printing press, neither Montaigne nor any of the other new voices could have been heard very widely. Without the new military technology and the new navigational technology (both the hardware of new ships and the software of new techniques for calculating longitude), neither discovery nor empire would have been possible.

New technology increased agricultural yields, too. Joyce Appleby (1977, chap. 3) argues that the taming of famine reduced the need for social solidarity and contributed to the rise of a new political discourse in the seventeenth century, one founded on individualism and self-interest—somewhat ironically, for if we follow Allen (1992), the gains in productivity were largely the work of yeomen enmeshed in community agricultural structures. The importance of solidarity was summarized by John Cook in *Unum Necessarium*, shortly before he became Solicitor-General of England (in which capacity he served as the lawyer for the parliamentary remnant, the "Rump," which tried King Charles I for treason in 1649): "The rule of charity is that one mans superfluity should give place to another mans conveniency, his conveniency to anothers necessity, his lesser necessities to anothers extreamer necessities, and so the mechanical poore to relieve the mendicant poor in their extreamer need, and this is but the Dictate of the Law of Nature" (quoted in Appleby 1977, 56).

Such a philosophy justified subordinating the market to the interests of the economically weak. As late as the sixteenth century, it was, for example, not unusual for direct consumers to be given priority over middlemen and speculators in English grain markets (Overton 1996, 135).

With the threat of famine fading from memory, this logic of solidarity seemed to many irrelevant. According to Joseph Lee, the rector of a parish church in Leicestershire (and beneficiary of the enclosure of the local commons), what mattered was that enclosure led to more efficient agriculture. *A Vindication of a Regulated Enclosure* (1656), published less than a decade after John Cook's defense of the old order, claimed that it did not matter if a switch from growing grain to raising sheep displaced peasants:

> Let it be granted that . . . fewer servants will be kept; are any bound to keep more servants then are needeful for their businese; or may they not cast how to do the same businese with least labour. . . . Is a man bound to keep servants to pill strawes or labour in vain? by what Law? if this principle

> be good, that all are bound so to carry on their affairs in the world, as to
> imploy servants, although to their own disadvantage; I dare say, the
> much applauded plough must be cast into the ditch, and much admired
> manufacture of tillage . . . be exchanged for digging with spades and mat-
> tocks, which would imploy more men than tilllage. (quoted in Appleby
> 1977, 61)

Even where technological change was minimal or altogether absent,
there was profound social change. As markets expanded, so did manufacture
and trade—long before the appearance of the new mechanized techniques
of production. With the growth of manufacture and trade, towns and cities
grew. The influx of people from different places, people without shared
histories and common understandings, people living in relatively anonymous and transient circumstances, contributed to the undermining of
community.

And, of Course, the Reformation

The Reformation was not intended as political and social reform. Indeed,
Martin Luther succeeded in breaking the hegemony of Rome where earlier
attempts failed precisely because Luther limited himself to restoring and intensifying the religious individualism of primitive Christianity. The Christian needed neither priest nor confessor to mediate with God; the inner
voice of conscience would guide the faithful along the path of righteousness.
At the same time, as his hostile attitude toward the peasant rebellion of
1525 clearly indicates, Luther had no intention of subverting the existing
social order.

By contrast, earlier reform movements did not acknowledge the distinction between religion on the one hand and politics, economics, and society
on the other. In contrast with Luther, whose support of local power rallied
the German princes to his cause, these proto-Protestant rebels brought
down the combined wrath of church and state upon themselves. Prelate
and prince put aside their bickering long enough to meet the attack from
below.

The flavor of the earlier movements is well conveyed in a speech by a de-
frocked priest named John Ball to the rebellious peasants and artisans as-
sembled at Blackheath, then on the outskirts of London, on a June day in
1381. Ball and the other leaders of the 1381 rebellion looked forward to the

realization of Christian ideals of freedom and equality within this world, in people's relations with each other, not just in their relation to God and eternity. In a contemporary account of the speech,[5] Ball began with a common medieval formula for the "original position":

When Adam delved and Eve span, Who was then the gentleman?

And continuing the sermon thus begun, [Ball] strove, by the words of the proverb that he had taken for his theme, to introduce and to prove that from the beginning all men were created equal by nature, and that servitude had been introduced by the unjust oppression of wicked men, against God's will; because, if it had pleased him to create serfs, surely in the beginning of the world he would have decreed who was to be a serf and who a lord. Let them consider, therefore, that a time was now given them by God, a time in which they might be able to lay aside the yoke of servitude, if they wished, and enjoy their hope for liberty. Wherefore they should be prudent men, and, with the love of a good husbandman tilling his fields and uprooting and destroying the tares which are wont to choke the grain, they should hasten to do the following things. First, they should kill the great lords of the kingdom; second, they should slay the lawyers, judges, and jurors of the country; finally they should root out all those whom they knew to be likely to be harmful to the commonwealth in future. Thus they would obtain peace and security in the future, if, when the great ones had been removed, there were among them equal liberty and nobility and like dignity and power. (Walsingham, *Historia Anglicana,* vol. II, 32; quoted in Myers 1969, 141)

Luther's brand of Protestantism did not pose the same immediate danger to secular power as Ball's because Luther distinguished between this world and the other, and he limited his claims for the authority and autonomy, and indeed the sovereignty, of the individual—not to mention the equality of individuals—to the spiritual world.[6] According to Luther, the inner voice would not speak out on politics or economics.

But even in the spiritual realm Luther's program was problematic, for he was unable to provide reliable guidance on listening. Predictably, there arose a cacophony of inner voices, often diametrically opposed to one another. An extreme case, no doubt, was reported by the French philosopher and critic Pierre Bayle: one young man's inner voice instructed him to cut off the head of his own brother, who like a pious *sati* went stoically to his death before a crowd of believers (reported in Aldous Huxley's study of diabolic possession in seventeenth-century France [1952, 86]).[7]

Even without going to such extremes, the multiplicity of voices that followed Luther helped to undermine existing social arrangements in the sixteenth and seventeenth centuries, for the more voices, the more doubt; the more truths, the less reason to accept any but the one most congenial to personal advancement. The Reformation turned out to be a powerful nail in the coffin of community, authority, and deference.

At one end of the Protestant spectrum was John Calvin. Calvin's English followers, known as Puritans for the strictness of their doctrines, dress, and demeanor, were extremely invested in the economy: worldly success was a marker of membership in the Elect, and this provided a novel and powerful justification for striving in the economic sphere. Like many a modern man, the Puritan found meaning and identity in economic success. In Max Weber's influential (if controversial) view (1958 [1904–1905]), the "Protestant ethic" was critical as a stimulus to the rise of capitalism in the early modern period.

This emphasis on economic success, it should be emphasized, did nothing to enhance work itself, as distinct from the economic rewards of work. If Luther embedded work in life, Calvin and his followers embedded money. The mildly nonconformist English divine Richard Baxter made this clear in his memoirs, written in the waning years of the seventeenth century: "If God show you a way in which you can lawfully get more than in another way (without wrong to your soul or to any other), if you refuse this, and choose the less gainful way, you cross one of the ends of your Calling, and you refuse to be God's steward" (quoted in Tawney 1938 [1926], 241).

For others closer to the middle of the Christian spectrum than the Calvinists, worldly success might have been a marker of nothing more than worldly success, for the economic arena was now open to the ambitious, talented, and lucky in a way that it had never been before. Economic success was a sure means to upward mobility in the social hierarchy.

Reform bred counterreform. Indeed, the Reformation was more than a spiritual crisis; it led to political crises on the Continent as well as in England. These controversies, simmering since the time of Martin Luther, embroiled France in the Wars of Religion in the sixteenth century and erupted in the seventeenth century as the Thirty Years' War on the Continent and as civil war in Britain.

The trials and tribulations of the Catholic Church in France continued even after the Protestant "heresy" had been suppressed. Jansenists struggle with Jesuits about the claims of local power in the "universal" church, lay versus priest, priest versus bishop, and king versus pope. And these struggles spilled over into the political arena, providing staging areas if not dress rehearsals for the political upheaval that culminated in the Revolution and its aftermath (Van Kley 1996, especially, 203, 217–218, 233–234).

Similarly in Britain. Once Protestant supremacy had been established, Puritans and Presbyterians struggled with high-church Anglicans about the degree of decentralization and popular participation in church governance, and the dispute threatened to spill over to the polity. In 1590, Elizabeth I of England wrote to her royal cousin James VI of Scotland (who would become James I of England upon Elizabeth's death):

> Let me warne you that ther is risen, bothe in your realme and myne, a secte of perilous consequence, such as wold haue no kings but a presbitrye, and take our place wile the injoy our privilege, with a shade of Godes word, wiche non is juged to follow right without by ther censure the be so demed. Yea, looke we wel unto them. Whan the haue made in our peoples hartz a doubt of our religion, and that we erre if the say so, what perilous issue this may make I rather thinke than mynde to write. *Sapienti pauca.* (Bruce 1849, 63–64)[8]

Indeed, as in France, religious disputes in England shaped political history—the civil war, the Restoration, and the Glorious Revolution.

The spiritual crisis also produced an intellectual crisis, which came to a head in the seventeenth century. Stephen Toulmin (1990) argues that the attempt of René Descartes to secure a new basis for knowledge came directly out of the failure of religious toleration. Both the pluralistic politics of Henry of Navarre (king of France as Henry IV, 1589–1610) and the pluralistic skepticism of Montaigne foundered on the rocks of intolerance.

Skepticism must itself be seen in the context of the social and intellectual disorder that accompanied the cacophony of claims to religious truth (Popkin 1979). It is hard to see the rise of skepticism in the early modern period other than as a response to the assertion of interior authority, self-evident truth—or truths, for there turned out, as we have observed, to be more than one—that Protestants invoked to counter the claims of papal authority. Skepticism, by attacking all claims to ultimate truth, sought to restore the legitimacy of claims most hallowed by time and tradition and, in Montaigne's version at least, to temper even these claims with moderation and tolerance.

The skeptics' project badly misfired, in part because Montaigne's temperate pluralism did not meet the requirements of the Catholic Church's attempt to defend itself against Protestantism. Instead of pluralism and tolerance, all sides pushed their claims to ultimate truth. Descartes cut through all this with a new system of knowledge that claimed to require no appeal to authority, intuition, or feelings, no appeal to experience, a system of knowledge reviving the Euclidean idea of knowledge based in rational deduction from self-evident first principles. As we shall see in our discussion of knowledge in economics, this new, Cartesian, knowledge eventually became a pillar of the ideology of economics.

Descartes began a project; he can hardly be said to have fashioned a complete system of knowledge. The immediate followers of Descartes in France, the so-called Port Royal logicians, made the first steps toward a new theory of probability, designed to bring uncertainty into the realm of the rationally knowable. Hobbes early on extended the Cartesian approach to the study of politics. Baruch Spinoza sought to explain the whole of nature by rational deduction based on self-evident first principles.

But it took the Enlightenment, that great eighteenth-century project of reordering knowledge, to bring the Cartesian project to fruition. The Frenchman Emmanuel Joseph Sieyès exemplifies the best and worst of the first attempt to translate Enlightenment thinking into political action. Abbé Sieyès's *Qu'est-çe que le Tiers État?* (What Is the Third Estate?), published on the eve of the convocation of the Estates General in 1789, made the case for replacing the ancien régime with a polity based on rational calculation alone.[9] Rational calculation gave to the world in turn the Revolution, the Terror, and the despotism of Napoléon Bonaparte.

What Are the Lessons?

Evidently, there is no single essence for the transformation—social, political, religious, technological as well as economic—that gave rise to modern society and to economics. There is no prime mover for modernity. Although it is accurate to pair the rise of the calculating, self-interested individual with the decline of community, the first is not the cause of the second, anymore than the second is the cause of the first. Rather, the two are twin results of wholesale change that affected every aspect of society. Changes surrounding landholding were basic, but so was the rise of manufacture and commerce, of towns and cities. So was the division of the Christian community. And so were technological transformations, from the art of printing to the art of navigating the seas to the art of killing.

My argument must frustrate those who are looking for simple answers in neat boxes. It resonates with Karl Marx in that it emphasizes the role of economic and technological change and, in particular, the role of enclosures in precipitating modernity out of the mix of relationships that governed landholding; indeed, Marx saw enclosure as the fundamental source of the so-called primitive accumulation from which capitalism developed. But unlike Marx (and, for that matter, most mainstream economists and economic historians), I do not see efficiency—the development of the forces of production in Marxian jargon—as the driving force of history. The Marxian story of enclosure, like mine, is replete with class struggle, but for Marx, classes contend with each other, consciously or not, to further the teleology of efficiency. By contrast, the enclosure movement is seen here in terms of a struggle over the distribution of the pie rather than as a way of making the pie bigger—without any teleology of efficiency operating behind the scenes.

Why does it matter which is the driving force? For this reason: to the extent that efficiency is the issue, it is more plausible that whatever might have been lost as a result—community, in the case of enclosure—is simply an unavoidable by-product of an increasing standard of living. Community just happens to be on the wrong side of the trade-off between social organization and economic growth. But insofar as history is driven by distribution, the case that what is lost stood in the way of economic progress dissolves.

If the argument advanced here departs from Marx in respect to the role of efficiency, neither is the argument at all Marxian in its stress on the Reformation and its aftermath as an independent source of a new ideology of knowledge. This new ideology comes not out of class struggle waged on behalf of the growth of the forces of production, but out of a struggle of people to make sense of their world, constrained by the need of seventeenth-century Europe for a unifying epistemology in the wake of the fratricidal French Wars of Religion, the Thirty Years' War, and the English Civil War.

Finally, we should not forget the role of economists themselves, or see this role as a mere superstructural reflection of an economic base, à la Marx. For four hundred years, economists have been active in the enterprise of constructing the modern economy and society, both by legitimizing the market and by promoting the values, attitudes, and behaviors that make for economic success. No apology is due for this—except for the pretense of scientific detachment and neutrality and the unwillingness to confront the ideological beam in our collective eye.[10]

CHAPTER 6

From Vice to Virtue in a Century

This chapter is about the changing valence of self-interest in the early modern period. It continues the discussion of how the foundational assumptions of economics came to be plausible ways of characterizing human beings. Here the focus is more on the history of ideas than was the case in the last chapter, but ideas and institutions are not separate realms: a main point of this chapter is to show how ideas about self-interest changed as facts on the ground changed.

Some will take issue with the notion that ideas are important at all. If you hold to the universality of the assumptions of economics, you are likely to dismiss my account of the transformation of self-interest: whatever a few intellectuals might have thought, self-interest is a constant of human nature. By now it will come as no surprise that I reject this view. The work of Robert Frank and his associates (Frank et al. 1993), cited in Chapter 1, seems to me to support the case that learning to think like an economist changes both how one views self-interest and how one acts. How people viewed self-interest changed dramatically in the early modern period.

It has been observed that self-interest, like community, like individualism, indeed, like many of the concepts this book takes apart, means different things to different people. In Chapter 4, I made the argument for defining self-interest narrowly, for opposing self-interest to regard for others, rather than defining self-interest broadly, as whatever people do. Accordingly, as in everyday English, self-interest will here mean a focus on one's own self, a situation where an individual's preferences are not only given but where his or her perceived well-being has nothing to do with what anybody else in society is consuming or doing.

Other-regarding behavior also permits of two different interpretations, one based on externalities—the direct effect of your actions on my utility—the other based on moral obligation. Again, Chapter 4 made a case for one of these interpretations over the other, namely, other-regarding behavior as a moral obligation. The question this chapter tackles is how, over the course of little more than a century, the moral element recedes in importance to the point that, in Adam Smith's hands, the notion of self-regarding behavior becomes not only legitimate but virtuous.

We begin with John Winthrop's sermon on board the Arbella in 1630, remembered for its allusion to the "city on a hill," the new Jerusalem that the Puritans would build in New England. For Governor Winthrop, the experiment of colonization was a test of Christian virtue against the natural inclination of the descendants of sinful Adam. Natural man was indeed self-interested, but Christian grace made him mindful of his obligations to his fellow man:

> Adam, rent himselfe from his Creator, rent all his posterity allsoe one from another; whence it comes that every man is borne with this principle in him to loue and seeke himselfe onely, and thus a man continueth till Christ comes and takes possession of the soule and infuseth another principle, loue to God and our brother, and this latter haueing continuall supply from Christ, as the head and roote by which he is vnited, gets the predomining in the soule, soe by little and little expells the former. (Winthrop 1838 [1630], 41–42)

The colonists would survive and prosper only if individual interests were subordinated to the greater good of the community:

> Now the onely way to . . . provide for our posterity, is to followe the counsell of Micah, *to doe justly, to love mercy, to walk humbly with our God.* For this end, wee must be knitt together, in this worke, as one man. Wee must entertaine each other in brotherly affection. Wee must be willing to abridge ourselves of our superfluities, for the supply of other's necessities. Wee must uphold a familiar commerce together in all meekeness, gentlenes, patience and liberality. Wee must delight in eache other; make other's conditions our oune; rejoice together, mourne together, labour and suffer together, allwayes haueing before our eyes our commission and community in the worke, as members of the same body. Soe shall wee *keepe the unitie of the spirit in the bond of peace.* (Winthrop 1838 [1630], 46–47)

As the God of the Old Testament held out to the children of Israel on the threshold of the Promised Land the choice between good and evil, plenty and famine, so did he to these new Israelites. If we act for each other, said Governor Winthrop,

> The Lord will be our God, and delight to dwell among us, as his oune people, and will command a blessing upon us in all our wayes. Soe that wee shall see much more of his wisdome, power, goodness and truthe, than formerly wee haue been acquainted with. Wee shall finde that the God of Israell is among us, when ten of us shall be able to resist a thousand of our enemies; when hee shall make us a prayse and glory that men shall say of succeeding plantations, "the Lord make it likely that of *New England*." For wee must consider that wee shall be as a citty upon a hill. The eies of all people are uppon us. (Winthrop 1838 [1630], 47)

But, should the members of the company disobey God's commandment to act unselfishly, calamity awaits:

> Soe that if wee shall deale falsely with our God in this worke wee haue undertaken, and soe cause him to withdrawe his present help from us, wee shall be made a story and a by-word through the world. Wee shall open the mouthes of enemies to speake evill of the wayes of God, and all professors for God's sake. Wee shall shame the faces of many of God's worthy servants, and cause theire prayers to be turned into curses upon us till wee be consumed out of the good land whither wee are a goeing. (Winthrop 1838 [1630], 47)

While the hardships, trials, and dangers of colonizing a far-away land may have made interdependence more urgent, Governor Winthop's sentiments were hardly unique. Chapter 5 summarized John Cook's eloquent plea for a "rule of charity" (*Unum Necessarium* 1648, quoted in Appleby 1977, 56), which echoed Winthrop's condemnation of self-interest. Cook, indeed, makes clear what was only implicit in Winthrop's sermon: not only do the needs of others come before our own when others' needs press more heavily, but the government should enforce charitable behavior: "Can any man question that the Magistrate is impowred by God to command every man to live according to the rule of nature and right reason" (Appleby 1977, 56–57).

Scarcely a century later, Adam Smith summarized his own rule of charity in what were to become the two most notable and quotable of the aphorisms of the *Wealth of Nations*. First,

It is not from the benevolence of the butcher, the brewer, or the baker, that we expect our dinner, but from their regard to their own interest. We address ourselves, not to their humanity but to their self-love, and never talk to them of our own necessities, but of their advantages. (Smith 1937 [1776], 14)

But self-love is not only a fact of life, but a good thing, too, for

every individual . . . necessarily labours to render the annual revenue of the society as great as he can. He generally, indeed, neither intends to promote the public interest, nor knows how much he is promoting it. . . . He intends only his own gain, and he is in this, as in many other cases, led by an invisible hand to promote an end which was no part of his intention. Nor is it always the worse for the society that it was no part of it. By pursuing his own interest he frequently promotes that of the society more effectually than when he really intends to promote it.[1] (Smith 1937 [1776], 423)

With respect to the possibilities of altruism, Smith is dismissive:

I have never known much good done by those who affected to trade for the public good. It is an affectation, indeed, not very common among merchants, and very few words need be employed in dissuading them from it. (Smith 1937 [1776], 423)

As for the magistrate in whom Cook was so ready to trust, Smith is positively scathing:

Every individual, it is evident, can, in his local situation, judge much better than any statesman or lawgiver can do for him. The statesman, who should attempt to direct private people in what manner they ought to employ their capitals, would not only load himself with a most unnecessary attention, but assume an authority which could safely be trusted, not only to no single person, but to no council or senate whatever, and which would nowhere be so dangerous as in the hands of a man who had folly and presumption enough to fancy himself fit to exercise it. (Smith 1937 [1776], 423)

This chapter explores the 180-degree turn that transformed self-regarding individuals from moral degenerates into social benefactors and even paragons of virtue. We get a better sense of the changing understanding of self-interest by looking at how the idea is treated in four influential works of this period: Hobbes's *Leviathan,* Locke's *Second Treatise of Government,* Mandeville's *Fable of the Bees,* and Smith's *Wealth of Nations.* The sharpness of the change in sentiment becomes clear when we realize that it took place in a period so short that, if one were born at the right time and the right place, it would have been possible to have a personal acquaintance with all four of these men: Hobbes died in 1679 and Smith was born in 1723.

From Hobbes to Smith, by Way of Locke and Mandeville

Thomas Hobbes, born in 1588, was brought up by his uncle, a Malmesbury glover who was sufficiently well-off to send young Thomas to Oxford. After receiving his Oxford degree, Hobbes obtained a position as tutor to the son of the Earl of Devonshire, which gave him the opportunity to expand his horizons through reading, conversation, and foreign travel while giving him an insider's vantage point on the decline of the old order—the Earl's household was in dire financial straits. Hobbes proved a shrewd observer of the decline of the old society based on status defined by birth, as well as the rise of the new society based on wealth and accomplishment.

For Hobbes, as for his contemporary John Cook, the self-regarding individual is the problem, but Hobbes and Cook part company here. For Hobbes, the self-regarding individual is also the solution.

Hobbesian human beings are motivated by relatively simple "appetites" for security and material success and "aversions" to pain, suffering, and—most of all—death. In the "state of nature," the political anarchy that Hobbes (along with many others) posits as a metaphorical original condition, these appetites and aversions put the self-interest of each at odds with the self-interest of everybody else. Because security is determined by relative power, my security can come only at the price of yours. Likewise material success: one more loaf of bread for me means one less for you. In short, we are each free in the state of nature to pursue our interests as best we can, but the search for security and well-being has bad consequences: "Where every man is Enemy to every man . . . there is no place for Industry; because the fruit thereof is uncertain: and consequently no Culture of the Earth; no Navigation . . . no Arts; no Letters; no Society; and which is worst of all, continuall feare, and danger of violent death; And the life of man, solitary, poore, nasty, brutish, and short" (Hobbes 1968 [1651], 186).

Absolute political power—*Leviathan*—is Hobbes's solution to the problem of security. My preferred solution is for you to be restrained while I am left free to satisfy my appetites. But you feel exactly the same way: restrain me, and let your appetites run rampant. So the state of nature continues. The way out is for all of us to agree to give up our inherent freedom to pursue our interests in any and all ways we see fit—as the condition of getting everybody else to submit to the rule of law. Each of us, in our own self-interest, submits to Leviathan as the price we pay for others to submit.

How can self-interest be both problem and solution? The Hobbesian state of nature is structurally equivalent to the cooperative game known as the "prisoners' dilemma," a situation in which two suspects in a criminal case have the choice of ratting on each other or keeping mum. The cooperative solution is to keep mum, depriving the authorities of testimony needed to convict and therefore exposing themselves to, at worst, a conviction on a minor charge.

The two prisoners may see the logic of cooperation, but how do they enforce this logic on each other? Without an enforcement mechanism analogous to Leviathan, the suspects are tempted to turn on each other by the promise of leniency in return for testimony favorable to the prosecution. In the absence of concerted action with my fellow prisoner, I have nothing to lose—save my honor—and everything to gain by ratting him out. And in the world of Hobbes, there is no honor among thieves—or among people in the state of nature. Leviathan spells the difference between what constitutes one's self-interest when one must act alone, in political isolation from one's fellows, and what constitutes one's self-interest when one acts in concert with others. In the first case, it's every man for himself; in the second, it's submission to the logic of cooperation.

John Locke, born almost half a century after Hobbes, was the scion of minor gentry of southwest England who made his career as physician and adviser to the Earl of Shaftesbury (and later as tutor to his grandson, the third earl). Shaftesbury was a leading, perhaps the leading, politician of Restoration England, and it was as part of the earl's entourage that Locke turned his energy and multifaceted talent to political theory. Locke differs from Hobbes in many ways, but one is of supreme significance for the present story: self-regarding individuals need not be mutually opposed to one another even in the state of nature. For Locke, "The plain *difference between the State of Nature, and the State of War,* which however some Men [Hobbes?] have confounded, are as far distant, as a State of Peace, Good Will, Mutual Assistance, and Preservation, and a State of Enmity, Malice, Violence, and Mutual Destruction are one from another" (1988 [1690], ¶19, 280).

In Locke's account, the state of nature does not pit each of us against the rest because there is enough to go around for everybody:

> As much as any one can make use of to any advantage of life before it spoils; so much he may by his labour fix a Property in . . . And thus considering the plenty of natural Provisions there was a long time in the World, and the few spenders, and to how small a part of that provision the industry of one Man could extend it self, and ingross it to the prejudice of others; especially keeping within the *bounds,* set by reason of what might serve for his *use;* there could be then little room for Quarrels or contentions about Property so establish'd. . . . Nor was this *appropriation* of any parcel of *Land,* by improving it, any prejudice to any other Man, since there was still enough, and as good left; and more than the yet unprovided could use. So that in effect, there was never the less left for others because of his inclosure for himself. (Locke 1988 [1690], ¶31, 290–291)

What would later be called enlightened self-interest[2] drives us to take just what we need, and resources are in effect unlimited if we do not waste nature's bounty. In the state of nature, therefore, whatever each takes for himself is a drop in the bucket, and far from hurting others by appropriating resources, we improve the lot of humankind by mixing our labor together with the natural endowment that God has provided for the lineage of Adam. Paradoxically, subtraction becomes addition: what is subtracted from the common fund is not missed and what emerges as private property by the admixture of an individual's labor is so much more productive than resources in the wild state. Locke's state of nature is originally a world in which land and other resources are free for the taking, and self-interest is directed to making these resources more productive.

Money changes things. The function of money is to provide a long-term store of value in a world in which goods are not durable. The existence of such a store of value provides an incentive for me to increase production and hence property beyond what I can consume from my own garden and by trading my lettuce for your tomatoes. Money in effect stimulates people's appetites, or rather removes technological constraints on satisfying these appetites.

Locke here rolls two very distinct arguments into one. First, it is not worthwhile to increase one's property beyond what will satisfy the desire for nondurable goods unless there is a way of converting the produce to a lasting store of value. Second, the absence of money limits the possibility of long-distance trade as a vent for surplus production.

> Where there is not something both lasting and scarce, and so valuable to be hoarded up, there Men will not be apt to enlarge their *Possessions of Land,* were it never so rich, never so free for them to take. For I ask, What would a Man value Ten Thousand, or an Hundred Thousand Acres of excellent *Land, . . .* where he had no hopes of commerce with other Parts of the World, to draw *Money* to him by the Sale of Product? (Locke 1988 [1690], ¶48, 301)

This description, needless to say, did not fit the England of Locke's day, but neither was it in his mind a just-so story. Through his association with Shaftesbury, Locke was involved in the management of trade between England and America as well as with the colonization of the New World, and like most Europeans, Locke saw the New World as an empty continent, with land free for the taking. (Native Americans were like the deer and moose, or perhaps the more predatory fox and bear, which roamed the land but had no rights in it.)

This unlimited availability of land is the consequence of the absence of money and hence of trade. "Men will not be apt to enlarge their *Possessions of Land,* were it never so rich, never so free for them to take," when there is no way to market the produce of the land. And America is a latter day example of the original state of the world: "In the beginning all the World was *America,* and more so than that is now; for no such thing as *Money* was any where known" (ibid., ¶49, 301).

Though Locke's conclusion—that money is central to the extension of property—is undoubtedly sound, his rationale leaves something to be desired. Locke recognizes—both as a practical and an ethical constraint—that one must not waste. Indeed, waste is the only constraint that Locke recognizes on acquisitiveness. Money, as a long-term store of value, solves the problem of spoilage by allowing what would otherwise go to waste to be exchanged and therefore consumed. Thus money solves both a practical and an ethical problem and legitimizes acquisition without limits.

But is money necessary for acquisitiveness? Even in a nonmonetary economy, a surplus over one's own needs provides the means of dominating others, which may well serve as an incentive to expand property and production. Perishable goods can be exchanged against subservience. Only a few centuries separated Locke from the feudal-manorial economy in which the power to command people was firmly allied to the power to command an economic surplus, and this in a primarily agricultural society in which money was used more as a unit of account than as a store of value. And Locke's own experience as an advisor to the Earl of Shaftesbury, in which capacity he became a member of the earl's household, might have impressed upon him the power over men that a surplus enables.

The argument about money and trade is equally muddled. Locke was certainly right that long-distance trade cannot absorb the surplus production of "an Hundred Thousand Acres of excellent *Land*" situated so far from its neighbors that there were "no hopes of commerce with other Parts of the World." But this doesn't tell us how money solves the problem. Suppose we start from a situation in which settlers in Virginia are willing to export tobacco in exchange for English manufactures, but transport costs are prohibitive. How does money change things?

In the most favorable case for Locke, the Virginia colonists become content to run up their London bank balances. In this case, transport costs are reduced, but probably not by much: the savings are only the difference between sending a loaded ship on the outbound voyage from England and sending an empty ship. If instead of running up London bank balances, the colonists insist on receiving gold in return for their tobacco, there still might be some savings if gold is cheaper to ship than are manufactures, but again the savings are limited to the difference in shipping costs.

In any case, the historical record amply demonstrates that the colonists did neither: the proceeds from exporting tobacco to England were used to finance a sumptuous lifestyle based largely on imports of English manufactures. In this case, it is hard to see how money fundamentally changes the picture. Of course, money facilitates trade since it obviates the double coincidence of wants that barter requires. But money doesn't alter the situation with respect to transport costs.

Even more problematic is Locke's failure to recognize the extent to which money undercuts his main argument: with the appearance of money, the state of nature is no longer a benign one in which individuals can live harmoniously because more for one does not mean less for others (C. B. Macpherson's introduction to Locke 1980, xvi–xix). Yes, appropriation may lead to greater production: "He, that incloses Land and has a greater plenty of the conveniencys of life from ten acres, than he could have from an hundred left to Nature, may truly be said, to give ninety acres to

Mankind" (Locke 1988 [1690], ¶37, 294), but nothing obliges the encloser to give the extra produce to his fellow human beings. However productive the land might be, if there is no bound on my acquisition or yours, my self-interest must surely at some point come into conflict with yours.

Moreover, as we shall see in Chapter 11, an important effect of money is to generalize scarcity, to make everything scarce as long as one thing is scarce. Appropriation and improvement may lead to more production, but abundance is undermined by the unleashing of appetites.

With Bernard Mandeville, born in 1670, things get even more complicated. Mandeville was born into a professional family in Holland, emigrating to England after completing his studies in Rotterdam. Like Locke, Mandeville was a physician by training and appears to have been a respectable if not eminent practitioner. Like Locke, Mandeville presents us with a paradox. If Locke's paradox is that less can be more, Mandeville's paradox is that the pursuit of self-interest can promote social well-being.

The *Fable of the Bees; Or, Private Vices, Publick Benefits* saw the light of day as an anonymous broadsheet in 1705 under the title *The Grumbling Hive: Or, Knaves Turn'd Honest.* Mandeville subsequently expanded on his allegorical fable by including several essays that developed the underlying philosophy, and it is this collection that comes down to us as *The Fable of the Bees.* In *The Grumbling Hive,*

> Insects liv'd like Men, and all
> Our Actions they perform'd in small.

Like the inhabitants of a prosperous nation, the bees act on the basis of hedonistic passions:

> Vast Numbers throng'd the fruitful Hive;
> Yet those vast Numbers made 'em thrive;
> Millions endeavouring to supply
> Each other's Lust and Vanity.

For Mandeville, it is not simply coincidence that prosperity coexists with lust, vanity, and worse. The subtitle, *Private Vices, Publick Benefits,* tips Mandeville's hand. As *The Grumbling Hive* puts it,

> Thus every Part was full of Vice,
> Yet the whole Mass a Paradise;
> Flatter'd in Peace, and Fear'd in Wars,

> They were th'Esteem of Foreigners,
> And lavish of their Wealth and Lives. . . .
> The Root of Evil, Avarice,
> That damn'd ill-natur'd baneful Vice,
> Was Slave to Prodigality,
> That noble Sin; whilst Luxury
> Employ'd a Million of the Poor,
> And odious Pride a Million more:
> Envy it self, and Vanity,
> Were Ministers of Industry;
> Their darling Folly, Fickleness,
> In Diet, Furniture and Dress,
> That strange ridic'lous Vice, was made
> The very Wheel that turn'd the Trade. (Mandeville 1988 [1714],
>   18, 24–25)

For Mandeville, individuals' vices—avarice, prodigality, pride, vanity, fickleness in fashion—were the very engines of the social good.

And the other way around. When the bees get religion and honesty replaces fraud, the hive shrivels to a shadow of its former glory and is unable to sustain either the domestic economy or the defense of the hive:

> Now mind the glorious Hive, and see
> How Honesty and Trade agree.
> The Shew is gone, it thins apace;
> And looks with quite another Face.
> For 'twas not only that They went,
> By whom vast Sums were Yearly spent;
> But multitudes that liv'd on them,
> Were daily forc'd to do the same.
> In vain to other Trades they'd fly;
> All were o'er-stock'd accordingly.
> The Price of Land and Houses falls. . . .
> The building Trade is quite destroy'd,
> Artificers are not employ'd. . . .
> All Arts and Crafts neglected lie;
> Content, the Bane of Industry,
> Makes 'em admire their homely Store,
> And neither seek nor covet more.

> So few in the vast Hive remain,
>
> The hundredth Part they can't maintain
>
> Against th'Insults of numerous Foes. (Mandeville 1988 [1714], 32–35)

Specialists have long debated whether Mandeville was for public virtue or against private vice, whether he is to be taken at face value or as a satirist of the hypocrisy of the public morality of his adopted country and society. (See Dumont 1977, 70–75, for discussion and references.) He apparently delighted in controversy and did not mind the ambiguity, and even scandal and notoriety, that accompanied the successive editions of *The Fable of the Bees.*

In the end, what matters is the distance traveled since Hobbes. Mandeville shares the Hobbesian view that humans are driven by self-regarding passions, but he is far from Hobbes's position that these passions are socially destructive, that social harmony requires the repression of actions based on self-interest. Rather, these passions are the spurs to economic prosperity and national glory.

But Mandeville is only half modern. Self-regarding behavior is good for society, but it is still an individual vice. With Adam Smith the circle is closed: at the individual level as well as at the level of society as a whole, self-regarding behavior becomes a virtue.

Smith was the son of a middling government official, comptroller of customs for the Scottish port of Kirkaldy, who died before Adam was born. Raised by his mother, Smith attended Glasgow and Oxford Universities. A career in the Church of England, for which Oxford presumptively prepared him, turned out not to be to his liking, and he returned to Glasgow and an academic career at his old university. Publication of *The Theory of Moral Sentiments* in 1759 brought Smith to the attention of the intelligentsia, not only in Britain but on the Continent as well. This led in turn to a position as a tutor and traveling companion to the young Duke of Buccleugh, in which capacity he met the intellectual leaders of the French Enlightenment. After this extended grand tour, Smith was to spend ten years of retirement in his native Scots village before *The Wealth of Nations* saw the light of day.

For Smith as for Mandeville, self-regarding behavior is socially virtuous— this is, after all, the import of the invisible hand. But unlike Mandeville, Smith holds self-love to be an individual virtue as well, or at the very least, morally neutral. In *The Theory of Moral Sentiments,* Smith writes:

Regard to our own private happiness and interest, too, appear upon many occasions very laudable principles of action. The habits of oeconomy, industry, discretion, attention, and application of thought, are generally supposed to be cultivated from self-interested motives, and at the same time are apprehended to be very praise-worthy qualities, which deserve the esteem and approbation of every body. . . . It is the great fallacy of Dr. Mandeville's book to represent every passion as wholly vicious which is so in any degree and in any direction. It is thus that he treats every thing as vanity which has any reference either to what are or to what ought to be the sentiments of others; and it is by means of this sophistry that he establishes his favourite conclusion, that private vices are public benefits. If the love of magnificence, a taste for the elegant arts and improvements of human life, for whatever is agreeable in dress, furniture, or equipage, for architecture, statuary, painting and music, is to be regarded as luxury, sensuality and ostentation, even in those whose situation allows, without any inconveniency, the indulgence of those passions, it is certain that luxury, sensuality and ostentation are public benefits. (Smith 1982 [1759], 304, 312–313)

With this background, the passage about the butcher, the brewer, and the baker appealing to our self-interest no longer appears as a simple reaffirmation of Mandeville. Smith has moved the debate to new ground, ground from which economics can claim to understand what ought to be along with what is.

Getting from Hobbes to Smith

How did England (and, with a little lag, Europe as a whole) get from Hobbes to Smith in such short order? There is no single cause for this sea change in the moral climate, but several facts stand out as important. First, the transition from war to peace. Hobbes lived through the English Civil War that pitted Parliament against king and ended only with the restoration of the monarchy in 1660. Indeed, Hobbes, whose writings had already made him controversial, sat out the civil war in France. The early part of the seventeenth century was no more peaceful on the Continent. The Thirty Years' War came to an end just as things were heating up in England, and by all accounts there was no European war more bloody or destructive—until the horrific twentieth century. By contrast, the period from 1660 to the rise of Napoléon was among the most peaceful that Europe experienced in the last millennium.

It is hardly surprising that Hobbes saw the "natural" condition of humans as a state of war of all against all, while his successors did not. Equally unsurprising is Hobbes's corollary that unquestioning obedience was the paramount need, while his successors were more attentive to the dangers of excessive authority. Unregulated self-interest was a luxury that a Hobbesian world could ill afford; it was an idea that a post-Hobbesian world could not only entertain but cherish. Self-preservation remains an issue for Hobbes's successors, but it is no longer an issue within society—an issue of a war of all against all; it is transformed into an issue of preserving the whole society, conflated with the nation-state, against threats from other nation-states. And this end is served by unleashing self-interest, not containing it. Mandeville, for example, sees the self-regarding behavior of his bees before they get religion as promoting not only prosperity, but also the military capacity of the hive.

A second factor, related but distinct, was the transition from a preoccupation with the distribution of goods to a focus on the production of goods—or, rather, to the growth of production. Various commentators noted the growing prosperity of the British economy in the second half of the seventeenth century; by the end of the century, it began to be plausible that growth could be a permanent feature of the economy. With this realization came a new concern: how to shape policies and institutional structures that would make the possibility of growth a reality (Appleby 1977, chap. 7).

The debate about enclosure illustrates this shift. There were always two issues, how enclosure would affect production and how it would affect the distribution of the produce. Proponents claimed (rightly or wrongly) important production advantages and downplayed distributional issues. Opponents emphasized distributional issues, from Francis Bacon's fiscal and military concerns (see Chapter 5 and Appendix B) to concerns about entitlement and famine. Fiscal and military issues diminished in importance as the growth of commerce, manufacturing, and technology shifted both the tax base and the basis of military might, and the growth of production both on and off the land made famine increasingly rare. With these changes, the concern for distribution diminished, and the proponents of enclosure could claim more and more of the high ground.

The Reverend Dr. Joseph Lee, whose argument was juxtaposed in Chapter 5 with that of John Cook, may have appeared callous in his assertion that it was nobody's business but his own whether he employed many or few servants, but Lee undoubtedly saw himself as a proponent of what would later be called "tough love," claiming that his concern for the poor was the equal of those who opposed enclosure, and claiming as well that he had a better policy for alleviating poverty. Self-interest would lead the encloser to employ the optimal number of laborers—optimal from his own point of view to be sure, but optimal as well from the point of view of the larger society: "If men by good husbandry, trenching, manuring their Land &c do better their Land, is not the Commonwealth inriched thereby?" (*A Vindication of a Regulated Enclosure* 1656, quoted in Appleby 1977, 62). The point is not whether Lee was right or wrong but that his argument carried much more weight in the context of a growing economy than in a stationary, cyclical, or declining one.

Growth transformed the economy from an arena in which your gain comes at my expense—a zero-sum game—to an arena where we could mutually profit—the rising tide that lifts all boats. Locke already presupposes a non-zero-sum economy when he argues that subtraction could mean addition, that in the state of nature society as a whole would benefit when an individual improves a piece of the commons and makes it his own. Indeed, the cost is small to the point of vanishing because, as we have seen, Locke's state of nature is one of unlimited resources—the only limit is the capacity of human labor.

America was the real-life example that justified Locke's theory of growth as a cooperative enterprise. But the abundance of free land in "America"—the America of Locke's fantasy—at best justifies the idea that I do not suffer from your subtracting resources from the common pool: how do I gain?

John Locke, as I have indicated, does not answer this question. But Adam Smith does. In *The Theory of Moral Sentiments,* Smith elaborated the idea of harmonious growth in terms that anticipated a central lesson of *The Wealth of Nations,* including the notion of the invisible hand:

> The rich only select from the heap what is most precious and agreeable. They consume little more than the poor, and in spite of their natural selfishness and rapacity, though they mean only their own conveniency, though the sole end which they propose from the labours of all the thousands whom they employ, be the gratification of their own vain and insatiable desires, they divide with the poor the produce of all their improvements. They are led by an invisible hand to the same distribution of the necessaries of life, which would have been made, had the earth been divided into equal portions among all its inhabitants, and thus without intending it, without

knowing it, advance the interest of the society, and afford means to the multiplication of the species. (Smith 1982 [1759], 184–185)

Contemporary economic theory expresses this proposition through the
idea that the accumulation of capital will increase the marginal productivity
of labor and hence the real wage.[3] So all of us benefit, not just those who do
the accumulating. Trickle-down was the answer to John Cook.

Another reason why self-interest became legitimate was the passage of
time and the growing familiarity of individualism, not as doctrine but as fact
on the ground. It would be an overstatement to say that Hobbes became
acceptable—"Hobbesian" is to this day a reproach in many circles. But as the
individualistic way of looking at the world became more a part of people's
everyday experience, the idea of a society functioning on the basis of individual pursuit of one's own interests became correspondingly less scandalous.
Familiarity may breed contempt, but it also leads to acceptance.

The rise of what philosophers call *consequentialism* gave a huge boost to
the fortunes of self-interest. Consequentialism is the doctrine that it is the
results of actions rather than the actions or the motives behind the actions
that matter in ethical assessment. Mandeville was no doubt riding a philosophical current rather than innovating in his implicit reliance on consequentialism, but his emphasis on the results of pride, prodigality, and related vices—employment for the poor, wealth for the entrepreneur and the
property owner—opens a new chapter in the history of self-interest. Indeed, Mandeville's central paradox stems from the partial application of the
new doctrine: the public sphere is judged by results, whereas the private is
judged by intention.

The tendency to view motivation in terms of interest rather than passion
was another change in the philosophic temper of the times, with important
implications for the present story. I have framed my discussion as being about
self-interest, but the more common phrase in the period 1650–1800 was
"self-love." The difference, as Albert Hirschman has argued in *The Passions and
the Interests,* is more than semantic. Ever since the classical Greeks, "passions"
have belonged to the lower part of the human psyche, "interests" to its higher
part.[4] Hobbes was inclined to assimilate the two aspects of motivation into a
single idea of appetite and aversion. The implicit subordination of the distinctive human faculty of rational calculation—which is what, after all, distinguishes interest from passion—was another reason why *Hobbesian* and *disrep-
utable* were closely entwined for many people. Locke, by contrast, famously

emphasized the rational aspect of human motivation, so with Locke self-regarding actions belong to the higher side of our makeup—another reason why self-interest would become respectable.[5]

Smith, we have seen, transforms Mandeville's vice into something between moral neutrality and positive virtue. We can now see that in part at least this change is the effect of relabeling. Smith's butcher, baker, and brewer act little differently from Mandeville's tradesmen, concerned with their own gain rather than service to others. But if they are cool, rational, and deliberate rather than hot, emotional, and impetuous, Smith can speak of their motives in terms of interest. This in itself goes some distance to absolving them of the charge that avarice, pride, envy, and vanity are the driving forces of their actions. In Smith's view, it is "the habits of oeconomy, industry, discretion, attention, and application of thought" that drive trade, and these traits, we have seen, "are apprehended to be very praise-worthy qualities, which deserve the esteem and approbation of every body" (Smith 1982 [1759], 304).[6]

There is some sleight of hand here. As in three-card monty, Smith shifts our attention from the consumer to the businessman and then shows us that his motives are very different from what Mandeville led us to believe. It helps Smith's case that the tradesmen on whom he focuses—the butcher, the brewer, and the baker, unlike, say, the draper, wigmaker, and interior decorator—deal in nondurables for which fashion and fickleness play a relatively small role.

In fact, by lauding frugality, Smith directly challenges Mandeville's juxtaposition of private vice and public virtue. "Capitals," according to Smith, "are increased by parsimony, and diminished by prodigality and misconduct" (Smith 1937 [1776], 321). How does Smith avoid Mandeville's paradox that individual frugality, by diminishing spending, is detrimental to the economy?

Simple: Smith revises Mandeville's economic model at a critical point. Mandeville is a proto-Keynesian for whom aggregate demand is an independent, and critical, factor in determining whether an economy will prosper. Thus all the vices that promote greater demand—whether demand for consumption goods or for investment goods—contribute to the prosperity of the hive.

By contrast, Smith is a pioneer of the worldview that has become dominant in economics, in which a central tenet is that aggregate demand does not matter. In contrast with Mandeville, Smith argues that saving cannot lead to a shortfall in demand since what is saved is spent—on capital goods rather than on consumption goods. In Smith's words,

> Whatever a person saves from his revenue he adds to his capital, and either employs it himself in maintaining an additional number of productive hands, or enables some other person to do so, by lending it to him for an interest, that is, for a share of the profits. As the capital of an individual can be increased only by what he saves from his annual revenue or his annual gains, so the capital of a society, which is the same with that of all the individuals who compose it, can be increased only in the same manner. . . . What is annually saved is as regularly consumed as what is annually spent, and nearly in the same time too. . . . That portion which [an individual] annually saves . . . is consumed by labourers, manufacturers, and artificers, who re-produce with a profit the value of their annual consumption. (Smith 1937 [1776], 321)

Well before John Maynard Keynes's revolutionary treatise, *The General Theory of Employment, Interest and Money,* appeared in 1936, economists had recognized that there might be short-run difficulties from a failure of people to spend their incomes; Keynes's stature gave new life and respectability to the idea that demand failure could undermine prosperity, and the superiority of his formulation gave context and system to the claim.[7] In one, fundamentalist, reading, the problem of demand failure was not limited to the short period. And this strand of Keynesian fundamentalism survived and even thrived in post–World War II Britain—its chief exponents were Roy Harrod at Oxford (Harrod 1948) and Joan Robinson at Cambridge (Robinson 1956, 1962). But the mainstream in the United States very early concluded that the applicability of Keynes's theory was limited to a short period, several years in the worst case, where some sort of market imperfection or friction prevented all markets, especially the labor market, from matching demand and supply. In the long run all was well—markets cleared as Smith and his followers imagined.

The resulting "neoclassical synthesis" in due course carried the day not only in the United States, but also in Britain and indeed throughout the world, a triumph, in my view, of technique over understanding. There remains a dispute within the economics mainstream between New Keynesians and New Classicals, the New Keynesians the inheritors of the neoclassical synthesis and its division between a short run of market frictions and a long run of market clearing, the New Classicals a band of market fundamentalists who believe that all markets clear all of the time.[8]

The important point for present purposes is the agreement between the two schools of thought about the long run. In the long run, fashion, fickleness, all the vices that Mandeville thought essential to maintain aggregate demand and hence prosperity, are not only unnecessary but counterproductive. Diligence, hard work, rational calculation will produce the prosperity that Mandeville thought could come about only through the profligacy of a critical mass of vice-ridden consumers. (Keynesian fundamentalists think prosperity requires optimism—buoyant "animal spirits" in Keynes's phrase—on the part of entrepreneurs. Consumers are considered to be passive agents who simply spend what they get.) If vice is not a necessary condition of prosperity, there is one less reason to object to self-interest.

There was not, I have suggested, a single cause for the legitimization of self-interest. The transition from war to peace, the discovery of growth, the growing familiarity of individualism, the emergence of consequentialism, the mutation of passions into interests, and the idea that demand was un-problematic—all these developments created a climate in which self-interest became not only legitimate but praiseworthy. By the end of the eighteenth century, advanced thinkers could see the private as well as the public virtue of self-regarding behavior. "Every man for himself and the Devil take the hindmost" had become inscribed on the doorposts of the church of economics.

My account of the radical transformation of the moral valence of self-interest was once challenged on the grounds that the difference between self-interest for Hobbes and for Smith was only that they had very different contexts in mind. Hobbes was thinking of bitter struggle, Smith of gains from trade. I didn't know exactly what to make of this challenge, since it was to my mind simply recapitulating a main point of my story, namely, that attitudes toward self-interest were—partly at least—a function of context. Smith reflected the context of the late eighteenth century, a context that differed markedly from that of the mid-seventeenth century, which framed Hobbes's take on self-interest. No wonder that Smith's understanding differed dramatically from Hobbes's.

Since Smith's day, the ideology of self-interest has taken hold in the general population. The advanced thinking of the eighteenth and nineteenth centuries became the conventional wisdom of the twentieth. To a great extent, ordinary people have bought into the virtue of self-interest, though as I have indicated, Economics 101 helps to drive the lessons home.

There remain important areas of economic and social life in which the reign of self-interest is contested, and there are others in which self-interest has only come recently to dominate. In the first half of the twentieth century, Americans considered wartime military service a patriotic duty rather than a job. Faced with national emergencies like World War II, most Americans felt that in principle all able-bodied men (the dominant gender ideology excluded women) had an equal obligation to risk life and limb. As a nation, we had rejected the Civil War idea that one could pay for a substitute and had not yet come to the idea of a volunteer army as the preferred way of fighting a war. It would be a mistake to suggest that the only issue was self-interest versus fairness, but it would be an even greater mistake to underplay the significance of this aspect of the debate over military service. It is a measure of the extent to which self-interest has become increasingly respectable in the intervening years that the issue of fairness rarely creeps into the debate over the relative merits of a volunteer army and a conscript army. Indeed, I am unaware of any debate at all.[9]

There is considerable debate in other areas. Most people, in the American heartland of self-interest as in other countries, believe markets in vital organs are a bad idea even though there are willing sellers and buyers. There are in fact many good arguments on both sides of this issue, but I think the paramount consideration for most noneconomists is once again the issue of fairness. It is one thing to allow markets to ration ordinary goods, so that I end up drinking Chateau Plonk while you, with ten times my income, are drinking Chateau Petrus. It is quite another to allow relative income and self-interest to determine who will live and who will die in consequence of how kidneys are allocated. More generally, much of the debate about health care is a debate about the relative roles of self-interest and fairness, and the issue is far from decided.

One of the important tasks of the twenty-first century is to find a better balance between the claims of self and the claims of others. We could do worse than to respect John Cook's admonition: "The rule of charity is, that one mans superfluity should give place to another mans conveniency, his conveniency to anothers necessity, his lesser necessities to anothers extreamer necessities" (*Unum Necessarium* 1648, quoted in Appleby 1977, 56).

CHAPTER 7

How Do We Know When We Do Not Know?

How do we know that we are ignorant in some realm or another? And how do we know when we can't know for sure? Both questions play some role in this chapter and the next two, but it is fair to say that my emphasis is on the second issue: what is the basis of knowledge in a world of uncertainty? My answer to this question is that uncertainty reveals the limits of knowledge based on logical deduction from self-evident first principles, the limits of action based on rational calculation—in short, the knowledge of *homo economicus.* In a world of uncertainty, in our world, we rely on convention, authority, and intuition—on our own, but even more so, on the community's, experience. When economics erases community, it at the same time erases, or at least marginalizes, an important source of the knowledge that individuals need to navigate an uncertain world.

John Maynard Keynes laid out the theme in his response to a symposium on his seminal work *The General Theory of Employment, Interest and Money:*

> We have, as a rule, only the vaguest idea of any but the most direct consequences of our acts. . . .
>
> By "uncertain" knowledge, let me explain I do not mean merely to distinguish what is known for certain from what is only probable. . . . The sense in which I am using the term is that in which the prospect of a European war is uncertain, or the price of copper and the rate of interest twenty years hence, or the obsolescence of a new invention, or the position of private wealth-owners in the social system in 1970. About these matters there is no scientific basis on which to form any calculable probability whatever. We simply do not know. Nevertheless, the necessity for action and for decision compels us as practical men to do our best to overlook this awkward fact and to behave exactly as we should if we had behind us a good

Benthamite calculation of a series of prospective advantages and disadvantages, each multiplied by its appropriate probability, waiting to be summed.

How do we manage in such circumstances to behave in a manner which saves our faces as rational, economic men? We have devised for the purpose a variety of techniques, of which much the most important are the three following:

(1) We assume that the present is a much more serviceable guide to the future than a candid examination of past experience would show it to have been hitherto. In other words we largely ignore the prospect of future changes about the actual character of which we know nothing.

(2) We assume that the *existing* state of opinion as expressed in prices and the character of existing output is based on a *correct* summing up of future prospects, so that we can accept it as such unless and until something new and relevant comes into the picture.

(3) Knowing that our own individual judgment is worthless, we endeavor to fall back on the judgment of the rest of the world which is perhaps better informed. That is, we endeavor to conform with the behavior of the majority or the average. The psychology of a society of individuals each of whom is endeavoring to copy the others leads to what we may strictly term a *conventional* judgment.

Now a practical theory of the future based on these three principles has certain marked characteristics. In particular, being based on so flimsy a foundation, it is subject to sudden and violent changes. The practice of calmness and immobility, of certainty and security, suddenly breaks down. New fears and hopes will, without warning, take charge of human conduct. The forces of disillusion may suddenly impose a new conventional basis of valuation. All these pretty, polite techniques, made for a well-paneled Board Room and a nicely regulated market, are liable to collapse. At all times the vague panic fears and equally vague and unreasoned hopes are not really lulled, and lie but a little way below the surface.

Perhaps the reader feels that this general, philosophical disquisition on the behavior of mankind is somewhat remote from the economic theory under discussion. But I think not. Tho this is how we behave in the market place, the theory we devise in the study of how we behave in the market place should not itself submit to market-place idols. I accuse the classical economic theory of being itself one of these pretty, polite techniques which tries to deal with the present by abstracting from the fact that we know very little about the future.

I daresay that a classical economist would readily admit this. But, even so, I think he has overlooked the precise nature of the difference which his abstraction makes between theory and practice, and the character of the fallacies into which he is likely to be led. (Keynes 1937, 213–215)

A colleague once sent me a paper about price-setting with this note: "Steve, This is not the way businessmen behave, but this may be the way economists could theorize about it!" Keynes would have had mixed reactions. He would doubtless be pleased to see that the map is distinguished from the territory but well might find my colleague too pretty and polite.

Milton Friedman had no such scruples. Taking as his text the postulate that individual behavior is governed by utility maximization, his classic 1953 paper on methodology argues that it really doesn't matter whether individuals actually perform such calculations. What matters is whether they act as if they maximize utility. Friedman offers a striking analogy to illustrate and defend the "as if" argument. He invites us to consider a superb billiards player lining up a delicate shot. This billiards player does not write down, much less attempt to explicitly solve, the complicated differential equations of the interactions of the billiard balls. It is enough, according to Friedman, that the successful player acts as if she were an expert in differential equations.

Economists have generally found the billiards analogy compelling, and indeed it is compelling—if we are prepared to grant that all knowledge is of a single kind. For in that case, the billiards player must willy-nilly be a closet mathematician and a superior one at that. But this homogenization of knowledge is precisely the point on which I propose to challenge economic method. Friedman has the weight of Western intellectual tradition behind him in his reduction of the billiards player to a mathematician, but I will argue that the relevant knowledge is better understood to be of an entirely different kind, belonging to a different system, and it is no more instructive to suggest that the billiards player lines up her shots as if she were a mathematician than to suggest that the mathematician solves her equations as if she were trying to make a score at the billiards table. Indeed, I will argue that the economic world is more billiards than mathematics, and that consequently the reduction of human action to maximizing behavior enfeebles our understanding and distorts our explanation. Let me give two examples, saving and investment behavior. I choose these examples deliberately, to avoid the accusation that the problems with the standard view of maximizing behavior—literal or "as if"—are limited to the margins of economics. Saving and investment are two areas of behavior that must be central to every economist's conception of the field.

Saving

Economists conceptualize consumer choice in terms of a well-informed individual who surveys the possibilities afforded by his budget and opts for the one that maximizes his well-being. This approach is probably harmless, and perhaps even useful, in conceptualizing the demand for canned peaches and canned pears, but significant sleight of hand is involved in extending the utility-maximization framework to saving behavior. Typically, saving decisions are modeled as a problem of intertemporal consumer choice: saving behavior falls out from a utility-maximizing consumption plan over one's entire life.

It is hard to know where to begin a critique of this approach. Maybe at the beginning. If the discussion is to go beyond formal mathematics, a fundamental question must be answered: where do preferences come from? In the context of peaches and pears, it can be plausibly argued that preferences emerge from a prehistory of trial and error: purchases of different mixes of the fruits (perhaps at random in the beginning) are followed closely by consumption, and preferences are formed in consequence of the relative satisfaction generated by consuming different commodity bundles. The essential point is that the results of choice are immediate, and the entire process can be repeated until preferences are honed to a fine edge, at which point the history of rational consumer choice can be imagined to begin. Indeed, if certain axioms hold, a utility function can be synthesized, or recovered, from the variations in the consumer's consumption of peaches and pears—her "revealed preferences"—as the relative prices of the two goods change.

Even as a "just-so" story, however, the trial-and-error development of preferences makes little sense in the context of long-term planning of consumption and saving, especially in the two most prominent versions of the theory, the permanent-income hypothesis (M. Friedman 1957) and the life-cycle hypothesis (due to Franco Modigliani and various collaborators, for instance, Modigliani and Brumberg 1954). In both of these models, individuals are assumed to save (and dis-save) in order to smooth consumption over time even though income fluctuates, and the consequences of one's choices are played out over one's lifetime. So there is limited scope for trial and error; as Oedipus learned to his chagrin, the lessons of one's lifetime choices emerge only when one's life is complete. (Reincarnation might do the trick of providing a prehistory of choice, except that even believers for the most part grant that there is little opportunity to apply the lessons of previous lives to the present one.) In short, it is difficult to tell a plausible story of how individuals acquire meaningful preferences between consumption today and consumption a decade or two hence, in the way one can imagine learning about peaches today and pears today.

But even if we sweep the problems of the preference map under the rug, there remain real difficulties in moving from the timeless peaches–pears framework to the intertemporal context. In the first, the budget constraint can be plausibly argued to be known with certainty, at least in the absence of checks and credit cards; the shopper goes to the supermarket with, say, one hundred dollars in his pocket. But in the intertemporal context, the budget is lifetime wealth, which for most of us consists primarily of our "human capital," the discounted present value[1] of our lifetime earnings. The inescapable fact, however, is that the variance around projections of earnings is in general so enormous as to make a mockery of the exercise: the prospects of interruptions in employment over one's lifetime, whether due to the vagaries of the business cycle or to the vagaries of enterprise or industry performance or even to the vagaries of one's own health, cannot be meaningfully quantified by most people. Neither can the prospects for occupational advancement. Lifetime earnings necessarily become a subjective and unmeasurable magnitude subject to continual revision, and without a well-defined budget constraint, a utility function can no longer (even in principle) be recovered from choices by so-called revealed preference. Under these circumstances, it is hard to imagine how an economist would ever know whether an individual was maximizing anything.

Observe that competition and the struggle for survival cannot be invoked to ensure conformity with the assumptions of utility maximization. Economists find deep meaning in the fact that $500 bills are not normally found on sidewalks: if one person fails to exploit an opportunity for gain, someone else will. The relentless predator waiting in the wings may adequately explain why the price of gold in New York does not differ much from its price in London or Tokyo, but it is difficult to find any $500 bills in my failure to optimize my saving behavior (Zeckhauser 1986; Grewal 1998).

This is not to say that no one uses the utility-maximization schema, or a reasonable facsimile, in saving decisions. People whose employment prospects are relatively certain, who follow a reasonably predictable career path, and whose lives are otherwise sufficiently ordered that long-term planning makes intellectual and emotional sense might conceivably make decisions in terms of rational comparison of alternative patterns of lifetime consumption. Middle-aged professionals come immediately to mind as a case in point. (My colleague Jim Duesenberry once observed that the life-cycle hypothesis is exactly what one would expect of a tenured college professor, just going to show that some people's quips are more profound than other people's theories.) But this group is hardly representative of the population as a whole—neither of the top 1 or 2 percent of the income distribution who account for a disproportionate amount of total saving and for whom motives other than provision for retire-ment must predominate, nor of the bottom 70 or 80 percent of the distribu-tion whose economic lives are insufficiently ordered to be describable in terms of deliberation and calculation.

The standard model is even more unconvincing when it is realized that, owner-occupied housing apart, family and individual saving, at least in the United States, has historically accounted for a relatively small part of total capital formation. In the period since World War II, corporate saving and, in-creasingly, pension-fund saving have provided the bulk of the funds for the accumulation of capital in the business sector. Measured personal saving rates, which include investment in owner-occupied housing and pension-fund saving as well as financial saving, have hovered around zero for most of the last decade, which is to say that personal financial saving, the saving households make available to business (and government), has been sharply negative.

Of course, in a theoretical framework dominated by the maximizing indi-vidual, household financial saving is not, or at least ought not to be, a central concept: the pension fund and the corporation are simply extensions of the household, and what matters is private saving, the sum of personal and cor-porate saving. Indeed, in U.S. national income accounts, private pension-fund saving is included both in the disposable income and the saving of households. Somewhat illogically, from the point of view of *homo economicus*, the retained earnings of the corporation are not integrated into the house-hold accounts. I say illogically because either the corporation is the agent of the shareholders, as economists most committed to the maximizing indi-vidual would have it, or—should corporate managers pursue saving policies adverse to an individual's perceived interest—the individual can adjust his direct saving in the light of the saving carried out by the corporations whose shares he owns. Either way, households can make total private saving whatever they wish even if they lack control over corporate investment.

In the jargon of the economics profession, households are supposed to "pierce the corporate veil," despite the inordinate time and resources, not to mention inclination, for the requisite calculations, that must be assumed to be available. The Rockefellers, with a bank at their disposal, may fit the model, but even allowing for the high concentration of share ownership, the Rockefellers are hardly the norm.

Of course, for Friedmanite positivists, the plausibility or implausibility of the assumptions is not an issue: one can always fall back on "as if" behavior if the numbers work out. And supporting evidence does exist, going back to Martin Feldstein (1973; see also Feldstein and Fane 1973). But subsequent empirical work, particularly the work of James Poterba (1987) and Edmond Malinvaud (1986), casts serious doubt on Feldstein's results.

It is a maxim of empirical economics that if you torture the data sufficiently, they will confess. Feldstein's evidence is problematic because consumption and retained earnings enter his regressions simultaneously, so that while Feldstein interprets changes in retained earnings as the cause and changes in consumption as the effect, causality could equally well go the other way. Indeed, it is much more plausible that causality runs from consumption to retained earnings, via aggregate demand and profits—the stickiness of dividends in the short run strengthening the effect of increases in consumption demand on retained earnings (S. Marglin 1984a, 379–382).

In short, saving behavior does not support the rational calculation paradigm. Much evidence is consistent with the maximizing hypothesis, but the data do not allow us to distinguish between hypotheses based on rational calculation and alternative hypotheses based on habit and rules of thumb (S. Marglin 1984a, chaps. 17–18). And with respect to the crucial question of whether people really pierce the corporate veil and integrate personal saving with institutional saving, the data are not consistent with veil piercing.

Investment

First, what is the difference between saving and investment? For the layman, investment is what one does with savings, like buying stocks and bonds. For the economist, the two are conceptually distinct: saving is abstinence from consumption, investment is the commitment of the abstract capital of saving to concrete physical forms. What the two have in common is that investment theory, particularly the theory of how businesses invest in plant and equipment, parallels saving theory in illegitimately extending the maximization paradigm to a domain where calculation can at best play a modest role.

One can plausibly imagine an agricultural enterprise deciding between growing wheat and growing rye on the basis of a profit-maximizing model analogous to the model of the utility-maximizing consumer. But once again, it stretches credulity to imagine that this framework illustrates the typical investment decision of a business. Once again, the time frame is critical. For the farmer deciding between wheat and rye, the costs and returns from the two crops are spread out over just a few months and, if hardly certain, can reasonably be imagined in terms of probabilities based on relatively objective distributions of outcomes. By contrast, the returns from business investment are typically spread out over a long time horizon and do not lend themselves to probabilistic calculation.

Contemporary investment theory summarizes the attractiveness of a project as a weighted sum of the future returns, its discounted present value. However, as Keynes emphasized in the quotation that began this chapter, the formalism of the theory obscures its real content, or perhaps I should say lack of content. The returns of any project, lying in the future, are not objectively given but are a subjective construction on the part of the investor. Both the returns and the utility of these returns depend on conjunctions of events about which the investor can have only vague notions and hunches, hardly the stuff of meaningful formal calculation. For Keynes, returns and utilities are vessels more or less filled according to the optimism or pessimism of the investor herself. For Keynes, the "animal spirits" of investors play a crucial role in investment demand, as do the conventional beliefs of the community of investors.

To be sure, in neoclassical hands, teaming up the states of mind of agents with the somewhat fanciful notion of complete contingent markets (see Appendix A) removes the investor's state of mind from an active role in the investment process. Individuals' saving decisions are realized through the purchase of contingent claims; individuals never need hold physical capital to back their hunches about the future. By contrast, firms, which do the investing in the complete markets model, respond to objective prices rather than to subjective utilities and probabilities. Objectively describable "states of the world" remove all vagueness from future project returns—the state of the world completely and uniquely determines investment returns—and the prices of contingent claims associated with particular states of the world guide the firm's investment decisions.

Although the stock market, as Peter Diamond showed in a seminal paper four decades ago (1967), can in principle play the role of a universal contingent market, the number of companies that would be required to span the economically relevant states of the world is beyond the capacity of financial experts to analyze, stock market pages to list, or computers to store in memory. In practice, contingent markets are the exception rather than the rule, materializing only under unusual circumstances; in the real world, opinions about the future are backed not by the purchase of contingent commodities but by commitments to particular forms of capital. In practice, firms' investment decisions are guided not by objective market prices, but by prospective investment returns, which, like the utilities associated with these returns, are seen "through a glass, darkly."

Indeed, much of economic life would dry up if it depended on calculation. A celebrated passage of Keynes's *General Theory* (1936, 161–162) expands on the theme of animal spirits:

> There is the instability due to the characteristic of human nature that a large proportion of our positive activities depend on spontaneous optimism rather than on a mathematical expectation, whether moral or hedonistic or economic. Most, probably, of our decisions to do something positive, the full consequences of which will be drawn out over many days to come, can only be taken as a result of animal spirits—of a spontaneous urge to action rather than inaction, and not as the outcome of a weighted average of quantitative benefits multiplied by quantitative probabilities. Enterprise only pretends to itself to be mainly actuated by the statements in its own prospectus, however candid and sincere. Only a little more than an expedition to the South Pole, is it based on an exact calculation of benefits to come. Thus if the animal spirits are dimmed and the spontaneous optimism falters, leaving us to depend on nothing but a mathematical expectation, enterprise will fade and die.

Joseph Schumpeter was poles apart from Keynes in his political views. Nevertheless, the two giants of twentieth-century economics agreed emphatically on the role of animal spirits. *The Theory of Economic Development* puts the issue thus:

As military action must be taken in a given strategic position even if all the data potentially procurable are not available, so also in economic life action must be taken without working out all the details of what is to be done. Here the success of everything depends upon intuition, the capacity of seeing things in a way which afterwards proves to be true, even though it cannot be established at the moment, and of grasping the essential fact, discarding the unessential, even though one can give no account of the principles by which this is done. Thorough preparatory work, and special knowledge, breadth of intellectual understanding, talent for logical analysis, may under certain circumstances be sources of failure. (Schumpeter 1934 [1911], 85)

For both Keynes and Schumpeter, calculation to justify one course of action instead of another is to "save the appearances" of ourselves as rational beings.

It is difficult to take Keynes and Schumpeter seriously and yet cling to the myth of economic man as a calculating, maximizing agent. For all the emphasis that economics gives to rationality, a chief virtue of the market is that it allows people to mobilize the nonrational component of their knowledge. In other words, markets allow us to transcend the limits to calculation, planning, and rationality. The market allows, indeed, obliges, us to put our money where our mouths are, and even more important to put our money where words fail us, where our mouths are not. (More on this point in Chapter 9.)

Uncertainty

In both cases, saving and investment, the central problem with the maximizing paradigm is uncertainty. To be sure, uncertainty has all but disappeared from the economist's sight, having been assimilated to risk by the device of subjective probabilities. The first step in the assimilation process was to blur the Knightian distinction (Knight 1940 [1921]) between risk (the case where we know the relevant probabilities) and uncertainty (the case where we do not). This was accomplished by transforming Frank Knight's binary opposition into a continuum and observing that, at the risk end of the spectrum, we can never really know an empirical (as distinct from logical) probability distribution; we only have more or less relevant information on particular samples. By the same token, at the uncertainty end, we are never totally without information about the likelihood of alternative outcomes. Moreover, the essential (for Knight) institutional difference between risky and uncertain events—the difficulties of insurance in the case of uncertainty—is also blurred: markets exist in a wide range of situations that are closer to uncertainty than to risk; for instance, futures markets in commodities and the ad hoc insurance contracts that have long been the specialty of Lloyd's of London.

The blurring in practice of the distinction between risk and uncertainty ignores the obvious in Knight's theory—that these categories are ideal types. (Knight was, after all, a student of the great German sociologist Max Weber.) The existence of mixed cases and fuzzy lines becomes the pretext for abolishing the distinction altogether. If one is disposed in that direction, it is an easy intellectual step from the fuzziness at the edges of the distinction to the idea that all probabilities are personal or subjective in nature. And this indeed is the dominant view in economic theory today. As with utility maximization, it does not matter for the theory whether individuals consciously calculate the subjective probability distributions required by the theory. "As if" behavior will do just fine.

Axiomatic treatments of subjective probability have been around for three-quarters of a century, but came to prominence only when game theory appeared to offer an approach to modeling behavior under uncertainty ("games against nature") as well as an approach to modeling strategic interactions among individuals and firms. In the wake of John von Neumann and Oskar Morgenstern's seminal work (1944), economists and statisticians became interested in the theretofore largely ignored work of Frank Ramsey (1980 [1926]) and Bruno de Finetti (1980 [1937]), an interest that culminated in the formal model of decision making elaborated by Leonard Jimmie Savage (1954), according to which optimal decisions are characterized by the maximization of expected utility, with the probability distribution given by the subjective evaluations of the decision makers in a way that parallels the utility function as the subjective valuation of different outcomes.

But even before Savage formalized the subjective probability approach, critics such as Nobel Laureate Maurice Allais registered objections (Allais 1953). Allais offered an example of a choice situation in which experimental subjects were inclined to violate the Savage axioms. (Savage himself was, on his own admission [1954], tempted, but upon reflection recanted his intuition in favor of the axioms.) A few years later, Daniel Ellsberg (1961) carefully constructed an example to separate risk from uncertainty and found once again that Savage (along with many other distinguished economists and decision theorists) was tempted to behave inconsistently with the Savage axioms, which have no room for the "ambiguity"—Ellsberg's word—of pure uncertainty. Much earlier, Keynes distinguished ambiguity (which he called the "weight of an argument") from probability understood as degree of belief. However, in *A Treatise on Probability,* a revised version of his fellowship dissertation of 1908, Keynes went only half-way down the street of subjective probability theory: he interpreted probability as degree of belief rather than relative frequency, but held the view that degree of belief could be given an objective, interpersonal meaning as belief rationally justified by the evidence.[2]

To be fair, some decision theorists—the names of Howard Raiffa and Savage himself spring to mind—never regarded consistency with the Savage axioms as innate. Generations of students have paid, and are still paying, good money to the leading business schools of the world to learn how to apply probabilities consistently. I do not wish even to hint that students don't get their money's worth, but I am very skeptical that their ability to deal with uncertainty is much enhanced.

More recent criticism, initiated by Daniel Kahneman and Amos Tversky (1979), has been even more damning, since it questions the very ability of people to make the kind of calculations required by probabilistic choice with any degree of consistency. For example, Tversky and Kahneman (1981) show that decision makers respond to the way in which the problem is posed, a 90 percent chance of surviving a medical procedure eliciting a different response than a 10 percent chance of succumbing. The line of investigation begun by Kahneman and Tversky has gathered a substantial following within economics, its value recognized in the award of a Nobel Prize to Kahneman in 2002. (Tversky died in 1996.)

Nonetheless, subjective probability has a firm hold on the economist's imagination. This, it should be understood, is not thanks to the predictive or normative power of the approach. The hidden agenda is to take human behavior, strip it of all its vagaries, conflicts, and contradictions, and then to compress it within the confines of the maximization paradigm. In the positivist euphoria of the mid-twentieth century, the appeal of subjective probability was doubtless enhanced by its consistency, at least in Savage's version, with the axioms of revealed preference: in principle, subjective probabilities, like subjective utilities, could be recovered from choices and actions. Coping with uncertainty, which ought to be regarded as a distinct form of action based on a distinct system of knowledge, is reduced to a logic of calculation and maximization in order to maintain the purity of the economic conception of knowledge and behavior.

Why does this conception have to remain uncontaminated by the inconvenient facts of human behavior? Simple: without the assumption of rational calculation, a key support of the claim that markets work well for people is undermined; the constructive agenda of building a world in the image of economic theory collapses.

Contrary to the economic conception of knowledge, my assertion is that under conditions of uncertainty, decision makers do not and cannot mobilize the apparatus of calculation and maximization. Without something to peg probabilities on, individuals necessarily fall back on quite different methods—on intuition, conventional behavior, authority—in short, on a different *system of knowledge* from that which drives maximizing behavior. This is a system of knowledge that is embedded in community, in the nexus of relationships that bind people to one another.

Systems of Knowledge

The term *algorithmic knowledge* is used here as shorthand for the knowledge of a calculating, maximizing *homo economicus.* Alongside algorithmic knowledge is *experiential knowledge,* a distinct form of knowledge characterized by its dependence both on authority and on intuition, insight, and hunch—in short, knowledge based on experience.

If knowledge is justified true belief, then the epistemological divide between algorithm and experience is where the two forms of knowledge stand on the questions of what are acceptable justifications for belief and for truth. My negative claim is that algorithm is not the only legitimate way of justifying belief and arriving at truth, that algorithmic knowledge does not provide a uniquely acceptable basis for justified true belief. I regard the idea that algorithm is the only way to justify belief as essentially ideological in nature, ideological in the sense that it rests on unproven (and possibly unprovable) assumptions about how we can know. My positive claim is that experience provides not only knowledge *how* (how to swim, how to ride a bike) but also knowledge *that* (that the earth is round, that cotton does not grow in cold climates).

I should emphasize at the outset that I have no criticism to make of algorithmic knowledge as one system of knowledge. On the contrary, we would not be human without our command of algorithmic knowledge. Rather, the problem is the claim made on behalf of algorithmic knowledge that it is all of knowledge, from which stems its proclivity to crowd out other ways of justifying belief. While algorithmic knowledge is essential to our humanness, so is experiential knowledge. Indeed, it is our ability to combine experiential and algorithmic knowledge that sets us apart both from other animals and from computers: animals have experiential knowledge and machines have algorithmic knowledge, but only we humans have both. Oliver Sacks's clinical histories (1985) are at once moving as well as entertaining evidence for the grotesque, bizarre, and even tragic distortions of human beings that result from a loss of either experiential or algorithmic knowledge.[3]

But I get ahead of my story; we cannot very well explore the relationships between different systems of knowledge before I lay out what I mean by this terminology. First, let me be clear about what a knowledge system is not: the term does not refer to a specific domain of knowledge. Economists and physicists, chemical engineers and personnel managers, deal with different domains of knowledge. But this in no way prevents us from sharing a common practice (or a common ideology) with respect to the systems of knowledge we employ.

My argument consists of three propositions: first, that knowledge and action are everywhere and at all times based on a combination, a synthesis, of at least two knowledge systems, algorithmic and experiential knowledge—and perhaps others (spiritual knowledge comes to mind as a distinctive system); second, notwithstanding this symbiosis in practice, modern Western culture has elevated algorithmic knowledge to a superior position, sometimes to the point that experiential knowledge is regarded not simply as inferior knowledge, but as no knowledge at all. In this ideological perspective, experiential knowledge remains unjustified belief, superstition, prejudice—except to the extent that this knowledge can be justified by algorithm. The third proposition is that the ideological hierarchy of knowledge has had a powerful influence on the way algorithmic and experiential knowledge interact in practice, rendering experiential knowledge illegitimate and even invisible.

I have found it useful to characterize systems of knowledge in terms of four dimensions: epistemology, transmission, innovation, and power. A particular system has its own theory of knowledge, that is, its own epistemology; it also has its own rules for acquiring and sharing knowledge, its own distinctive ways for changing the content of what counts as knowledge, and, finally, its own rules of governance, both among insiders and between insiders and outsiders.

Why system? The point of the term system is twofold. Its first purpose is to suggest that epistemology, transmission, innovation, and politics are not attributes of knowledge in general but characteristics of particular ways of knowing. There is no single epistemology, but specific epistemologies that belong to distinct ways of knowing. Equally, there are distinctive ways of transmitting and modifying knowledge over time. And each particular way of knowing may go along with a different set of power relationships among the people who share knowledge and between insiders and outsiders.

The links among the several characteristics by which we describe a system of knowledge are a second reason for using the term. How we know and how we learn and teach, how we innovate and how we relate politically—these characteristics of knowledge mutually interact.

The difference between algorithmic and experiential knowledge begins with the distinctiveness of their epistemologies. I have said that algorithmic knowledge can be identified with rationality. Its form in the modern West is knowledge based on logical deduction from self-evident first principles; Euclidean geometry and the Cartesian method are perhaps the canonical exemplars. The Western form of algorithmic knowledge thus combines induction and deduction. Induction plays an important role in determining first principles (parallel lines never meet), and deduction allows us to reach conclusions at some remove from these first principles (the Pythagorean theorem). "Logical deduction" implies proceeding by small steps with nothing left out, nothing left to chance or to the imagination. Thus, besides the mathematical theorem, the computer program comes to mind as a model of algorithmic knowledge.

Observe that the necessity for induction to establish first principles for this form of knowledge raises the issue of whether there can be, even as an ideal type, such a thing as pure algorithmic knowledge. The problem is that the notion of self-evidence requires a form of experiential knowledge—how else do we recognize what is "self-evident"? How do we distinguish illumination from delusion?[4]

Let us look more closely at the distinguishing features of the epistemology of algorithmic knowledge. First, algorithmic knowledge is analytic. It decomposes a body of knowledge into its components. It is thus directly and immediately reproducible. It is fully articulate, and within algorithmic knowledge it may be said that what cannot be articulated does not even count as knowledge. As noted in Chapter 1, Lord Kelvin famously opined that only when knowledge can be expressed in numbers does one really know something.

Algorithmic knowledge is purely cerebral. Mind is separate from body, and algorithmic knowledge pertains to the mind alone. The statement "I feel there is something wrong with what you are saying," which is to say "I sense something is wrong, but I cannot articulate what or why," has no place within algorithmic knowledge.

Even when pressed into action, algorithmic knowledge is theoretical. Once the tentative and provisional nature of any axiomatic scheme is recognized, algorithmic statements are necessarily hypotheses. Indeed, without entering into the nuances of the debate between Karl Popper (1968 [1935]) and his critics (Kuhn 1970 [1962]; Lakatos 1970; Putnam 1974), it can be said that algorithmic knowledge is geared one way or another to falsification and verification. Its very procedure, the insistence on small steps that follow immediately and directly on one another, precludes discovery and creativity. To discover or to create through algorithmic knowledge would be like the proverbial monkey typing Shakespeare: he might some day do it, but we would be hard-pressed to find the wheat among the chaff.[5]

Finally, algorithmic knowledge, like the God of the New Testament, is impersonal and impartial; it is in principle accessible to all on equal terms (Romans 2:11; Colossians 3:10–11). Thus algorithmic knowledge is not only theoretical knowledge; it becomes theoretical knowledge of theoretical equals. So far so good: who would not applaud a bias toward equality? The problem is that as the idea of a universal God led Christians to deny the possibility of salvation to unbelievers, so the idea of a universal algorithmic knowledge has led to the disenfranchisement of those judged (rightly or wrongly) to be less adept at navigating this system of knowledge. It is an easy step to the view that those lacking in algorithmic knowledge are lacking in knowledge itself.

If algorithmic knowledge is another name for the knowledge acquired through our rational faculties, experiential knowledge runs the gamut from the authority of recognized masters (and mistresses) to one's own intuition. Keynes's emphasis on convention in his response to critics of *The General Theory*, with which I began this chapter, is an important aspect of experiential knowledge. More than many of us would like to admit, we hold beliefs because others similarly situated in society hold these beliefs—and we appeal to convention as a justification for the truth of what we believe. We also know independently of what others believe, through direct and immediate apprehension unmediated by any process of rational deduction, that is, through intuition. Different as these two ways of knowing may appear, they share a common core of lived experience, in the one case our own experience, in the other the experience of contemporaries (or of those who have gone before).

Opposed to the small steps of algorithmic knowledge are both received doctrine and the imaginative leap—the great aha!—which all at once enables one to fit the jigsaw puzzle together. Received doctrines and imaginative leaps are both knowledge of the whole, difficult to break down into parts. In contrast with the analytic nature of algorithmic knowledge, experiential knowledge is indecomposable.

Experiential knowledge is often difficult if not impossible to articulate. Those who possess it may be aware that they possess special knowledge, but their knowledge is implicit rather than explicit. It is revealed in weaving an intricate design, in creating a sculpture, in performing a ritual, or in forecasting gross domestic product, not in textbooks for student weavers, sculptors, priests, or economists.

Whereas algorithmic knowledge may be claimed to be universal, it is difficult to make such a claim for experiential knowledge. Experience is by its very nature specialized and closely allied to time and place. It is, in short, contextual, existing for a particular purpose.

Experiential knowledge belies the mind–body dualism that is basic to algorithmic knowledge. Under experiential knowledge, one knows with and through one's hands and eyes and heart as well as with one's head. Experiential knowledge is knowledge that gives due weight to Keynes's animal spirits, to what Martha Nussbaum and Amartya Sen (1989, 316) have called the "cognitive role of the emotions." It is also the knowledge of touch. Feeling, in both senses of the term, is central to experiential knowledge; it is at once both tactile and emotional.

Experiential knowledge is intensely practical, to the point that, as has been suggested, it reveals itself only through practice. This is not to deny the existence of an underlying theory, but the theory is implicit rather than explicit, not necessarily available, perhaps not even usually available, to practitioners.

Experiential knowledge is geared to creation and discovery rather than to falsification and verification. Even a mathematical theorem is largely the product of experiential knowledge, although the proof must, by the very requirements of the knowledge system on which mathematics is formally based, be cast in terms of algorithmic knowledge.

The transmission mechanisms of experience and algorithm are as different as the epistemologies. Algorithmic knowledge in principle is accessible through pure ratiocination, but in practice, it is generally acquired through formal schooling. Indeed, knowledge in the West has more and more come to be equated with what is taught in the schools, and the schools in general are dedicated to algorithmic knowledge—so much so that a nephew once suggested opposing "book knowledge" and "street knowledge" in place of the opposition between algorithm and experience.[6]

The canonical way of transmitting experience is through a personal nexus epitomized by the master–apprentice relationship. The master's example more than any precept instructs the apprentice, who absorbs almost unconsciously what he is taught. Almost anybody can acquire the rudiments of a craft in this way, but quality is a matter of intuition as well as of a heightened sense of touch and feel developed through years of practice.

Algorithmic innovation leads a double life. The formal model allows one only to replace an erroneous logical derivation with a correct one or to change the assumptions. One can supplement existing axioms, or, more rarely, replace existing axioms by new ones, as Newton did for his predecessors and Einstein did for Newton. With new axioms, one can proceed to new theorems by old methods: the new theorems are simply logical entailments of the new assumptions. In practice, as has been noted, a considerable admixture of experience is involved even in algorithmic innovation: the innovator has to know where she is going, and the map is provided by her intuition rather than her logic. Experiential innovation is largely a matter of trial and error. This is not to say it is haphazard, but the underlying structure of experiential innovation is often hidden from the innovator herself.

If knowledge is a text, the canonical form of algorithmic innovation is criticism. Innovation takes the form of a direct assault, a challenge to logic or to first principles themselves. For this reason, algorithmic innovation can flourish only in a group of equals, where respect for personal authority is relatively attenuated.[7] The canonical form of experiential innovation, by contrast, is commentary, emendation, and explanation of the text. The authority of the fathers is not challenged but reinterpreted.

Algorithm and experience reverse internal and external power relations. If algorithmic knowledge presupposes a group of equals, knowledge based on experience presupposes a hierarchy of knowledge and a corresponding hierarchy of power within the charmed circle.

Experiential knowledge is not and cannot be the knowledge of theoretical equals. It normally exists in networks of relationships and cannot be transmitted or even maintained apart from these relationships. The normal avenues of transmission—parent–child, master–apprentice, guru–shisha—are intensely personal and invariably hierarchical.

These hierarchies blend age, power, and knowledge. Sometimes the hierarchy is as wide at the top as at the base, so that those at the bottom have a reasonable expectation of moving up to the top with the passage of time. An example is the hierarchy of the guild, where every apprentice could hope to be a master, not that of the factory, where few workers can become foremen, let alone executives.

There are, of course, hierarchies, such as those based on gender or skin color, in which one does not move up as one gains experience. Hierarchies based on exclusion are, however, as likely to be justified in terms of algorithm as in terms of experience: arguably, an important element in the subordination of women and blacks in the modern West has been the claim that white men have superior algorithmic capacity.[8]

If experiential knowledge is internally hierarchical, it is more open externally. Laying no claim to universality, recognizing limits of time, place, and purpose, people whose knowledge is based on experience do not generally exhibit the tendency of those whose knowledge is algorithmic to nullify other ways of knowing. If your knowledge is rooted in experience, you may not be egalitarian in terms of your relations with people whose experiences differ, but you are more likely to live and let live.

As with many of my favorite "original" ideas, once having elaborated the notion that algorithm and experience constitute separate and distinct systems of knowledge, I found similar ideas elsewhere, in fact everywhere. One of the better known is Robert Pirsig's distinction between "classical" and "romantic" knowledge in *Zen and the Art of Motorcycle Maintenance*. The details are different, but Pirsig's classical knowledge clearly resonates with algorithm and romantic knowledge with experience. Michael Polanyi (1962 [1958]) characterized "tacit" knowledge as a distinct way of knowing in which touch and feel play an important role—as they do in my notion of experiential knowledge. In another context, Jerome Bruner (1979 [1962]) distinguished "right-handed" from "left-handed" knowledge, the first based on logic, the second on intuition—a distinction that also characterizes algorithm and experience.

Within economics, distinctions similar to mine have arisen at various times. Thorstein Veblen (1990 [1908]) distinguished between "speculative knowledge" and "work-day knowledge," Nicholas Georgescu-Roegen devoted a whole chapter of *The Entropy Law and the Economic Problem* to "Science, Arithmomorphism, and Dialectics," and Deirdre McCloskey (1985) wittily and forcefully argued for acknowledging the limits of "scientific" economics (algorithm) and recognizing the role of rhetoric (experience) in our arguments.

Why does it matter how we know? The short answer is that how we actually know differs from our beliefs about knowledge. In practice, we moderns know in multiple ways just as nonmoderns know, but with this difference: our knowledge and understanding are distorted by our beliefs about knowledge, in particular by an ideology that subordinates experience to algorithm. The next two chapters explore the ideological component of how we know, and how this ideological component limits and constrains how we actually know.

CHAPTER 8

Sources of the Modern
Ideology of Knowledge

I have suggested that economists' ideology of knowledge, which prioritizes algorithmic knowledge, is at odds with good economics, which requires a synthesis of algorithmic and experiential knowledge. Not only economics but any activity, from repairing a motorcycle to running a business to proving a mathematical theorem, must necessarily combine algorithmic and experiential knowledge. This is a common feature of otherwise disparate cultures. Economics has a huge problem coming to grips with this fact of life, a problem that reflects an ideology that marginalizes experience. Whereas non-Western cultures appear to strike an ideological balance roughly congruent with the actual coexistence of the two systems of knowledge, the ideology of the modern West puts the first on a pedestal and denigrates the second. Why?

The glorification of algorithmic knowledge in Western culture goes way back. I have elsewhere (Marglin 1990, 1996) used the Greek terms *episteme* and *techne* for what I have here called algorithmic and experiential knowledge. In part, I used the Greek to allow me to treat different systems of knowledge as black boxes that I could fill as I saw fit, something that is much harder to do with ordinary English words, which—Humpty Dumpty to the contrary notwithstanding—create certain expectations.[1] But there was another reason for the Greek: to signal the age of the dispute about knowledge.

A formal distinction between episteme and techne along the lines of algorithm and experience is made by Aristotle in the *Nicomachean Ethics* (1139 b 14–1140 a 24, 140–142), except that Aristotle restricts episteme to knowledge *of* and techne to knowledge *how*. Earlier writers, including Plato, used the terms almost interchangeably (Vernant 1982 [1965], 59 fn36; Lyons 1969; Nussbaum 1986, 444). Plato's term for knowledge lacking algorithm is *empeiria*.[2]

For our purposes, it doesn't matter very much whether we choose to contrast episteme with techne or with empeiria, or for that matter with *ortha doxa* (mere correct opinion, which is to say knowledge without proper justification); techne, empeiria, and ortha doxa, as the province of the craftsman, are closely bound up with one another. Greek theories of knowledge, the French classicist Jean-Pierre Vernant has suggested, led to the devaluation of experiential knowledge precisely because the craftsman's experience inevitably allowed unpredictable events to contaminate pure knowledge, which deals with the unchanging and the certain. Unlike episteme, experiential knowledge deals with approximation, "to which neither exact measure nor precise calculation applies" (Vernant 1982 [1965], 51). For this reason,

> Artisanal *techne* is not real knowledge. The artisan's . . . *techne* rests upon fidelity to a tradition which is not of a scientific order but outside of which would hand him over, disarmed, to chance. Experience can teach him nothing because in the situation in which he finds himself placed—between rational knowledge on the one hand and *tuche,* chance, on the other—there is for him neither theory nor facts capable of verifying theory; there is no experience in the proper sense. By the strict rules which his art necessitates, he imitates blindly the rigor and sureness of rational procedure; but he has also to adapt himself, thanks to a sort of flair acquired in the practice of his profession, to the unpredictable and the chancy, which the material on which he acts always has in greater or lesser degree. (Vernant 1982 [1965], 59)

Music provides Plato with a good example of the problem of knowledge that lacks the certainty of algorithm: "It attains harmony by guesswork based on practice, not by measurement; and flute music throughout tries to find the pitch of each note as it is produced by guess, so that the amount of uncertainty mixed up in it is great, and the amount of certainty small" (*Philebus* 56 A, 359–361). Citing the poet Agathon, Aristotle says the same thing about *techne:* "Art [*techne*] loves chance, and chance art" (*Nicomachean Ethics,* 1140 a 20, 141).

Plato's *Republic* is categorical about the inferiority of the craftsman's knowledge. Socrates contrasts the knowledge of the horseman who uses the bit and bridle and the craftsman who makes them. "Is it not true," Socrates asks, "that not even the craftsmen who make them know [how they should be made] but only the horseman who understands their use?" (601 C, 332).[3] He continues:

It follows, then, that the user must know most about the performance of the thing he uses and must report on its good or bad points to the maker. The flute-player, for example, will tell the instrument-maker how well his flutes serve the player's purpose, and the other will submit to be instructed about how they should be made. So the man who uses any implement will speak of its merits and defects with knowledge, whereas the maker will take his word and possess no more than a correct belief, which he is obliged to obtain by listening to the man who knows. (601 E, 332)

For Aristotle, too, the craftsman left to his own devices could lay claim only to an inferior grade of knowledge. Indeed, Aristotle takes over the parable of the flute maker and the flute player and with Plato stigmatizes the craftsman's knowledge as simply "right opinion" (*Politics,* 1277 b 27–30, 195).[4] Aristotle believed that there could be an episteme—albeit an inferior one—of even the slave's work, an episteme, for instance, of cooking (ibid., 1255 b 21–40, 29–31). In this respect, Aristotle is the true precursor of Frederick Winslow Taylor, the father of scientific management. (See the next chapter for more on Taylor.)

The subordination of the craftsman's knowledge of production went hand in hand with the subordination of the craftsman himself. But if Plato is any guide, the upper-class conception of the craftsman must have been ambivalent: the craftsman figures prominently in the Platonic origin myth, creation itself being the work of a *demiurgos,* a craftsman; and the craftsman's techne appears and reappears in the Platonic dialogues as the model of purposive knowledge (Klosko 1986, 28, 41; Vidal-Naquet 1983, 293). The ambivalence may stem from a very real tension between the essential role of the craftsman and his knowledge to the well-being of the *polis* on the one hand and the inferior position of the craftsman on the other (Vidal-Naquet 1983, chap. 5).

This tension was part of a more general political and social tension that could only have amplified the attractions of episteme. The Greeks identified chance with disorder, and episteme was thus the knowledge system not only of eternal truth but of social order as well. The craftsman and his techne represented—to borrow a phrase used by the French historian and activist Pierre Vidal-Naquet in a different context—"disorder and the individual exploit" (1983, 174).

The very transition from the Homeric to the archaic age, which saw the birth of Greek philosophy, was, according to the British classicist Eric Dodds, a period of a heightened sense of insecurity, "not a different belief but a different emotional reaction to the old belief" (Dodds 1951, 30). Undoubtedly, the rise in insecurity had many causes, but the political and economic upheavals that marked the seventh and sixth centuries BCE loom large in Dodds's account (Dodds 1951, 44ff). He suggests that the breakdown of the family—the primary community in most human societies—and, specifically, the erosion of the authority of the father played an important role in the perception of growing social disorder. Personal authority is central to experiential knowledge, and one of the attractions of algorithmic knowledge is precisely the challenge to this authority that it poses. It is certainly possible that in ancient Greece a precocious individualism was strengthening, and being strengthened by, algorithmic knowledge.

It is evidently too much to assert that the conception of knowledge, and particularly the low view of craft knowledge, held by certain Greek philosophers determined the Western conception for all time to come. In any case, we do not need to go all the way back to the Greeks. My characterization of the modern Western idea of algorithmic knowledge could have been cribbed from Descartes (and very likely was, albeit unconsciously—I thought I was copying Euclid), for it practically paraphrases the procedure for arriving at true knowledge expounded in the *Discourse on Method and Meditations on First Philosophy* (Descartes 1980 [1637 and 1641]). But in a sense, Descartes is a Greek once removed: mathematics was for him the model, and the model of the model was Euclid's geometry.

The context in which Descartes elaborated his project is important, for it sheds more light on the appeal of algorithmic knowledge. As for the Greeks, algorithmic knowledge was for Descartes and his times the answer to the disorder that threatened to undo society. I have already indicated a relationship between the breakdown of the medieval synthesis and the rebirth of algorithmic knowledge in Chapter 5, but it is worth reiterating the main point here.

The Reformation shattered more than the Church. Established ways of knowing were cast into doubt by Martin Luther's insistence on a direct channel between the Christian and God. But the channel turned out to be noisy, and the signal weak. As was noted in Chapter 5, one young man thought God had commanded him to kill his brother: it is not always easy to distinguish illumination from illusion. Skepticism reappeared after a hiatus of more than a millennium. In the hands of a "liberal" like Michel de Montaigne, skepticism could form the basis of open-minded tolerance at the level of religious belief as well as the level of religious politics. But the project of tolerance misfired on both levels, and the seventeenth century turned into the bloodiest in European history—at least until the world wars of the twentieth century surpassed the horrors of the Thirty Years' War.

Descartes showed that, carried to the limit, skepticism would founder on the rocks of the indubitable fact of consciousness: *I think, therefore I am.* The *cogito* (Latin for "I think") could serve as a model for logical deduction from self-evident first principles. Algorithmic knowledge mimicking the form of the mathematical theorem was the answer to the "disunity and uncertainty" of contemporary knowledge, an answer resounding with "certainty, necessity, and precision" (Descartes 1980, editor's preface, vii).

In view of the central role that uncertainty plays in this story, it is also very much to the point that shortly after the death of Descartes, the intellectual attack on uncertainty and doubt took a decisive turn. As Ian Hacking (1975) tells the story, the Greeks, lacking a theory of probability, did not consider random variability as something of which one could have real knowledge. The modern idea of probability required both a new conception of stochastic events and a new understanding of doubtful knowledge as differing in degree rather than in kind from certain knowledge. The first text to reflect these notions, the so-called Port-Royal Logic, was Antoine Arnauld's *The Art of Thinking*, originally published in 1662.

Hacking's work is a tour de force, brilliant as it is entertaining. But it errs, I think, in seeing probability as an attack on the Greek idea of knowledge as certainty. Hacking rightly sees the Greek correspondence

knowledge : certainty = opinion : uncertainty

being ruptured by the modern notion of probability. In Hacking's view, probability shifts the boundary between knowledge and opinion so that knowledge can be brought to bear on uncertainty. Instead, Descartes and the Port-Royal logicians seem to me to affirm the boundary between knowledge and opinion but to break down the boundary between certainty and uncertainty so as to bring chance within the framework of certainty.

Probability is thus the opposite of an attack on certainty; it is an attack on uncertainty. The probability calculus assimilates the uncertain into the realm of true, certain knowledge. Uncertainty and approximation—hallmarks of experiential knowledge—are banished by the certainty and exactness of algorithmic knowledge. Uncertainty becomes risk, the object of calculation and maximization, as experiential knowledge yields to algorithmic knowledge.

That, at least, was the project. But like the skeptics' project, the proba-bilists' didn't quite come off. Much has been achieved, as the insurance in-dustry attests. Thanks to our understanding of probabilities, we can buy life insurance, fire insurance, and even medical insurance at more or less their actuarial value, plus administrative costs and sometimes a healthy profit for the insurers. But no amount of calculation can move the incalculable from the realm of experiential knowledge to the realm of the algorithmic. (The poet Agathon was surely on to something important when he noted the affinity of techne and chance.) In short, experiential knowledge is the knowledge system of uncertainty, and uncertainty is the blessing—or curse, depending on one's point of view—of life.

Ideology and Practice

The history of the ideological commitment to algorithm over experience would matter relatively little if practice and ideology occupied water-tight compartments. But the modern ideology of knowledge is partially respon-sible for the failure of economists to offer convincing explanations of eco-nomic phenomena, and (as we shall see in the next chapter) for the distor-tions in the prescriptions that economics offers for the ills of the economy.

There are, of course, many reasons for the failure of economics to explain, and many of these reasons have little to do with the ideology of algorithm. For one thing, the subject matter is exceedingly difficult, not the least because it changes practically before our very eyes (Galbraith 1967, 409–412). The worlds studied by physicists and biologists change sufficiently slowly that Galileo and Einstein, Darwin and Haldane, confronted the same underlying phenomena. Interpretations might differ, but the structures being interpreted did not. By contrast, economic structures have changed drastically, not only over five hundred or one hundred or years, but within a generation. Chasing a moving target, economists are at a disadvantage relative to natural scientists. Thus, what I referred to in the last chapter as "post-Baconian science"—the iterative revision of first principles according to experimental evidence—may be a plausible procedure for the natural sciences (whether or not this is how natural scientists really work) but totally impractical for a field of social in-quiry like economics.

This difficulty is compounded by the ease with which values, beliefs, and preconceptions rush in to fill the vacuum created by our ignorance. Since its beginnings, mainstream economics has served the triple purpose of explaining the market, justifying market arrangements, and constructing a world in the image of economics. The mainstream, by the way, has had no monopoly over the confusion of ends: Adam Smith and Karl Marx were in many respects polar opposites, but in mixing normative and descriptive they set the same standard for their followers.

Most of us willingly concede the role of ideology in theories we reject, while denying it for our own brand of truth. Perhaps it cannot be otherwise. A theory, after all, must be seen as at least a possible path to truth. And as long as truth and ideology are seen as opposites, inconsistent with one another, the denial of an ideological component becomes a necessary condition for the development of a theory.

Joseph Schumpeter's magisterial *History of Economic Analysis* makes the useful distinction between vision and analysis, between the "preanalytic act" that provides the "raw material for the analytic effort" (Schumpeter 1954, 41) and analysis itself. For Schumpeter, visions are necessarily suffused with ideology:

> Vision is ideological almost by definition. It embodies the picture of things as we see them, and wherever there is any possible motive for wishing to see them in a given rather than another light, the way in which we see things can hardly be distinguished from the way in which we wish to see them.

The role of analysis is to refine and test the vision

> The first task is to verbalize the vision or to conceptualize it in such a way that its elements take their places, with names attached to them that facilitate recognition and manipulation, in a more or less orderly schema or picture.

Analysis also winnows the vision; Schumpeter continues:

> But in doing so we almost automatically perform two other tasks. On the one hand, we assemble further facts in addition to those perceived already, and learn to distrust others that figured in the original vision; on the other hand, the very work of constructing the schema or picture will add further relations and concepts to, and in general also eliminate others from, the original stock. Factual work and "theoretical" work, in an endless relation of give and take, naturally testing one another and setting new tasks for each other, will eventually produce *scientific models*, the provisional joint products of

their interaction with the surviving elements of the original vision, to which increasingly more rigorous standards of consistency and adequacy will be applied.

In the end, the grain of truth is separated from the ideological chaff:

> The rules of procedure that we apply in our analytic work are almost as much exempt from ideological influence as vision is subject to it. Passionate allegiance and passionate hatred may indeed tamper with these rules. In themselves these rules, many of which, moreover, are imposed upon us by the scientific practice in fields that are little or not affected by ideology, are pretty effective in showing up misuse. And, what is equally important, they tend to crush out ideologically conditioned error from the visions from which we start. It is their particular virtue, and they do so automatically and irrespective of the desires of the research worker. The new facts he is bound to accumulate impose themselves upon his schema. The new concepts and relations, which somebody else will formulate if he does not, must verify his ideologies or else destroy them. And if this process is allowed to work itself out completely, it will indeed not protect us from the emergence of new ideologies, but it will clear in the end the existing ones from error. (Schumpeter 1954, 42–43)

Schumpeter might paraphrase Agathon to read: "Ideology loves techne, and techne ideology." The advance from vision to analysis is the taming of experiential by algorithmic knowledge.

I take a different view. In the first place, opposing truth and ideology is in my view a methodological error. What is ideology, after all, but the unproved assumptions, beliefs, and values that must underlie any intellectual inquiry, or for that matter, any form of contemplation or action? Ideology need not be immutable; today's ideologies may become the subject of searching scrutiny tomorrow. But whatever the fate of today's particular ideologies, it is in the very nature of ideology that the issue of truth or falsity lies beyond our intellectual grasp, at least our algorithmic grasp. A core of assumptions—necessarily susceptible to ideology—remains in our theories and models no matter how much we might test and refine them. Imre Lakatos (1970) has distinguished between this inviolable core and a "protective belt" of auxiliary assumptions, the individual elements of which are continually being examined, amended, and even replaced if need be. This examination, amendment, and replacement is what Thomas Kuhn's "normal science" is all about (Kuhn 1970 [1962]).

The point is that normal science, however much it may change the protective belt, leaves the core intact and inviolable. Many economists discovered Lakatos in the 1980s when they realized that resistance of data to torture did not require them to give up cherished beliefs; the tests were, it turned out, of "joint hypotheses" drawn from the core and the protective belt, so it was always possible to disown the hypotheses from the protective belt and maintain the one(s) from the core.[5] But this is just a way of avoiding the ideological beam in one's own eye. As long as we deny the ideological components of our theories, we shall never transcend them.

Alongside the inherent difficulties of economics and the preconceptions we bring to it lies a methodological failure, namely, our insistence on explaining economic behavior in terms of algorithmic knowledge alone. I should reiterate that I have nothing against algorithmic knowledge—in its place. Its clarity and precision are rightly esteemed, and it is the language of choice for unambiguous communication. Problems arise not from algorithmic knowledge itself but from abuse of algorithmic knowledge, abuse that begins when the system in which we communicate is confused with the system we are communicating about, the system of knowledge of the playwright with the system of knowledge in which the actors operate. A colleague's distinction between how businessmen set prices and how economists think about price setting (see the beginning of the last chapter) is a step in the right direction.

Indeed, we might carry Schumpeter's opposition between vision and analysis one step further and distinguish vision from theory and theory from model. I would accept Schumpeter's characterization of vision as "preanalytic"—experiential in my language—and apply his notion of analysis as purely algorithmic (at least in its ideal type) to models. This leaves theory. For me, theory about human interaction should be a mixture of the experiential and the algorithmic—like real life. A good theory has enough algorithmic knowledge to make the vision tractable and enough experiential knowledge to reflect the richness, mystery, and evanescence of the human condition.

In my view, it is the theory rather than the model that ought to interest us. Models are means to apprehending theories, not ends in themselves. Yet, we characteristically become so wrapped up in our models, indeed, enchanted by them, that we lose sight of their purpose. In the extreme, we convince ourselves that it doesn't matter whether agents actually play by the rules of our models; or worse, we insist for reasons of isomorphic purity that agents' behavior conform to the formalisms of the model. The experiential knowledge of agents and the experiential knowledge of the theorist disappear equally from view.

So what? Even if agents operate largely in terms of experiential knowledge, what is wrong with describing their behavior in terms of algorithmic knowledge? What is wrong with "as if"? There are several reasons for rejecting the representation of experiential knowledge in terms of algorithmic knowledge. For one thing, now that the positivist euphoria has worn off, most of us are quite willing to admit that we are interested in understanding as well as, perhaps more than, in explanation (to use Max Weber's terms), and explanation—accounting for the observed data in an econometric sense—is the most that can be claimed for as-if economics.

But even within a positivistic framework, in which the sole criterion is the consistency of a hypothesis with data, there are serious difficulties. If, like the physicist's or the biologist's worlds, the economic world were unchanging, or changed very slowly, Milton Friedman's dictum—that the assumptions do not matter as long as they "work"—might be extended to the system of knowledge itself: an algorithmic rendering of what is in fact experiential knowledge might turn out okay (Friedman 1953). However, as has been noted, economic structures change at such a rapid rate that we cannot trust that a model that captures the past will also predict the future. I think it was the economist Abba Lerner who remarked that while we don't need to know how a car works to drive, it sure helps when it comes to fixing one.

Nonetheless, Friedman's as-if is undoubtedly superior to the basic idea of so-called rational expectations, according to which agents actually embody the assumption of the rational, calculating individuals of neoclassical theory, a clear case of nature as the mirror of philosophy. I have considerable sympathy for the view that the economist's theory ought to be isomorphic to agents' behavior, but it is more difficult to accept the dictum that it is agents who must shape up to the theory rather than theorists who ought to reflect the behavior of agents. It is at the very least more tolerant to allow agents their experiential knowledge, as Friedman does, even if we insist on representing this experience in terms of algorithmic knowledge. Better still would be to accept the virtue of isomorphism between theory and practice, but to turn rational expectations on its head: to reflect agents' experiential knowledge in a theory that is as much experiential as algorithmic. Keynes, Schumpeter, and Marx remain worth reading today not for their formal models but for their insight and intuition into the workings of capitalism reflected in the theories that precede the models. The losses inherent in translating experiential into algorithmic knowledge are substantial. Rendering the experiential knowledge of coping with uncertainty into an algorithmic calculus of subjective probabilities is like rendering Shakespeare in French or Racine in English.

Worse. The loss is compounded by the distortions that take place under the influence of our unacknowledged ideological preconceptions. In this respect, the fate of "satisficing" provides a cautionary tale. Nobel Laureate Herbert Simon's response (1955, 1956) to the limitations of maximization in real-world settings was to argue that people concentrate on finding satisfactory rather than optimal solutions. But translated from the experiential to the algorithmic, satisficing becomes just another form of maximization, an extended maximization that takes account of the costs of processing information, of calculating the benefits and costs of alternative courses of action. One is reminded of the fate of rebellion against the caste system in India. Rebels are assimilated as a new caste—the caste opposed to the caste system.

Recognizing the importance of uncertainty and the consequent role of satisficing will make some of our most cherished problems quietly disappear. Do businessmen maximize profits? Do households take account of future tax liabilities implicit in deficit spending? These questions, sensible as they are within an algorithmic economics, will likely be regarded by future historians as the economist's equivalent of the scholastic concern with how many angels can stand on the head of a pin. Once the preponderance of uncertainty in any intertemporal context and the corresponding vagueness of returns and costs or future tax liabilities is acknowledged, it is hard to see the assumptions of profit maximization and so-called Ricardian equivalence as other than indicators of the limits of algorithmic knowledge.

I reiterate that my objections would not matter very much if economists were primarily concerned with a consumer's basket of peaches and pears or a farmer's mix between wheat and rye. The algorithmic model of maximizing behavior probably does little harm and may provide some understanding about the outcomes of the choice process even if it is of limited use in understanding the process itself.

But economics is much more than peaches and pears, wheat and rye. Even in a focus so narrow and short-term as that of conventional macroeconomics, saving and investment are central elements of everyone's story, and consequently uncertainty must play a leading role. And coping with uncertainty is—I insist—predominantly a matter of experiential knowledge, and will remain so no matter how adept at climbing decision trees or manipulating subjective probabilities we might become. The difference between saving decisions and allocating the consumer's budget between peaches and pears or between investment decisions and allocating farmland between wheat and rye may be one of degree, but the degree is so great that quantity becomes quality; the uncertainties are so overwhelming that a purely algorithmic model breaks down completely. In such contexts, the role of calculation may, as Keynes (1937) suggested in the *Quarterly Journal of Economics* piece cited at the beginning of the last chapter, be limited to justifying what agents are inclined to do on the basis of authority, habit, convention, or intuition.

The takeaway is that the practice of economics itself provides a useful lesson about the limits of algorithmic explanation, as well as the distortions introduced by minimizing the role of experience. Economists in effect confront the task of explaining economic phenomena with one hand tied behind our collective back.

Community and Knowledge

The denial of experiential knowledge is closely tied to the denial of community. For some elements of experiential knowledge, the identification with community is almost definitional: transmission of experiential knowledge typically takes place, I have suggested, within a network of personal relationships—for example, parent–child, teacher–student, master–apprentice. The authority of parents is rooted in the small community of the family, and the authority of teachers and masters in the community of school, workshop, craft, and profession. The chemist and philosopher Michael Polanyi puts the importance of community in perspective:

> The . . . transmission of [the] immense aggregate intellectual artifacts from one generation to another takes place by a process of communication which flows from adults to young people. This kind of communication can be received only when one person places an exceptional degree of confidence in another, the apprentice in the master, the student in the teacher. . . . This assimilation of great systems of articulate lore by novices of various grades is made possible only by a *previous act of affiliation,* by which the novice accepts apprenticeship to a community which cultivates this lore, appreciates

its values and strives to act by its standards. This affiliation begins with the fact that a child submits to education within a community, and it is confirmed throughout life to the extent to which the adult continues to place exceptional confidence in the intellectual leaders of the same community. . . .

The learner, like the discoverer, must believe before he can know. But while the problem-solvers' foreknowledge expresses confidence in himself, the intimations followed by the learner are based predominantly on his confidence in others; and this is an acceptance of authority. (Polanyi 1962 [1958], 207–208)

It is not only personal authority that is rooted in community, but convention as well. Convention, for Keynes an important basis of knowledge in a world of uncertainty, carries weight because of the ties that bind us to one another.

Convention has come in for hard knocks from those who subscribe to the modern ideology of knowledge. In one section of *Identity and Violence*, headed "The Priority of Reason," Amartya Sen extols Akbar, the sixteenth-century Mughal ruler of a large part of India, not only for his religious tolerance, for which he is deservedly famous, but for his commitment to reason over convention. According to Sen, "Akbar . . . claimed that his own Islamic religious beliefs came from reasoning and choice, not from 'blind faith,' nor from what he called 'the marshy land of tradition'" (2005, 162).

I wonder what Akbar would have made of his contemporary, Michel de Montaigne. It is clear what Montaigne would have made of Akbar: for Montaigne, one of the great revelations of increasing contact between Europe and the rest of the world was the relativity of religious belief. Montaigne, as we saw in Chapter 5, viewed reason as playing a modest role in religious convictions. In his essay "Apology for Raymond Sebond" he is even more explicit: "We receive our religion . . . not otherwise than other religions are received. We happen to have been born in a country where it was in practice. . . . We are Christians by the same title that we are Perigordians or Germans" (Montaigne 1965, 324–325).

There is a middle ground between the skepticism of Montaigne and the rationalism of Akbar. The founder of Hasidic Judaism, Israel ben Eliezer, better known as the Baal Shem Tov, was distinguished by his embrace of feeling and emotion, in contrast with the ascetic rationalism of Talmudic

Judaism. But he found a place both for rationality and for the conventions of the Jewish community:

> Why do we say "Our God and God of our fathers?"
>
> There are two kinds of people who believe in God. The one believes because it is handed down to him by his fathers; and his belief is strong. The other has come to his belief through searching. And this is the difference between them: the superiority of the first is that his faith cannot be shattered no matter how many arguments one may bring against it, for his faith is firm because he has taken it over from his fathers; but it has a defect: that his faith is only a human command, learned without meaning and understanding. The superiority of the second lies in the fact that because he has found God through searching, he has arrived at his own faith; but for him too there remains a defect: that it is easy to shake his faith through proof to the contrary. To him who unites both, however, none is superior. Therefore we say: "Our God," because of our searching, and "God of our fathers," for the sake of our tradition. (Buber 1958, 183–184)

The sticking point in relating experience to community is intuition, which might appear to be quintessentially individualistic. Intuition, no doubt, has an individualistic component, but this should not make us lose sight of its social dimension. Alexander Luria, the eminent Soviet psychologist, did considerable fieldwork on the psychology of knowledge in the 1930s in the central Asian provinces that the Soviet regime had inherited from the czars. He chose central Asia for these investigations, Luria tells us in his autobiographical memoir, because, in the wake of "rapid change [brought about by] the advent of collectivization and mechanization of agriculture, . . . great discrepancies between cultural forms promised to maximize the possibility of detecting shifts in the basic forms, as well as the content of people's thinking" (Luria 1979, 60).[6] Age-old villages existed side by side with new collective farms; Luria's question was how these changes affected the way people think.

Luria's foray into cultural anthropology has had a curious history—on second thought, maybe not so curious in the Soviet Union of Stalin and his successors. Fieldwork conducted in the 1930s was published only in the 1970s, when a more open political climate made it possible to disseminate results that did not accord with the latest twist in the party line. Luria's American editor provides a biographical sketch in which he attributes Luria's difficulties to his attachment to a German Romantic view of culture as "the progressive accumulation of the best characteristics of mankind in science, art, and technology, . . . [which] orders human societies on an evolutionary scale" (Luria 1979, 214).

It seems to me that this evolutionary view is instead part of a common Eurocentric ideology that unites Whigs, Marxists, and German Romantics: history as the ascent along an inclined plane (to use a favorite phrase of Ashis Nandy) leading all cultures to the mountaintop of the modern West, with non-European peoples spread out along the slopes behind. But no matter: wherever Luria was coming from intellectually, the core beliefs he expressed in a preface written for the English translation when his work was at last published, shortly before his death, would not jar the sensibilities of most Western readers—not in the 1930s, the 1970s, or the first decade of the twenty-first century:

> Despite the high levels of creativity in science, art, and architecture attained in the ancient culture of Uzbekistan, the masses had lived for centuries in economic stagnation and illiteracy, their development hindered among other things by the religion of Islam. Only the radical restructuring of the economy, the rapid elimination of illiteracy, and the removal of the Moslem influence could achieve, over and above an expansion in world view, a genuine revolution in cognitive activity. (Luria 1976, v–vi)

My concern is not with evolution but with difference. And this difference is clear whether or not, like Luria, one finds central Asian intuition primitive; whether or not, like Luria's editor, one finds it "unusual, not to say bizarre" (Luria 1979, 194). Two examples will suffice. Luria invites his Uzbek subjects to examine patterns like those that two generations of American preschoolers have encountered on *Sesame Street:* which of these things is not like the other? Rakmat, an illiterate middle-aged man from an outlying district who rarely has been to the city, is shown drawings of a hammer, a saw, a log, and a hatchet. Rakmat refuses the *Sesame Street* game, insisting that all four belong together: "They're all alike. I think all of them have to be here. See, if you're going to saw, you need a saw, and if you have to split something, you need a hatchet. So they're *all* needed here" (Luria 1976, 55). Rakmat rejects all prompts and clues that the unifying principle is "tool": "One fellow," Luria offers, "picked three things—the hammer, saw, and hatchet—and said they were alike." Rakmat attempts a compromise: "A saw, a hammer, and a hatchet all have to work together. But the log has to be there too." Luria persists: "Why do you think he picked these three things and not the log?" Rakmat relies on his intuition: "Probably he's got a lot of firewood, but if we'll be left without firewood, we won't be able to do anything." Luria tries one final time. "True, but a hammer, a saw, and a hatchet are all tools." "Yes," counters Rakmat, "but even if we have tools, we still need wood—otherwise we can't build anything" (Luria 1976, 56).

To drive his evolutionary point home, Luria presents several cases in which his subjects refuse the most elementary tool of algorithmic knowledge, the abstract syllogism. Here's one, an interview with a man named Abdurakhm, another illiterate from a remote village (Luria 1976, 108; Luria's running commentary on the answers is omitted; his questions of Abdurakhm are given in italics):

Cotton can grow only where it is hot and dry. In England it is cold and damp. Can cotton grow there?

I don't know.

Think about it.

I've only been in the Kashgar country; I don't know beyond that. . . .

But on the basis of what I said to you, can cotton grow there?

If the land is good, cotton will grow there, but if it is damp and poor, it won't grow. If it's like the Kashgar country, it will grow there too. If the soil is loose, it can grow there too, of course.

[*Luria repeats the syllogism.*] *What can you conclude from my words?*

If it's cold there, it won't grow; if the soil is loose and good, it will.

But what do my words suggest?

Well, we Moslems, we Kashgars, we're ignorant people; we've never been anywhere, so we don't know if it's hot or cold there.

Rakmat and Abdurakhm are not alone. According to Luria, whose interviews with other Uzbeks from traditional villages are of a piece with Rakmat's and Abdurakhm's, it is only when a subject has been exposed to the modern ways of life of the collective farm that he or she accepts the primacy of the categories Luria has brought with him from Moscow.

As I have said, when it comes to interpretation, I part company with Luria. I see difference where he sees evolution. The Uzbek's intuition is rooted in his community, but no more than Luria's is rooted in his. These Uzbeks regard Luria's categorization principles as every bit as odd as Luria (and his American editor) regard the Uzbeks'. In another point in the interview, Rakmat is told, once again, that "another fellow" had a different view of grouping objects (in this case, a glass, saucepan, pair of spectacles, and a bottle). Rakmat doesn't seem to be phased by this news: "Probably that kind of thinking runs in his blood. But I say they all belong here" (Luria 1976, 57).[7]

However much we may disagree on evolution versus difference, Luria and I agree on a more fundamental point: experiential knowledge is rooted in community. The critical point is that the effacing of community has contributed to the ideological subordination of experiential knowledge. Most moderns, just like Abdurakhm, have no experience of whether cotton grows in England, but we are willing to bracket that gap in our knowledge and apply a syllogism to answer the question. It runs in our blood. In the limit, a secular fanatic (Nazis come to mind) or a religious fanatic (many sorts come to mind, from all the world's great religions) may even suspend all his human experience to follow a logic of extermination based on deduction from first principles as real to him as the nonmeeting of parallel lines was to Euclid.

Experiential knowledge, like community, survives in the interstices of modern society, more or less underground, despite the ritual affirmation of community by politicians of every stripe during election season. Both experiential knowledge and community survive because we can't do without them, but neither receives the nurturing and attention it requires and merits.

CHAPTER 9

Taking Experience Seriously

How would economics change if one were to take the previous two chapters seriously? This chapter answers this question in two ways. First, we examine some examples of how economics has been distorted by an uncritical acceptance of the dominant ideology of knowledge. Second, we look at an important example of the politics of knowledge, the attempt to insulate monetary policy from the normal political process.

None of this proves that a different kind of economics would be more friendly to community. But an economics that takes experience seriously would necessarily be an economics open to human relationships, and human relationships are the keystone of community. Community would no longer be invisible to the economist. In any case, whatever the effect of taking experience seriously on how economics understands community, I have no doubt that taking experience seriously would improve the ability of economists to make sense of the world. Let me begin with a critical perspective on some work of my own.

How Do Bosses Know?

In "What Do Bosses Do?" and its progeny (Marglin 1974, 1979, 1984b, 1990, 1991), I argued that the most important innovation of the Industrial Revolution was not technological, but organizational: the linear hierarchy (master–journeyman–apprentice) typical of crafts in the premodern era was replaced by the pyramidal hierarchy (boss–foreman–worker) of the modern, capitalist enterprise. How did this happen? What hold did the capitalist have on the worker that permitted this new form of organization to thrive and eventually to dominate?

The conventional answer is superior efficiency, a better mousetrap. If the capitalist enterprise comes into existence because of its superior efficiency, then the boss can entice the worker by offering him more money than the worker could earn on his own. The greater efficiency of the capitalist enterprise (more efficient than the guild, more efficient than a sole proprietorship or any other form of worker-owned enterprise) would provide both more pay for the worker and a profit for the capitalist.

By contrast, the answer in "Bosses" is that the capitalist organization of work came into existence not because of superior efficiency but in consequence of the rent-seeking activities of the capitalist. As in the case of the enclosure movement (see Chapter 5), distribution, not efficiency, drove this momentous institutional change. But if the capitalist enterprise was not more efficient, how was the capitalist able to survive a Darwinian struggle of alternative forms of enterprise? If the capitalist firm is less efficient than, or only as efficient as, worker-owned alternatives, then by assumption there is no surplus (relative to worker-owned alternatives) with which to entice the worker and reward the capitalist. If the capitalist is to turn a profit, workers must accept a lower wage. But why should they? Why don't workers produce on their own, in worker-owned enterprises that do away with the capitalist rent seekers?

One reason is that capitalists not only organized work, they provided *capital*—the buildings and equipment that enhanced the productivity of workers manyfold during the course of the Industrial Revolution. There is obvious merit in this argument—the boss did not get the name of capitalist for nothing. And it is clear that workers had limited access to capital markets. So the greater productivity of the capitalist's machinery might make a space for the capitalist and his profit: if the choice is between handwork in an underequipped worker-owned enterprise and machine work in a capitalist enterprise, then the higher productivity of capital might allow the worker a higher wage and the capitalist a profit.

But in many of the leading industries of the Industrial Revolution, the equipment remained rudimentary for a long time. Woolens are a case in point: capitalist manufacturers and putters-out ran their businesses with the same equipment as the independent weaver used in his cottage. And since the capitalist organization came to dominate here as well, barriers to entry posed by capital goods cannot be a general explanation of the dominance of the capitalist enterprise. In this case, absent superior organizational efficiency, the capitalist enterprise has no obvious competitive advantage.

The argument in "Bosses" is that the capitalist organization of work, based on a highly refined specialization of labor, was designed to make the capitalist indispensable. In this view, the division of labor was pursued by capitalists not as a means of increasing efficiency, but as a means of enhancing the control of the boss over the workers—indeed, as a means of ensuring a place for the boss in the enterprise. By specializing particular individuals to particular tasks and reserving to himself an essential task that integrated the parts into a whole, the boss prevented these workers from acquiring the knowledge of the whole—and thus ensured his own indispensability. "Divide and conquer" may have been invented by the Romans,[1] but it served these capitalists equally well. As one early-nineteenth-century manufacturer said in his testimony before a parliamentary committee investigating woolen manufacturing: "Suppose a man goes into a room and is confined in a room where there are twelve, thirteen, or fourteen looms, how is that man to be proficient in any part of the business [other] than that?" (*Report from the Select Committee to Consider the State of Woollen Manufacture in England*, British Parliamentary Papers [1805], vol. 1, p. 74; quoted in Morris 1972). In short, division of labor at the subproduct level was the result of rent seeking rather than the quest for efficiency.

Imagine a capitalist of Adam Smith's time who introduces a new product or process. Imagine, to fix ideas, that an entrepreneur decides to manufacture pins in an area in which pins have never before been produced. Imagine further a pool of readily available workers. Suppose that the technology of pin making is neutral with respect to organization, that is, that pins can be manufactured equally efficiently by a single workman moving from one task to another (presumably with sufficient continuity in each task that setup costs are amortized over a large production run) as by twenty workmen specialized to individual tasks. Suppose further that the input of capital goods to the production process is minimal, and that training costs are also minimal.[2] How does the capitalist organize production in order to achieve and maintain a high rate of profit?

The first part, achieving a high rate of profit, is the easier part. The existence of unemployment, let us assume, keeps wages down, and for a while retaining workers would not be a major concern, given the assumption that training costs are minimal. So the capitalist need not be overly concerned with structuring the enterprise of pin making in a way that makes it difficult for workers to leave.

But what happens once the industry expands to the point that the labor surplus no longer exists? How does the capitalist maintain profits in a tight labor market if workers exit to set up their own shops? Answer: he can't. So, if he is prudent, he takes steps early on to ensure that his workers don't have sufficient knowledge to set up on their own. He specializes some workers to making pinheads, some to making pin bodies, some to the task of attaching the heads to the bodies, some to the whitening process, and some to putting the finished pins on cards. Nobody, except for him, knows all the processes. Nobody but him is in a position to set up for himself.

The claim of "Bosses" is that the failure of any rival to the capitalist enterprise to emerge is consistent with both competition and free entry and yet represents an inefficient allocation of resources. The capitalist's profit is a rent, a return to his ability to organize work in a way in which he has a crucial role in integrating the separate processes of production into a marketable whole, but which contributes nothing to overall product.

This brings us to the key question: how does the capitalist's organizational rent survive in conditions of free entry? If training costs are minimal, why don't schools or individual "trainers" emerge that, for a fee, impart to workers the knowledge of the whole, the knowledge deliberately withheld by capitalists that would permit the workers to get along without bosses?

In one of the papers spawned by "Bosses" (Marglin 1984b), I attempted to answer this question by arguing that particular qualities, both intellectual and psychological, are required either to figure out for oneself how to put together all the things necessary for a successful business operation or to be able to train others to do so. Without taking a position on the extent to which these traits are the result of nature or of nurture, on whether these traits are acquired or innate, we may suppose a bell-shaped distribution of the population similar to the distribution of other physical, mental, and psychological traits, from height to mathematical ability to acquisitiveness. Given the limited supply, those who possess the necessary capabilities and the motivation to act on these capabilities find it more rewarding to become capitalists themselves than to set up as sole proprietors or train others to do so. There are no incentives to upset the capitalist applecart.

This way out may appear to be giving up the game. If the necessary knowledge is scarce because certain traits are in limited supply, then isn't the competitively determined reward to this knowledge—the capitalist's profit—simply the measure of the social value of the underlying traits?

My answer hinged on the economist's distinction between public goods and private goods: yes, business knowledge is scarce because of the limited supply of certain underlying personality traits, but this knowledge is a *public good,* a good characterized by the peculiar condition that making a unit available for one person does not diminish its availability to anyone else. The canonical example of a public good, Adam Smith's own example, is a lighthouse, which can provide warning to one ship in a channel without diminishing the warning to others. To be sure, the availability of light will affect the value to those who possess it. If only one ship avoids the shoals and is able to deliver its cargo of pepper and spice from the Indies, these commodities will command a higher price in the market, and accordingly, the "derived demand" of a single vessel for the light will be the greater, the fewer ships have access.

Similarly with knowledge. The rent a capitalist can command for his knowledge of integrating the production process into a marketable commodity will depend on how generally available the knowledge is.

There was a spirited debate in the years following Paul Samuelson's formalization of the attributes of public goods (Samuelson 1954, 1955). For some, the absence of a mechanism for excluding agents from consuming a good was as important a condition as the nonrivalrous nature of consumption. Public goods were those that were both nonrivalrous and nonexcludable. For others the issue was solely one of nonrivalry.

I have no reason or desire to rekindle that debate here. But the issue of excludability is at most a secondary one for our purposes. Whether or not agents can be excluded from consuming a public good, it is inefficient to do so. If utilization of the lighthouse's services by Noah's ark does not diminish the light available to other ships, then even if exclusion is costless, it reduces the total economic pie to exclude the ark as long as Noah derives even a penny of benefit from the light. (See Appendix A for further discussion of the issues of excludability and rivalry.)

Thus it is that a capitalist regime can constitute a competitive equilibrium yet be inefficient. Neither existing producers nor potential entrants have any incentive to introduce a noncapitalist form of enterprise that will simply eliminate the rent that accrues to the entrepreneur. But as long as the knowledge can be made available to others without diminishing its availability to existing entrepreneurs, it is inefficient for some to hoard their knowledge.

Capitalism is not the only economic system in which the transmission of knowledge is constrained by the incentives to agents to restrict or facilitate knowledge flows. Medieval guilds placed severe constraints, both positive and negative, on the sharing of knowledge. Guild masters, for example, were enjoined from sharing knowledge with outsiders but enjoined to share the same knowledge with apprentices. Indeed, every community, at the peril of the destruction of its cohesion, must have rules and customs for the transmission of knowledge of production. In hunting and gathering societies, in peasant societies, this transmission takes place mostly within the household, which is a unit both for production and consumption. As social organization becomes more complex, so does the transmission mechanism.

What distinguishes the capitalist era is that, as guild regulations fell into desuetude, the incentives to restrict knowledge became dominant—with no community to oblige sharing of knowledge, the individual became free to follow his self-interest to keep knowledge to himself. While knowledge is nominally free, in the sense that there are no legal restrictions on its dissemination, the capitalist has every reason to maintain a monopoly of crucial knowledge and no reason to share this knowledge with potential rivals.[3]

There is no necessary inconsistency between the assumption that, left to their own devices, most workers could not get it together to manufacture pins independently and the assumption that it is costless to share the necessary knowledge among these same workers. Consider your likely fate if you are one day set down in the middle of nowhere to grow your own food, albeit with all the requisite tools—seeds, fertilizers, plow, harrow, and so forth. If you have had some experience on the land, you would probably do just fine. But if you are not a farmer, or at least a gardener, I dare say you could not get your act together in time to avoid starvation even if you had a generous supply of edibles to tide you over for one or two growing seasons. Unlike Daniel Defoe's Robinson Crusoe, most would be hard-pressed to figure out how to plant, when to plant, and how deep to plant—issues that are difficult to resolve only if you don't know how. But our inability to figure out the process on our own is perfectly consistent with it being costless for the few farmers and gardeners among us to share their knowledge with the rest of us. They might be reluctant to do so, in order to protect the power, status, or prestige that the scarcity of knowledge bestows on them, but that is an altogether different matter.

Until I began thinking about knowledge from the viewpoint of this book, I did not realize that characterizing knowledge as a public good relied on a very particular conception of knowledge. For knowledge to be a public good, it must take the form of algorithmic knowledge, for it is only algorithmic knowledge that is freely available to anybody who can read the book. One more copy of any book is virtually costless, no more than the cost of the paper, ink, and the time of the pressman—or in the present age, no more than the cost of a diskette (or CD-ROM or flash drive—how quickly technology changes) and the time to copy the data.

But to the extent that production is based on experiential knowledge, it ceases to be a public good. If the transmission of knowledge requires a personal network, for example, of parent and child, master and apprentice, or teacher and student—that is, a community—then it can never be costless to share knowledge. So a major premise of my argument is called into question by the recognition that business knowledge is in large part experiential knowledge, necessarily embedded in community. If I were writing "Bosses" now, I would still be guided by the preanalytic vision (to use Schumpeter's term—see the previous chapter) that relations between various people involved in production are not determined by efficiency, much less by technology; that how we relate to each other in the production process is the result of struggles over distribution. But I would also be sensitive to the interplay of systems of knowledge in the production process. I would certainly not simply assume that the relevant knowledge was algorithmic in nature.[4]

There is a related issue that "Bosses" does not address. If the knowledge of production was within workers' collective grasp, even if not available to most of them individually, why did workers acquiesce to a series of steps aimed at organizing work to facilitate capitalist control? Why did workers' collective resistance—determined, even heroic, in the fight for higher pay, shorter hours, greater security—generally stop short of challenging control over the production process?

In part, the answer lies in the weakness of collective organization and a failure of community. But only in part. Even where workers were well organized, the record shows little systematic resistance to the successive steps capitalists took in order to control the production process.

The capitalists' project was taken to an extreme in Frederick Winslow Taylor's dream of a "scientific management" that would transform the experiential knowledge of workers into an algorithmic knowledge that would serve as the basis for managerial control. In Taylor's words (1967 [1911], 36–38),

> Under scientific management, the managers assume . . . the burden of gathering together all of the traditional knowledge which in the past has been possessed by the workmen and then of classifying, tabulating, and reducing this knowledge to rules, laws, and formulae. . . . These replace the judgment of the individual workman. . . . Thus all of the planning which under

the old system was done by the workman, as a result of his personal experience, must of necessity under the new system be done by management in accordance with the laws of the science.

Taylor, to be sure, never achieved his dream. Running a factory on algorithmic knowledge was a fantasy, but the project that gave legitimacy to this fantasy was very real indeed, and the dominant ideology of knowledge was crucial to its ultimate success in deterring workers from challenging capitalist control of the production process. In short, the belief that capitalist control is based on a superior form of knowledge has been critical in disarming resistance (S. Marglin 1990). Even where workers have understood the ideological underpinnings of this belief, it has empowered successive generations of capitalists. Capitalists, like most of us, find it easier to act when God as well as self-interest is on their side. And public opinion, the day-to-day expression of cultural norms, however sympathetic to the fight for a living wage or a reasonable working day, has offered little support for what has been perceived as backward and retrograde opposition to progress.

The general lesson is that the cultural dimensions of knowledge ought to be given a more central role in our understanding of class and class struggle. Classes do not act in history until they are armed by culture, and culture sets the terms of class conflict. Culture determines what is on the agenda of conflict and what is not. Class interest is nothing without a cultural justification. For all these reasons, both the power of the capitalists to take and maintain control of the production process and the limits of resistance to this project cannot be understood without reference to the modern ideology of knowledge. The notion that real knowledge, truth, resides in algorithmic knowledge, that the knowledge of experience is trustworthy only insofar as it is validated by algorithm, has undermined the knowledge of experience to the point that it has lost value in the eyes of the workman as well as the boss. The capitalist has held the high ground culturally as well as economically and politically.

Efficient Socialism?

Let me turn now to another area of economics in which the nature of knowledge is critical. Once upon a time economists and others were vitally interested in the "feasibility of socialism." The question they had in mind was not really feasibility, but efficiency: economists hotly debated how a system in which the market was not the principal means for allocating resources could function without inordinate waste. Ludwig von Mises is generally credited with the opening salvo in this debate (von Mises 1935 [1920]). Von Mises argued that without prices, there was no meaningful basis on which to allocate resources among competing ends, and that without markets there could be no meaningful prices.

Fred M. Taylor's[5] presidential address to the American Economics Association presented an answer to von Mises's challenge, namely, that apart from the determination of incomes, the socialist economy could and should imitate the workings of a regime of competitive markets (Taylor 1929), with consumers ultimately calling the tune through dollar (or ruble) voting. I don't know that von Mises ever responded to Taylor, but I could imagine him saying that with friends like Taylor, socialists didn't need enemies: Taylor effectively throws in the towel by accepting the market and market prices as the means for determining the allocation of resources.

A few years later, H. D. Dickinson suggested a two-part procedure for determining prices. In the first stage, prices of consumer goods would indeed be established in the market place: sellers of consumer goods would choose prices that just equated demands and supplies. But the second stage would substitute centralized calculation for the play of market forces. On the basis of the prices of consumer goods, producers could draw up demand schedules for factors and supply schedules of products, and the entire system of equations would be solved for the equilibrium quantities (Dickinson 1933).

Oskar Lange took the argument a step further by suggesting that the daunting task of solving Dickinson's equations could be accomplished à la Léon Walras, the pioneering nineteenth-century theorist of market equilibrium, by an iterative procedure: a central planning board (CPB) would announce trial prices, and firms would calculate the profit-maximizing levels of outputs and inputs on the basis of these prices; firms would communicate these trial quantities to the CPB, which would then revise prices according to the trial balance of demands and supplies—prices would be increased where demands exceeded supplies and reduced where supplies exceeded demands.[6] When demand and supply balanced out all around, the trial quantities would become the actual production levels. But the trial prices, having served their purpose of guiding the CPB to the optimal allocation, need never take effect as actual market prices. Lange had in effect discovered the shadow prices that a decade later would emerge from the new technique of linear programming as the "dual" to the allocation problem

(Lange 1936). Lange's virtual market achieves the informational economy of real markets—firms need not send explicit information about production functions to the CPB, limiting their communication to quantity signals that respond to price signals sent out by the CPB.

Lange's demonstration of the theoretical possibility of an efficient, "as if" market socialism challenged received ideas about planning: was the iterative algorithm he proposed centralized or decentralized? The answer is both. Relative to Dickinson's procedure, Lange's "trial and error" (his phrase) process is highly decentralized since it involves the firms in an iterative exchange of information with the CPB. But relative to a real market process, it is highly centralized since the firms are in effect solving the CPB's supply–demand equations one step at a time.

Like many debates in economics, this one was never settled. Friedrich Hayek, von Mises's student, brought up many telling points against Lange (some of which had earlier been raised by von Mises), including the problems of incentives, innovation, and the allocation of investment (Hayek 1940, 1945). But on the whole I think it is fair to say that Lange's position came to be the conventional wisdom, gaining support, ironically, from the increasingly central role of the Arrow–Debreu model of the competitive economy (Arrow and Debreu 1954; see also Arrow 1963–1964 and Debreu 1959).

My own take on this debate has changed drastically over the years. Early on I came to the view that the most glaring omission in Lange's approach was the problem of incentives, but my understanding of the incentive problem has changed in a very important way. I first came to focus on incentives almost circuitously, as a corollary of concluding that the informational claims on Lange's behalf were overblown. Lange's algorithm shares with Walrasian iterative search *(tâtonnement)* the property that prices are the only signal that firms require from above (above being the CPB in the one case and the market in the other) and that quantities of outputs and inputs are the only information that firms send back. But this does not add up to significant economizing on information flows. A firm willy-nilly transmits information about the shape of its production functions—the information the CPB would need to formulate an economy-wide plan—whenever it transmits information about factor demands and product outputs: when trial quantities change in response to changes in trial prices, the firm is implicitly transmitting information about the shape of its production function, just as surely as if it were responding to a direct request from the CPB for information about marginal productivities (S. Marglin 1969).

So if Lange's so-called decentralized system had little to recommend it on informational grounds, what might recommend it over alternatives in which firms communicate directly about production conditions and the CPB assigns production quotas based on the information it has gathered? Evidently if firms reaped the profits associated with the plans that result from tâtonnement guided by profit maximization, then—provided there are enough firms—each firm has an appropriate incentive both to find the optimum and to implement the optimal plan (S. Marglin 1969). In this perspective, the shadow element in Lange's prices becomes problematic: either prices are real—they become actualized in terms of the rewards the firms reap—or prices will not be effective in planning or implementation. Just like in capitalist markets.

Observe that the need for incentives is not limited to Lange's algorithm. Any algorithm for eliciting information from enterprises to a CPB necessitates appropriate incentives for the firms to acquire and accurately transmit this information—not to mention incentives for implementing the production plan that the CPB ultimately determines.

I now believe that the problem of incentives is the tip of an iceberg; the deeper problem is the nature of economic knowledge. Hayek put his finger on this problem in 1945. His central point in "The Use of Knowledge in Society" is that the market economizes on knowledge—each agent need know only his own local conditions to respond to market prices. At first sight, this might seem a willful misreading of Lange, or at least a failure on Hayek's part to appreciate Lange's argument. The point of "as if" market socialism was that imitating the market allowed planners to take advantage of the compartmentalization of knowledge. As long as knowledge is all of a piece, there would seem to be nothing the market can do that cannot be done as well by a CPB.

But this response misunderstands Hayek, whose central point is precisely that knowledge is not of one piece. Hayek begins by posing the question of the relative efficiency of central planning, defined as "direction of the whole economic system according to one unified plan," and of competition, defined as "decentralized planning by many separate persons." He begins his answer with the statement that it "depends mainly on the question under which of them we can expect that fuller use will be made of the existing knowledge" (Hayek 1945, 521). He then explains why he thinks competition is superior:

> It will at once be evident that on this point the position will be different with respect to different kinds of knowledge; and the answer to our question will

therefore largely turn on the relative importance of the different kinds of knowledge; those more likely to be at the disposal of particular individuals and those which we should with greater confidence expect to find in the possession of an authority made up of suitably chosen experts. If it is today so widely assumed that the latter will be in a better position, this is because one kind of knowledge, namely, scientific knowledge, occupies now so prominent a place in public imagination that we tend to forget that it is not the only kind that is relevant. It may be admitted that, so far as scientific knowledge is concerned, a body of suitably chosen experts may be in the best position to command all the best knowledge available—though this is of course merely shifting the difficulty to the problem of selecting the experts. What I wish to point out is that, even assuming that this problem can be readily solved, it is only a small part of the wider problem.

Today it is almost heresy to suggest that scientific knowledge is not the sum of all knowledge. But a little reflection will show that there is beyond question a body of very important but unorganized knowledge which cannot possibly be called scientific in the sense of knowledge of general rules: the knowledge of the particular circumstances of time and place. *It is with respect to this that practically every individual has some advantage over all others in that he possesses unique information of which beneficial use might be made, but of which use can be made only if the decisions depending on it are left to him or are made with his active cooperation* [emphasis added]. We need to remember only how much we have to learn in any occupation after we have completed our theoretical training, how big a part of our working life we spend learning particular jobs, and how valuable an asset in all walks of life is knowledge of people, of local conditions, and special circumstances. To know of and put to use a machine not fully employed, or somebody's skill which could be better utilized, or to be aware of a surplus stock which can be drawn upon during an interruption of supplies, is socially quite as useful as the knowledge of better alternative techniques. And the shipper who earns his living from using otherwise empty or half-filled journeys of tramp-steamers, or the estate agent whose whole knowledge is almost exclusively one of temporary opportunities, or the *arbitrageur* who gains from local differences of commodity prices, are all performing eminently useful functions based on special knowledge of circumstances of the fleeting moment not known to others.

It is a curious fact that this sort of knowledge should today be generally regarded with a kind of contempt, and that anyone who by such knowledge gains an advantage over somebody better equipped with theoretical or technical knowledge is thought to have acted almost disreputably. To gain an advantage from better knowledge of facilities of communication or transport is sometimes regarded as almost dishonest, although it is quite as important that society make use of the best opportunities in this respect as in using the latest scientific discoveries. This prejudice has in a considerable measure affected the attitude toward commerce in general compared with that toward production. Even economists who regard themselves as definitely above the crude materialist fallacies of the past constantly commit the same mistake where activities directed toward the acquisition of such practical knowledge are concerned—apparently because in their scheme of things all such knowledge is supposed to be "given." The common idea now seems to be that all such knowledge should as a matter of course be readily at the command of everybody, and the reproach of irrationality leveled against the existing economic order is frequently based on the fact that it is not so available. This view disregards the fact that the method by which such knowledge can be made as widely available as possible is precisely the problem to which we have to find an answer. . . .

This is, perhaps, also the point where I should briefly mention the fact that the sort of knowledge with which I have been concerned is knowledge of the kind which by its nature cannot enter into statistics and therefore cannot be conveyed to any central authority in statistical form. The statistics which such a central authority would have to use would have to be arrived at precisely by abstracting from minor differences between the things, by lumping together, as resources of one kind, items which differ as regards location, quality, and other particulars, in a way which may be very significant for the specific decision. It follows from this that central planning based on statistical information by its nature cannot take direct account of these circumstances of time and place, and that the central planner will have to find some way or other in which the decisions depending on them can be left to the "man on the spot." (Hayek 1945, 521–522, 524)

Translated into my terminology, Hayek is arguing that experience is an irreducible part of economic knowledge, a part that is impossible to articulate and communicate in the formal procedures of a Lange-type mechanism. The knowledge at issue may not even be available to the agent as more than a hunch, a feeling, an intuition. The point is that it is only in an actual market, with its rewards and punishments, that the knowledge can be actualized—not as a hypothetical response to a hypothetical set of conditions, but as a real-life commitment of the agent. An analogy may help: like many people with a penchant for the kitchen, from time to time I am asked for a recipe for some dish or other. I am always happy to provide a list of ingredients, but I can never give the proportions. For I myself do not know the proportions until I am in the kitchen actually preparing supper, and then only after I have mixed the ingredients together.

The crucial role of experiential knowledge, I believe, is the lesson of the italicized portion of this long extract from Hayek's article. For if knowledge is algorithmic in character, there is no reason for knowledge to become available only if the agent is an active participant in implementing his (or her) knowledge. It is when the knowledge in question has an irreducibly experiential component that *use can be made* [of it] *only if the decisions depending on it are left to him or are made with his active cooperation.* In today's jargon, agents have private information, or, rather, hyperprivate information: the knowledge is so private that the knower herself becomes knowledgeable only when translating the knowledge into action.

If people really could formulate all their knowledge in algorithmic terms and calculate as economic theory assumes, there would be no need for real-life markets. Lange's pretend markets would do just fine. The virtue of the real market is precisely that it calls forth knowledge that people cannot explain, justify, or defend intellectually, knowledge that economic agents themselves may not fully understand. It calls forth this knowledge by the incentives it provides for action and the ruthlessness with which it weeds out error. Ironically, the symbiosis between markets and economic growth depends on a reality of knowledge that is strikingly at odds with the ideology of knowledge as algorithmic.

The Hayekian argument harks back to the justification of markets, prices, and profits that preceded the conception of a system of markets as an analog computer. It is, I believe, a powerful defense of capitalism as an engine of growth and accumulation in the context of a world in which experiential knowledge is critical and radical uncertainty endemic—in marked contrast with the post-Lange, Arrow–Debreu defense that presupposes a static world of algorithmic knowledge and complete probability distributions.

But we should be aware of a crucial hidden assumption in the Hayekian justification—namely, that scarcity is the economic problem, and the solution lies in ever greater production. Whatever the case in the past, the nations of Western Europe, North America, and Japan are long since past the point that their primary need is for more goods and services. Three cheers

for Hayek for his insight into the nature of economic knowledge and its relation to economic action. But no cheers for the conception of modernity
that gives full reign to markets, prices, and profits. Modernity may once
have been part of the solution to scarcity, but it is now part of the problem.

If incentives are the tip of the iceberg of socialist calculation, the debate
about the possibilities of socialist calculation is itself the tip of another iceberg. The Arrow–Debreu framework sharpens our understanding as well as
out wits, but it diverts attention from significant issues. I have already noted
the irony in the role played by the ascendance of the Arrow–Debreu model
of a capitalist economy in the triumph of Lange over von Mises and Hayek,
but—as Nobel Laureate Joseph Stiglitz (1994, 65ff) pointed out in his
reprise of the socialism debate—the problems of Langean socialism and the
problems of Arrow–Debreu as a description of the capitalist economy are
closely intertwined. By collapsing time into a form of product differentia-
tion and assuming that agents have complete knowledge of production and
consumption possibilities, Arrow–Debreu makes it difficult to think about
what happens outside of equilibrium when agents have only partial and incomplete information. The Arrow–Debreu framework sets too easy a task
for economics.

The rational expectations defense of the market goes even further, arguing that in the absence of external institutional constraints, price-taking
agents will move immediately to the competitive equilibrium. The logic is
simple enough: the competitive equilibrium is also a Nash equilibrium,
which is to say that nobody can do better than her "play" in a competitive
equilibrium—given what other agents are doing, this is the best she can do
for herself.

But what happens when consumers know only that the marginal rate of
substitution of peaches for pears exceeds the ratio of the price of pears to
the price of peaches, but not the utility-maximizing allocation of their bud-
gets? What happens when producers know only that the marginal productivity of labor exceeds the wage, but not the precise point at which the two
are equal? Presumably, they adjust in the direction of increasing utility or
profit, but the local nature of knowledge makes it impossible to go to the
utility- or profit-maximizing equilibrium all at once. Agents learn about
their utility or productions functions by and through the adjustment process. A world of experiential knowledge is necessarily a world of leaning by
doing, in which the failure of agents to move at once to the competitive
equilibrium is inherent in the very nature of knowledge. We ought to worry

more about how agents behave, about dynamics outside of equilibrium, and less about the existence of equilibrium. In fact, if we understood these disequilibrium dynamics, we could let equilibrium take care of itself.

Why Are Contracts Incomplete?

Finally, let us look briefly at how a more adequate theory of knowledge might inform another area of economics, namely, contract theory. A central innovation in this field is the idea that contracts are in general incomplete, but there is a surprising variety of explanations for this fundamental incompleteness. Various authors emphasize different reasons, ranging from bounded rationality and the associated inability of the contracting parties to specify all the relevant contingencies, to uncertainty and transaction costs that make it either impossible or suboptimal to write a complete contract.

Oliver Hart has emphasized the distinction between the *observable* and the *verifiable* as the key to incompleteness (Hart 1995; Grossman and Hart 1986; but see Hart 1995, 76 and Hart and Moore 1988, 1125–1126 for an explanation that emphasizes transaction costs rather than verifiability). In this view, some variables are observable to the contracting parties, but not verifiable by third parties. This is important because contract provisions that are not verifiable by third parties (judges and juries) cannot be enforced.

Hart offers two examples:

The quality of [a] book is observable, in the sense that anybody can read it. (Of course, some are in a better position to evaluate it than others.) However, it [would be] difficult . . . to [write] a contract making . . . royalties a function of quality, since if a dispute arose it would be hard . . . to prove that the book did or did not meet some pre-specified standard. . . . In other words quality is not verifiable. A second example is a university tenure decision. In an ideal world, the conditions for being granted tenure would be specified in advance in minute detail (quantity and quality of publications, teaching performance, prominence in the profession, etc.). In practice this is impossible to do, and so the criteria are left fairly vague. At the same time, many aspects of a candidate's performance are observable (certainly the publications record is). The difficulty is to prove that someone's work does or does not meet the appropriate standard to justify tenure, in other words, whether the standard is met is not verifiable. (Hart 1995, 37–38n)

The distinction between observable and verifiable, I believe, requires us to accept the distinction between algorithmic and experiential knowledge. In algorithmic knowledge, what is observable is verifiable, and the distinction between observation and verification breaks down. It is only when experiential knowledge is recognized as a separate system of knowledge that we can make sense of the distinction. Take Hart's examples: the very notion of the quality of a book or the quality of a candidate's dossier makes sense in terms of experiential knowledge but not within algorithmic knowledge.

Central Bank Independence and the Politics of Knowledge

The economic ideology of knowledge legitimizes the view that economics is a neutral science standing above the crude give and take of politics. This has consequences not only for economics as a discipline but for the economy as well. For one thing, it helps to explain the lack of resistance to the project of making central banks—like the Federal Reserve in the United States—independent of political control and accountability, a lack of resistance that would otherwise be a puzzling anomaly, especially in the country that prides itself on being the world's leading democracy.

The independence of the Federal Reserve has a long history, and I do not mean to oversimplify. Writing in the 1950s when the power and prestige of the Fed were at a considerably lower ebb than today, John Kenneth Galbraith suggested that, in the first place, the Fed's independence was exaggerated and, in the second, that such independence as the Fed enjoyed was a reflection of "the belief that monetary policy is the highly professional prerogative of the financial community. As such," Galbraith noted archly, "it must be protected from the crude pressures of democratic government" (Galbraith 1958, 227). I hardly wish to be accused of minimizing or underestimating the power of Wall Street, but I think that there remains more than can be explained simply in terms of the power of the banks and their allies. That the Fed's Board of Governors and, more specifically, the Federal Open Market Committee (FOMC) and its chair are accountable neither to the President of the United States nor to the Congress, not to mention the American people, can in my view only be understood in the context of a society in which the idea of economic *science* is well embedded in the public consciousness.

Economists claim that their discipline is part and parcel of post-Baconian science (see Chapter 7, note 5), which is to say that economics, like physics, is based on the algorithmic deduction of propositions that are in turn subject to rigorous testing in a confrontation with hard empirical data. It doesn't matter for this purpose whether economic agents themselves are calculating and maximizing, but it is of signal importance that these agents are understood in terms of a rigorous, axiomatic system, and therefore that the conclusions of economics are entitled to the deference due science. Just as one would not wish the criteria for the safe capacity of a bridge to be the subject of politics, so with economic questions like inflation and unemployment: economic policymakers need not be—indeed, ought not to be—politically accountable.

The issue of central bank independence is dramatized by recurring proposals for the Fed to follow explicit rules rather than be guided by its own experiential assessment of the economy. Such proposals would give new meaning to the idea of independence: the Fed would in effect be neutered as a player in the economy.[7]

The most well known of these proposals is Milton Friedman's idea that the Fed should maintain a constant growth in the money supply in line with the rate of growth of the real output, which is assumed to be exogenously given. More interesting for our purposes is a proposal by John Taylor (1993, 1998), who has been both a leading academic economist and a prominent practitioner, serving as Undersecretary of the Treasury from 2001 to 2005. According to Taylor, U.S. monetary policy should follow a simple rule: for each 100 basis points that inflation exceeds its target rate, the federal funds rate[8] should increase by 150 basis points; for each percentage point by which output falls short of potential gross domestic product (GDP), the federal funds rate should fall by 50 basis points. (Taylor's 1998 paper suggests that the coefficient on output should be 100 rather than 50.)

Taylor's rule is interesting for two reasons. First, unlike Friedman's, Taylor's recognizes a trade-off between output and inflation. Second, this rule appears to track actual Federal Reserve policy rather well in the era of Alan Greenspan, who was the top dog, indeed the only dog of note, at the Fed from 1987 until 2006. If Taylor's rule captures a trade-off implicitly guiding the FOMC, we are entitled to ask how the parameters are set. Why not be more aggressive against inflation? Why not put more emphasis on shortfalls in GDP? The point of these questions is not that I have a better answer than Greenspan or his successor Ben Bernanke, but that whoever makes these decisions ought to be accountable through the political process.

Some years ago, Mobil Oil (before it merged with Exxon to become Exxon-Mobil) made the case for the independence of the Fed in one of a series of paid political advertisements. The occasion was a legislative proposal (which as far as I know died on the vine) to change the way regional Fed presidents were selected, to which Mobil responded in these terms:

> The nation needs a Fed free of short-term political influence and free also to make the difficult, unpopular long-term decisions that elected officials often find too painful to carry out.
>
> Very simply, the Fed, through its regulation of money supply and interest rates, attempts to create a stable economic environment and thereby minimize uncertainty. As a result, the American people can make fundamental economic decisions that foster the saving and investment which, in turn, increase productivity and ensure higher growth and improved living standards over the long term. . . .
>
> Running the Fed is no easy task. It's a tightrope walk between too much expansion and just enough—with consequences that would make it akin to performing without a net. It is not a job for elected officials. . . .
>
> Giving elected officials additional power over the Fed politicizes the process of setting interest rates and determining the money supply. And make no mistake. These are not arcane functions. . . . They affect every American.
>
> For example, if you're looking to buy a house or sell one, interest rates are often the determining factor in such a decision. Starting a business, or expanding one? You may need to borrow money and, again, you'd be concerned about interest rates. . . . In short, the Fed impacts our lives in very different and very direct ways.
>
> Politicizing it makes absolutely no sense.
>
> The Congress has enough to worry about and should leave well enough alone. (Mobil Corporation 1993)

A powerful argument. Trouble is that the same argument can be made about virtually everything Congress does. Monetary policy, like other kinds of policy, is necessarily political in the sense of being a central function of modern governance, whether it is "politicized" or not. There are winners and losers from any monetary policy, and it remains the art of good policy to balance these gains and losses. One man's politicization is another's democratic politics.

A change of administration or a change in the composition of the Senate or the House may, as the Mobil ad argues, create tremendous uncertainty, but it is usually the Suhartos, the Pinochets, and the Saddam Husseins of this world who have made the argument for the stability and certainty of dictatorship against the instability and uncertainty of democracy. The implications of Mobil's arguments are profoundly antidemocratic, and no sugar-coating of the pill can hide that.

The common thread in these stories is the limits and distortions of a purely algorithmic economics. Knowledge turns out to be key in very different arguments about the functioning of the economic system—from the organization of work to the limits on economic calculation absent markets to why contracts cannot be specified completely. As long as economics holds to the view that the knowledge of the people it studies is essentially algorithmic, it cannot give satisfactory answers to any of these questions.

But the problem goes beyond what is assumed about agents' knowledge: how do economists themselves know? The claim that economics is science legitimizes the idea that economics is above politics, and that economic policies are the equivalent of the kinds of safety measures that are rightly the province of technical experts, not the subject of political debate. Applied to central banking, the result is to undermine political accountability and, ultimately, to undermine democracy itself.

In the end, the attempt to separate economics from politics rests on what I would regard as a mistaken attempt to separate the size of the pie from how it is sliced, efficiency from distribution. In the next chapter, we examine a key pillar in this separation: the nation-state.

CHAPTER 10

Welfare Economics
and the Nation-State

Mainstream economics asserts that, subject to some fine and not-so-fine print, a market system makes society as a whole as well-off as is possible given the resources available. Even if we suspend disbelief that individuals are as standard economics assumes them—rationally calculating a very limited self-interest—even if we assume that markets meet all the conditions that make for efficient outcomes—summarized in Appendix A—this is still a very strong claim. First off, we have to separate distribution from efficiency, and then we have to justify the focus on efficiency. The last step is crucial: in effect, we have to assume that somehow or other, it is legitimate to ignore distribution, that the state is able to distribute resources in a just manner. This chapter examines the assumptions behind this argument.

Why be concerned with society at all? The "Iron Lady," former British prime minister Margaret Thatcher, once said—famously or infamously, depending on your point of view—that society does not exist. Unlike Ms. Thatcher, mainstream economists are not by and large libertarians for whom "society" is a figment of the imagination and "state" a four-letter word spelled with five letters.[1] Economics is very much concerned with the well-being of society, provided societal well-being is reduced to one aggregate or another of individual utilities.

In principle, "society" is a concept that can be applied to any group of individuals. But in the history of economic ideas, society is far from arbitrary: the nation-state has been the privileged social group since at least Adam Smith. *The Wealth of Nations* focused not on how the aristocracy might become more prosperous or, for that matter, on how widows and orphans might be made better off. To be sure, Smith thought the fortunes of the working class were bound up with the fortunes of the nation, but it is telling that he nevertheless did not choose *The Wealth of Workers* as his title. When economists, in Smith's day or ours, say "society would be better off if . . ." or indeed "society would be worse off if . . . ," they generally have the nation-state in mind. What ties economics to nationalism is the idea that economics (and economists) are above the fray of special interests, the guardians of the interest of the people as a whole, the guardians of the nation.

Why is the nation-state *the* legitimate group? Why is a focus on workers, or on subnational communities, parochial, and if not totally illegitimate, certainly less legitimate than a focus on the nation as a whole?

The short answer is that in the modern world, governments gain legitimacy from their claim to represent a nation. Authority is legitimacy plus power, and while the state part of the equation

$$society = nation\text{-}state$$

provides the power, the nation part provides the legitimacy. Power and legitimacy to what end? Power and legitimacy to manage the conflicts that inevitably accompany change, particularly change associated with economic growth. Change means losses as well as gains, losers as well as winners; conflict is built into change even within the parameters of standard economics.

The longer answer, with which this chapter is concerned, must begin with a brief reprise of the distinction between description and prescription. Descriptive (or positive) economics makes assertions like "The top 10 percent of the population receives 35 percent of society's income"; or "If income taxes are reduced, people will work more." Prescriptive (or normative) economics makes claims such as "It would be better if the top 10 percent received half as much income"; or "If people worked more, society would be better off." The two parts of economics are generally thought by economists to be logically distinct and separable, but the conventional basis of the distinction, fact versus value, has come under increasing attack in recent decades (Putnam 2002). In any case, as argued in Chapter 1, the prescriptive agenda has shaped the foundational assumptions of the discipline. And this prescriptive agenda is not only evaluative; it is also an agenda for constructing the world in the image of economics. Economics is not only epistemology; it is also ontology. It is not only about how to understand the world; it is about how to be in the world.

John Neville Keynes, father of John Maynard Keynes and father as well of the subdiscipline of economic methodology, made the distinction between description and prescription central to economic argument, but subsequent generations have used Keynes's labels while changing the content in important ways. For the senior Keynes, as for the present-day economist, the box labeled *positive* contains the search for economic laws. This is the science box, supposedly value free. Keynes and today's economists may be on the same page in their belief in a value-free positive economics, but this is because both are blind to the values implicit in the calculating self-interested individuals always striving for more. In fact, the very assumptions of economics, conditioned by the prescriptive agenda, are full of implicit values.

By contrast, prescription, what ought to be, rests on explicit value judgments. This is the box that has changed its meaning since Keynes. For Keynes, prescription involved "economic ideals"; in the twenty-first century, prescription presupposes efficiency as the goal of economic life.

To confuse matters, Keynes had a third category, the art of economics, defined as the "rules for attaining a given end" (J. N. Keynes 1917 [1890], 34–35). This box survives, but the label is lost. The confusion is compounded by the fact that today's normative box—*welfare economics* in the current jargon—bears little resemblance to what Keynes called normative and considerable resemblance to Keynes's "art."

The reason is simple. The universe of economic ideals has shrunk to a single point: instead of competing images of a good economy, the only ideal in today's economics is efficiency. So all we have left to talk about are competing mechanisms for attaining the stipulated end—that is, all we have left to discuss is the "art" of achieving efficiency.

Is this discussion descriptive or positive? Unclear. For Keynes, the art of economics does not involve value judgments since the ends are not in question. This logic would suggest that today's normative economics, too, is not really normative, concerned as it is with finding rules for minimizing waste. But it can be argued against Keynes as against present-day economists that value judgments enter through the back door even if the goal is not in dispute: the choice of a metric for comparing alternative means requires value judgments every bit as much as does the choice of ends—even if in the end the value judgment is that the means don't matter.

From Normative Ends to Normative Means

How did we get from Keynes's conceptualization of economics to today's? From a normative economics concerned with alternative goals that the economy might serve to a normative economics concerned with the best means for achieving an efficient allocation of resources? The generation that followed Keynes shared Keynes's view of the descriptive/prescriptive divide. Arthur Pigou was the author of the leading treatise on welfare economics in the first half of the twentieth century, *The Economics of Welfare*. Much of this book is given over to the question of whether a more equal distribution of income conflicts with maximizing output, a descriptive question that rests on a prescriptive judgment, namely, that a more equal distribution of income would improve overall social well-being. The prescriptive logic was straightforward: Pigou subscribed both to the idea of diminishing marginal utility, the idea that successive increments of consumption in general provide smaller doses of satisfaction, and to the idea that human beings are basically similar. For Pigou, comparisons between rich and poor were fundamentally similar to comparisons of different amounts of income or consumption for a single individual. Generally speaking, it increases society's well-being to transfer income from the rich to the poor because a dollar taken away from the average rich man provides him little utility, while the same dollar in the hands of an average poor man provides a lot of utility. (On occasion this proposition may be confounded by a rich man whose ability to transform income into pleasure is extremely well honed while the poor beneficiary of the transfer is so insensitive—perhaps insensitized by a lifetime of poverty—that extra income produces little extra pleasure [Pigou 1952 (1920), chap. 8 and appendix 11].)

The open question was whether such transfers would be at the expense of the overall size of the economic pie. On the whole, Pigou minimized the conflict, but this is less important for present purposes than the recognition that economics ought to consider both the size of the economic pie and how it is sliced.

In this context, Lionel Robbins represents a watershed in economic thinking. His *Essay on the Nature and Significance of Economic Science* banished distribution to a limbo of value judgments that he viewed as necessarily subjective and personal—unscientific—and therefore illegitimate. For Robbins, science was the apex of human knowledge because it does not rely on value judgments. The only economics worthy of the name *science* was a supposedly value-free positive economics, economics defined (as it still is today) as "the science which studies human behaviour as a relationship between ends and scarce means which have alternative uses" (Robbins 1948 [1932], 16). Economics for Robbins is no more or less than the logic of opportunity costs, the lost opportunities that are the inevitable result of scarcity: if you come to a fork in the road, you go one way or the other—the cost of taking one road is that you must forgo the opportunity to take the other. Economics thus reduces to constrained maximization (see Appendix A), and prices are simply the implicit ratios that measure trade-offs at the margin.

Robbins in effect closes down the normative box, or rather transforms it into the box that Keynes labeled the art of economics. Economics is defined in terms of *positivism*, for which the scientific touchstone is the ability to test a proposition against objective, empirical evidence. Welfare economics, as the study of economic ideals, was not part of economic *science*—and for this reason was illegitimate—because its propositions incorporated value judgments and therefore defied such testing.

The first problem for Robbins was that evaluating the well-being of society requires us to compare the well-being of one individual with the well-being of another. Robbins rejects Pigou's utilitarian framework for making ethical judgments about the relative deserts of these individuals. For Robbins, the comparison is necessarily subjective. Here he explains the difference between evaluating one individual's utility and comparing two different individuals:

> Suppose that a difference of opinion were to arise about A's preferences. Suppose that I thought that, at certain prices, he preferred *n* to *m*, and you thought that, at the same prices, he preferred *m* to *n*. It would be easy to settle our differences in a purely scientific manner. Either we could ask A to tell us. Or, if we refused to believe that introspection on A's part was possible, we could expose him to the stimuli in question and observe his behaviour. Either test would be such as to provide the basis for a settlement of the difference of opinion.
>
> But suppose that we differed about the satisfaction derived by A from an income of £1,000, and the satisfaction derived by B from an income of twice that magnitude. Asking them would provide no solution. Supposing they differed. A might urge that he had more satisfaction than B at the margin. While B might urge that, on the contrary, he had more satisfaction than A. We do not need to be slavish behaviourists to realise that there is no scientific evidence. *There is no means of testing the magnitude of A's satisfaction as compared with B's.* (Robbins 1948 [1932], 139–140)

The difference between Robbins and Pigou shows clearly the role of assumptions in economics. There is, to be sure, no difference with regard to their willingness to universalize the characteristics of nineteenth-century

Englishmen as "human nature." But they differed dramatically on the substance of these assumptions. For Pigou, it was obvious that human beings are essentially similar, and on average at least, the satisfactions of one individual can be compared with the satisfactions of another (1952 [1920], 850–851). For Robbins, it was equally obvious that there was no objective way to compare satisfactions, and hence that by introducing subjective judgments, welfare economics strayed off the reservation of economic science.

Robbins won the day. By mid-century Milton Friedman (1953, 7) could argue explicitly that economics was mostly about means—not only could there be no meaningful discussion about ends, but such discussion was unnecessary because all were in agreement. Robbins paved the way for Friedman because underlying Robbins's vision of economics as the study of opportunity costs was the belief that a clear understanding of opportunity costs would narrow if not eliminate the debate about politically contentious issues. Knowledge of opportunity costs might not bring us to agreement on the menu for today's dinner, but it would certainly focus the debate about, say, the relative merits of capitalism and socialism—a raging issue in Robbins's day, writing as he was in the depths of the Great Depression:

> Without economic analysis, it is not possible rationally to choose between alternative *systems* of society. We have seen already that if we regard a society which permits inequality of incomes as an evil in itself, and an equalitarian society as an end to be pursued above all other things, then it is illegitimate to regard such a preference as uneconomic. But it is not possible to regard it as rational unless it is formulated with a full consciousness of the nature of the sacrifice which is thereby involved. And we cannot do this unless we understand, not only the essential nature of the capitalistic mechanism, but also the necessary conditions and limitations to which the type of society proposed as a substitute would be subject. . . . And, in this supreme weighing of alternatives, only a complete awareness of the implications of modern economic analysis can confer the capacity to judge rationally. (Robbins 1948 [1932], 155)

From here it was a relatively easy step to the view that it was not the ends themselves that were in question but the means to achieve those ends. In a world of self-interested individuals, distribution is "my blood or thine." But if one way or another we can put distribution to one side (for example, by focusing on changes that do not diminish any individual's slice of the pie), these same self-interested individuals will all agree on the desirability of a bigger economic pie. Once distribution and production are separated, economics can focus on the realm of harmony—that is, on producing the largest pie possible—and leave the realm of conflict, the realm of distribution, to politics and philosophy.

In short, a welfare economics of agreed-upon ends requires us to finesse the problem of distribution. This in turn requires a measure of social well-being that does not rely on interpersonal comparisons of individual utilities. A tall order, but not one beyond the ingenuity of the economics profession. Actually, Robbins's *Essay* was not the first to develop the outline of such a welfare economics. The Italian economist Vilfredo Pareto elaborated just such a measure during his tenure (from 1892 to 1912) as professor of economics at the University of Lausanne, and others, such as Pareto's contemporary, the English economist Francis Edgeworth, worked the same street. This approach made little headway, however, until Robbins's attack on interpersonal comparisons.

The New Welfare Economics: Efficiency, Distribution, and the Pareto Criteria

The basis for the so-called New Welfare Economics that emerged in the wake of Robbins's strictures came from Pareto: efficiency—the largest possible pie—is defined in terms of outcomes that cannot be improved upon for everybody, outcomes that in the jargon are called *Pareto optimal.* By extension, *Pareto improvement* refers to a change that makes everybody better off. The core of the New Welfare Economics consists of two propositions: the *first welfare theorem* is that a system of competitive markets, once it settles down to equilibrium, is Pareto optimal; starting from a competitive equilibrium, it is not possible to improve everybody's lot. In other words, the prices that clear competitive markets by bringing supplies and demands into line with one another also bring about outcomes that cannot be improved upon for everybody. The *second welfare theorem* is more sweeping: any Pareto optimal outcome can be achieved by means of a competitive market equilibrium—provided the distribution of resources among individuals is completely flexible. This is to say that the initial distribution can be adjusted to suit the needs of the desired distributional outcome. (Appendix A provides some detail on what is entailed by competitive equilibrium and the adjustment of the initial distribution of resources.)

The New Welfare Economics reflects the shift from a discussion of the various ends the economy might serve to a discussion of how to achieve the largest economic pie. And the New Welfare Economics answers the question of means: subject to the fine print of the structural assumptions discussed in Appendix A, a system of markets leads to the largest pie that existing resources allow us to produce.

The New Welfare Economics appears to offer a way of talking about societal well-being without invoking value judgments. But appearances, as is often the case, deceive: value judgments continue to be present, hidden in the foundational assumptions that social well-being consists of satisfying the rational, calculating individual's self-interested pursuit of consumption.

Even on its own terms, the New Welfare Economics is hardly compelling: indeed, why should anybody care about efficiency or Pareto optimality, not to mention competitive equilibrium, especially if the outcome involves a highly unequal distribution of income?

Imagine a dialogue between economist E and a member of the unwashed public, U. E says, "Efficiency means that Bill Gates, with his $40 billion (plus or minus), trades off transportation services for housing services or medical services at the same rate as Jane Doe, a nurse's aide who lives hand to mouth on $10 per hour. Since Bill and Jane have equal *marginal rates of substitution,* you can't make them both better off by shuffling the mix between houses, cars, and doctors, or tinkering with the prices that arise spontaneously from the interaction of buyers and sellers."

U say, "Why should I care about efficiency if it means that Bill Gates has 100 cars and 10 houses and a doctor who comes to his house whenever he has a sniffle, while Jane Doe has 1 car (held together with baling twine and duct tape at that) and a crummy apartment, and can't afford to see a doctor but once a year? Why should I care that they have the same marginal rates of substitution among the goods they consume? Wouldn't the world be a better place if, at the very least, doctors were allocated among patients according to the severity of their illnesses rather than the depth of their pockets?"

"Perhaps," says E, "but that involves value judgments and gets us into the realm of the subjective. How can you compare Bill's suffering with Jane's? Maybe Bill is a sensitive soul who dies a thousand deaths with each sneeze, while Jane is a stoic, oblivious to pain. In any case, redistribution need not be at the expense of efficiency. By simply rearranging the starting point for Bill and Jane, just like we handicap horses by adding weight to make the race more even, we can achieve the same distributional results that U want to achieve by meddling in particular markets, without the wastes that such meddling inevitably involves. Take $1 billion from Bill and give it to Jane, and then let the market work its magic. [This, in effect, is the second welfare theorem.] Relative to the kind of meddling U are advocating, competitive markets offer the possibility of Pareto improvement."

"That's fine," U object. "But what happens if the wealth transfer is not made? How can you argue in this case that efficiency is not in conflict with the more desirable outcome that might be achieved by distributing some things—health care for starters—through nonmarket channels?"

"Not to worry," responds E, quick as a whip, sharp as a razor. "A move from a nonequilibrium situation to a competitive equilibrium is a potential Pareto improvement because society could, if it wished, redistribute resources among its members so that everybody has more than at the original nonequilibrium."

The key point in this dialogue is the subtle shift from Pareto improvement to potential Pareto improvement. Pareto improvement can be criticized because of its reliance on contestable foundations (individualism and the rest), but on its own terms, it is compelling. Potential Pareto improvement is not even compelling on its own terms. E can't claim any more than that "society *could* . . . redistribute resources . . . so that everybody has more." Because actual compensation is not necessary, a potential Pareto improvement can leave some folks worse off than before. And this, not Pareto improvement, is the real world. The example of Chapter 1, in which a trade initiative like NAFTA increases total output but some people lose their jobs, is a case in point.[2]

This is crucial. As Appendix A makes clear, the kind of rearrangement of resources envisaged in the second welfare theorem is not very helpful in the real world; the division between a harmonious realm of production and a conflictual realm of distribution is highly artificial. In practice, changes in production and distribution are a spider's web of reciprocal entanglements. A new technology may be more productive and add to the size of the pie, but it may change the nature of the product and require both a new set of skills and a new organization of work. The automobile proverbially put buggy manufacturers and their employees out of work or obliged them to switch from horse-drawn to self-propelled carriages. In our own day, outsourcing might make the pie bigger overall, but it does not make the slices bigger for the folks who lose their jobs in call centers in Maine or in automobile plants in Michigan.

Second, there is an important difference between the way potential Pareto optimality and Pareto improvement is treated in elementary and advanced texts. Advanced texts typically note the distributional problem associated with changes like outsourcing when compensation does not actually take place. And then move on (for instance, Mas-Colell et al. 1995, 830). By contrast, elementary texts typically avoid the issue altogether. The best-selling elementary text asks rhetorically whether the market can be improved upon—and replies with a resounding "no": "Can the social planner raise total economic well-being by increasing or decreasing the quantity of the good [corresponding to the equilibrium price]? The answer is no" (Mankiw 2004, 149). This "no" simply sweeps distribution under the rug, so that Pareto optimality becomes an appropriate criterion of well-being, and potential Pareto improvement become an appropriate measure of changes in well-being.

All this might be of little interest were it not for the fact that when economists move from epistemology to ontology, from the academy into the policy realm, their argument and advice is more in tune with the elementary text than with the advanced one. Economists' strictures on matters as diverse as international trade, health and safety regulations, and price controls generally reflect a criterion of potential Pareto improvement as the relevant test of the soundness of a policy proposal. "There are," according to one leading undergraduate text on international trade, "three main reasons why economists do *not* generally stress the income distribution effects of trade." The reasons are as follows:

1. Income distribution effects are not specific to international trade. Every change in a nation's economy, including technological progress, shifting consumer preferences, exhaustion of old resources and discovery of new ones, and so on, affects income distribution. If every change in the economy were allowed only after it had been examined for its distributional effects, economic progress could easily end up snarled in red tape.

2. It is always better to allow trade and compensate those who are hurt by it than to prohibit the trade. (This applies to other forms of economic change as well.) All modern industrial countries provide some sort of "safety net" of income support programs (such as unemployment benefits and subsidized retraining and relocation programs) that can cushion the losses of groups hurt by trade. Economists would argue that if this cushion is felt to be inadequate, more support rather than less trade is the right answer.

3. Those who stand to lose from increased trade are typically better organized than those who stand to gain. This imbalance creates a bias in the political process that requires a counterweight. It is the traditional role of economists to strongly support free trade, pointing to the overall gains; those who are hurt usually have little trouble making their complaints heard. (Krugman and Obstfeld 2000, 57)

How the Nation-State Justifies Potential Pareto Improvement

Is there any way to justify ignoring those who lose out because of a focus on the size of the pie? Can we rescue the criterion of potential Pareto improvement? Yes, but it's a torturous road: if we are willing to assume that the state reflects the will of a nation, then we can make an argument for separating efficiency from distribution and focusing on efficiency.

In principle, as was noted in the beginning of this chapter, society can be any social aggregate, from the family or a network of friends to the entire human population on this earth. But, as was also noted, economists have identified society with the nation-state ever since Adam Smith. One reason is purely pragmatic. Economics was born out of policy discussions, debates, and disputes, and economists have always thought of themselves as speaking to power—preferably speaking truth to power, however much they might disagree on the content of truth—but in any case speaking to power. And power is lodged with the state.

There is a moral dimension that goes beyond the merely pragmatic. Why does the economist identify with the state, rather than, say, with the working class, or the local community, or the members of his or her religious faith? Surely naked power is not a sufficient moral reason for the state to claim the economist's allegiance, as against the claims of class, community, or religion. Here is where the nation comes in. The state represents power, whereas the nation gives legitimacy to this power; the nation-state is an entity that transcends the particular interests of individuals or, rather, synthesizes particular interests into a general interest. If

$$\text{authority} = \text{power} + \text{legitimacy},$$

a basis in the nation is what makes the power of the state legitimate and confers authority on the nation-state.

The point is that—paradoxes aside (see note 2)—potential Pareto improvement becomes a sufficient condition for an improvement in overall well-being if the nation-state can always take the requisite actions to make sure that losers are actually compensated. And compensation does not have to be paid. Compensation will be paid only if the losers are deserving. How do we know if the losers are deserving? We look to whether compensation is paid.

The reasoning may appear circular, but to cut through the circularity we need only the assumption that the political process is legitimate. The legitimacy of the political process is guaranteed by the assumption that the government speaks for the nation, for the whole rather than for some of the parts; for the people, not for king or emperor; for all of us, not for an aristocracy or an oligarchy. This absolves economists of the responsibility to think about distributional issues, freeing us to concentrate our attention on how to increase the size of the pie; we can leave it to the political process to figure out how to distribute the pie.

The Nation as *Vox Populi*

This logic, to be sure, requires a very special theory of the nation-state. A Marxian theory, in which the state serves the interests of the dominant economic class, would hardly be compatible with the legitimate political process imputed to the nation-state within standard economics. Neither would the state as conceived by the likes of Anthony Downs and James Buchanan. Their "public-choice economics" understands public service and politics in terms of the same assumptions that standard economics applies to the private activities of agents: rational calculation of individual self-interest. There is no more room in this view for a state that transcends the particular and special interests of economic agents than in the Marxian view. Both lack the key element of legitimacy.

This is not the place to review the gamut of theories of the nation-state. But it is appropriate to distinguish between two broad strands in the vast literature on nationalism: those that see the nation as artificially constructed to serve the needs of the powerful or the would-be powerful, and those that see the nation as the outgrowth of a groundswell of popular emotion. Clearly, if one accepts the idea that nationalism is an invented ideology, the nation-state loses its allure of transcending special interests; but if nationalism is a bottom-up phenomenon, there is a presumption of legitimacy. We need not settle the dispute; indeed, this is a dispute in which both parties can be right, or at least half right—nationalism can be a reflection of popular sentiment, and at the same time that sentiment can be manipulated by elites.

To convey the flavor of the debate, let me sketch two theories, one from each camp. In *Nations and Nationalism,* Ernest Gellner sees the nation as an invention in the service of industrialization. Before industrialization, people are organized in terms of local groups having comparatively little interaction with each other. Even language is fragmented into dialects that might not be mutually intelligible if one travels just a short distance. This works fine for a predominantly agricultural society, but fails utterly to meet the needs of an industrial society. Industrial development requires explicit and precise communication among a large number of individuals. Because of the dynamic nature of industrial society, these individuals must be not only mutually intelligible to one another; they must be mutually substitutable, just like the interchangeable parts of standardized manufactures. This requires a common culture, which is where nationalism comes in: the "nation" represents the imposition of a common culture in the service of expanded communication. As Gellner puts it,

> Let us recapitulate the general and central features of industrial society: Universal literacy and a high level of numerical, technical and general sophistication are among its functional prerequisites. Its members are and must be mobile, and ready to shift from one activity to another, and must possess that generic training which enables them to follow the manuals and instructions of a new activity or occupation. In the course of their work they must constantly communicate with a large number of other men, with whom they frequently have no previous association, and with whom communication must consequently be explicit, rather than relying on context. They must be able to communicate by means of written, impersonal, context-free, to-whom-it-may-concern type messages. Hence these communications must be in the same shared and standardized linguistic medium and script. The educational system which guarantees this social achievement becomes large and is indispensable. . . .
>
> Nationalism is, essentially, the general imposition of a high culture on society, where previously low cultures had taken up the lives of the majority, and in some case of the totality, of the population. It means that generalized diffusion of a school-mediated, academy-supervised idiom, codified for the requirements of reasonably precise bureaucratic and technological communication. It is the establishment of an anonymous, impersonal society, with

mutually substitutable atomized individuals, held together above all by a shared culture of this kind, in place of a previous complex structure of local groups, sustained by folk cultures reproduced locally and idiosyncratically by the micro-groups themselves. (Gellner 1983, 33, 57)

In terms of our earlier discussion of knowledge,[3] Gellner is saying that the communication required by industrialization must be in terms of algorithmic knowledge, the knowledge of logical deduction based on self-evident premises, and this in turn requires common education, language, and—most important of all—a common culture. This is what nationalism supplies.

I am tempted to turn Gellner's argument on its head. If all that were required was a common algorithmic knowledge, industrialization would hardly require a common culture. The virtue of algorithmic knowledge is precisely its ability to transcend culture. Rather, a common culture is required because of the limitations of algorithmic knowledge. A common culture provides a common experience and a common experiential knowledge. It is the tacit, not the explicit, that must be generalized across the disparate groups that inhabit a state's territory; by unifying culture, nationalism provides a basis for a common experiential knowledge.

Gellner's view of how the role of culture changes with industrialization seems to me to support this interpretation:

Culture is no longer merely the adornment, confirmation and legitimation of a social order which was also sustained by harsher and coercive constraints; culture is now the necessary shared medium, the life-blood or perhaps rather the minimal shared atmosphere, within which alone the members of the society can breathe and survive and produce. For a given society, it must be one in which they can *all* breathe and speak and produce; so it must be the *same* culture. (Gellner 1983, 37–38)

Either way—whether nationalism facilitates algorithm or supplements algorithm with a common body of experiential knowledge—Gellner's is not a theory of transcendence. By contrast, in *Nationalism: Five Roads to Modernity,* Liah Greenfeld sees nationalism as a new identity created by and for rising classes—businessmen, civil servants, intellectuals, agricultural capitalists—to justify upward social and economic mobility. For Greenfeld, *"National identity is, fundamentally, a matter of dignity.* It gives people reasons to be proud" (1992, 487). National identity opposes the elite identity of the higher orders or, rather, transfers the notion of elite status from these orders to the people as a whole.

In this view, nationalism emerged first in England precisely because of the precocious social mobility of sixteenth-century Tudor England. But there is more to the story than social mobility: national identities throughout Europe were shaped, as Anthony Marx has argued, by the Reformation (Marx 2003).

Henry VIII's break with Rome infused Christianity with an English identity, but for a time the divisiveness of the split between Protestantism and Catholicism was masked by a deliberate downplaying of the Protestant element in English national identity. Case in point: Sir Thomas Wyatt, the leader of the eponymous and unsuccessful rebellion of 1554 against the Catholic Queen Mary, wrote a fellow rebel, " 'You may not so much as name religion, for that will withdraw from us the hearts of many' " (quoted in Fletcher and MacCulloch 2004 [1968], 101). Mary's successor, Queen Elizabeth I, said famously that she wished no window into her subjects' souls, requiring only national loyalty and outward conformity.

In contrast to the sixteenth century, the seventeenth saw a hardening of religious lines, a decreasing tolerance for the Catholic minority. Locke's eloquent plea for religious toleration, penned toward the end of the century, was a plea for tolerating dissident Protestant sects. Tellingly, Locke drew the line at toleration for Catholics (A. Marx 2003, 175–184).

Across the channel, Henry IV also attempted to minimize the division between Catholics and Protestants. A convert to Catholicism ("Paris is worth a mass," in the undoubtedly apocryphal words attributed to him by cynics), Henry attempted to replace the motto "one faith, one law, one king" with a policy of toleration: "I wish members of the [Christian] Faith to live in peace in my kingdom. . . . We are all French and fellow citizens of the same country" (Marie-Madeleine Martin 1951, 144). But the policy of toleration failed in seventeenth-century France, just as it did in England. Henry was assassinated by a Jesuit who thought him soft on dissent, and with Henry died the experiment in religious pluralism. Henry's Edict of Nantes, guaranteeing religious liberty to Protestants, was revoked by century's end, and the policy of toleration was revived only in the last days of the Old Regime.

There are, according to Greenfeld (1992), three types of nationalism. First, there is the good kind associated with the United States and England, based on individualism and "citizenship." (By citizenship Greenfeld means an open and voluntary commitment based on shared values, making citizenship something between membership in a community of affinity and a libertarian association.) And there are two bad kinds: French nationalism, based on citizenship but with the individual subordinated à la Rousseau to the collective and authoritarian power embodied in the state; and German and Russian nationalism, based not on citizenship but on ethnicity, and therefore, for Greenfeld, necessarily collective and authoritarian.[4]

Greenfeld's *Nationalism* portrays the formation of national identity, at least in England, as primarily a bottom-up process that fills a void as identity based on religion breaks down under the onslaught of schism and as identity based on nobility is eroded by social mobility. But in a later book devoted to understanding the relationship between the rise of the two leading "isms" of modernity, capitalism and nationalism, *The Spirit of Capitalism: Nationalism and Economic Growth*, Greenfeld amends the picture significantly.

At the level of the individual, *The Spirit of Capitalism* depicts English nationalism as arising from the need to legitimize self-interest in terms of a morally acceptable group interest. The spirit of capitalism, in Greenfeld's view, is precisely the moral cover that the nation provides for the individual's striving on his or her own account: self-interest becomes okay morally because it serves the interest of the nation, à la Smith. Greenfeld presents this view as Max Weber without the Protestant ethic, or, rather, with the Protestant ethic replaced by a national ethic.

At the level of the state, capitalism is seen as providing the resources for the state to pursue goals of military power and national prestige, so that traditional disdain for "trade" gives way to acceptance and even honor. So even in Greenfeld's friendly account, nationalism takes on something of a contrived character: the state promotes national feeling to facilitate capitalism, the better to enlarge the economic pie and the state's slice.

So who is right? Is nationalism bottom-up or top-down? The irreducible reality is that nationalism mixes the spontaneous and the contrived into a stew, and it is impossible to sort out the ingredients. Joan of Arc's passion for France was spontaneous, however much the Maid of Orleans was contrived into a legend. In World War I, millions died on the battlefields of Europe for their respective nations, again a mixture of spontaneous patriotism and manipulated loyalty. Years ago, I was struck, reading the history of a small town in the state of Maine, by the large number of volunteers for the Union Army during the Civil War: 84 in the very first weeks of the war out of a total of 138 who served—all this out of a total population of less than 1,000 (West 1923, 35–37; the population figure is from the U.S. Census of

1860 [Kennedy 1864, 204]). Considering that roughly half the population were women, and two-thirds of the males were under or over age, the number of volunteers is staggering—almost half the eligible population.[5] What moved these men and boys to go off to war? Some may have been bored by life on the frontier—this town was on the fringe of the settled territory (and still is: people stopped pushing the Maine frontier northward once the trans-Appalachian West was opened in the early part of the nineteenth century). Some no doubt were stirred by abolitionist calls to put an end to the disgrace of slavery. But many fought for Lincoln's avowed war aim of preserving the Union, preserving the nation. And even those who took up arms to free the slaves must have been moved in part by the national aspect of the disgrace, that slavery took place in their nation, a nation nominally dedicated to freedom and equality—there were no volunteers from this town, so far as I know, to free the slaves in Brazil.

The Nation as Community

There is another way of viewing the nation: in at least two influential accounts, the nation derives its legitimacy from its role as surrogate community. We have already (in Chapter 1) encountered the idea that the nation filled the vacuum created as subnational communities were undermined in the early modern period. This is the basic idea of Robert Nisbet's study *The Quest for Community*, which sees the state, rather than the market, as the culprit in the assault on community. The state offers the nation as a substitute for the village, church, family, guild, and the myriad associations that lay claim to the individual's loyalties in the absence of modernity—both in terms of material support and in terms of psychological and spiritual meaning. For Nisbet, the nation as surrogate community is an underlying theme of modernity, a theme uniting the political Right, Left, and Center, which differ from one another only in the degree that community is obliterated or tolerated.

The nation as community is also the basis of Benedict Anderson's *Imagined Communities*. For Anderson, the modern nation is "an imagined political community," imagined because the members of the national community do not know each other personally, indeed have never laid eyes on most of their compatriots and never will: "yet in the minds of each lives the image of their communion . . . regardless of the actual inequality and exploitation that may prevail . . . the nation is always conceived as a deep, horizontal comradeship" (Anderson 1983, 15–16).

This last point is crucial to the legitimacy of the nation. Jean-Jacques Rousseau is the bête noire of Nisbet as well as of Greenfeld, a prophet of totalitarian dictatorship in the guise of egalitarian democrat. Rousseau's idea of forcing men to be free opens the door to the single party states of Left and Right, the leadership of which exacts compliance to the leader's intuition of the general will in the very name of the freedom of the people. Even if we accept Nisbet's and Greenfeld's take on Rousseau at face value, it remains that the leader's legitimacy, every bit as much as the legitimacy of parliamentary democracies, rests on the conception of the nation "as a deep, horizontal comradeship." It is this comradeship that inspires in ordinary people not only a range of extremes, from heroic sacrifice on the battlefield to the acceptance and even willing participation in genocide, but also deference to the political leadership on everyday questions of policy, including decisions on the distribution of the economic pie.

Anderson is at great pains to distance himself from Gellner on the crucial point of whether the nation is an artificial, top-down imposition, or a spontaneous, bottom-up creation (Anderson 1983, 15; Anderson's reference is to an earlier work, Gellner 1964). The idea of comradeship is hard to assimilate to an idea of invention and imposition from above.

But Anderson and Gellner are perhaps not so far apart. Gellner, for whom top-down invention and imposition is a central point of his narrative, in effect concedes the importance of popular consciousness in the development of nationalism. He summarizes his theory in his account of how the Ruritanian nation is created out of the Empire of Megalomania (Gellner 1983, 58–62), a tale that emphasizes the idea that whereas some nation is necessitated by the cultural needs of industrialization, the emergence of any particular nation is accidental. The Ruritanians could just as easily have remained Megalomanians. But tucked into Gellner's story is the recognition of the importance of the demise of other forms of community to the rise of nationalism:

> Ruritanians had previously thought and felt in terms of family unit and village, at most in terms of a valley, and perhaps on occasion in terms of religion. But now, swept into the melting pot of an early industrial development, they had no valley and no village: and sometimes no family. But there *were* other impoverished and exploited individuals, and a lot of them spoke dialects recognizably similar, while most of the better-off spoke something quite alien; and so the new concept of the Ruritanian nation was

born of this contrast. . . . And it was not an illusion: the attainment of some of the objects of the nascent Ruritanian national movement did indeed bring relief of the ills which had helped to engender it. . . . In this national form, it also brought forth a new high culture and its guardian state. (Gellner 1983, 62)

"No valley and no village," it should be clear, means no community. And "the new concept of the Ruritanian nation . . . was not an illusion"—it was a newly imagined community.

We have a choice. We can see the nation as a collection of individuals—calculating self-interested individuals. The alternative is to see the nation as a community.

I suppose the first question to ask is what difference this makes. In the first case, the state is a black box whose workings we don't really have to understand, confident that its very visible hand will legitimize the invisible hand of the market, confident in a division of labor in which the state concerns itself with the politics of distribution and the market takes care of economic efficiency. In the second case, in which the nation is a form of community, politics and economics are inexorably intertwined, and the existence of an economic realm that focuses on efficiency alone cannot be defended.

From the point of view this book, the choice should be an easy one: why not simply embrace the idea of the nation as a community that coexists with "parochial" interests, with other communities? If it is true, as I have asserted, that normative economics morphs into constructive economics—the building of society in the image of economic theory—why not turn this to good account?

There is much to say for the imagined community of the nation. For one thing, it has provided inspiration paralleled only by the inspiration of religious faith. When the signers of the American Declaration of Independence pledged their lives, their fortunes, and their sacred honor to the fledgling United States, they were hardly engaging in hyperbole. Not only would they have been disgraced and destitute had the War of Independence been remembered instead as the War of Rebellion; many of them would have ended up on the gibbet. And in succeeding generations, the nation has been a continuing focus of willing sacrifice, as well among followers as among leaders. Neither is the American example in any way unique: sacrificing oneself for one's country, I have noted, is a familiar part of the litany of nationalism all over the world.

Even if we limit ourselves to the more mundane realm of the economic, I would argue that a sense of shared community has been important in spreading the benefits of a growing economy. The national community to which you belong, every bit as much as the skills and resources you control, is central to the standard of living you enjoy. Particularly if you are a wage earner.

To be sure, community is irrelevant in the mainstream version of how wages are determined. Standard economics posits a competitive labor market (unless unions muck things up) in which wages are determined by "marginal productivities": people are rewarded according to their contribution to the production process. But there is some sleight of hand here. In one sense, marginal productivity theory is simply the logic of constrained maximization: it follows from profit maximization. The sleight of hand comes in the form of two powerful assumptions that mainstream economics adds to profit maximization, namely, that all markets, including the labor market, are perfectly competitive, so that there is no such thing as involuntary unemployment (see Appendix A for a discussion of perfect competition); and that the labor supply is exogenous, fixed by forces outside the economy. Without these "auxiliary" assumptions, marginal productivities don't determine the level of wages; rather, the level of wages determines marginal productivities.

Some years ago, I contrasted the mainstream marginal-productivity theory (profit maximization plus perfectly competitive labor markets plus the exogeneity of the labor force) with a "classical" theory of wages inspired by the insights of Adam Smith, David Ricardo, and Karl Marx (Marglin 1984a). The classical theory holds that wages are determined by "subsistence," in quotation marks because subsistence in Adam Smith's Britain and all the more so in the contemporary world, certainly in the rich countries where capitalism has held sway for a long time, is not a biologically determined level, but a conventional level determined by the interplay of a variety of forces—economic forces to be sure, but also social, political, cultural, and even moral forces. It is through this second set of "noneconomic" forces that community becomes important. The wage is conventional in two senses, first in that it reflects custom, and second in that it represents an agreement between parties with different interests.

This is not to say that technology and productivity are unimportant. Overall (not marginal) productivity determines the size of the pie to be divided among the parties, but the other elements—social, political, and so forth—determine how the pie is sliced.[6] Thus nineteenth-century British output had to be of a certain size before workers could obtain a share large enough to permit them to buy refined white bread rather than the coarse grains to which the lower classes had accommodated themselves in earlier times; twentieth-century American production had to be of a certain size before workers could successfully struggle for a share large enough to include an automobile as part of the wage packet. But a productive technology did not guarantee that either the nineteenth-century British pie or the twentieth-century American pie would be sliced in a way that would allow workers to achieve their aims. For this to happen, certain community standards were essential.

These community standards underlie, for example, the very idea of a legal minimum wage—and the erosion of community, I would wager, is an important factor in the erosion of the minimum wage in the United States over the last three decades. Nor is it just the minimum that is at issue. The last thirty years have also witnessed an ever-widening gap between workers in the middle of the income distribution and the richest 1 percent of the distribution, which includes both top managers and large stockholders. There is no longer even the pretense that we are all in it together, that the United States is a community when it comes to economic matters.

As I write this, the issue of immigration, particularly the rights of undocumented workers, is very much a front-burner issue, very much a focus of electoral and legislative politics throughout Western Europe and North America. Immigration has many dimensions, but it does not oversimplify to point out the clear resonance of many of these dimensions, both economic and noneconomic, with fundamental questions about what constitutes the national community and who qualifies for membership. Certainly, questions of wages, employment protection, and the like are bound up with the question of community. Should a Mexican worker who emigrates to the United States benefit from the U.S. minimum wage of $5.85 per hour, as opposed to the Mexican minimum wage of $4.50 per day?[7] Why? Does mere physical presence on U.S. soil make him a member of the national community? Ten years' residence? Must he learn English? Must he cease to be a member of the Mexican national community? Should a green card matter? Formal U.S. citizenship? What, in short, constitutes the imagined national community and who is eligible for membership?

These are vexing questions, and, as I write this, there is certainly no political consensus on how to answer them. Nor is there consensus on analogous questions in other countries with large immigrant populations. But the very fact that these questions are being asked tells us that the question of whether and how the nation is to be considered a community is very much on the table. It will not advance the discussion to respect the economist's dichotomy between efficiency and distribution and to put markets off limits for the pursuit of distributional goals.

The Dark Side of Nationalism

But only two cheers for the national community. There is another side to the nation-state that makes me reluctant to accept the imagined community of the nation, and more than reluctant to accept it as trumping all other forms of community: all nationalisms contain an element of xenophobia, as all religions—at least the major ones—contain an element of fundamentalism. The most extreme example is of course German National Socialism. For the Nazis, German nationalism was inseparable from a murderous hatred toward Jews and other Others. But even more benign nationalisms have not been free of intolerance and even genocide. Take England, the leading representative of a "civic" national identity that for Greenfeld and others represent the good face of nationalism. There religious pluralism, as we have seen, early on gave way to exclusion from public life of the Catholic minority, just as French national identity, after a brief experiment in pluralism, became bound up with Catholicism and the consequent exclusion of Protestants (A. Marx 2003). Political disabilities for Catholics in England continued into the nineteenth century and for Protestants in France until the end of the Old Regime.

Nationalism is inherently suspicious of other loyalties, as if loyalty to one's religion, class, or ethnicity compromises loyalty to the nation—unless the religion, class, or ethnicity is the dominant one, in a position to claim the aura of the nation itself. The revolutionary National Assembly, which overthrew the French monarchy and proclaimed "Liberty, Equality, and Brotherhood," famously extended citizenship to its Jewish population—but on one condition: "To the Jew as an individual—everything," declared Count Stanislas de Clermont-Tonnerre, "to the Jews as a nation—nothing" (quoted in J. Carroll 2001, 415). Jews would in effect have to choose between being Jews and Frenchmen: "They must not constitute a political body or a [separate] order within the state. They must be citizens individually" (quoted in Boualili 2001).[8]

The idea that a Jew who was unwilling to subordinate loyalty to the Jewish community to his French (or German) identity could not be a real Frenchman (or German) united liberals, conservatives, and fascists. But the liberals offered a choice, the choice embodied in the words of Clermont-Tonnerre. Central to the vision of the nation embodied in German and French fascism (and perhaps in the conservative view of the nation as well, but certainly less fanatically) was the idea that nationality was rooted in blood and that, accordingly, Jews could not be anything but Jews, regardless of what religion they practiced or, indeed, even if they practiced no religion. And in Nazi hands this idea became the basis for the murder of six million men, women, and children, from the deeply observant to the devoutly atheist.

But it would be a mistake to see the intolerance of nationalism only through the lens of anti-Semitism or the lens of a mutual antagonism between Catholics and Protestants. In England, we noted in Chapter 5, Protestants fought among themselves (dissenters versus the established church), as did Catholics in France (Jansenists versus Jesuits). And on the Iberian peninsula, too, where religious harmony had once prevailed among Christians, Muslims, and Jews, but from which Muslims and Jews had long since been banished, there was no lack of religious division. In the mid-eighteenth century, the Jesuits were expelled from Portugal and Spain (as well as from France), on precisely the same grounds that Jews were held by Nazis and their ilk to be a danger to the body politic. The Jesuits were accused of putting their loyalty to Rome before their allegiance to country. Here is what Bernardo Tanucci—adviser both to Charles III (who reigned as king of Naples before he ascended the throne of Spain in 1759) and to Charles's son and successor in Naples—wrote to various emissaries of the Kingdom of Naples. (The letters all date from 1761, a few years before the expulsion of the Jesuits.) To the representative of Naples in Paris:

It is necessary to extinguish completely the Order of the Jesuit Fathers, or to placate these gentlemen. If the said Order is not extinguished, it will become stronger day by day because misfortunes teach one to pull oneself together and to multiply vigilance. (Danvila y Collado 1894, 284)

And to another:

The Jesuit theologians have produced this evil with their diabolical and criminal doctrines. Ah, if the sovereigns had time to study the customs and doctrines of the said gentlemen, as the Crown Prince has said, they would have been thrown out of their states a long time ago. (Ibid., 284)

According to Manuel Danvila y Collado, the Spanish historian to whom we owe this account of Tanucci's animus towards the Jesuits,

> So alive and deep was the idea of expulsion that in addressing the representative of Naples in Lisbon, he [Tanucci] considered the expulsion of the Jesuits suitable [*conveniente*] for his sovereign and his nation because foreign bodies could not create anything but inflammations and gangrene, finding themselves in a country where they have a spirit and a life contrary to that of the body in which they insinuate themselves. They were always suspicious, always curious and always intriguing, in favor of a foreign superior to whom they have sworn loyalty and obedience. They were, in consequence, seditious spies in the country in which they were staying, rapacious and insidious, and when it suited them, they would be rebels, traitors, assassins, and enemies of the laws and of the sovereign of the country in which they found themselves. (Ibid., 284–285)

It may sound like something out of Josef Goebbels or Alfred Rosenberg, complete with a medical analogy to foreign bodies and gangrene, but it antedates the Nazis by almost two centuries—and it is directed by one Catholic toward another.

The point is that nationalism needs an Other, not a particular Other. In the United States, there have been a succession of exclusions: manifest destiny provided a pretext and an excuse to slaughter Native Americans when they would not accept the treachery and chicanery that European Americans employed to deprive them of their traditional lands. And even within the European population, American nationalism until very recently included an element of suspicion that only white Anglo-Saxon Protestants were real Americans. Catholics, particularly Irish Catholics, Jews, Southern and Eastern Europeans, and Hispanics have at one time or another been subjected to discrimination of varying degrees. Not to mention the bondage in which African Americans were held and the restricitions imposed on immigrants of East Asian descent. (It was in my lifetime that Japanese Americans were interned in concentration camps as a racial enemy.) Today it is the turn of Muslims to play the role of Other. Many Americans, including some in official Washington, appear to regard

Muslims, particularly Muslims of Middle Eastern origin, as unindicted co-conspirators of Osama Bin Laden.

The point of this history for economic ideology is to temper enthusiasm for the national community, to heighten suspicion of any theory that assumes or purports to establish the transcendence of the nation over "special interests," especially when, in the hands of economists, the national interest is limited to the size of the economic pie.

I guess it depends on which ox is gored. I am quite happy to be associated with my fellow economists in protesting the rip-off of the American consumer by the import quotas that sugar barons have secured to protect their inefficient operations from foreign competition.[9] But this does not make economists the natural defenders of a national interest against more parochial interests or groups. I do not view workers in a manufacturing plant in mid-America whose jobs are outsourced, nor for that matter do I view the typical worker who has managed to hold onto his job but whose wages have stagnated over the past quarter-century or more, as a parochial interest on a par with the sugar barons.

This is not to idealize subnational, or indeed transnational, groups in opposition to the nation. Indeed, the problem with the imagined community of the nation is of a piece with the problems of community noted in Chapter 2. Historically, neither the subnational community nor the nation has passed the test of tolerance with flying colors. How groups that do not have the privileged status of nation, whether constructed on ethnicity, religion, culture, or some other basis, ought to relate to one another and to states is a serious issue that deserves serious attention. But it will no more do to preempt such a discussion by opposing subnational communities to the nation, and declaring ipso facto the illegitimacy of such communities, than it will do to idealize them and ignore the oppressions large and small that people experience within these communities. Pending that discussion, I would urge a healthy skepticism toward the claim that the economist is the natural guardian of a national interest, the "counterweight," in the words of Krugman and Obstfeld (2000, 57), to the organized special interests that promote inefficient uses of resources because of the benefits they enjoy at the expense of the nation.

The historical symbiosis between economics and the nation-state is far from accidental. The economist serves the nation-state by legitimizing not only an analytic division between the size of the pie and its distribution but by legitimizing the claim that the focus on the size of the pie is devoid of politics. The nation-state serves the economist by providing a cover for economics to ignore the inconvenient side of change and conflict: real hardships to real people, whose livelihoods and sometimes the very meaning of whose existence are sacrificed on the altar of a larger economic pie.

But short of defensive war, isn't enlarging the pie as close to a unifying national goal as one could possibly imagine? My answer comes in the form of another question: whatever happened to "enough"? The next chapter addresses this question.

CHAPTER 11

Why Is Enough Never Enough?

Robert Cline has had trouble making ends meet. A *New York Times* article in the spring of 2001 reported that Dr. Cline "worries about retirement. He worries about paying for college for his six young children, not to mention weddings for his five daughters" (Yardley, 2001). So what—who doesn't worry about having enough to provide for family and self?

What makes Dr. Cline newsworthy is that, at the time the *Times* article was written, he was a surgeon making almost $300,000 per year and living with his family in a house that cost two-thirds of a million dollars. In the year 2000, his nanny bill came to more than $25,000. Dr. Cline's income puts him in the top 2 percent of the U.S. income distribution, which one might think would free him from the kind of economic worries that are the lot of most Americans.[1]

Not so: one of the paradoxes of our age is that abundance is always one step beyond our reach. Despite the enormous growth in production and consumption, we are as much in thrall to the economy as were our parents, grandparents, and great-grandparents. We worry about mortgage payments, car payments, retirement plans, and the rising cost of day care and college for our children and nursing homes for our parents. Most American families find one income inadequate for their needs. This is true not only at the bottom of the distribution, where stagnant real wages over the past three decades have made a rising standard of living dependent on a second paycheck, not only in the middle, but also—as Dr. Cline's situation reminds us—in the upper ranges of the distribution as well.

My purpose in this chapter is to explore the connection between modern culture and economics on the one hand and, on the other, our inability to realize the promise of abundance.

Economics and the Nonproblem of Abundance

In mainstream economics, it is axiomatic that wants are unbounded. Unbounded wants are the root of scarcity, and scarcity is the keystone of economics. Scarcity in turn causes rivalry—division of the pie is normally treated as my blood or thine rather than as a moral issue (see Chapter 10). "Every man for himself and devil take the hindmost," I have noted, is taken to be a verse from Holy Scripture.[2]

There is an obvious problem with the idea of unbounded wants: survey evidence suggests that relatively modest sums would satisfy most people's felt wants.[3] Ask somebody with an income of $50,000 how much she would need to satisfy her wants, and you will get a modest response, like $70,000.

But the modesty of responses to enquiries about felt wants is not an insuperable difficulty to the idea that wants are unlimited. Economists will say, and I think with reason, that more income is only a temporary fix. An income of $70,000 will do only for the moment because wants grow with income. In 2005, PNC Advisors, an investment advisory firm associated with PNC Bank, surveyed several hundred wealthy individuals: "When asked how much they needed to feel financially secure in the future, respondents consistently cited a need to approximately *double* their current level of assets. Those with $10 million or more felt they needed a median of $18.1 million; those with $5 million or more needed $10.4 million, and those with a half million to $1 million said they needed $2.4 million" (PNC Advisors 2005). There is, in short, a dynamic interaction: wants now exceed the means to fulfill them, and wants will always grow faster than means.

There is no inherent problem in modeling how preferences are formed and how preferences change, and economists have done so from time to time. The problem is that even the very restrictive set of results that are the core of present-day welfare economics—the first and second welfare theorems discussed in Chapter 10 and Appendix A—no longer mean very much if preferences are changing; we cannot say whether a change in consumption has made an individual better off if the measure of her well-being is itself transformed by changes in consumption. Positive or descriptive economics is held hostage to the agenda encapsulated in the profession's paean to the invisible hand, which requires an invariant measure of individual well-being.[4]

So, instead of modeling preference change, economists fall back on static models that collapse the evolution of desire into a single set of preferences defined over both present and future goods and posit that wants have no limit. "Unbounded wants" becomes shorthand for dynamic assumptions about the coevolution of ends and means. It is a convenient, but hardly harmless, fiction that allows economists to elide the problem of how wants evolve and thereby to avoid the slippery slope of departing from the assumption that preferences are given, a primitive of the problem of choice.

The harm comes from assuming that unlimited wants, even in its more realistic formulation as a dynamic tendency of wants to outstrip the means for satisfying those wants, is deeply embedded in human nature, valid for all people at all times. Economics can posit unlimited wants as a universal axiom only because it takes the assumptions of modernity as its own while imputing them to human nature.

This chapter lays out an alternative view, namely, that this Sisyphean relationship between means and wants is a product of the development of the modern West over the last four hundred years.

Keynes and the Possibilities of Abundance

In 1930, the world was entering the Great Depression. Indeed, Great Britain had been mired in recession since the mid-1920s, while most of Europe and North America were enjoying unprecedented prosperity. Against this scene of economic gloom, John Maynard Keynes—who a few years later would become the founder of the new field of macroeconomics—tried to cheer up his countrymen with an essay celebrating long-term growth. Times may be bad, Keynes wrote, but the present difficulties are but a blip in an onward-and-upward trajectory that will eventually liberate mankind from the constraint of economic scarcity.

Keynes's essay "Economic Possibilities for Our Grandchildren" made an even bolder assertion, namely, that his generation's grandchildren might well live to see the end of scarcity. If the rate of growth that had been achieved in recent decades could be maintained, "the *economic problem* may be solved, or at least in sight of solution, within a hundred years" (Keynes 1931 [1930], 366).

The secret is compound interest. If output and consumption per capita grow at 2 percent per year, we will see a doubling approximately every thirty-five years. In a century (103.5 years to be precise), consumption and income will increase to eight times its current level. In another thirty-five years, consumption and income will have expanded sixteenfold.

Keynes perhaps thought it obvious that a sixteenfold abundance of goods and services would vanquish the economic problem; in any case, he did not spell out an argument why this should be so. Pressed, however, Keynes might have argued along the following lines. Suppose that a household at the ninety-fifth percentile of the income distribution (which means 94 percent of households have less income and 5 percent have more) always enjoys an income some sixteen times as great as one at the tenth percentile, more or less the pattern in the United States at the end of the twentieth century.[5] If—*pace* Dr. Cline—we are justified in supposing further that the top 5 percent had no economic problem in 1930, it follows that, after 140 years have passed, people above the bottom tenth won't either. A household at the tenth percentile in 2070 will have the same income and consumption that one at the ninety-fifth percentile had in 1930. In 2070, when the last of Keynes's "grandchildren" are popping off, people near the bottom of the totem pole will be at the level of the richest in 1930. And even those at the very bottom, below the tenth percentile, will be much better off than most people were in Keynes's own time.

If we look at the distance we have come over the last century, it is easy to see the force—and the limits—of this logic. In the last century, U.S. output per capita pretty much followed the 2 percent trajectory that Keynes supposed would solve the economic problem. Over the period from 1900 to 1999, the compound growth rate was 1.9 percent, and since 1930 growth has been a tad stronger, which is perhaps surprising since the Depression took most of a decade to overcome.

At first blush, such an expansion vindicates Keynes's claims. All the more so because Keynes identified the economic problem with the satisfaction of what he called absolute needs—food, clothing, shelter, health care—those needs that "we feel . . . whatever the situation of our fellow human beings may be." The solution to the economic problem will be achieved "when these needs are satisfied in the sense that we prefer to devote our further energies to non-economic purposes" (Keynes 1931 [1930], 365).

There is an ambiguity here. Does "further" mean after some particular date is reached? Is Keynes equating a solution to the economic problem with satiation? With the idea that somehow our absolute needs will be met with so little effort that we will be free of all economic necessity? Free to pursue whatever fancies us? Or is "further" a statement about the margin, namely, that at the margin we will decide to allocate more of our energy to the noneconomic and less to the economic?

The first interpretation is problematic because satiation might well require productivity increases well beyond the 2 percent growth figure that Keynes took as his benchmark. The second is equally problematic, for economists at least, because our standard position is that people make choices at the margin all the time. No need to wait until 2070 or any other future date for people to choose to allocate more energy to leisure and less to goods, more to noneconomic and less to economic pursuits. As a statement about the margin, Keynes's criterion for the solution to the economic problem is hardly very helpful.

In my view, Keynes had neither satiation nor marginal analysis in mind. His perspective is rather a psychological, or perhaps even a cultural, one. The problem for Keynes is that our lives are focused on the economic. We not only get our daily bread from the economy; we live in the economy. We not only nourish our bodies, but also our minds and souls, through the economy. We will have solved the economic problem when it no longer presses on us to the extent that our primary engagements are economic.

In other words, Keynes foresaw a gradual withering away of the economy as the dominant force in our lives. The economic problem would recede as more and more people became emancipated from the need for full-time remunerative employment. Eventually economic matters would press on us no more than daily chores like walking the dog or putting out the trash.

He was agnostic on how a future without economic compulsion would sort itself out. For with the withering away of the economy would come two very different possibilities. At one pole was the possibility of a flowering of human potential that the economic problem had held in check. At the other was the possibility that eons of conditioning in terms of scarcity might make the vast majority of human beings unfit for the new freedom from economic need. "We have been," Keynes tells us, "expressly evolved by nature—with all our impulses and deepest instincts—for the purpose of solving the economic problem. If the economic problem is solved mankind will be deprived of its traditional purpose" (1931 [1930], 366).

Keynes finds no grounds for optimism in the behavior of the vanguard, the wealthier strata of his own times. Look, he says, at "the wives of the well-to-do classes, unfortunate women, many of them, who have been deprived by their wealth of their traditional tasks and occupations—who cannot find it sufficiently amusing, when deprived of the spur of economic necessity, to cook and clean and mend, yet are quite unable to find anything more amusing" (1931 [1930], 367).

Nor are more ordinary folk very promising. The working-class imagination is as limited in its own way as is the imagination of the rich. The "traditional epitaph written for herself by the old charwoman" says it all:

> Don't mourn for me friends, don't weep for me never,
> For I'm going to do nothing for ever and ever.
> . . . . .
> With psalms and sweet music the heavens'll be ringing,
> But I shall have nothing to do with the singing. (1931 [1930], 367)

Such passivity may be understandable for people whose lives have been spent at alienating work—the charwoman's ambition is not, after all, so different from that of the present-day couch potato whose work may be physically easier and economically more rewarding but in the end no more meaningful than hers. "Yet," as Keynes says, "it will only be for those who have to do with the singing that life will be tolerable—and how few of us can sing" (1931 [1930], 367).

Keynes's most striking observation is that freedom from economic want will at last allow us to free ourselves from a system of ethics geared to solving the economic problem but opposed to goodness and decency, opposed to life:

> We shall be able to rid ourselves of many of the pseudo-moral principles which have hag-ridden us for two hundred years, by which we have exalted some of the most distasteful of human qualities into the position of the highest virtues. We shall be able to afford to dare to assess the money-motive at its true value . . . a somewhat disgusting morbidity, one of those semi-criminal, semi-pathological propensities which one hands over with a shudder to the specialists in mental disease. All kinds of social customs and economic practices, affecting the distribution of wealth and of economic rewards, and penalties, which we now maintain at all costs, however distasteful and unjust they may be in themselves, because they are tremendously useful in promoting the accumulation of capital, we shall then be free, at last to discard. . . .
>
> I see us free, therefore, to return to some of the most sure and certain principles of religion and traditional virtue—that avarice is a vice, that the exaction of usury is a misdemeanour, and the love of money is detestable, that those walk most truly in the paths of virtue and sane wisdom who take least thought for the morrow. We shall once more value ends above means

and prefer the good to the useful. We shall honour those who can teach us how to pluck the hour and the day virtuously and well, the delightful people who are capable of taking direct enjoyment in things, the lilies of the field who toil not, neither do they spin. (1931 [1930], 369–370, 371–372)

Keynes, as always, gives us much to chew on. First, his conception of the contingent nature of customs, practices, and even ethics. Yet the devil is in the details, and I have real problems with the particulars of his idea that we construct our lives around markets because up to now we have needed markets for the sake of material progress.

For Keynes, social attitudes—"all kinds of social customs and social practices," including ethics—reflect the needs and requirements of an economic base. As long as the base is geared toward the accumulation of capital, the cultural superstructure conforms: Not only should policy foster economic growth; "we must pretend . . . that fair is foul and foul is fair; for foul is useful and fair is not" (1931 [1930], 372). Only after sufficient capital has been accumulated can we abandon policies and pretenses appropriate to an earlier age.

"Base" and "superstructure" are part of a terminology that belongs to Karl Marx and his followers. But even though Keynes took great pains to distance himself from Marx,[6] and certainly never uses the words base and superstructure, the shoe fits. Keynes's perspective differs little from Marx's economism, the idea that the economy shapes the society. Marx and Keynes share the view that capitalism dictates the culture of contemporary society, and this culture must be tolerated until capitalism has had enough time to lay the material foundations for a more decent society.

And if the Revolution comes before these material foundations are complete? As Keynes was writing "Economic Possibilities," Joseph Stalin was putting a more murderous version of the economistic vision into practice. Forced-march socialist accumulation also was to be temporary, and only for a limited time to require us to "pretend to ourselves and to every one that fair is foul and foul is fair; for foul is useful and fair is not."

I am not suggesting any affinity between Keynes and Marx (and not between either of them and Stalin) beyond their shared economistic convictions. But that is no little affinity. It is precisely his economism that prompts Keynes to see the elimination of work as requiring us to learn to sing. Were Keynes to have started from a broader conception of life, he might easily have come to the opposite conclusion: the problem is not that we must learn to sing once freed from economic necessity; rather, our fundamental problem lies in our inability to make our work sing even while we fulfill our economic needs.

Keynes, it should be noted, is hardly alone in his insistence that work precludes the pursuit of loftier goals. For Edward Bellamy, the nineteenth-century utopian socialist, the abolition of work was the precondition of a spiritual life (Bellamy 1996 [1888], 95). In this, Bellamy and Keynes follow a long tradition in Western thought, going back at least to the Greeks. Nor is it simply a class view. The Judeo-Christian tradition has for the most part remained faithful to the biblical idea that labor is a punishment for the transgression of Adam and Eve. And thus, like chicken pox, something to be got over as quickly as possible. This is in marked contrast to various non-Western traditions, in which work may itself be a means for spiritual expression (see S. Marglin 1990 for more on this theme).

Are We There Yet?

By Keynes's own standard, the striking gains in material abundance do not appear to have brought us very close to solving the economic problem: if we measure its severity by the space that the economic takes up in our lives, we have hardly made a dent. There is little evidence that, as a people, we "prefer to devote our further energies to non-economic purposes." Middle-class folks—who, according to Keynes, should be toward the front ranks of the march away from the economy—work longer hours today than our parents did a generation ago (Schor 1991). Moreover, we enjoy our work less and fear more for our economic futures (Fraser 2001).

Why has Keynes's prediction of economic emancipation fared so badly? One reason, of particular relevance to the United States, is the changing distribution of income, especially in the last quarter of the twentieth century. Between 1973 and 1998, income at the ninety-fifth percentile increased by more than a third, while income at the tenth percentile went up by only 7 percent. Income stagnation was not just a phenomenon of the bottom of the distribution. Over this same period, median household income also increased by about 7 percent (Jones and Weinberg 2000, 5, table 3). Half the U.S. population might be forgiven if they were to be skeptical about the miracle of compound interest.

Elizabeth Warren and Amelia Warren Tyagi (2003) argue that the middle class has not just stood still but actually lost ground, even in—they would say *especially* in—families in which both parents are holding down jobs. Even when families are making more in real terms, they do not have higher real incomes once one takes account of the higher "fixed costs" of housing, medical insurance, child care, and transportation. Some of these costs (like housing) have risen because of the pressures families feel to settle in desirable school districts. Some (child care and transportation) have risen because of the added expenditure associated with having a second earner in the paid labor force. But the worst aspect of the eponymous "two-income trap" is the added vulnerability that comes with having both parents permanently in the paid labor force. In the past, with dad working outside the home and mom inside, the possibility of mom joining the paid labor force was a kind of insurance policy against disasters like the primary breadwinner losing his (or, theoretically but rarely in practice, her) job or becoming incapacitated. But having both parents in the paid labor force all the time is like raiding a rainy-day fund to finance ordinary expenditures; it is no longer there in reserve for extraordinary events.

We might not have to go any further in search of the explanation of how the economic possibilities of Keynes's grandchildren got derailed. Except for one thing: the top of the income distribution, which has done very well, especially in the recent past, doesn't seem any closer to economic nirvana than the bottom. It is hard to imagine that Dr. Cline's father and grandfather were any more hard pressed than Dr. Cline himself. There is clearly something else at work besides a worsening income distribution.

Keynes gives himself an out, for he recognizes at the outset of "Economic Possibilities" that in addition to absolute needs, there are relative needs: "those [needs] which . . . we feel . . . only if their satisfaction lifts us above, makes us feel superior to, our fellows." Relative needs, Keynes allows, know no limits. "Needs . . . which satisfy the desire for superiority, may indeed be insatiable; for the higher the general level, the higher still are they" (Keynes 1931 [1930], 365).

A word of clarification is in order. Absolute needs sound very much like necessities, and relative needs like luxuries. Beware. Although absolute needs, defined à la Keynes as those needs that we feel independent of what others might or might not have, may overlap with necessities, they are not the same thing. I may have a taste for licorice that depends not a whit on whether you, too, are partial to licorice, but in no way regard licorice as a necessity, as something I cannot do without. Neither must necessities be needs that we feel independent of what others might or might not have—unless we arbitrarily restrict the meaning of necessities. Adam Smith (1937 [1776], 821–822) argued, to the contrary, that necessity has a social dimension:

> By necessaries I understand, not only the commodities which were indispensably necessary for the support of life, but whatever the custom of the country renders it indecent for creditable people, even of the lowest order, to be without. A linen shirt, for example, is, strictly speaking, not a necessary of life. The Greeks and the Romans lived, I suppose, very comfortably, though they had no linen. But in the present times, through the greater part of Europe, a creditable day-labourer would be ashamed to appear in public without a linen shirt, the want of which would be supposed to denote that disgraceful degree of poverty, which, it is presumed, no body can well fall into without extreme bad conduct.

More striking than a linen shirt is the desire for a decent funeral. Avoiding a pauper's burial was a reason for joining one of the "friendly societies" that flourished in the nineteenth century (see Chapter 1). And in the late nineteenth and early twentieth centuries, a time when the rate of infant and child mortality per thousand births was typically measured in three digits, insurance policies on the lives of the very young became a big business (Gosden 1973, chap. 5). Despite the urgings of middle-class reformers that the working class abandon its predilection for expensive funerals, the bereaved themselves, encouraged no doubt by the insurance companies and the collecting societies (nominally large friendly societies but functioning in practice for the profit of the officeholders), held to their own norms of decency and propriety (Behlmer 1982, chap. 5, especially 120).

Thus there may be a large overlap between relative needs and luxuries, but these two categories do not describe the same phenomenon. Smith's "creditable day-laborer" desires linen because in eighteenth-century European society a linen shirt was a badge of a decent standard of living and therefore a badge of a decent human being, not for its aesthetic qualities or for its physical comfort. A worker at the turn of the twentieth century paid a substantial sum to bury his child—more than he could afford in the view of his betters—because not to do so would stamp him, as the absence of a linen shirt would have stamped his great grandfather, with a "disgraceful degree of poverty, which . . . no body can well fall into without extreme bad conduct." Relative needs take up so much space in our universe of desires precisely because they come to be defined as necessities.[7]

Relative Needs over Time: From the Age of Accumulation to the Age of Abundance

It is tempting to blame "insatiable" relative needs for the continuing economic pressure even the Clines and their ilk feel, not to mention people with more modest incomes. But if this is the case, how can Keynes so easily put relative needs to one side in arguing that a solution to the economic problem is at hand? Why would even the full and complete satisfaction of absolute needs lead us to devote our energies to other realms?

Nicholas Xenos (1989, 46) attempts to solve the puzzle by suggesting that for Keynes relative needs have a very different character in the age of capital accumulation from the character they will acquire after the age of abundance has arrived. These needs are functional to the accumulation of capital and the growth of output. Envy, greed, and the other vices that we must for the time being call virtues serve an economic purpose in motivating individuals to maximum exertion and effort.

As Mandeville explained four centuries ago (see Chapter 6), envy and the like are the locomotive of the economic train—to the benefit of all the passengers.[8] No envy, no trickle-down. Adam Smith was no less effusive about the incentive effects of envy:

We are . . . charmed with the beauty of that accommodation which reigns in the palaces and oeconomy of the great; and admire how every thing is adapted to promote their ease, to prevent their wants, to gratify their wishes, and to amuse and entertain their most frivolous desires. If we consider the real satisfaction which all these things are capable of affording, by itself and separated from the beauty of that arrangement which is fitted to promote it, it will always appear in the highest degree contemptible and trifling. But we rarely view it in this abstract and philosophical light. We naturally confound it in our imagination with the order, the regular and harmonious movement of the system, the machine or oeconomy by means of which it is produced. The pleasures of wealth and greatness, when considered in this complex view, strike the imagination as something grand and beautiful and noble, of which the attainment is well worth all the toil and anxiety which we are so apt to bestow upon it.

And it is well that nature imposes upon us in this manner. It is this deception which rouses and keeps in continual motion the industry of mankind. It is this which first prompted them to cultivate the ground, to build

houses, to found cities and commonwealths, and to invent and improve all
the sciences and arts, which ennoble and embellish human life; which have
entirely changed the whole face of the globe, have turned the rude forests
of nature into agreeable and fertile plains, and made the trackless and barren
ocean a new fund of subsistence, and the great high road of communication to the different nations of the earth. (Smith 1982 [1759], 183–184)

The "deception" of which Smith speaks is quickly transformed into the
invisible hand that we encountered in Chapter 6, which makes self-
interested behavior serve the common good. We all benefit from improvements "which ennoble and embellish life" even if we had no hand ourselves
in promoting them: "They [the improvers] are led by an invisible hand to
the same distribution of the necessaries of life, which would have been
made, had the earth been divided into equal portions among all its inhabitants, and thus without intending it, without knowing it, advance the interest of the society, and afford means to the multiplication of the species"
(Smith 1982 [1759], 184–185).

In short, avarice, greed, and envy are functional in promoting hard work,
accumulation, and economic growth—and thus the fulfillment of absolute
needs as well as relative wants. My efforts to keep up with the Joneses
benefit the whole society. Not only do I benefit from my hard work and
from the capital I accumulate; you, too, benefit from the growth in the stock
of machines and other forms of capital. An enlarged and improved capital
stock increases your productivity even if you work no harder, and higher
productivity allows higher wages as well as greater returns to the owners of
capital—in short, a higher standard of living all around. In the mainstream
account, wages go up in tandem with the increased demand for labor: an
increasing marginal productivity of labor shifts demand upward against an
exogenously given supply. Real wages rise, thanks not to the workers but to
the additional capital goods that accumulation makes available. (Nonmain-
stream accounts differ in terms of the mechanism by which wages increase,
but the result is the same: general prosperity follows from the accumulation
of capital [S. Marglin 1984a].)

It is thus a good thing for society that individuals do not get together to
limit consumption to the fulfillment of absolute wants. In the language of
economics, the positive externalities, the incentive effects of relative wants,
outweigh whatever negative externalities rivalry produces.[9]

But once the age of abundance arrives, envy and similar unsavory motives are no longer functional, and Keynes implicitly assumes that, accordingly, relative needs will fade away. Emulation may continue, but it will be transformed: "We shall honour those who can teach us how to pluck the hour and the day virtuously and well, the delightful people who are capable of taking direct enjoyment in things, the lilies of the field who toil not, neither do they spin" (Keynes 1931 [1930], 372).

Xenos would thus compound Keynes's economism by imputing to him a naive functionalism: once relative needs no longer serve a legitimate social purpose, they will cease to exist. Instead of trying to keep up with the Joneses in the consumption of BMWs and Jacuzzis, we will perhaps try to match Mr. Jones in meditation and Mrs. Jones in awareness of the beauty of the world around us. How the requisite psychological transformation and, dare I say it, spiritual transformation might take place is not even raised as a question, much less answered.

The affinity between Keynes and Marx has been noted, and both are part of a broader tradition of utopian thinking born of the Enlightenment. John Kenneth Galbraith's two-volume magnum opus, *The Affluent Society* (1958) and *The New Industrial State* (1967), is the latest work, and perhaps the last, in this line. Like Marx, Galbraith recognizes that the economy will not wither away just because we possess sufficient resources to fulfill our absolute needs. Galbraith, again like Marx, sees the main obstacle as the power of producers, but for Galbraith it is not the power of the capitalist class but the power of the "technostructure," a group comprising "all who bring specialized knowledge, talent or experience to group decision-making. This, not management, is the guiding intelligence—the brain of—the enterprise" (Galbraith 1967, 71). For this group, status, identity, and creativity—their whole lives, not just their economic well-being—are bound up with the corporation. They will not let go of the very meaning of their lives just because it is in our economic capability to fulfill our absolute needs.

Where Marx saw revolution as the answer, or at least as a precondition for the transformation that would emancipate us from the economy, Galbraith put his faith in the ability of the university to shape the men and women of the future. Scientists and social scientists in particular occupied a critical place in the care and feeding of new recruits to the technostructure. This critical position gives the academic establishment a power and influence disproportionate to its numbers, indeed a power that might be used to subvert the commitment of the technostructure to more (and better) ever more useless things.

Four decades after the publication of *The New Industrial State,* the university has yet to show itself as a plausible white knight that might rescue us from the technostructure, or rather the technostructure from itself. Galbraith's contribution lies not in his proposed solution, but rather in his recognition of noneconomic obstacles to an age of abundance.

Keynes was dead wrong. Economic growth will not lead to the conquest of scarcity. Whether or not absolute needs can be met, relative needs will not conveniently disappear once they are no longer functional in motivating growth and the fulfillment of absolute needs.

Yet Keynes here, as so often is the case, is provocative in the best sense of the term. He leads us to a fundamental question: why are relative needs so deeply embedded in our psyche?[10] To answer this question, we must look at the difference between scarcity in premodern societies and scarcity in the modern world.

The Birth of Scarcity

Keynes may have thought of relative needs as a switch that society turned on to encourage capital accumulation, and through accumulation general prosperity. As a switch that could just as easily be turned off when the work of capital accumulation—providing the economic base for a society that no longer need be preoccupied by the quest for more—was done. Bernard Mandeville, by contrast, saw the role of relative needs much more in terms of generating the aggregate demand necessary to keep the labor force employed, a position Keynes came to embrace in the *General Theory.* But if relative needs reflect consumption as a means to status and respectability, then their role antedates Mandeville and his seventeenth-century predecessors by several hundred years. It was already true in the predawn of modernity that consumption conveyed status.

One salient difference between the premodern and the modern world is that in premodern societies, status is a means to economic goods, whereas in the modern world, economic goods are a means to status. We have a window into understanding this reversal in the attempts of kings and parliaments to suppress the display of finery. According to the medieval historian Sylvia Thrupp, the first English "sumptuary laws," laws controlling what would later be called conspicuous consumption, were enacted in part at least "because fashion was tending to obscure class distinctions" (Thrupp 1989 [1948], 148). Dress was the first and most visible indicator of one's station in life and had previously been governed by norms that assigned different forms of dress to different social orders.[11] By the fourteenth century, these social norms were already failing to enforce dress codes; it was in 1363 that an English monarch first felt it necessary to impose legal prescriptions on matters of dress.[12]

Where did the merchant ever get the idea that he might be as worthy as a knight and, more to the point, entitled to the same show of self-worth? Or the well-to-do peasant the idea that he was as good or better than a down-at-the-heels lord? Why did social inferiors cease to accept their inferiority and begin to proclaim their equality through the way they dressed? I have briefly sketched an answer to these questions in Chapter 5, an answer that hinges on the breakdown of the manorial economy and the feudal polity, the challenge to received wisdom by the Reformation and the challenges of exploration and the beginnings of empire, the elaboration of new technologies for fighting wars and diffusing ideas, and the beginnings of a new economy based on manufacture and centered in towns and cities.

Premodern England is hardly the only example of a society trying to regulate conspicuous consumption through legislation. Many societies, finding the social order threatened by the presumption of nonelites to affect elite manners and behaviors, have experimented with sumptuary laws. These experiments have generally ended in total failure. The reason is that when sumptuary laws are enacted, it is generally the case that an elite is trying to lock up the barn after the horses have been stolen: when it comes to controlling dress and other forms of display, the law is no substitute for the sanctions that face-to-face communities are able to impose.

Communities have an array of weapons, ranging from ridicule to witchcraft, for dealing with those who transgress the unwritten law on appropriate forms of display. The Amish provide an example: their dress code requiring women to wear subdued pastels and men to wear Gothic black has earned them the name of the "plain people." Once again, quaintness conceals an important purpose, in this case maintaining social equality in the face of differing material circumstances. These sanctions are not only negative: maintaining the social order may at times require the opposite of restraint—sumptuous display in order to level out material differences. Feasts such as the potlatch of the Native Americans of British Columbia are a case in point.

The significance of sumptuary laws is not their effect but rather what they tell us about social change: sumptuary laws are a sign of social breakdown, an indication that the internalized regulating mechanism has stopped working, that social sanction no longer is effective. Informal sanctions can work in tight-knit rural communities, where face-to-face relationships enforce these sanctions on a day-to-day basis. And in small towns too: the medieval *bourgeois gentilhomme*, the townsman affecting the airs of a noble, might have been cured of his pretensions by ridicule.[13] But in cities, which in Europe grew rapidly after the fifteenth century, the anonymity of life makes it well-nigh impossible to enforce informal sanctions and leaves no option other than legal prohibitions—even though these too proved ineffective in the end.

Once it ceases to be unthinkable for a bourgeois to appear in public dressed like a noble, the game of controlling display by legislation is up. From then on, the economy offers not only access to goods but a ladder to climb up (or fall down) the social hierarchy. With the breakdown of medieval society, rivalry gets channeled into the economy, not because of human nature but because of the erosion of the social constraints that once limited the role of wealth as a counter in the game of social status.

It is not my contention that scarcity exists only in conjunction with modernity. It is rather that scarcity takes on a specific form in the modern world and comes to dominate our lives. Suppose, for the sake of argument, that the seventeenth-century English philosopher Thomas Hobbes was right when he argued that competition, diffidence (mistrust in today's English), and glory are universals (Hobbes 1968 [1651], chap. 13, 183–188). Suppose, that is, that rivalry is basic to the human condition.[14] Nonetheless, the means by which we compete, the means by which we demonstrate our diffidence, and the means by which we achieve glory vary from society to society. Rivalry may be expressed through oratory or song, mistrust may be expressed through spells and witchcraft, and admiration may be sought through display of physical courage on the battlefield or intellectual adroitness in the seminar room. It is peculiarly modern to channel this rivalry into the economy.

This is not to say that all rivalry is channeled into the economy. The modern era has had its share of war, athletic spectacle, and academic display. Rather, the point is that in modernity the economy emerges as a prime site for the expression of rivalry, as wealth becomes the measure of human worth.

Scarcity and scarcity

There is another important difference between modern and premodern scarcity: scarcity becomes generalized. Isolated and incommensurable scarcities have characterized human existence since time out of mind. Remember Jacob's son, Joseph, who made his name interpreting Pharaoh's dreams and laying up grain against the famine these dreams foretold. In the world of the modern West, we no longer have such scarcities—indeed, the greatest scourge, famine, has long since been eliminated. Instead, we have one big scarcity, Scarcity with a capital S. Scarcity structures our existence: since everything is interconnected, everything is scarce.

How does this interconnection come about? Once consumption becomes relative, the specifics of goods become more important in some ways but less important in others. If you are hungry, no amount of silk or jewelry will answer your need. But if the need is for display, then goods are much more fungible. We may strive to keep up with the Joneses in some dimensions but not in others.

That is part of the story, the demand side so to speak. The other part of the story, the supply side, is the growth in commerce and monetization of the economy, which facilitates the substitution of goods and services for one another. King Midas may have thought he would never lack for consumption goods because he would always be able to exchange his gold for other commodities. The poor fellow was simply ahead of his time. In the modern world, such exchange is indeed possible.

Finally, scarcity becomes Scarcity because the means become available to alleviate Scarcity. This sounds paradoxical, but Karl Marx and Sigmund Freud separately came up with the same explanation of the paradox, albeit at different levels. Karl Marx (1970 [1859], 21) said, "Mankind inevitably sets itself only such tasks as it is able to solve." Freud somewhere made a similar remark, I believe, about individuals undergoing psychoanalysis, to the effect that the ego allows only those problems to emerge that it possesses the capacity to resolve.

Hobbes's war of all against all was in the first instance a struggle over a fixed economic pie. The struggle for power becomes an economic struggle because, according to Hobbes, "The value, or worth of a man, is as of all other things, his price; that is to say, so much as would be given for the use of his power" (1968 [1651], chap. 10, 151). Hobbes's successors, beginning with Locke, finessed this struggle by proposing that the right policy would increase the pie overall, so that everybody could have a bigger piece. The love affair with trickle-down began in earnest, and Growth has been chasing Scarcity ever since. But like the mechanical rabbit at the dog races, Scarcity has always managed to stay comfortably ahead of its pursuer.

There are several things going on here that are worthy of our notice. The first is that only when the engine of production was sufficiently well developed to deliver steady growth could the genie of Scarcity be let out of the bottle. Not until the conditions were in place to meet desire at least halfway could rivalry be safely channeled into the economy.

"Halfway" because growth tames scarcity only to the extent that people compare themselves not with their contemporaries but with their parents or themselves some time back. To this extent, the game of growth is not zero-sum—everybody can be a winner (see B. Friedman 2005 and S. Marglin 1975, 24). Ernest Gellner (1983, 22) calls this "universal Danegeld, buying off social aggression with material enhancement." It was only in the seventeenth century that the European economy became sufficiently oriented toward expansion that god Growth could even pretend to be a match for demon Scarcity.

"Halfway" also because it may be that we are living in a fools' paradise in imagining that growth is a permanent fixture, a secret that we have unlocked rather than a Pandora's box we have opened. The anthropologist George Foster believed that the various social contrivances by which poor peasant communities manage demand in order to keep Scarcity at bay are necessary only because these communities have not figured out how to get the stopper out of the growth genie's bottle (Foster 1965). Once the genie is released, and people see that growth makes for larger slices of the economic pie all around, that growth is a non-zero-sum game, these strategies become unnecessary and, according to Foster, will rightly fall into desuetude. But if the ecological pessimists are right (see Chapter 3), a growth-oriented economy is not the permanent condition of mankind, but a snare and a delusion. Growth is not the god but the demon.

"Halfway" also because producers have found it possible and advantageous to manipulate consumers. The need to keep up with the Joneses is promoted by advertising and other forms of persuasion that together form the peculiarly modern art of salesmanship. Mid-twentieth-century critics like Galbraith may have exaggerated the power of salesmanship, but there can be little doubt that marketing reinforces the demand for goods that we value because others have them. Advertising teaches us what will truly allow us to keep up with the Joneses. In Galbraith's words, "[advertisers] are effective only with those who are so far removed from physical want that they do not already know what they want" (1958, 158).[15]

Finally, "halfway" because growth can be seen not as universal Danegeld but as a pact with the devil to undermine the cohesion of a community in which people know their place (in more ways than one), a community that is not torn apart by the ceaseless striving of its members for more. The Faust legend is perhaps the archetype of the restless striver, who is willing to bargain his soul against the possibility that he might ever, even for a moment, achieve fulfillment of his wants.[16] It is hardly accidental that the Faust legend took shape against the backdrop of early modernity, in which the process of economic growth must have seemed no less magical—and no less dangerous—than alchemy (Watt 1996, chaps. 1–2). Similar tensions have been observed by anthropologists in South America and Africa: in the Cauca Valley of Colombia, a sugarcane worker can supposedly contract with the devil to increase his productivity and wage but at the cost of the health of the land as well as the health of his own body and spirit (Taussig 1980, chaps. 3–7); among the Luo of Kenya, tobacco, a plant traditionally associated with enhancing conversation with the spirits of one's ancestors, produces "bitter" money if it becomes a cash crop (Shipton, 1989).

Modernity and Absolute Needs

The relativity of wants, the generalization of scarcity, and its transformation from scarcity to Scarcity are reasons why scarcity persists in an age of abundance. But this is not the whole story: absolute needs keep growing, too.

Product innovation is one reason. New goods continually come on the market and only gradually diffuse throughout the population. Today's luxury, valued largely for its prestige and enjoyed by a small fraction of the population, becomes tomorrow's necessity, desired—at least at the conscious level—independently of the status it confers. In 1900, a negligible fraction of the American population owned automobiles. By 1989, 83 percent of urban families and 89 percent of rural families owned cars. Three percent of American families had electricity at the beginning of the century, compared with 99 percent in 1960. In 1910, 46 percent of white families and 71 percent of black families in American cities shared a toilet with at least one other family; in 1989, the figure was less than 1 percent for white and black urban dwellers alike. (All figures in this paragraph are from

Lebergott 1993.) These goods have both relative and absolute aspects, but if pressed I would place them all closer to the absolute than the relative pole. And one could go on: the twentieth-century expansion of the array of goods and services on offer would have been incredible to earlier generations.

It would be easy to stop with a technological explanation of the growth of absolute needs, but it would be a mistake to do so. Technology explains supply, but what explains demand? Why, even apart from relative needs, does *stuff* play such an important part in our lives? Here is where the culture of modernity and, in particular, individualism come in. In societies in which the individualistic worldview is the dominant map, commodities—goods and services purchased in the market—become the means of solving existential problems.

One example will serve to illustrate if not to prove this point. It is generally recognized that over much of the last century, cities became increasingly unattractive and undesirable places for living, not to mention for raising a family. Whereas in the nineteenth century, and perhaps even in the first decades of the twentieth, the amenities of urban life improved markedly, by the middle of the past century, cities were becoming increasingly deficient, dirty, and dangerous. The solution, for some at least, was escape to the suburbs. Suburban homes may involve a certain amount of conspicuous consumption, but they also serve absolute needs. In the absence of strong communities, people are unable to take joint action to solve social problems. Lacking "voice," individual "exit" may be the only solution (Hirschman 1970).

Belief in the power of commodities—suburban homes in the present example—need not be simply a form of fetishism nor a form of false consciousness, as Marxists often claim, but a realistic assessment of the available options. The mistake is not the idea that being is based on having, but to suppose that this is the human condition rather than an artifact of the limited range of options available in modern society.

Health care provides perhaps the best example of a good, the consumption of which can grow (and is growing[17]) without apparent limit, but which cannot reasonably be classified as a relative need: no one, to the best of my knowledge, has ever wanted a triple bypass because Mr. Jones down the street just got one, or because advertising seduced him into hankering after the delights of the operating room or the pleasures of convalescence.[18] Part of the explanation is a high rate of innovation on the supply side, but for our purposes it is more to the point to focus on demand, in particular, on what health care tells us about the role of individualism in creating limitless demand.

How do economists analyze the demand side in the health-care sector? Hobbes again led the way: though there may be no agreed-upon ends, no highest good (Hobbes 1968 [1651], 160), *Leviathan* assumes, as Michael Oakeshott has pointed out, that death is the supreme evil (Oakeshott 1991, 250). Indeed, one can read *Leviathan* as a course of instruction in what people might do to avoid untimely death and pain. The obvious difference between then and now is that in Hobbes's day health care did precious little to prolong life no matter the extent of one's resources. Today's economics can plausibly extend the language of trade-offs to include a trade-off between longer life and other goods.

Formally, the problem becomes the choice of an optimal life span. The representative individual maximizes lifetime utility as a function of momentary utility and length of life. At its most simple, momentary utility is expressed as a numerical magnitude associated with each point of time, and lifetime utility is simply the sum of this series of numbers over one's whole life from the starting point at birth to the terminal point at death. Momentary utility depends in turn on two variables, ordinary consumption and health. Consumption goods promote momentary utility directly, while investment in health may (or may not) in the first instance lower momentary utility, but pays back the investment in greater momentary utility and longer life.[19] In this model, the "optimal" time of death for an individual is determined by the combination of consumption and length of life at which lifetime utility is maximized: life span becomes a choice because the individual can allocate his resources between consumption goods and investment in health.

This formulation elides many problems, such as the difference between preventive medicine and treatment that responds to a diagnosis of disease. It also lumps consumption into a single good, despite the considerable evidence of different health consequences of different patterns of consumption. It oversimplifies by ignoring the complex relationships between momentary utility at different moments of time. But for all its simplicity, it captures the way mainstream economics—if not most contemporary individuals, who, after all, are only half-modern at best—approach health-care decisions.[20]

In this model, under plausible assumptions about production, individuals will never be satiated in consumption goods: their nonmedical wants, along with health care, will always outstrip the means of fulfilling these wants. To see this, suppose to the contrary that the utility of the last bit of ordinary consumption (its marginal utility) is zero. At the same time, suppose that investment in health still has a payoff at the margin in terms of either improving momentary utility or extending the period over which a positive momentary utility can be sustained. In the language of economics, the marginal returns from health expenditure exceed the zero marginal return from ordinary consumption. So it pays to reallocate one's budget in the direction of more health care and less ordinary consumption, and to keep on reallocating resources until the marginal returns from health care and ordinary consumption are equal. Thus either the marginal return from health care falls to zero, or the marginal return per dollar of expenditure on ordinary consumption rises to the level of the marginal return on health care as the consumer's budget shifts in the direction of more health care and less consumption of other things. Satiation in one area—defined as the point where the marginal return is zero—can come only at the same time as satiation in the other.

The lesson is that as long as there is a prospect for even very small extensions of life expectancy or improvements in momentary utility by investing in health, satiation will never come either in investment in health care or in consumption of other goods. As long as medical technology improves over time, the returns to health investment will continually grow and provide an attractive outlet for expenditure, which will prevent people from reaching satiation in ordinary consumption goods as well.

This model does not logically rule out the possibility of satiation. The point is rather that satiation cannot come unless and until the possibilities for expanding the reach of medical technology are exhausted. The underlying supply-side assumption is that technical progress in medicine will continue.

It thus sounds like technology, not individualism, is the culprit, if that is the word. To be sure, there is a strong empirical assumption about the "production function" for health,[21] but the conclusions of the standard model depend as much on the framework of the individual weighing investments in health care against consumption as they do on the assumption of a high rate of technological change in health care.

But is there any other way to think about health-care decisions? If technological progress in health care offers an ever-expanding array of interventions, will we not take advantage of them—once we have the resources to do so?

Not necessarily. Suppose the objective is not to maximize lifetime utility but to sustain the community. This is not to suggest a callousness or indifference to individual human life, but a different set of priorities. Conceivably, the individual returns to health-care expenditures might count for little compared with one's sense of obligation to the community. Even if health care were free, undermining the community might be unacceptable.

This is not an exercise in imagination. In Chapter 1, we encountered an Amish couple who let their baby die rather than compromise the independence of their community, a tragic example of another way of viewing health care.

Modernity has created both the possibility and the impossibility of abundance. The possibility part is better understood. Modernity unleashed an unprecedented and unparalleled growth of productivity and thus a potential abundance unimaginable in earlier epochs. It wasn't so long ago that it would have seemed loony to imagine that 1 percent of the population could possibly feed the remaining 99 percent, with quite a bit left over for export. Yet that is the reality in the United States today.[22]

But no matter how productive we become, abundance remains an impossibility so long as wants are boundless. The unboundedness of wants has two sides to it. First, the economic sphere has become a primary site for expressing rivalry, a site in which worth is achieved (and displayed) by wealth. Second, individualism has become the dominant map of social organization.

As a general rule, human societies, including premodern Europe, erect formidable obstacles to expressing rivalry in economic terms. Outside the modern West, it is generally understood, or rather intuited, that economic rivalry imperils social cohesion. The odd man out is the society that took root on English soil in the seventeenth century and has spread to Europe, North America, and beyond in the intervening centuries. As this society developed, it could be (and was) argued that unleashing the forces of growth turned consumption into a non-zero-sum game. Winning no longer meant that someone else must lose. The sanctions that communities are able to impose in order to maintain social cohesion became less and less necessary, as indeed—once individualistic society replaced community—these sanctions became ever less feasible.

The discovery of growth and the erosion of community did more than diminish the necessity as well as the possibility of restricting economic rivalry. The pursuit of wealth actually became a plausible basis for social cohesion, and success in this pursuit became the only distinction that mattered.[23] As the bumper sticker puts it, "Whoever dies with the most toys wins."

Modernity undermines the promise of abundance in another way. Even for goods that are not relative in nature, the individualistic worldview promotes scarcity. As long as commodities are a primary means of solving existential problems, goods will be scarce. Denying, as individualism does, the primacy of relationships, all that's left is stuff. Goods and services in effect substitute for meaningful relationships with family, friends, and community.

No better example exists than health care. As long as good health is a commodity, there is no way—short of a halt in the progress of medical technology—that health care could cease to be scarce within the individualistic worldview. There is no limit on an individual's desire for health care except the other goods he or she has to give up for the sake of better health, so neither health care nor ordinary consumption goods can be superfluous. In this calculus, the claims of the community must get short shrift, and the values that support community will correspondingly atrophy.

But the individualistic calculus itself is not the only way to think about consumption, be it of ordinary goods or of health care. We think about consumption in a particular way because we are the products of a particular history and culture, not because human beings are programmed to think in this way. It is not, as Keynes suggested, that we can rethink the premises of society once we have "enough." Rather, we shall have enough when we rethink the premises of modernity.

CHAPTER 12

The Economics of Tragic Choices

Chapter 3 began with a deal proposed by Lawrence Summers, then a senior World Bank official: Africans could alleviate their hunger by agreeing to absorb the industrial world's pollution, in effect renting garbage-disposal sites to the industrialized countries. Guido Calabresi and Phillip Bobbitt (1978), as well as Martha Nussbaum (2001), call such choices tragic. Michael Walzer (1983) calls them desperate. These scholars all have the same thing in mind: choices where there is no good outcome, where the best outcome is the least of evils. One of Nussbaum's examples is Antigone's choice between subverting the political order and denying her brother the funerary rites necessary for passage to the next world. No good outcome here: Antigone must dishonor her obligation to the state, personified by Creon, or her obligation to her dead brother, Polynices. She chooses Polynices—and pays with her life.

Is Working in a Sweatshop a Tragic Choice?

Do sweatshops qualify as a tragic choice in the realm of economics? Workers, often young women and even children, are obliged to choose from a set of three unattractive choices: (1) long hours in difficult, unhealthy, and sometimes dangerous conditions stitching shoes, clothing, or soccer balls; (2) even more degrading work, like begging or prostitution; or (3) going hungry.

An Oxfam report on how poor women in the paid labor force have fared under globalization points to the toll sweatshop labor has on health and well-being: "Garment factory workers from Bangladesh to Morocco commonly suffer headaches, coughing, vomiting, fever, and physical exhaustion. Poor ventilation in lint-filled rooms can lead to debilitating respiratory diseases. Hired in jobs that demand highly dexterous and repetitive movements, many women suffer joint injuries and back, leg, and shoulder pain."

In sweatshops in the fields, agricultural laborers suffer even greater health risks:

> Pesticide use on farms has an appalling history in some countries. A decade-long study found that members of California's United Farm Workers organization had elevated rates of leukemia and cancers associated with pesticide exposure. A study conducted in a hospital in Rancagua, Chile, between January and September 1993 found that all 90 babies born with neural defects were children of temporary fruit workers. ([Raworth] 2004, 27)

In mainstream theory, these health consequences give rise to a *compensating variation,* a wage premium that balances the deleterious effects on body, mind, and spirit. Is the compensating variation adequate? Defenders of sweatshops argue that the very willingness of individuals to go into sweatshops and continue to work there is conclusive evidence that they regard sweatshops, warts and all, as the best option available.

In fact, economists regard the choice between sweatshops and more dire alternatives as no more tragic than any other. Many years after Summers left the World Bank, he offered the following homily at morning prayers in the chapel of Harvard University, of which he was then serving as president:

> Many believe that it is wrong to buy imported products produced by workers who are paid less than a specified minimum wage of some sort. We all deplore the conditions in which so many on this planet work and the paltry compensation they receive. And yet there is surely some moral force to the concern that as long as the workers are voluntarily employed, they have chosen to work because they are working to their best alternative. Is narrowing an individual's set of choices an act of respect, of charity, even of concern? From this perspective the morality of restrictions on imports or boycotts advocated by many is less than entirely transparent. (Summers 2003)

Sweatshop conditions may be deplorable but still better than the alternatives.

Suppose we accept that individuals freely and knowingly choose to work in sweatshops as the best of a bad lot of alternatives.[1] It is still a leap to the conclusion that the production and distribution of clothes, footwear, and many other goods meets even the minimal goal of efficiency (Pareto optimality in the jargon): the defense of sweatshops makes many doubtful assumptions, beginning with the structural assumptions that economists themselves recognize as necessary for markets to meet (see Appendix A). For starters, these industries are hardly the model of perfect competition that the case for the market presupposes. For another thing, externalities abound. Here is what the Oxfam report had to say about the externality borne by the children of sweatshop workers:

> Some working mothers can only cope with their double duties [housework on top of wage work] by taking their eldest daughters out of school to look after younger children, but the girls lose their chances of a more skilled job in the future. In Morocco, 80 per cent of women with older children had taken daughters under 14 out of school to do so—no wonder that many eventually follow their mothers into the factories. ([Raworth] 2004, 26)

But even if, for the sake of argument, we put to one side the standard objections to sweatshops that come directly out of mainstream theory, defenders of sweatshops are still not home free. Again, from the Oxfam report: "When women migrate for work, they often lose their ties with their traditional communities which had provided support such as childcare, informal credit, and neighbourhood security" ([Raworth] 2004, 28). Not only is there a loss to the individual of an important system of support, but the community itself is weakened as individuals substitute market relationships for community ties.

We already know the economist's response: if people choose to migrate, it must be better for them than the alternatives. As we have seen in earlier chapters, this logic is unassailable—*if* we accept the assumption of the rational, calculating self-interested individual. Within this foundational framework, one assumption leaps out: the idea that sweatshop workers really have agency, that they are players whose choices do not differ in kind from the textbook model of college men and women on a study break choosing between various combinations of pizza and cola; in short, that there is no coercion involved in the process through which people end up in sweatshops.

Why might workers, especially young female workers, lack agency? For one thing, their decisions may be coerced by a parent, husband, or other authority. But maybe not. Maybe they are, as Summers says, "working to their best alternative," freely choosing the sweatshop because the alternatives are so dire. Does the poverty that limits the choice set so drastically count as coercion? Poverty is a constraint, the economist will readily admit, but we are all constrained in our choices by the alternatives available to us, as well as by what we bring to the table in terms of skills and other resources. Poverty is a difference of degree, not a difference of kind.

This is a very strong assumption. Coercion may lie not only in the power of a father or husband, but in the circumstances of choice. In Chapter 4, I argued that in the context of the kind of choice in which there is no good outcome (the example there was trade in hazardous wastes between a rich Californian, Mr. C, and a poor African, Mr. A), it is not by any means obvious that a decision maker has real agency, as assumed in the standard economic account. In a situation where Mr. A must either go hungry or face health risks, the assumption of agency, insofar as it relies on deliberation and calculation, may be misplaced. Note that I say *may* be misplaced. Dire necessity does not inevitably rule out deliberation. But it does change the equation of decision making sufficiently that a burden of proof should attend the assumption that all decisions are the same, that there is a universal logic to choice. It is up to the economist to justify the assumption that tragic choices, particularly those made in the context of dire poverty, differ only in the degree to which scarcity is a constraint—rather than representing a difference in kind.

In standard economics, sweatshops benefit the individual—she would not choose this kind of work if it didn't. But sweatshops benefit the larger world as well. Not only do they provide consumers in the rich countries with cheap apparel and other goods; they provide people in the poor countries the opportunity to accumulate capital, improve skills, and learn the discipline necessary for industrial work. Everybody—workers as well as capitalists—benefits from the new investment that sweatshop profits make possible, and from more skill and better discipline. As Chapter 11 suggested (in arguing that relative wants promote growth by stimulating effort), the benefits of capital accumulation will eventually trickle down to all workers. Higher levels of capital improve worker productivity just as do higher skill levels and greater discipline, and higher productivity eventually leads to higher wages, so workers generally benefit. The externalities are positive.

This is not just the economic theory of the academy. Nicholas Kristof, who covered Asia before becoming an op-ed columnist for the *New York Times,* and his wife Sheryl WuDunn, also a distinguished journalist, published one of the more thoughtful accounts of sweatshops in the *New York Times Sunday Magazine* a few years back. Here is their take on the sweatshop as an engine of accumulation:

> The truth is, those grim factories in Dongguan and the rest of southern China contributed to a remarkable explosion of wealth. In the years since our first conversations there, we've returned many times to Dongguan and the surrounding towns and seen the transformation. Wages have risen from about $50 a month to $250 a month or more today. Factory conditions have improved as businesses have scrambled to attract and keep the best laborers. (Kristof and WuDunn, 2000)

So there is a case to be made for sweatshops: new opportunities are created for both the individual and the society. In the economist's view of the world, the decision to work in a sweatshop is no different from any other economic choice, and the sufferings of sweatshop workers, however deplorable, do not count as tragedy. In a word, there is no tragic choice involved.

Case closed? It all depends on what constitutes the tragedy. The standard interpretation of Antigone's tragedy is the absence of any course of action that preserves both the political order and the divine order, and analogously the tragedy of the sweatshop worker is the absence of any course of action that preserves physical well-being and a modicum of human dignity and spirit. But perhaps the real tragedy in both cases lies elsewhere: in Antigone's case, in the failure of the political order to conform to the divine order;[2] in the case of sweatshops, in an economics—and an economy—based on individualism, rational calculation, unlimited wants, and the nation-state. Yes, this economy makes it possible for a Chinese, Haitian, or Bangladeshi to earn more than she might absent sweatshops, but it is also this economy and its justification in economics that makes it necessary for her to work long hours in unpleasant, and often unhealthy and unsafe, conditions, to subject herself to the arbitrary authority of bosses who daily give new meaning (or perhaps simply revive old meanings) to the word "exploitation."

The real tragedy is that at little cost to consumers in the rich nations, who form the market for sweatshop products, the choices of these workers could be transformed into nontragic choices. I observed in Chapter 6 that the Californian in a hypothetical trade in hazardous wastes will have no qualms about his African counterpart who is obliged to accept pollution to avoid hunger—as long as Mr. C is guided by self-interest. By contrast, if we endow

Mr. C with a modicum of ethical sensitivity, he might well see an obligation to his fellow human being to help him avoid hunger and pollution. The problem with a market in pollution is not Mr. A's participation; whether or not we call it coercion, Mr. A may have little effective choice. The problem, rather, lies with Mr. C's participation in this market without accepting responsibility for the consequences, without doing the little that would be necessary to transform tragic into nontragic choices.

Consider this: athletic shoes are a $15 billion business in the United States. At the turn of this century, over 100 million pairs were bought for American children (*Washington Post* 2002, 4). An $80 pair of sneakers includes perhaps $3.00 of wages for a worker in China, South or Southeast Asia, or the Caribbean—less than 4 percent of the total price. The rest is materials (say $11), rent and other operating costs of the factory owner (another $3.00), and the profits of the factory owner (another $2.00 or so). All this brings the cost to Nike (or Adidas or any of the smaller athletic shoe manufacturers) to $18. Then there are the costs of promoting and advertising the brand and developing the next wave of athletic shoes, as well as the cost of distributing the shoes to the retailer (about $13 in all), taxes ($1.50), and operating profits (another $6.50). This brings the cost to the retailer up to about $39: the $18 that Nike or its competitors pay for the finished shoe plus some $21 of "value added" promoting, advertising, and developing the brand. The rest, approximately half the total, is the retailer's costs and profits: rent, salaries and wages, other operating costs, and operating profits (maybe $10 for each of the four categories). Add another $1.00 of taxes and we've reached the $80 price tag. The cost breakdown appears in Table 12.1.

Nike, which has been much attacked for its labor practices—unfairly in the company's view—has responded to criticism. After breaking down the costs of a pair of its shoes (in more or less the same fashion as I have just done), Nike poses—and answers—the question that troubles noneconomists:

Q&A: Why not simply double the wages of the worker? As with any other cost, changes in wages can have a significant effect on the cost of the product and ultimately on the amount of the product produced and sold. . . .

These increased costs would have to be passed on to consumers in the form of higher prices. Since the market for athletic footwear responds to the laws of supply and demand, higher prices would likely mean fewer units sold. Of course Nike's shareholders would earn less money. But lower sales

Table 12.1 Where the Money Goes: How the Costs of an $80 Pair of Athletic
Shoes Are Divvied Up

At the factory in Asia		
Wages	$ 3.00	
Materials	10.00	
Other operating costs	3.00	
Operating profits	2.00	
= Cost to manufacturer		$18.00
At the manufacturer (Nike, Adidas, etc.)		
Advertising, etc.	13.00	
Operating profits	6.50	
Taxes	1.50	
= Cost to retailer		39.00
At the retail store in the United States		
Salaries and wages	10.00	
Rent	10.00	
Other operating costs	10.00	
Operating profits	10.00	
Taxes	1.00	
= Cost to consumer		$80.00

Sources: This cost breakdown is my synthesis of two documents: data for 2001 from
"Labor Practices," from Nike's *Fiscal Year 2001 Corporate Responsibility Report* (Nike, Inc.
2001, 12) and more detailed data for 1995 from *Washington Post* 2002, 7.

also mean fewer jobs and lower earnings for Nike suppliers, employees and
factory workers. (Nike, Inc. 2001, 12)

There is certainly some truth to this response, but it is misleading to lump
Nike owners, suppliers, employees, and factory workers together as a group
for whom higher wages necessarily means lower earnings. For the stockholders, Nike's suppliers, and its U.S. employees, it is true that a wage increase for the shoe stitchers well may reduce sales if it is passed on to the customers. (The economist will point out that if a rise in price did not reduce
sales now or in the future, presumably Nike would have already increased
prices—that is the logic of profit maximization.) Consumers who find it difficult to choose between Nike and Adidas might find an extra $3.00 in the
price of Nikes enough to tip them toward the competition. And even Nike
loyalists might decide to buy new shoes less frequently, preferring to purchase

more of other things as the relative price of Nikes climbs. So, yes, higher prices predictably will lead to lower sales. And this may eventually mean fewer Americans will be needed to sell and distribute Nikes. As well as lower sales and profits for the factory owners who produce the shoes in Indonesia or China, not to mention lower profits and lower returns to Nike stockholders.

But the situation is very different for the factory workers, who, we are assuming, would earn twice as much money. It would take a tremendous reduction in sales to offset this windfall, a 50 percent reduction to be precise. In fact, though Nike's market share has varied greatly over the years, it has always been the predominant player, with close to half the total U.S. sales of running shoes in 2006;[3] it is far from a price taker in a competitive market for whom a price increase would mean the total loss of its market. So it is more than a bit disingenuous to imply that Indonesian or Haitian factory workers would, like other categories of stakeholders, lose out if their wages were increased.

This hardly clinches the argument for higher wages. Nike can still argue, along with Calvin Coolidge, Milton Friedman, and other votaries of the market, that the business of business is business, that Nike's obligations are to its stockholders, that Nike's management would be failing in its fiduciary duty if it were to transfer income from its owners to its workers, perhaps especially remiss since the Asian and Latin American workers are not even Nike employees, but the employees of its suppliers. There is nothing to prevent a North American from donating $3.00 to a fund for Indonesian shoe stitchers along with the purchase of a pair of athletic shoes. Customers, and indeed shareholders as well, can contribute to charity if they are so moved, but with their own money rather than with company funds. This way the impulse to charity does not affect the efficiency of the market as an allocative device, does not interfere with the ability of the market to direct resources to their highest valued uses.

And what makes the critic think that the Haitian who is lucky enough to get a job as a shoe stitcher is the most needy? It was a left-of-center economist who once said that, for the poor, the only thing worse than being exploited by capitalism was not being exploited. If one feels moved to help the poor of Haiti, why not contribute to the poor who don't manage to land sweatshop jobs rather than to their relatively well-off brothers and sisters who do?

In short, the concern of consumers, particularly younger consumers, for the people who make the products is either irrelevant or downright harmful to the proper functioning of the economy. Charity belongs to a separate sphere, a sphere that ends at the doorstep of the market.

This way of looking at sweatshop wages and working conditions obviously has no room for the Fair Labor Association, which monitors suppliers to the garment and footwear companies for compliance with the companies' codes of conduct. Or for the fair trade initiative, which for some years has attempted to provide a floor price for small coffee growers and is now expanding into chocolate and bananas, and even into manufactured goods, starting with soccer balls. This way of looking at sweatshops is something else too: a reflection of the poverty of economics.

Fair Trade as a Search for Community

Coffee is instructive. The fair trade initiative offered small growers a floor price of approximately $1.25 per pound for conventional arabica[4] and $1.40 for organic arabica at a time when prices received by growers were less than half that level. Should the producer price of coffee rise above the floor, a small premium of $0.05 per pound is still paid to the grower.

The price for so-called green or unroasted coffee has fallen dramatically since the United States pulled out of the international coffee agreement as the Cold War was coming to an end. The price of arabica on the New York Coffee Exchange fell from over $1.20 per pound in the last years of the international agreement to less than $0.50 per pound in the first years of the twenty-first century. (The price has improved since, but it has been forecast to remain below $1.00 for the next decade [Lewin et al. 2004, 15].)

The producer does not receive the full value of the coffee on the New York exchange. Typically, it costs something like $0.25 per pound to clean, dry, and ship coffee from the farm to the roaster in the United States or Europe, and most of these activities, even the ones that could be done by the grower (like cleaning and drying) are normally carried out by the local middleman or the exporter, who captures for himself the value added. With the New York Coffee Exchange price at $1.25, the grower may get as much as $1.00; when the price falls to $0.50 on the New York exchange, the grower may get only $0.25. (My figures are rough and ready: there is surprisingly little data on the actual distribution of the dollar value of a pound of coffee delivered in New York, London, or Rotterdam. And there is, of course, considerable variation, depending on the distance of the grower from a port, the intensity of competition among middlemen, and related factors. But these figures, however imprecisely, convey the relevant magnitudes.)

Meanwhile, retail prices in the United States are about the same today as when the international coffee agreement fell apart in 1989, around $3.00 per pound. In effect, the cost of processing, promoting, and selling coffee once it arrives on U.S. shores has risen from less than $2.00 per pound to $2.50 per pound, in line with the general increase of 50 percent in consumer prices over the period from 1989 to 2005. The result is that the grower's share declined from about one-third to less than one-tenth, better than the shoe stitcher's 4 percent share of the price of a pair of Nikes, but shockingly low by historical standards, not to mention by a standard of survival of the coffee producers, their families, and their communities. Doubling the income of the grower, the price floor adds only a small percentage—perhaps 15 percent—to the price paid by the consumer.

The underlying cause of low market prices is the breakdown of the International Coffee Agreement, which the United States and other capitalist nations supported as a way of buying the allegiance of coffee-producing countries in the Cold War. With the fall of the Soviet Union came an end to the export quotas that were the principal means for maintaining a balance between supply and demand. Coffee production expanded rapidly both in old coffee-producing countries like Brazil and in new ones like Vietnam. The new plantations are extremely productive.[5] In an interview with Oxfam, a coffee trader observed: "To give you an idea of the difference, in some areas of Guatemala, it could take over 1000 people working one day each to fill the equivalent of one container of 275 bags, each bag weighing 69 kg. In the Brazilian cerrado, you need five people and a mechanical harvester for two or three days to fill a container. One drives, and the others pick" ([Gresser and Tickell] 2002, 18).

Against this background, paying a premium seems to economists just the wrong strategy. The world needs less coffee, but the signal fair trade sends—a price higher than the market will accept—is one calculated to induce more coffee production. In the economist's view, the only saving grace of fair trade is its negligible impact: fair trade accounted for something like one-half of one percent of coffee consumption in the United States in 2002, and only 4 percent in the Netherlands, where the movement was born some two decades ago (Lewin et al. 2004, tables 7, 43, and 123). If free trade were to succeed in capturing a significant proportion of the market, then—according to the logic of economics—a premium price would be nothing short of disaster.

As Brink Lindsey of the market-friendly Cato Institute observes, things are already difficult enough:

> The story of the current coffee glut is at bottom a story of falling costs and productivity improvements on both the supply and the demand sides. In other words, the coffee market is delivering what markets are supposed to deliver—economic progress. Admittedly, it is never pleasant for market incumbents to be displaced by more efficient new entrants, and such displacement can be especially painful when those incumbents live in poor countries that offer few alternative livelihoods. [In Peru and Colombia the "alternative livelihood" is growing coca—the raw material for cocaine—to which coffee growers are turning in increasing numbers.] But creative destruction lies at the very heart of the market process; it is not a market failure. (Lindsey 2003, 5)

Fair trade can only make matters worse. For Lindsey, fair trade is simply one more "activist campaign to browbeat roasters and retailers into carrying products that consumers don't want" (Lindsey 2003, 7). So retail prices will increase, and unsold coffee will pile up on retailers' shelves—while growers get a (false) signal to produce more coffee.

This analysis may be straightforward Economics 101, but it misses the point of an initiative like fair trade. People might react to a price increase that feeds the bottom line of the roasters and processors by buying less coffee, as textbooks say they will. This corresponds to moving up a negatively inclined demand curve. But the same consumers, or some of them anyway, might be willing to spend more for coffee when the extra expenditure feeds the families of coffee growers—an outward shift of the entire demand curve. The evidence? First of all, the rapid growth of fair trade and allied initiatives in coffee and other goods suggests that some consumers react differently to price increases associated with raising the incomes of producers than standard theory predicts (Lewin et al. 2004, 123). This conclusion is also borne out by polls—for example, a *US News and World Report* poll, which indicated that 70 percent of Americans would be willing to pay "a few dollars more per item" for goods not made under sweatshop conditions (December 16, 1996, quoted in Varney 1998, 3).

The whole point of fair trade is to elicit a response from the consumer based on solidarity with producers, a pole apart from an economics that understands consumers in terms of the calculation of individual self-interest. From the economist's perspective, as has been observed, fair trade mixes up two things that ought to be kept separate, charitable redistribution and efficiency. But in terms of its own perspective, fair trade introduces a whole new dimension into the analysis, a dimension that cannot be comprehended within standard economics.

In short, the idea behind fair trade is that consumers will pay more for their coffee if it comes with a credible commitment that the lion's share of the price increase will end up in the hands of the growers rather than flowing to the bottom line of Procter & Gamble (Folgers) or Kraft (Maxwell House). In the jargon of economics, the right question is not how much a price increase would reduce coffee sales along a negatively inclined demand curve, but how much sales would change when a price increase is coupled with an outward shift in the demand curve. To the extent the fair trade movement is successful in stimulating demand for fair trade coffee, the signal to producers is that there is indeed a market for their coffee at premium prices—prices that will sustain the grower, the grower's family, and the grower's community.

There is more than one way to understand the willingness of (some) consumers to pay more for coffee or bananas or athletic shoes when these commodities are produced in conditions that provide something approaching a decent standard of living for the producers themselves. It is possible, for example, to cast the argument in more or less individualistic terms, in a language of human rights to which nobody steeped in Immanuel Kant's individualism could object (see Chapter 4). But I believe the motivations underlying consumers' participation in fair trade efforts go beyond the individualistic. If the motivation were simply one of abstract human rights, there would be no reason or need to personalize the producers. But, in point of fact, promoters of fair trade and the like go to considerable efforts to make the producers and their communities real to consumers, to foster a sense of relationship between the consumer and producer.

In my judgment, the fair trade movement is tapping into something very important. Benefit–cost analysis includes a large literature on the difference between the way people implicitly value a "statistical" life, meaning the life of a random member of a population class, like "motorist" or "coal miner," and the way the same people implicitly value an "identifiable" life, like the life of a little girl named Jennie trapped in an abandoned well.[6] Identifying a fellow human being implies some kind of relationship, and relationship is the basis of community.

It may seem a stretch to suggest that consumers in North America or Europe are searching for community with the Bangladeshi shoe stitcher or the

Peruvian coffee grower. Why would people expect to bond with the woman who stitches the shoes they wear or the man who grows the coffee they drink in the morning? My answer is that in a world starved for community, people look for connection in odd places. This search need not even be at a conscious level, but without this element it seems to me hard to make sense of the fair trade and antisweatshop movements, especially when it is recognized that the victims of low commodity prices and low wages may be less deprived than their fellow countrymen who don't have land to grow coffee or access to sweatshop jobs.

We favor the people who tend to our needs over those who (having missed out on capitalist exploitation) might be more needy for the same reason—a sense of connection—that we favor our own children despite the fact that they are unlikely to be the most needy. Indeed, we would think ourselves lacking in human emotion if we were to treat all children symmetrically in economic terms regardless of how close our connection to them, if we were to deprive our own children in order to free up resources for the children of the slums of Port-au-Prince or Calcutta, who are prima facie more lacking in material goods.

I am struck by the similarity of motives of the university students (and others) who support initiatives like fair trade and the motives of the Harvard University students who supported the living wage movement some years back, some of them to the point of risking punishment by occupying the offices of the university administration. The premise of the living wage movement is that workers ought to receive high enough wages to support an adult worker and a child at a level above the poverty line. Until 2001, when the sit-in at Harvard took place, the principal successes of the movement were in getting various municipalities across the country to enact ordinances requiring service providers for these cities to pay wages that would allow a single worker to support a family of two or three at the poverty level (Pollin and Luce 1998). The Harvard students demanded similar treatment for Harvard workers and the workers of companies that hold maintenance, repair, and construction contracts with the university.

Economists, with rare exceptions, reacted predictably. Greg Mankiw, later to become chair of the Council of Economic Advisers under George W. Bush, first questioned whether higher wages would actually be good for workers— because fewer workers would be hired at a higher wage, especially workers at the bottom of the employment ladder holding the low-skilled jobs that the living wage movement targeted. But Mankiw's trump card echoed the argument that a business like Nike owes its allegiance to its owners, not to other stakeholders. Harvard has a fiduciary duty to its donors, who give money for educating its students, not for ameliorating the lives of its workers:

> The living-wage protest raises the issue of Harvard's mission in society. The benefactors who give to the University do so to support education, not income redistribution. (And if Harvard were to take up the cause of income redistribution, it would have to acknowledge that even the poorest workers in Cambridge [Massachusetts, where Harvard is located] are rich by world standards.) Harvard needs to pays its workers—janitors and professors alike—enough to attract and motivate them. But it shouldn't pay more than it needs to. . . . To do so would compromise the University's commitment to the creation and dissemination of knowledge. (Mankiw 2001, 70)

Once again, this misses the point. In the economist's worldview, in which there is a strict separation between efficiency and redistribution, paying a living wage might indeed "compromise the University's commitment to the creation and dissemination of knowledge." But the students were implicitly rejecting the premises of the economist's argument. The students were not asking for charity for the people who clean their bathrooms, serve their food, and sweep their floors, so it is not to the point to argue that there are more needy folk elsewhere in the world. Rather than asking for charity, the students were expressing their solidarity with these workers, searching for a bond between themselves as children of privilege and the people whose menial work facilitates their privileged existence, searching for community across a sea of economic, social, and cultural difference. Naive? Illusory? Perhaps, but nonetheless a strong indictment of the claim that the premises of mainstream economics are universal.

The Devil in the Details

There is plenty of room for discussion about the details of the antisweatshop movement, fair trade, and related initiatives. Does fair trade adequately address the lopsided division of value along the supply chain? Is the distributional problem the consequence of processing and distribution being concentrated in a few hands whereas the shoe stitchers, shirt makers, and coffee growers are unorganized and operate in markets that resemble more closely the "perfect" competition of the economics text? Should solidarity be expressed by a general boycott of goods from countries that allow sweatshops?

Are roasters who include a modest amount of fair trade coffee in their product mix to be congratulated (on the theory that half a loaf, or even 10 percent of a loaf, is better than none) or castigated (on the theory that these roasters are talking the talk but not walking the walk, opportunistically gaining legitimacy from their association with the fair trade movement)? Is child labor an absolute taboo?

These are difficult questions. The first question is the lopsided division of the value of a pair of athletic shoes or a pound of coffee: the shoe stitcher gets $3.00, and everybody else along the way gets $77.00; the coffee grower gets a larger share, but it is at best a relatively small percentage of the retail price of a pound of coffee and an even smaller percentage of coffee sold by the cup. Even if fair trade doubles the wages of the shoe stitcher, she still would be getting less than 8 percent of the total value of the product; even if fair trade brings the grower's price of coffee up to $1.25 per pound, he would be lucky to get one-third of the total value.

What justifies such a distribution of the pie? Why aren't the needs of producers factored into the prices of commodities? Once again, ordinary folk and economists part company. People who have not been washed in the blood of Economics 101 are deeply troubled by these questions; economists consider them naive. Standard economics posits a competitive labor market, with the result that markets distribute value according to "marginal productivity": people are rewarded according to their contribution to the production process. If the Bangladeshi shoe stitcher receives 4 percent of the price of a pair of athletic shoes, it is because that is what her labor is worth. That's the demand side. She accepts this wage because she has no better alternative. That's the supply side. (If her labor were worth more, shoe manufacturers would bid her wages up. If she had better alternatives, she would not work for sweatshop wages.)

Marginal productivity theory, as noted in Chapter 10, is a powerful theory based on dubious assumptions of competitive labor markets and an exogenously given labor force. Without these "auxiliary" assumptions, marginal productivity theory reduces to profit maximization and is compatible with a very different logic of wage determination, one in which community is central.

I believe a similar argument applies to the distribution of value across the supply chain of a pair of athletic shoes or a pound of coffee. Productivity determines the size of the pie, but not how it is distributed. Distribution, once again, depends on a host of factors we might sum up as community standards. But the issue raised in Chapter 10 has to be faced here as well: what, or rather who, constitutes the community?

The answer implicit in the actual determination of the distribution of value, absent fair trade, is that there is no community that binds sweatshop worker or coffee grower to other agents in the supply chain or to consumers: there are therefore no transnational community standards to invoke on behalf of the sweatshop worker or the coffee grower like those that guaranteed a British worker circa 1850 a loaf of white bread as a matter of right, or an American worker circa 1950 an automobile as a matter of right. In the absence of community among producers and consumers, there is nothing but the local community, constrained by local productivity, to prevent the returns to labor from falling to the level of the opportunity costs of Third World people, who, needless to say, have precious few opportunities. That is, what I termed a "conventional wage" in the discussion of wage determination within a national community may still be relevant, but it is a wage determined by the conventions of Bangladesh or Peru rather than by a convention emerging from international solidarity. (Marginal productivity in shoe or coffee production enters into the demand for Third World labor, as marginal productivity enters into the demand for labor in the United States or Europe, but with virtually unlimited supplies of labor at the conventional wage, demand affects the level of employment rather than the wage itself.)

Fair trade puts the question of community front and center. If the appeal of fair trade is bound up with the idea of creating community with those who produce the goods and services on which we rely, then the very logic of fair trade ought to lead to a community that transcends national borders and to a very different income distribution.

Chapter 10 introduced the notion of the nation as "imagined community" (B. Anderson 1983). But the nation is not the only possible imagined community; religious groups with scattered memberships—Muslims, Jews, Christians, and no doubt others—have long wrestled with the issue of defining "imagined" communities (see J. Marglin 2006, chap. 3, for one example, the community imagined by Jews finding themselves between tradition and modernity in Morocco circa 1900). It is a leap, but not an impossible one, to imagine a community of producers and consumers across national borders.

How far consumers or, for that matter, producers—Americans, Europeans, or citizens of other rich countries—involved in the supply chain are willing to follow this logic is an open question. It is one thing for a consumer to be willing to pay an additional $3.00 for a pair of Nikes or $0.75

more for a pound of coffee. It is quite another to consider the Bangladeshi shoe stitcher or the Peruvian coffee grower as entitled to a decent level of living by our own standards of decency, to include the education of the Bangladeshi's children or the health care of the Peruvian's in the calculus of a conventional wage. It is too early to tell whether the idea of a community of consumers and producers across national borders is an idea whose time has come or a utopian vision.

Needless to say, community is not the only lens through which to view the problem of distribution. Earlier, I asked whether the actual distribution of the value embodied in athletic shoes or coffee is the consequence of market power—one alternative to seeing the problem in terms of community. There is no question that powerful companies like Nike and Procter & Gamble occupy key positions in the supply chain that begins with the raw materials and ends with the finished product, and it is plausible that their market power allows the Nikes and Procter & Gambles of the world to capture a disproportionate share of product value in the form of oligopoly profits. (Oligopoly is the economist's term for a market with few sellers.) If so, the remedy is to challenge the market power of the oligopolists, perhaps with the countervailing power of producers' associations or trade unions.[7]

In my view, oligopoly is part of the problem, but not the biggest part. I do not say this to defend Nike and its ilk, but to argue that the problem lies less in oligopoly than in the differences between wages, salaries, and the returns to property of all kinds (including intangibles like knowledge) in the countries in which apparel makers and coffee growers work and live and the levels of productivity and income at the end stages of the chain of value. My assertion, in other words, is that the excess profits of oligopolies—excess relative to the economist's standard of a competitive return—are small relative to the differences in income levels between, on the one hand, Europe, North America, and Japan and, on the other, the poor countries of the world where coffee is grown and apparel is manufactured, and it is the difference in income levels across countries that accounts for most of the difference between how much of the value of a product ends up in one place and how much ends up in another. An agricultural laborer in the High Amazon of Peru may be lucky to get $3.00 per day, as compared with a federal minimum wage in the United States of $5.85 per hour. According to Nike's own statistics, in dollar terms a worker in a Nike factory in the United States makes twenty times the earnings of her Indian counterpart and six times the earnings of her Peruvian counterpart (Nike, Inc. 2001, 11). Advertising costs big bucks. Mall rents have to be paid. It is these differences rather than Nike's profits that account for the lion's share of the difference between the small amount of value added up to the time products reach the shores of the United States and the large amount of value added from the time products are unloaded at the dock to when they reach the consumer. According to the estimates for athletic footwear, over three-quarters of the purchase price of $80 represents "value added" within the United States, and of this three-quarters, hardly one-quarter—20 percent of the total price—represents the operating profit of both Nike and the retailer. This 20 percent is hardly negligible, but it is not the lion's share of the lion's share.[8]

This suggests that despite superficial resemblances, movements like fair trade should not be assimilated to trade unions or producers' cartels, the principal aim of which is to raise prices and ration the (reduced) demand among the union or cartel members, in effect to redistribute value along the chain that links producers to each other and to consumers. The aim of fair trade is less to redistribute income from Nike or Nestlé to the shoe stitcher or coffee grower than to create new value in the solidarity between the consumer and the stitcher or grower. If such movements are to succeed, they must be able to raise demand for nonsweatshop athletic shoes or fair trade coffee. It remains to be seen, I have suggested, how far it is practical to take this process.

Clearly some control over production would be necessary; the potential supply of coffee or athletic shoes at prices that allow producers what we in the consuming countries consider a decent standard of living far exceeds the available demand. And this leads inevitably to some odd results. Such as denial of fair trade status to coffee plantations that would, transplanted to the world of sweatshops, be beacons of virtue. In 2002, Bradley Meacham reported in the *Seattle Times:* "The 200 workers at Eddy and Mausi Kuhl's coffee farm [in Nicaragua] are paid living wages and have homes with electricity, running water and concrete floors. They help make decisions about the operation of the 560-acre farm, and their 400 dependents receive benefits, including an on-site school and health clinic" (Meacham 2002, E-1).

Why would such an enlightened enterprise be excluded from the benefits of fair trade certification? Because certification is limited to cooperatives and excludes large growers like the Kuhls. To be sure, the umbrella organization of the fair trade movement, Fairtrade Labelling Organizations International (FLO; www.fairtrade.net), deals with large employers in other product areas such as bananas and soccer balls; indeed, FLO has two sets of standards, one tailored for small farmers, the other for large employers such as factories and plantations. But in coffee it draws the line, including small farmer cooperatives within the privileged circle and excluding large producers such as the Kuhls, regardless of how worker friendly, or eco-friendly, they might be.

This may appear arbitrary, but it makes more sense on reflection. For some goods, the reality is that production takes place in large units: the benefits of fair trade can reach the folks at the bottom of the chain of value only if large production units based on wage labor are included. For other goods, of which coffee is a leading example, large and small production units coexist. Indeed, small units are the norm, at least for the higher quality, shade-grown arabicas that dominate the specialty coffee market. This, together with the reality that only a small fraction of the eligible coffee is actually sold at fair trade prices,[9] makes the small-farmer bias more understandable. Yes, it is ideological—it reflects the republican ideology of Thomas Jefferson, who saw an economic democracy of small farmers and craftsmen as the only sure basis for political democracy.

Ideology notwithstanding, in a world in which the demand for fair trade coffee exceeded the supply, there need be no circle that would limit who is chosen; fair trade certification would be open to the Kuhls as well as to the proprietor of a two-hectare plot, as long as the benefit of higher prices reached the target population. In the world as it is, if fair trade certification represents the difference between bare survival and a decent life for the small farmer—by the standards of the farmer's own community if not of ours—it makes ethical sense to extend the benefits of fair trade to him (or her) before turning one's attention to the large plantation.

Should solidarity with workers in poor countries be expressed through a general boycott of the exports of these countries when their governments fail to enforce standards of wages or working conditions? To pose the question in these terms is almost to answer it. A general boycott is like hunting ducks with an elephant gun. As its name implies, a general boycott is totally unselective, punishing the innocent along with the guilty, and above all punishing the worker along with the sweatshop owner.

Collective punishment may be acceptable when there is no other way of bringing about compliance and when governments are capable of enforcing compliance with wage and other labor standards. But both premises are shaky. Monitoring by Nike and others is difficult and expensive but not impossible, so the premise that there is no other way of securing compliance may not hold. And governments may lack the resources (as well as the will) to improve working conditions, so the second premise may not hold either. In short, it seems there is generally a better way to show solidarity than broad boycotts, and in practice nongovernmental organizations active in the antisweatshop movement prefer monitoring individual factories to outright countrywide bans on imports.

What about the question of whether to keep at arm's length the large roasters with only a fraction of their coffee labeled fair trade? This kind of purity with regard to the roaster's commitment seems to me a virtue the movement can hardly afford. A foot in the door of a large roaster like Procter & Gamble or a medium-sized roaster like Green Mountain is tremendously important to promoting the fair trade idea, not only for coffee but for a whole spectrum of goods. It is up to the movement rather than up to the roasters to build demand for fair trade—demand to which I have no doubt the large- and medium-sized roasters will respond. Here, the logic of the film *Field of Dreams*, "if you build it, they will come," is wishful thinking. The right logic is "if you come, they will build it." If consumers want fair trade coffee and are willing to pay the extra few cents, the roasters will provide the coffee. Case in point: Procter & Gamble announced in the fall of 2003 that it would add fair trade–certified coffee to its offerings.

Child labor is perhaps the most vexing problem. I have many questions about a school curriculum that, on purpose or not, promotes the mainstream economist's view of the world as composed of calculating self-interested individuals, but I have no doubt that a modern education, even with all its cultural biases, is part of the package of survival of noneconomistic modes of understanding the world and being in the world. Yet even families who fervently wish to preserve their own view of the world while recognizing the need for the survival skills that come with formal education might send their children to labor in field or factory instead of to school. Most, faced with what is among the most tragic of choices a parent faces, do so to eke out survival for the family. The solution, however, is not to ban child labor, which critics of antisweatshop movements rightly point out will simply drive children into even worse occupations than stitching soccer balls or sewing shirts—begging and prostitution for starters.

Is it reasonable to hope that a significant increase in children's wages might relieve the burden of this tragic choice and trust the market to provide a good—education—for which there would, in consequence of higher wages, be increased demand? I am not terribly optimistic about such a market solution. For many families who send their children to work for a pittance sewing soccer balls or shirts or shoes, the gap between resources and needs is so great that even a substantial increase in wages would not change the parents' choice: indeed, the so-called substitution effect, according to which child labor becomes a relatively more attractive option the better paid it is, works in the opposite direction.

Here it seems to me that a better approach than an outright ban is to require employers of child labor to provide schooling for their young employees. Large employers might be required to provide schools on the factory premises, smaller employers to band together to construct and operate schools that would be accessible to the children, with released time (compensated by the employer) for school attendance.

Evidently such a project is not likely to be undertaken by a single country. If India were to institute such a policy, Bangladesh and Pakistan would be able to undercut India's costs of production since their "fringe benefits" would be substantially lower. But if Nike or FLO were to require schools as a condition of doing business, no country would have a competitive advantage: all would be faced with the same additional costs.

This would not be a light undertaking. The requirements of physical infrastructure, of teachers, not to mention the need for enforcement, dizzy the mind. But as an alternative both to condemning yet another generation of poor children to go without education and to condemning them and their families to go hungry, school-plus-work merits consideration.

These brief comments hardly begin to address, much less do justice to, the myriad issues that initiatives to transcend the market must contend with. It does, I hope, put some flesh on an otherwise abstract debate about the limits of the market.

Viewed from the perspective of an alternative economics, the proposals of the fair trade movement, the antisweatshop movement, and the like appear very different from the straw men set up by people who have never met a market they didn't like. These initiatives are not about denying choice to the poor of Latin America, Africa, and Asia, but about changing the array of choices so that the people who make our apparel and grow our food do not have to choose between having a job and worker safety, between being able to buy medicines for their aged parents and worker dignity, between feeding their kids and educating them. These movements are about giving priority to a holistic vision, a vision in which, as John Donne, chaplain to James I of England and dean of St. Paul's Cathedral, put it, "No man is an island entire of itself; every man is a piece of the continent, a part of the main" (Donne 1975 [1624], Meditation 17). These movements are about giving priority to a vision in which duty, particularly our duty to those who labor for us, rather than self-interest, guides our actions; about giving priority to feelings of connectedness to the shoe stitcher and the coffee grower over calculations of utility; about taking a few baby steps back from the idea that our consumption is the measure of our worth; about envisaging a different kind of world from the one in which our absolute allegiance is to our own nation-state.

Whatever the disagreements about details or ultimate limits, one can only applaud this vision, a vision that at so little cost to people who have so much, can mitigate the tragedy of the choices that so many poor people all over the world make as the price of survival.

CHAPTER **13**

From Imperialism to
Globalization, by Way of
Development

Up to now, we have considered the impact on community both of markets and of economic ideology mostly in the context of the modern West. I have touched on the spread of Western culture, and the last chapter addressed a specific problem that links the rich West with the poor rest. The present chapter carries the argument a step further by going back to a question that originally set me on the path that led to this book: What is lost as economic development proceeds in India, Peru—throughout the so-called Third World? More specifically, how has development impacted Third World cultures? This question has more to do with economics than one might suppose. Not only is economics the cutting edge of modern Western culture; economics possesses (or perhaps is possessed by) its own theory of culture.

The destruction of culture has been a leitmotif of the West's interaction with the rest of the world. Ever since that interaction got underway in earnest in the decades following the voyages of discovery and (soon after) conquest in the last decades of the fifteenth century and first decades of the sixteenth century. This is the common thread linking imperialism, development, and globalization, three successive epochs of the story of West meets rest.

By "culture," I do not mean artistic sensibility or intellectual refinement. Culture is used here the way anthropologists understand the term, to mean the totality of patterns of behavior and belief that characterize a specific society. Culture in this sense is sustained by and through community, the set of connections that bind people to one another economically, socially, politically, and spiritually. Traditional communities are not simply about shared spaces, but about shared participation in producing and exchanging goods and services; about governing, entertaining, and mourning; and about generating and regenerating people physically, morally, and spiritually.

The culture of the modern West, with its emphasis on the market as the organizing principle of life, is the exception to the link between culture and community. Market culture undermines traditional communities wherever it penetrates—just as it has undermined community on its home turf for the last four hundred years.

My view of culture is not an essentialist one that juxtaposes a rational, individualistic, self-interested Westerner concerned only with material goods and an irrational, community-minded, spiritual non-Westerner. As I have tried to indicate at various points in this book, I see the difference between the culture of the modern West and other ways of understanding and behaving as a difference of balance. Non-Westerners and nonmodern folk within the West (which means all of us to some extent) are perfectly capable of thinking rationally, of pursuing self-interest, and of enjoying material prosperity. But individualism is balanced by holism, self-interest by obligation, algorithm by experience, materialism by spirituality, the nation-state by other allegiances. The culture of the modern West is, in my judgment, defined precisely by the absence of such balancing factors.

If you ask what does a culture here or a culture there matter if this is the price of material progress, I have three answers. First, I am not persuaded that cultural destruction is a necessary corollary of the technologies that extend life and improve its quality. Western technology can be decoupled from the commitment of Western culture to the market. Second—if I am wrong about the first claim—I would ask, as Jesus does in the accounts of St. Mathew (16:26) and St. Mark (8:36), "What shall it profit a man, if he shall gain the whole world, and lose his own soul?" Third, for all the material progress that we in the West have achieved, we pay a high price: the weakening to the point of breaking of ties of community. We have much to learn, and the cultures that are being destroyed in the name of progress are perhaps the best resource we have for restoring balance to our own lives.[1] Finally, if none of these answers persuades, I would ask my readers to reflect for a moment on the ethical implications of destroying ways of being that are different from our own.

The project of cultural destruction has succeeded remarkably well with Third World elites. From Delhi to Lima, elite culture is based increasingly on the individual rationally calculating and acting in terms of self-interest. Worth, moral as well as economic, is measured in terms of income and wealth. Allegiance to the nation-state trumps all other allegiances.

Economics as Cultural Theory

What does this have to do with economics? Just this: the presuppositions of this now worldwide culture are the assumptions of economics. Economics, this book has argued, is the formalization of the dominant worldview of the modern West.

There are, in fact, two views of culture among economists. For the mainstream, culture is but a thin veneer over a common way of being in the world based on calculating and maximizing individual self-interest. Ignoring cultural differences, a common human nature is assumed: people all over the world are the same—and therefore like us.

According to this view, the Indian subsistence-oriented peasant is no less calculating, no less competitive, no less individualistic, no less self-interested, than the American commercial farmer. Indeed, encountering a Bengali in his rice paddy, the economist imagines a Kansas wheat farmer, a *homo economicus* striving to maximize his well-being as a self-interested individual.

This view of culture has a singular merit: throwing out the baby of culture also throws out the bathwater of racism, with its logic of intrinsic differences based on skin color or other physical features, real or imagined. It is hard to be both faithful to the assumptions of mainstream economics and to the tenets of racism.[2] Case in point: as we saw in Chapter 2, John Stuart Mill's economic logic led him to a conclusion about human equality very much out of step with his time and place (Victorian England), a position that put him at odds with the originator of the term "dismal science" on the so-called Negro Question. Indeed, well before Mill, Adam Smith expressed the idea of human equality in these terms: "The difference between the most dissimilar characters, between a philosopher and a common street porter, for example, seems to arise not so much from nature, as from habit, custom, and education. When they came into the world, and for the first six or eight years of their existence, they were, perhaps, very much alike" (Smith 1937 [1776], 15).

It would be misleading, however, to suggest that economics is monolithic in this respect. There is a second approach that, far from minimizing cultural differences, emphasizes these differences. This may be a minority view within economics, but outside economics cultural difference commands much broader allegiance. It is perhaps the dominant view.

In this approach, cultures, implicitly or explicitly, are ranked, along with income and wealth, on a linear scale. As the West is richer, Western culture is more progressive, more developed. Indeed, the process of development is seen as the transformation of backward, traditional, cultural practices into modern practice, the practice of the West, the better to facilitate the growth of production and income.

What the two views share is confidence in the superiority of Western culture. The first, in the guise of denying culture, attributes to other cultures Western values and practices; the second, in the guise of affirming culture, posits an inclined plane of history (to use Ashis Nandy's phrase once again) along which the rest of the world is, or at least ought to be, struggling to catch up with the West. Both views agree on the need for "development." In the first, the Other is a miniature adult, and development means the tender nurturing by the market to form the miniature Indian or African into a full-size American. In the second, the Other is frankly a child who needs structural transformation and cultural improvement to become an adult.

The concept of development makes sense in the context of an individual person as long as there is an agreed-upon standard of adult behavior against which to measure progress. Personal development is measured by progress from intuitive, inarticulate, cooperative, contextual, and personal modes of behavior toward rational, principled, competitive, universal, and impersonal modes of behavior, that is, from "weak" modes generally regarded as feminine and based on experience to "strong" modes regarded as masculine and based on algorithm. Carol Gilligan (1982) challenged the gender bias implicit in this progression, which brought a whole new set of questions into the study of child development, but the development of nations continues to be seen in these terms.

The Age of Imperialism

If the elites of Asia, Africa, and Latin America have successively endorsed imperialism, development, and globalization, nonelite cultures have been a tougher nut to crack. The two views of culture reflected in economics were set out early in the race for conquest in the Americas (see Todorov 1984, 146–167 for an illuminating discussion). The dominant view of the Europeans who encountered the indigenous peoples of the Americas was one of difference and hierarchy, according to which the Americans were little different from beasts, hardly human.

The alternative view was based on identity and equality, close to the view of mainstream economics today. This view was put forward most strongly by the Spaniard Bartolomé de las Casas, an adventurer turned priest—he eventually joined the Dominican order—who arrived in the New World as a young man in 1502 and lived into the seventh decade of the sixteenth century. Las Casas had an epiphany after seeing the conquistadores in action and became a champion of native rights. He had a long and distinguished career and acquired considerable access and influence within the councils of the king of Spain. In this capacity, Las Casas won an important debate with Juan Ginés de Sepúlveda, a leading proponent of the view that the indigenous peoples of the Americas were more bestial than human. ("Won" in the sense that his opposition prevailed on a council convened to determine whether to allow Sepúlveda's views to be published. Evidently, Las Casas lost the larger war in terms of how the indigenous people were actually treated.[3]) Las Casas was known in his lifetime and beyond as an indefatigable defender of native rights. Indeed, while articulating the principles of identity and equality, he actually found the natives closer than his fellow Spaniards to the ideal Christian in their gentleness, simplicity, and humility.

The danger to indigenous culture from conquistadores imbued with notions of difference and hierarchy needs no explanation. But Las Casas's idea of identity and equality was in its own way even more subversive of non-European ways of understanding and being in the world. Anticipating mainstream economics, it came with its own syllogism: everybody is the same; thus, you are like me. . . . And my Truth is your Truth. Like his opponents who believed in difference and hierarchy, Las Casas had no doubt that he was doing the natives a favor by bringing them Christianity and European culture. And flavored with honey rather than vinegar, Las Casas's missionary message was harder to resist. At least with Las Casas's opponents, Native Americans knew where they stood: the only good Indian was a dead one, or one reduced to slavery.

In one form or another, imperialism took root in most of the non-European world. We Americans did much the same thing in the United States as the Spanish did in Latin America. However, white Americans found it easier and more profitable to enslave African blacks than American natives, so the indigenous people were pushed ever westward—by slaveholders and free-soil men alike—until there was no more West into which to push them, at which point in time, roughly the end of the Civil War, genocide began in earnest.

The missionary justification never waned during empire's long sway, although with the rise of secularism, missionary zeal was cloaked in nonreligious garb. Three centuries after the Spanish debated whether spreading

Christianity to the West Indies justified their wars of conquest, Thomas Macaulay was urging upon the British government the mission of spreading English language and culture to India, clear across the globe. In a celebrated memorandum on educational policy, Macaulay laid out the case for re-shaping the colonial world in the image of the West:

> What we spend on the Arabic and Sanscrit Colleges is not merely a dead loss to the cause of truth. It is bounty-money paid to raise up champions of error. . . . (Macaulay 1920 [1835], 114)
>
> It is said that the Sanscrit and the Arabic are the languages in which the sacred books of a hundred millions of people are written, and that they are on that account entitled to peculiar encouragement. Assuredly it is the duty of the British Government in India to be not only tolerant but neutral on all religious questions. But to encourage the study of a literature, admitted to be of small intrinsic value, only because that literature inculcated the most serious errors on the most important subjects, is a course hardly reconcil-able with reason, with morality, or even with that very neutrality which ought, as we all agree, to be sacredly preserved. It is confessed that a lan-guage is barren of useful knowledge. We are to teach it because it is fruitful of monstrous superstitions. We are to teach false history, false astronomy, false medicine, because we find them in company with a false religion. . . . (Macaulay 1920 [1835], 115)
>
> It is impossible for us, with our limited means, to attempt to educate the body of the people. We must at present do our best to form a class who may be interpreters between us and the millions whom we govern—a class of persons Indian in blood and colour, but English in tastes, in opinions, in morals and in intellect. To that class we may leave it to refine the vernac-ular dialects of the country, to enrich those dialects with terms of science borrowed from the Western nomenclature, and to render them by degrees fit vehicles for conveying knowledge to the great mass of the population. (Macaulay 1920 [1835], 116)

At the end of the nineteenth century, Rudyard Kipling, the poet laureate of British imperialism, urged the United States to follow Britain's lead. On the morrow of the American occupation of the Philippines and Puerto Rico, after the War of 1898 demolished the last remnants of the Spanish overseas empire, Kipling exhorted Americans to

> Take up the White Man's burden—
> Send forth the best ye breed—

> To bind your sons to exile
> To serve your captives' need;
> To wait in heavy harness
> On fluttered folk and wild—
> Your new-caught, sullen peoples,
> Half-devil and half-child.[4]

We must never lose sight of the arsenal that permitted the white man to bear his burden when the natives objected. As Hilaire Belloc put it so pithily, "Whatever happens we have got, The Maxim Gun, and they have not" (1923 [1898], 41). But the soft power of ideology is not to be ignored: ideology has played an important role in undergirding the hard power of the machine gun.

Imperialism unified European opinion on cultural ideology as on no other political question. At one end of the political spectrum was the Englishman Lord Cromer, the effective ruler of Egypt from 1883 to 1907, who summarized the difference between West and East in terms of the command of algorithm:

> The European is a close reasoner; his statements of fact are devoid of any ambiguity; he is a natural logician, albeit he may not have studied logic . . . his trained intelligence works like a piece of mechanism. The mind of the Oriental, on the other hand, like his picturesque streets, is eminently wanting in symmetry. His reasoning is of the most slipshod description. Although the ancient Arabs acquired in a somewhat higher degree the science of dialectics, their descendants are singularly deficient in the logical faculty. They are often incapable of drawing the most obvious conclusions from any simple premises of which they may admit the truth. (*Modern Egypt*, chap. 34; quoted in Said 1978, 38)

Pity the poor Egyptian. With only experiential knowledge at his disposal, how could he hope to survive without the European to reason for him?

Karl Marx was at the other end of the European political spectrum from Cromer; Marx recognized the oppression inherent in colonialism, but for Marx colonial oppression, like capitalist oppression at home, served the teleological goal of emancipation of the individual. Indeed, Marx was, if anything, harder on the natives than Cromer. In Marx's eyes, the village communities of precolonial India were so "contaminated"—his word—

by distinctions of caste, and by slavery, that they subjugated man to external circumstances instead of elevating man into the sovereign of circumstances, that they transformed a self-developing social state into never changing natural destiny, and thus brought about a brutalizing worship of nature, exhibiting its degradation in the fact that man, the sovereign of nature, fell down on his knees in adoration of Hanuman, the monkey, and Sabbala, the cow. (*New York Tribune*, June 25, 1853; reprinted in Marx and Engels 1959 [1846], 480)

Marx was under no illusions with respect to the motives behind colonialism, but motives mattered less than consequences—once again the thinking is familiar to anyone acquainted with Marx's analysis of capitalism on its home ground: "England . . . was actuated only by the vilest interests [in India]. . . . But that is not the question. The question is: Can mankind fulfill its destiny without a fundamental revolution in the social state of Asia? If not, whatever may have been the crimes of England, she was the unconscious tool of history in bringing about that revolution" (ibid., reprinted in Marx and Engels 1959 [1846], 480–481).

Marx, it was observed in Chapter 3, shared with his bourgeois antagonists a belief in the power and glory of the rational individual set free to pursue his self-interest. The difference was not about goals but about means, about whether capitalism allowed people in general, and the working class in particular, to realize their individual potential; about whether it was sufficient for the market to dissolve the community, or whether instead this was a necessary step that had to be transcended in due course by a socialist revolution. For the bourgeois, the answer was an emphatic and absolute "yes" to capitalism: yes, it was necessary; yes, it was sufficient. For Marx, the problem with "Freedom, Equality, Property and Bentham" (Marx 1959 [1867], 176) was that the working class gets so little of any of them, not that these goals are undesirable in themselves. In the modern West, the worker might struggle for a socialist revolution. The Indian enmeshed in community could not even hope for revolution until a foreign agency like the British dissolved community bonds.

The term *development* was not unknown during the colonial era. But it had more to do with land and natural resources than with people. Indeed, experienced colonial administrators perceived a tension between development and social well-being. John Furnivall, longtime civil servant in colonial Burma, gave the devil his due: "There was good reason to believe that the cultivators, as individuals, were better off from a material standpoint under British than under Burmese rule" (quoted in Arndt 1987, 29). But there was more to social well-being than individual prosperity: "The mere maintenance of law and order set free economic forces which dissolved the village into individuals. . . . The annexation [of Burma by Britain] destroyed the Burmese social order and probably nothing less catastrophic would have cleared the way for reconstruction; but the destruction of a civilisation is in itself an offence against humanity" (quoted in Arndt 1987, 29).

Many years later, a Thai forest dweller, asked his view of "reconstruction," might well have endorsed Furnivall's assessment that destroying a civilization is a crime against humanity—without necessarily accepting that this crime would enhance productivity and increase prosperity. A European consulting firm had devised a plan for the exploitation of Thai forests that involved "enclosing" the forest—that is, transforming the communally owned and managed forest into separate parcels:

> The . . . consultant put three hypothetical choices to the villager, [including an option whereby] individual families could be assigned rights to separate small forest plots to manage as they wished. . . . The villager rejected all three alternatives. . . . First, he objected to the manner in which the choice was put to him. If such matters were to be discussed and considered, they could only be discussed and considered as a community, not through approaches to separate individuals or "preference polling." Second, the villager said that each alternative would lead to destruction of the forest on which the villagers depended for water and other goods. Putting the forest in the hands of discrete individuals, he explained, would destroy the community and thus the forest. (Lohmann et al. 1994)

The Development Moment

By the end of World War II, the exhausted European members of the victorious coalition were unable, and—some of them at least—unwilling to maintain their colonies. First Asia, and then Africa, experienced a wave of decolonization. With the passing of the age of imperialism, development acquired a new meaning. Jawaharlal Nehru, the first prime minister of independent India, spoke for many Third World leaders when he embraced development as the means "to raise the standard of the masses, supply them with their needs, give them the wherewithal to lead a decent life, and help them to progress and advance in life not only in regard to material things, but in regard to cultural and spiritual things also" (1958, 141).

The Cold War made the Third World a battle ground between the First World—the part of the world in which capitalism dominated—and the Second World—where Soviet socialism dominated. But one thing on which the First and Second Worlds agreed was their cultural superiority vis-à-vis the Third World. Socialist Russians echoed the tropes of Marx while capitalist Americans echoed Cromer. Both saw non-Western culture negatively, in terms of the obstacles that indigenous cultures threw in the path of growth. Development meant the removal of these cultural obstacles. Their Third World interlocutors accepted the need for cultural transformation. Nehru wrote *The Discovery of India* while imprisoned by the British during World War II, that is, before he assumed the reins of government. But the outbreak of war had changed expectations all around, and some form of home rule, if not total independence, was in the air even as he wrote. *The Discovery of India* treads a fine line between, on the one hand, radically rejecting traditional India—which would have blurred the lines between Nehru's social democracy and the revolutionary project of the Communist Party of India—and, on the other hand, completely embracing the past, stained by the oppressions of caste and class. In the end, Nehru leaves no doubt that he is a modernizer, albeit a Brahmin modernizer with respect for India's history. "It is therefore with the temper and approach of science, allied to philosophy, and with reverence for all that lies beyond, that we must face life" (Nehru 1946, 514), wrote the man who once styled himself the last Englishman who would rule India.

Globalization

The development moment, like the age of imperialism, has passed. The watchword now is globalization, world integration through the market. Globalization brings one new feature. The market, this book has argued, destroys community, leaving only the imagined community of the nation. Globalization takes the process the final step by putting even the national community at risk: what else does it mean that globalization is making national boundaries obsolete?

But, as the French say, the more things change, the more they stay the same—at least in matters of culture. Except for the marginalized voices of a few nongovernmental organizations, the cultural dimension of globalization gets short shrift.

Consider the recent defense of globalization provided by Jagdish Bhagwati, a distinguished economist who has specialized in international trade and development for more than four decades (Bhagwati 2004). Much of Bhagwati's argument is highly nuanced, but there is little nuance to be found in the single chapter he devotes to the cultural consequences of globalization. He complains that critics who argue the case against globalization in terms of the effects on indigenous cultures offer little evidence to justify their criticisms (2004, 27, 115). Fair enough, perhaps, but Bhagwati offers no evidence to support his own view that the globalization omelet is worth breaking a few cultural eggs: "In the end, the indigenous peoples will have to confront the fact that the old yields to the new. Only active nurturing of the collective memory and a selective preservation of cultural artifacts can be a response, not the impractical fossilization of traditional attitudes and values" (2004, 116).

Bhagwati sets up a straw man. The issue was never one of "fossilization of traditional attitudes and values." Cultures fossilize only when their backs are to the wall. Otherwise, the first rule of cultural survival is and always has been the ability to change and to adapt. The question is change on whose terms? Adaptation according to whose program?

The Amish once again are a case in point. Amish communities do not reject modern technology out of hand. They carefully consider which elements of the technology of the "English" (as they call their non-Amish neighbors) are compatible with maintaining their communities, and which are not. It is clearly a balancing act, and Amish communities have fractured on the issue of technological choice. Outsiders may find some of the choices the Amish make somewhat bizarre—stationary engines are okay; moving engines are not—but it is just plain wrong to argue that the Amish are Luddites.[5]

I agree with Bhagwati and other defenders of globalization that people everywhere want the technological benefits that have come to the West with modernity. No mother wants to see her children die in infancy; no husband wants to see his wife die in childbirth. Nobody wants to work as a beast of burden, as I have seen both men and women working in India, looking sixty or seventy years old as they approach thirty. But people do not necessarily want the cultural entailments in which imported technologies of improving health, alleviating physical drudgery, providing material comfort, come wrapped. For starters, they do not necessarily want their lives governed by the market. They may want (in both senses of the word) enough to lead a dignified life, the goal assumed by Adam Smith, but they do not necessarily wish for lives of quiet desperation (in Henry David Thoreau's memorable phrase) as individuals calculating how to get more, and still more. Whatever our view of T. S. Eliot's dictum that there is no life without community and no community without God (see Chapter 2), Eliot is surely closer to most people on the receiving end of globalization than is Bhagwati.

It is an act of faith and optimism that new technologies can be decoupled, delinked, from the cultural entailments in which globalization delivers them. But as John Maynard Keynes said in an early defense of his idea that in a world of uncertainty decisions are driven by animal spirits, "There is a subtle reason . . . why faith may work. For if we consistently act on the optimistic hypothesis, this hypothesis will tend to be realized" (1931, vii). The opposite is certainly the case: if we act on the hypothesis that technology inevitably comes in a package with modernity, then we doom any attempt to keep a space open for cultures other than the culture of the modern West.

Cultural Intervention and Its Limits

How far do we go in leaving a space open for a variety of cultural flowers to bloom? How do we tell the beneficial plants from the weeds? What about cultures whose practices threaten us physically or outrage our sensibilities by the cruelties they inflict on their own? Sometimes the answer is simple: "cultural necessity" cannot be a license for murder, terror, or other violent crimes, whoever commits these horrendous acts. It is not necessary to list examples; all one need do is pick up the newspaper for a daily recital of crimes committed in the name of the necessity of preserving a way of life, crimes perpetrated by states, communities, and individuals.

In other contexts, the answer must be more complex. Take what has become the litmus test—at least since widow burning and foot binding have fallen into desuetude: do I wish to preserve a space for cultures that practice female genital alteration, to avoid both the anodyne term *circumcision* or the tendentious term *mutilation?*

For the same reasons that I do not see community through rose-colored glasses which mask oppression or, for that matter, intolerance and bigotry, I do not take an "anything goes," relativistic view of culture. Neither am I a preservationist in the sense of supporting the continuation of whatever practices, values, or ideologies happen to exist. In short, I do not apply the radical subjectivism of the economist (see Chapter 4) to matters of culture.

And I am not categorically opposed to intervention to change practices and values, behaviors and attitudes. But I would be very cautious, whether the issue is military intervention, trade sanctions, or aid conditionality; the constraints we place on parents with respect to how they bring up their children; or the uncontrolled proliferation of the market, with its inevitable "collateral damage" to Third World communities. (By "intervention," I thus mean both the conscious, purposive attempt of the more powerful to change the ways of the less powerful, and the possibly unintended, but equally predictable, consequences of the spread of the market.)

My caution comes partly from skepticism about the efficacy of intervention. But more important is my conviction that there is no universal set of principles to which one can appeal in judging cultural practices. This recognition does not make me a relativist, but rather obliges me to recognize that, like everybody else, I start from someplace definite; by the same token, it obliges me to examine the biases and presuppositions implicit in my own starting point. From this examination it should be a relatively easy step to the moral necessity for humility proportionate to the disparity of power that exists between us (governments, Westernized elites, foreign experts) and them (slum dwellers, peasants, immigrants).

I also believe in the moral necessity of reciprocity in cultural intervention. Instead of the monologue that fits the conviction that cultures can be arranged on an inclined plane, with one's own culture at the top, there must be dialogue, a willingness to listen as well as to speak. And intervention should be based on a commitment to joint participation, to sharing the burdens as well as the benefits of change, to learning as well as teaching, to linking our fate with the fate of those in whose lives we intervene—in short, to building community across the gulfs of economics, ethnicity, and religion.

Intervention is thus a last resort because it commits us morally to an involvement that we may not be able or wish to sustain but that we cannot morally avoid. In any case, the purpose of preserving a space for autonomous cultural development (as distinct from preserving cultures as we would preserve artifacts in a museum) will generally be better served by less intervention rather than by more.

How does all this apply to a concrete case like female genital alteration? First, we should recognize that this term covers a wide variety of practices, ranging from a token, ritual incision, to excision of the clitoris, to infibulation (sowing the genitalia together except for a small passage for urine and menstrual fluids). These procedures obviously differ greatly in their health risks, the pain and suffering they cause, and in their impact on sexual sensitivity. Yet they are lumped together under the name of female circumcision by those who would minimize the consequences, or under the more provocative name of female genital mutilation by those who wish to end these practices. Which of these practices outrage our sensibilities? All of them? Only the most extreme?

Second, what are the grounds of our opposition? If our opposition is based on the health risks associated with operations performed by traditional practitioners (often elderly women with neither knowledge of nor access to sanitary practices), or on pain and suffering, medicalization would seem to provide an adequate alternative. Instead of outright opposition, why not advocate the use of antiseptics and anesthetics and, if necessary, hospitalization?

Feminists will object that medicalization does nothing to preserve the right of women to sexual pleasure, nothing to challenge a system that subordinates women in a regime frankly designed to reduce, if not eliminate, female sexuality in the interests of patriarchy, nothing to protect a girl's right to decide for herself on such an intimate matter. This argument, too, has to be unpacked.

Patriarchy is a real issue, but it is unlikely to hinge on a single practice and, indeed, is unlikely to be weakened by a ban on female genital alteration. In any case, if patriarchy offends our sensibilities, we need not go to Africa to find instances galore.

Similarly with the rights of children. There is a real issue here, but it is disingenuous to pretend that the decisions made by parents with regard to female genital alteration are different in kind from the life-shaping decisions that parents routinely make for their children in every society, our own included.

Patriarchy and the right of the child to decide for herself apart, what about the specifics of female sexuality? The problem with basing opposition to female genital alteration on its effects on sexual pleasure is that precisely the same objection can be raised to male circumcision. Why is this a problem? Because male circumcision is widely practiced not only in the "backward" Third World, but in the "advanced" First World; not only by "natives," but by "us."

The salient difference is that the defenders of female genital alteration have only superstition to back up their practice, while we have medical science—or did until the pendulum began to swing against routine male circumcision in the 1970s. In its latest word on the subject, the American Academy of Pediatrics took the position that the health benefits are too marginal for the Academy "to recommend routine neonatal circumcision" (Lennon et al. 1999, 686).

More embarrassing still is that the Jewish injunction for male circumcision has been rationalized by an argument that is essentially identical to the argument that offends our sensibilities when it comes to African women. The great medieval Jewish philosopher and physician, Moses ben Maimon, Maimonides, defended the *brit milah* (covenant of circumcision) precisely because circumcision reduces sexual pleasure:

> One of the reasons for [circumcision] is . . . the wish to bring about a decrease in sexual intercourse and a weakening of the organ in question, so that this activity be diminished and the organ be in as quiet a state as possible. . . . Violent concupiscence and lust that goes beyond what is needed [for procreation] are diminished. The fact that circumcision weakens the faculty of sexual excitement and sometimes perhaps diminishes the pleasure is indubitable. For if at birth this member has been made to bleed and has had its covering taken away from it, it must indubitably be weakened. The *Sages, may their memory be blessed,* have explicitly stated: *It is hard for a woman with whom an uncircumcised man has had sexual intercourse to separate from him.* In my opinion this is the strongest of the reasons for *circumcision.* (Maimonides 1963 [1191], 609)

To what end? Maimonides gives a general answer that the purpose of the commandments specifically binding upon Jews, of which circumcision is the first, is "to quell all the impulses of matter. It behooves him who prefers to be a human being in truth, not a beast having the shape and configuration of a human being, to endeavor to diminish all the impulses of matter—such as eating, drinking, copulation" (1963 [1191], 433–434).[6]

The scientifically disposed may not accept the authority of even so great a sage as Maimonides as to the effects of circumcision on sexual pleasure, but evidence in the form of controlled experiment is inherently difficult to marshal. Even if the evidence were to support Maimonides on this point, I doubt that there would be an outcry against male circumcision. The nonreligious arguments that Jewish parents make for circumcision based on conformity (to the physical appearance of the boy's father, to the wishes of the boy's grandparents, to the expectations of the Jewish community), not to mention the religious commandment, would trump arguments for a boy's right eventually to decide for himself whether he wished to undergo circumcision.

I obviously do not intend to settle the issue of female genital alteration (or the issue of male circumcision, for that matter) by these remarks; I have the more limited purpose of showing that what seems to be a simple, clear-cut issue turns out to be a multifaceted, complex one. All the arguments that can be leveled against a practice that appears strange, if not barbaric (the word barbaric comes from *barbaros,* a Greek word that means foreign), can with equal effectiveness be leveled against a practice that is unremarkable in our own culture, and indeed was the medical norm in the United States until relatively recently. It is hardly one that simply pits cultural relativism against universal human rights.

The Language of Intervention

If in the end we are to intervene in cultural matters—again, by "we" I mean a variety of actors, governments, elites, and experts—in what language do we intervene? I mean this question to some extent literally, but more as a shorthand for the way in which cultural interaction is conducted. The problem is that cultural intervention normally takes place under conditions of asymmetrical power, and there is a real danger that with all good intentions we intervene as children of Las Casas. Armed with the syllogism "Everybody is the same; thus, you are like me. . . . And my Truth is your Truth," we will insist that others speak our language. Like Alexander Luria with the Uzbeks (see Chapter 8), we will insist on the language of syllogism, when our interlocutors may well prefer a language of experience.

Amartya Sen illustrates the problem in his recent book *Identity and Violence.* A major focus is the conflict between cultural freedom and cultural preservation. Sen's concern is that the individual be free to pick and choose among the diverse elements of the culture into which he or she happens to be born:

> Cultural freedom may include, among other priorities, the liberty to question the automatic endorsement of past traditions, when people— particularly young people—see a reason for changing their ways of living. (Sen 2005, 114)

So that the freedom be real rather than illusory, Sen conditions it on reasoned consideration, on whether the persons involved would choose . . . particular practices given the opportunity of critical scrutiny and an adequate knowledge of other options and of the choices that actually exist. . . .

The decision to stay firmly *within* the traditional mode would be an exercise of freedom if the choice is made after considering other alternatives. In the same way, a decision to *move away*—by a little or a lot—from the received behavior pattern, arrived at after reflection and reasoning, would also qualify as such an exercise. (Sen 2005, 114, 157–158)

There are at least two reasons to be wary of this argument: the first is that it takes away with one hand what it offers with the other. My friend, you are free to choose your culture, but only if the results conform to the dictates of reason. You are not free to choose on the basis of emotion, intuition, or what your parents or grandparents think makes for a decent and fulfilling life. And to make sure that you choose reasonably, we—the government, the elite, the experts—will use our best efforts to prevent your parents from choosing the kind of education they think will form you suitably for life, unless it conforms to our standards of reason.

In Sen's hands, the argument for cultural freedom easily slides into an argument against parental choice, especially if the parents are likely to opt for faith-based education. Indeed, Sen is sharply critical of British government policies extending the support given Christian schools to the schools of other faiths:

Adding . . . Muslim schools, Hindu schools, and Sikh schools to preexisting Christian ones . . . can have the effect of reducing the role of reasoning which the children may have the opportunity to cultivate and use. And this is happening at a time when . . . the ability to undertake reasoned decision-making is of particular importance. The limitations imposed on the children are especially acute when the new religious schools give children rather little opportunity to cultivate reasoned choice in determining the priorities of their lives. Also, they often fail to alert students to the need to decide for themselves how the various components of their identities . . . should receive attention. (2005, 117–118)

The test for Sen is "what would best enhance the capability of the children to live 'examined lives' as they grow up" (2005, 160), and faith-based schools do not pass muster.

I share Sen's doubts about education that reduces identity to the single dimension of religion, but I part company at the point where the argument turns into one against parental choice. Parents never have full control over their children's upbringing, and where cultural minorities face the threat of assimilation, this control is attenuated even further. Choosing the schools in which one's children are educated is important to maintaining a space for cultural evolution. No community—other than the national community—can be sustained without the active participation of parents in regenerating the community. No culture—other than the dominant national culture—will long survive unless parents are empowered to instill in their children their own values, customs, traditions, and expectations. This is not to minimize other values—including the capacity to make reasoned choices. But to impose an education in which the primary value is the capacity for rational deliberation, overriding parents if need be, is willy-nilly to foster a particular way of engaging the world. It is, in my view, to give undue weight to thinking like an economist.

The second reason to be on guard against Sen's notion of cultural freedom is that he sets this goal in opposition to the straw man of cultural preservation. Like Bhagwati, Sen confuses two very different ideas: on the one hand, preserving a space for cultures to change and develop, and, on the other, preserving each and every cultural practice—that is, fossilization of a culture. Cultural freedom surely conflicts with fossilization, but it need not conflict with keeping open a space for cultural evolution.

How this evolution takes place is another matter. Sen would force a complex and even mysterious process into the narrow channel of reasoned deliberation. My own intuition, a reasoned intuition but an intuition nonetheless, is that if subjected to the scrutiny of algorithm, most cultures will disappear in the melting pot of globalization. For Sen this may not be regrettable; he favors cultural diversity for the enrichment it offers, but only "to the extent that it is freely chosen as possible by the persons involved" (Sen 2005, 150). I can only repeat what I said at the outset of this book: "The claims of the individual and the claims of the community conflict. And not a bad thing: this tension is normal, healthy, and even creative. It should not be resolved once and for all in favor of either the individual or the community. But over the past four hundred years, the ideology of economics has fostered both the self-interested individual and the market system, and has undermined, and continues to undermine, the community."

Sen argues for a very specific language of intervention in the guise of universal principles. In reality, Sen's language makes sense only if we subscribe to the culture of the modern West, to the foundational assumptions of economics. The primacy of the individual over the relationships that constitute community justifies the subordination of cultural evolution to cultural freedom. The primacy of the imagined community of the nation implies that local communities, based on religion, ethnicity, or neighborhood, count for little. And the ideology of modern knowledge that favors algorithm over experience justifies the emphasis on developing the skills of rational deliberation. If algorithm is the only form of knowledge, or even a superior form of knowledge, then an experiential dimension, not to mention a spiritual dimension, adds little or nothing to our abilities to determine the priorities of our lives.

On the other hand, if we reject this ideology of knowledge in favor of one that gives greater weight to experience, or to spirituality, we might argue against an overly narrow focus on rational deliberation. If we reject the primacy of the individual over the relationships that constitute community, we might be sensitive to both the rights of individuals and the rights of communities. If we reject the primacy of the national community, the claims of local communities become more legitimate. Starting from a different set of assumptions, we may well discover a different set of priorities for ourselves and for our children.

There are many ways of resolving the tensions between individualism and holism, between self-interest and obligation to others, between algorithm and experience, between the claims of various communities on our allegiance, between material prosperity and spiritual health. Economics offers one way, but as presently constituted, economics is hobbled by an ideology in which these tensions are replaced by a set of pseudo-universals about human nature. A dismal science indeed.

The Limits of Dissent

I will be accused of exaggerating the agreement among economists. Surely, economics is a broad enough tent that there is room for disagreement, including dissent with respect to the appropriate scope of markets and the impact of markets on communities.

There *is* dissent and disagreement in economics. Harry Truman is said to have longed for a one-armed economist—an economist who was not constantly hedging his bets with "on the one hand . . ." and "on the other hand. . . ." And dissent and disagreement are not limited to policy. Indeed, economics provides the basis for searching self-criticism: if you take seriously the fine print on the warranty that mainstream economics provides for the market, your celebration of the market is likely to be rather subdued, or at least nuanced (McMillan 2002). Nor is the fine print accessible only to the priests, to people steeped in many years of graduate training. Most elementary texts discuss a variety of structural assumptions that must be satisfied if markets are to produce desirable outcomes, ranging from assumptions about market organization to assumptions about information flows. Nonetheless, writers of elementary texts, like professional economists in general, play down the limiting nature of these structural assumptions. Most would agree with Greg Mankiw, whose text, as we saw in Chapter 10, argues that equilibrating demand and supply maximizes "total economic well-being" (Mankiw 2004, 149).

This appendix lays out a critique that comes from inside mainstream economics, based on the assumptions about market structure that underlie the idea that markets produce good results. A major reason for exploring this internal critique in some depth is to highlight a major difference between it and an external critique based on the foundational assumptions of self-interested individualism, rational calculation, the nation-state, and unlimited wants. No matter how searching on its own terms, the internal, structural, critique stops short of challenging the basic tenet of economics that markets are good for people. On the contrary, the takeaway from the structural critique is that defects of markets can be fixed by more and better markets. Does the market for electric energy fail to maximize total well-being because the local utility has monopoly power over prices? Replace the monopoly with competition. Does the energy market fail because of the pollution that accompanies the generation of power, pollution that harms people who are not party to the transaction of buying and selling energy? Create markets in pollution permits. (If this strikes you as bearing more than a faint resemblance to the drunkard's predilection to cure a hangover with a hair of the dog that bit him, so be it.) By contrast, a critique based on the foundational assumptions inevitably leads one to challenge the economist's presumption in favor of markets. It is not surprising that economists favor the structural critique over the foundational one.

Chapter 1 made the point that the apparatus of economics is largely about the normative claims made on behalf of markets, however much economists might claim that the discipline is really about describing the world. This appendix is intended to clarify this fundamental point. The structural assumptions, like the foundational assumptions, are not needed for describing *how* markets work—as distinct from *how well* markets work. Let us begin with the central organizing principle of welfare economics, *Pareto optimality.*

Pareto Optimality

Just what does the economist claim for the market? Adam Smith's famous remark about the invisible hand leading individuals to promote the social good while pursuing their self-interest is a convenient starting point. As observed in Chapter 6 (note 1), economists have come to see the invisible hand as a metaphor for the idea that a competitive market system leads to the largest economic pie available from the given resources at a society's disposal, that markets maximize the efficiency of production—although it is doubtful that Smith had anything so grandiose in mind.

To begin at the beginning: can we measure the size of the pie? Size of the pie is unambiguous as long as there is only one flavor. If the only thing we produce and the only thing we care about is apple pie, there is no conceptual difficulty in measuring how much pie is produced or consumed in a given year. But size becomes ambiguous as soon as there is more than one flavor, and the relative difficulty of producing different kinds of pie varies with the amounts produced—and people's tastes differ with respect to various flavors of pie. Imagine there are two groups of people, some who like apple pie, some who like pumpkin. Suppose further that it is harder to produce pumpkin pie and that it becomes increasingly harder to produce either kind of pie the more of that kind is produced. Evidently, the more the distribution of income favors the apple-pie lovers, the more apple pie will be produced. But can we say there is more "pie" as we shift the mix in favor of apple pie? No, for it becomes impossible to sort out changes in the size of the pie from changes in how the pie is sliced up among consumers. Apple pie is by assumption easier to produce, so as we shift from pumpkin pie to apple pie, there is more pie in terms, say, of weight. But it is not clear that this constitutes more pie in terms of value. Nor will it do to simply add up the dollar value of pie in the two circumstances since the prices of the two kinds of pie will depend on the mix. Because apple pie becomes more difficult to produce the more there is of it, the value of apple pie measured at market prices will rise with the quantity available. By the same token, the value of pumpkin pie will fall by a larger percentage than the quantity. Size of the pie is elusive once we move beyond the most simplistic of models, a world with only one good. In the more general case, we cannot separate the size of the pie from how the pie is sliced, or as the economist would say, we cannot separate efficiency from equity.

A more cumbersome language is necessary to define efficiency in a way that allows the economist to talk about efficiency without explicitly measuring the size of the pie. The more cumbersome terminology is summarized in two propositions, conveniently labeled the first and second welfare theorems. The first theorem asserts that a system of competitive markets leads to an outcome that cannot be improved upon for everyone. Any departure from a competitive market system must make at least one person worse off. The term of art for a situation that cannot be improved upon for everybody is Pareto optimality, or *Pareto efficiency*. The second theorem is more sweeping: any Pareto optimal outcome can be reached by allowing free play to a system of competitive markets, provided the starting point, the initial distribution of resources, is suitably adjusted.

Together, these two propositions allow us to define efficiency in a way that finesses the objection that markets may lead to wide disparities in income and consumption. A market outcome in which a few people have the lion's share of income qualifies as Pareto optimal just as much as an equilibrium in which the benefits are distributed equally. In both cases, it is impossible to make one person better off without making someone else worse off. In the first case, to improve matters for John Doe would make a Bill Gates or a Warren Buffett worse off; however much one might embrace such a move, the fact remains that in terms of Pareto optimality, it is not a move from an inferior to a superior situation—that is, it is not a move that makes everybody better off. And all that is claimed by the first welfare theorem is that a market system cannot be improved upon for everybody.

Once its distributional limitations are understood, the first welfare theorem must be recognized as providing a very weak defense for the market. Conversely, if society can reach any Pareto optimal outcome through the market, as the second theorem asserts, the distributional objection does not loom so large. If society doesn't like one particular outcome, the starting point can be changed by redistributing resources from one individual to another, by taxing some and subsidizing others, and then the market can be let loose to work its magic.

It is another matter how to arrange the requisite redistribution. One of the takeaways from elementary economics is that taxes and subsidies distort market outcomes—"distort" in the sense that taxes and subsidies drive a wedge between prices and costs and so prevent agents from adjusting demand and supply, consumption and production, to a Pareto optimum. All taxes and subsidies distort: taxes on widgets distort the widget market; subsidies on tegdiws distort the tegdiw market. Even a tax on everything, a general tax on income, distorts because one can't effectively tax leisure or shirking. So an income tax is in effect a subsidy to leisure and laziness. And distorts both how much people work and how hard they work. Every elementary text has a section devoted to measuring the so-called deadweight loss associated with various taxes. The name is suggestive: deadweight losses purport to measure the welfare losses occasioned by taxes; there is no attempt to measure the welfare gains.

We may need taxes and subsidies to accomplish the redistribution implicit in the second welfare theorem, but if all systems of taxes and subsidies distort incentives, we appear to be forced to compromise either efficiency or distribution. The economist's way out of the problem of deadweight loss is the so-called lump-sum transfer, a tax and subsidy scheme in which taxes and agents are taxed or subsidized according to their talent and potential for producing income, or perhaps according to differential moral worth, but taxes and subsidies are not conditional on actual economic performance, as an income or sales tax is. The point of a lump-sum transfer is to get the agents to the right starting point, so that the resulting market outcome brings about not only efficiency but the desired distributional result. The economy then enjoys (in theory at least) the best of both worlds, efficiency and distribution.

Lump-sum transfers are tailored to each agent's individual condition, in order to bring about a fair distribution—though the mainstream economist will generally insist that fairness is in the eye of the beholder, unlike efficiency, which can be objectively defined. For the economist, imposing lump-sum transfers is much like adding different amounts of weight to the saddles of racehorses, in the sense that both are ways of distributing handicaps to insure a fair race. The point is not necessarily to reach equality of outcomes, but to ensure that distribution does not get in the way of efficiency.

Lump-sum transfers are not a realistic policy instrument, but an ideal type that shows the properties taxes and subsidies would have to possess in order to be nondistorting. Even if lump-sum taxes and subsidies were feasible, there is a problem with relying on this instrument to achieve a distributional goal without sacrificing efficiency: the self-denying ordinance implicit in the idea of a social consensus on what constitutes a fair distribution, a fair starting point. If some are going to end up with more than others (which might be judged fair because some are capable of producing more than others), then what is to prevent the fortunate from using their position to make the race less fair rather than more fair? Even absent tyranny and oligarchy, economic power conveys political power, not only because politicians are for sale, but because economic power provides the means to persuade.

In practice, the economist's contribution to policy debates is not to help in choosing one Pareto optimal point over another. It is rather to argue in favor of the market on the grounds (supported by the two welfare theorems) that when markets do not have full sway, the results are inefficient: more reliance on markets can produce *Pareto improvements*, across-the-board improvements in the lives of people.

But as soon as we leave the world of the textbook, we inevitably find that market-friendly policy initiatives normally do not lead to Pareto improvements. (Neither do most other policy initiatives!) Rather, some people gain and others lose. Recognizing this, economists often appeal instead to the concept of *potential Pareto improvement*, a change that would make it possible to improve everybody's lot because those who gain from the change are sufficiently better off that they could compensate the losers and still have something left over for themselves. Trade liberalization policies are a case in point: as we saw in regard to the North American Free Trade Agreement in Chapter 1, consumers may benefit from a greater array of goods and lower prices, and some people will find better jobs in newly created or newly expanded export industries. But many people will lose their jobs as a result of trade liberalization. This leads directly to the question of how potential Pareto improvement could possibly be a convincing criterion when compensation is not paid—a question explored in Chapter 10.

Despite the cumbersomeness of the language, the first and second welfare theorems, along with the idea of potential Pareto improvement, allow us to see an order in markets that is not apparent to the naked eye. These ideas, in theory, make formal sense of the intuitive notion that markets are good for people. I say "in theory" because in addition to the distributional problems, there are a series of assumptions about the conditions of production and consumption that must be satisfied for the two theorems to hold, structural assumptions squarely within the realm of mainstream economics.

It is to these assumptions that we now turn.

Competitive Equilibrium

First, the two theorems are couched in terms of market outcomes that constitute a "competitive equilibrium." An equilibrium is defined as an outcome of the actions of all the participants in which no agent can improve upon his or her own situation—given his or her resources (so many machines, so much capacity to work with a particular set of skills) and possible actions (buy more of this, sell more of that, produce X instead of Y). It is an equilibrium precisely because nobody has any interest in doing something different from what he or she is already doing. This is fairly straightforward.

By contrast, the idea of competition does not mean in economics what it means in everyday language, and "perfect competition" is even more at odds with ordinary speech. Outside of economics, competition suggests active struggle against other competitors. Like the 100 yard dash. Or chess. Or competition for grades. But in economics perfect competition describes a situation of the utmost passivity. Perfect competition is the term for a market in which anybody can buy or sell whatever amount he or she wishes at the going price.

This takes some getting used to. The "going price" means that, as on a stock or commodity exchange, there is at every moment of time a price that presents itself to all interested parties as *the* price, as distinct from a price that is negotiated between the parties to a transaction. So sellers do not have to compete in the usual sense of the term in order to sell their goods. I have no need to convince buyers of the merits of my wares, nor do you, my "competitor." We can both sell as much as we wish, so neither of us has anything to gain by promoting our own brand.

I just used the word *brand,* a familiar word to anybody who lives and breathes in the real economy outside the texts. But it is a word that has no place in the world of perfect competition. For there to be a single going price, it must be the case that goods on offer are uniform in their qualities, so that there is nothing to be gained by branding. Number 2 Hard Red Winter Wheat delivered in Kansas City is one example, common stock of IBM another. But beyond primary commodities and stocks and bonds, there are precious few instances of homogeneous goods like KC Winter Wheat, which is why the textbook examples of perfectly competitive markets are rather monotonous—commodity markets and stock markets pretty much exhaust the list.

Price-taking is the term for describing people's behavior in a perfectly competitive market. The importance of price-taking behavior is that agents adjust production and consumption decisions to the same signals—the system of market prices—with the result that relative prices reflect relative scarcities: neither production nor consumption can be changed to yield an all-around improvement. When agents rationally calculate how to spend their incomes, each makes sure that the relative values he or she places on the last units of the various goods are brought into line with relative prices, and hence into line with the relative valuations of other agents (who are doing the same thing in their choices). When agents rationally calculate how much to produce of a particular good, they make sure that the market price of the good—which reflects its relative value to consumers—is just equal to the cost of producing the last unit of the good. (If it were more, producers would add to production because they would make more profit; if it were less, they would cut back production for the same reason.) Because universal price-taking behavior means that all producers act this way, "cost" has a double meaning. It is at one and the same time the cost to the producer in terms of outlays on labor and other inputs to the production process and the cost to society in terms of the other goods that are forgone in devoting resources to any particular good. The condition that consumers have identical relative valuations of, say, the last slice of pizza they eat and the last bottle of cola they drink and the condition that the cost of producing one more pizza is equal to its price, as is the cost of one more bottle of cola, together provide the basic reasoning behind the two welfare theorems linking competitive equilibrium to Pareto optimality: under these conditions, it is impossible to shift goods from one consumer to another, or to alter the mix of goods produced, in a way that would benefit all agents.

Economists sometimes make price-taking behavior a basic assumption about the structure of markets and accept the idea that goods are homogeneous as an implication of price-taking. Sometimes economists instead justify price-taking behavior in terms of more primitive assumptions including the assumption that goods are homogeneous. Homogeneity shifts from being an implication of price-taking behavior to being an assumption underlying price-taking behavior. For our purposes, it doesn't matter which alternative is adopted: in both cases, price-taking behavior and homogeneous products go hand in hand.

If we go the route of justifying price-taking behavior in terms of more basic ideas, another primitive assumption is that people act independently of one another (no coalitions, cartels, or associations), and each buyer and seller accounts for a small percentage of market activity. This, in turn, presupposes that there are no significant cost advantages to large-scale production, large being understood in relation to the size of the market. A third assumption is that buyers and sellers can easily move in and out of the market. Their hands are not tied by long-term contracts or other barriers to entry and exit. Finally, it is assumed that participants are well informed about market conditions.

The basic idea of perfect competition is thus a world of many producers and consumers, each one too small to affect market outcomes and therefore not in a position to dictate to the market. A world of wheat farmers, for example. But in actual cases where the number of participants on both sides of the market would make perfect competition feasible, markets rarely operate according to the textbook model in which prices and production are regulated by demand and supply. The wheat market is a good example: beginning with the extended crisis of the 1880s, U.S. wheat farmers were in the forefront of a political movement that swept the prairies, the point of which was to have the government intervene to modify the operation of demand and supply; with the depression of the 1930s, this movement succeeded, and for the last two generations, one version or another of price and production controls has been the norm in the United States, despite the recurring paean to the free market. It will not escape the European reader that the European Union has, if anything, been more aggressive in its intervention in agricultural markets.

It is not only in agricultural markets that producers resist competition. Where there is no possibility of changing the market environment to favor the interests of producers, firms simply pack up and leave. Just one example: a few years back IBM got out of a long-time bread and butter business, the manufacture and sale of personal computers, because computers were becoming "commodities," too much like KC wheat, to afford an adequate profit. Producers thus use both the strategies that the economist Albert Hirschman outlined in his manual for dissidents, *Exit, Voice, and Loyalty:* either change the market to fit the interests of the producers (the voice option favored by farmers and their allies) or leave the market for greener pastures (the exit option adopted by IBM to deal with the changing nature of the computer business). Both kinds of action make it harder to suspend disbelief when it comes to the competitive market as a model for actual markets.

Nonetheless, some markets are plausible approximations to perfect competition, even if they do not fit the mold as neatly as the market for Number 2 KC Hard Red Winter Wheat. But it isn't enough that there be some specimens of competitive markets. In order to guarantee that the two welfare theorems hold, it must be the case that all markets are perfectly competitive. And that strains credulity: most markets are a long way from perfect competition. In many product markets, large scale confers an advantage in production, and this precludes there being the large number of sellers that make price-taking behavior plausible. And even in the absence of cost advantages, producers may erect barriers to entry in order to profit from the ability a monopolist (single seller) or oligopolists (few sellers) have to control prices and production. I have already mentioned brand names. Branding is a formidable barrier to entry for a newcomer who would have to mount a costly marketing campaign to offset the advantages that familiarity confers on existing brands.

But the most glaring inconsistency with the assumption of perfect competition is a market that virtually everyone is personally familiar with, the labor market. For the labor market to be perfectly competitive, each potential worker must be able to work as many or as few hours as he or she would like to work at the going wage. There is, in short, no such thing as unemployment in the perfectly competitive model of the economy. People may not be working 24/7, but that is a matter of their preferences with regard to leisure and rest, not a matter of being unable to find work.

A whole branch of economics would have no reason to exist if labor markets conformed to the assumption of perfect competition. *Macroeconomics*, the study of the behavior of output and employment in the aggregate, came into existence as a result of the Great Depression, when massive unemployment took hold of the capitalist world.[1]

Not only did the failure of labor markets to be perfectly competitive necessitate a whole new branch of economics; this failure accounts for much of the damage caused by simple translations of economic theory into economic policy. The use of comparative advantage to justify free trade is a good example.

From Theory to Polemic: Does Comparative Advantage Justify Free Trade?

Comparative advantage is the jewel in the crown of economic theory, providing deep insight into how societies gain from concentrating their productive energies not necessarily on the things they do best, but on the things they do better than other societies. The abuse of comparative advantage provides a good example of the mischief caused by economic theory when the fine print—in this case, fine print about competitive markets—is ignored. Here the damage is compounded by the lack of attention to class and class divisions. Economics can be problematic even when one accepts its foundational assumptions.

Comparative advantage tells us that each country should specialize in the commodities that it can produce relatively easily—relative, that is, to what is possible in other countries. The theory of comparative advantage was first put forward by the nineteenth-century British economist David Ricardo to explain how Portugal and England could mutually benefit from the differences in their endowments of natural resources: hot, sunny Portugal ought to specialize in wine; temperate, rainy England in woolen cloth (Ricardo 1951 [1817], chap. 7, especially 133–140). Ricardo's theory was an innovation that went against the prevailing wisdom (and intuition) that absolute advantage, as measured by costs of production, governed trade. Absolute advantage was the theory of no less an economist than Adam Smith (1937 [1776], 424), but it is now held up as a canonical example of how even the best of economic minds can go astray. If my productivity in every line of work is exactly twice yours, I have an absolute advantage in everything, but a comparative advantage in nothing. There is no reason to trade.

By contrast, assume that, owing to a favorable climate, I can produce 1,000 gallons of wine in a year; or alternatively, working all year, I can produce 100 yards of cloth. You have less favorable opportunities: you can either produce 50 yards of cloth or 100 gallons of wine. Suppose further that the production technologies are "linear," so that each of us can substitute production of wine for production of cloth at a constant rate. I am able to produce 10 gallons of wine for each yard of cloth I give up, whereas you will get 2 gallons for each yard. Turn the relationship around, and it is clear that by giving up 1 gallon of wine, I get only 0.1 yard of cloth, whereas you get 0.5 yard for each gallon of wine. I have an absolute advantage in both wine and cloth production, but a comparative advantage in wine. You have a comparative advantage in cloth.

Suppose in the absence of trade, I devote half my time to wine production and half to cloth production, ending up with 50 yards of cloth and 500 gallons of wine, while you, oenophile to the core, produce and consume 100 gallons of wine and go around in the all-together. Now suppose trade is introduced into the picture and that we have the possibility of trading 5 gallons of wine for 1 yard of cloth—or, vice-versa, 1 yard of cloth for 5 gallons of wine. Then by specializing in wine production and trading one-fourth of my wine for cloth, I end up with 50 yards of cloth and 750 gallons of wine. I produce 1,000 gallons of wine and trade 250 gallons for 50 yards of cloth. Trade permits specialization in the industry in which I enjoy a comparative advantage and allows me to increase my consumption of wine by 50 percent without any reduction in cloth consumption. You gain by specializing in the other direction: trading all your cloth (you are now producing at the rate of 50 yards per year), you receive 250 gallons of wine rather than the original 100 gallons, an increase of 150 percent.[2]

The beauty of comparative advantage is that, barring ties such as exist if I can produce everything exactly twice as efficiently as you can, everybody has a comparative advantage in something. With each country playing to its relative strengths, all gain from trade.

How easy it is to move from theory to polemic! A *Wall Street Journal* editorial that appeared at the height of the furor about trade-related job losses in 2004 seamlessly connected wine and cloth to outsourcing:

Comparative advantage means that if country X does or makes something with relatively less cost than country Y, then country X should do it. Country Y is thus released to earn higher returns on something else. The magic is that both countries are better off through this arrangement. In the current trade debate, country X stands for India and country Y is the U.S. By moving some data entry, customer service and software engineering activities to India, the economies of both countries gain. (*Wall Street Journal* 2004, A12)

If everybody has a comparative advantage in something, if everybody gains from trade, why are there persistent complaints in the United States about job loss to Mexico, job loss to China, job loss to India?

Let's look at the comparative-advantage argument more closely. As we have seen, Ricardo had in mind a world in which natural resource endowments differ between countries: sunny Portugal specialized in wine and rainy England in cloth, to their mutual advantage. How does comparative advantage work today when natural resources—agriculture and oil apart—play such a minimal role in determining trade flows? To dramatize the question, how does comparative advantage work in a world where there is only one good, edible widgets, which can be used for every purpose under the sun, a world in which an American can produce, say, 5 times as many widgets as an Indian in the same time? Where is India's comparative advantage in this world?

Economics says that India's comparative advantage lies in the sale of its labor to the United States. How is that a comparative advantage? It's not really; it makes more sense to think about this kind of trade in terms of the much maligned theory that preceded comparative advantage, namely, absolute advantage. To use comparative advantage to describe trade in this context is like using an earth-centered model to describe the motions of the planets. It can be done, but such an explanation is cumbersome at best; it is an explanation only in the sense of providing a set of equations that fit the data, not in helping us to understand what is going on. Much better to make the sun the center, and even better to move the sun a bit off center.

But here, for the light it sheds on how far-reaching are the consequences of assuming perfect competition and ignoring class divisions, is the earth-centered explanation of widget trade, using the language and concepts of comparative advantage. First of all, the economist points out, there are really two commodities, widgets and the worker's time. Leisure, for the economist, is time spent not working. So if there are 24 hours in a day, and I work 8 hours, then I "produce" 16 hours of leisure. If the American technology churns out widgets 5 times faster than the Indian technology, then the United States has a comparative advantage in widgets, and India has a comparative advantage in leisure. The sale of labor by Indians is really the sale of Indian leisure, which means the utilization of Indian labor with the American technology instead of with the inferior Indian technology. The movement of jobs from the United States to India is simply the increase of American leisure in response to the new possibilities of exchange opened up by free trade.

To see this, take another look at the explanation of trade in terms of comparative advantage. Replace wine with widgets and cloth with leisure. Sam, an American, has 100 available hours that he can transform into widgets at the rate of 10 widgets for each hour of leisure he is willing to give up. Bharat, an Indian, also has 100 hours at his disposal, and he can transform leisure into widgets at the rate of 2 widgets per hour. Working all 100 hours, Sam can produce 1,000 widgets, and Bharat can produce 200 widgets.

Suppose that in the absence of trade, each chooses to devote half of his available 100 hours to producing widgets, the other half to leisure. Then Sam ends up with 50 hours of leisure and 500 widgets, whereas Bharat ends up with 50 hours of leisure and 100 widgets. How does trade improve matters? Assume that trade takes place at the rate of 5 widgets for one hour of labor time, and that Sam and Bharat each changes production in the direction of specializing in the good in which he has comparative advantage. Specifically, assume that Sam buys 50 hours of Bharat's leisure and utilizes Bharat's time to produce 500 more widgets, combining Bharat's labor with Sam's more productive technology. Bharat stops producing altogether with his own technology to free up the time. In return, Sam pays Bharat 250 widgets (5 widgets per hour × 50 hours). If Sam continues to work 50 hours, then he ends up with 50 hours of leisure and the 500 widgets he produces, plus the difference between what Bharat produces, namely, 500 widgets, and what Sam has to pay Bharat in wages, 250 widgets—750 widgets in all. Sam is a clear gainer.

But Sam's gain is not at Bharat's expense. Bharat works the same amount of time as before, but he is now working with a more productive technology, and even after Sam's cut, he ends up with 2.5 times what he was able to produce with his own technology, 250 widgets instead of 100. Both partners gain from trade.

Indeed, Sam might decide to cut back on his hours, working only 40 hours instead of 50. Then he would gain both in leisure and widgets: instead of his original 50 hours of leisure and 500 widgets, he would have 60 hours of leisure and 650 widgets (250 of the widgets Bharat produces and 400 widgets from his own 40 hours of work).

The argument so far follows Ricardo's original example in presupposing a world of yeomen, who, like Ricardo's English and Portuguese yeomen, are at once producer and consumer, worker and owner. Sam and Bharat produce, trade, and consume widgets and leisure, just as the Englishman in Ricardo's story raised sheep and manufactured cloth, consuming part of his production and trading the rest for Portuguese wine, and the Portuguese grower–vintner produced wine for his own table as well as to trade with his English counterpart.

It is doubtful that such a model captured the reality of Ricardo's own day. But whatever the case then, the reality today is that few Americans (and few Indians too, for that matter) are worker-owners, and even fewer consume a significant part of what they produce. Both Bharat and Sam most likely sell their labor to an employer, and buy their consumption goods on the market. It is not just a simplification to ignore these realities but a distortion: the distinction between worker and owner is basic to capitalism, as is the distinction between producer and consumer. If we are to understand the costs and benefits of trade in the world beyond the textbook, we must abandon the yeoman model and distinguish among various groups—workers, managers, owners, consumers—distinctions obscured by the yeoman model.

For simplicity, let's focus on two of these groups, workers and owners. Suppose, as before, that Americans produce 10 widgets per hour and Indians produce 2 widgets per hour. But now imagine that Sam and his fellow Americans work for U.S. Widget, the world leader in widget manufacture, each of them receiving 8 widgets per hour. This leaves 2 widgets per hour as profit for U.S. Widget. To keep matters simple, let Bharat and his fellow Indians remain self-employed, at least for the moment, as in the original case of worker–owners, consumer–producers.

Imagine that before trade, 50 Americans and 50 Indians are working. On an hourly basis, Americans are producing 500 widgets, split 400 for workers, 100 for owners; Indians have 100 widgets at their disposal. Assume that, as before, "trade" consists of putting the Indians to work with American technology: 50 Indians become employed by an Indian subsidiary of U.S. Widget. Indian output increases from 100 to 500 widgets per hour, of which, we shall continue to assume, Indians receive 250 as wages; the other half goes to U.S. Widget. Suppose finally that output in the United States falls by 20 percent, from 500 to 400, which partially offsets the increased production in India. In India the hourly gain is 150 widgets, from the 100 that 50 workers can produce with their own technology to the 250 they receive as wages from the Indian subsidiary of U.S. Widget. In the United States, the overall gain is also 150 widgets per hour—a profit of 250 widgets from the Indian subsidiary, less 100 widgets in lost production in the United States. These overall numbers are the same as before, as is the reduction in hours worked in the United States. So what is the difference between the two cases?

Americans gain across the board—if all 50 workers voluntarily reduce their work time by 20 percent to 48 minutes, and the workers get all the profits of U.S. Widget. In this case each worker will enjoy a proportionate share of the gains from trade: when workers voluntarily adjust their working time and receive all the profits, we are in effect back to the original case of trade between Sam and Bharat. Under these circumstances, American workers balance labor and leisure as they will, and lost wages will be compensated by an increase in the value of their U.S. Widget shares, as higher profits reflect the cost savings of locating widget production abroad.

But the reality is that American workers don't in general own the companies for which they work, and American labor markets are far from the competitive model in which the worker gets to choose how much to work. It is, as I have said, doubtful that the abstraction of "Englishmen" and "Portuguese" captured the reality of Ricardo's time, but it is a sure thing that in today's world the consequences of outsourcing are dramatically different for different groups within the countries engaged in trade.

The owners of U.S. Widget stock will be better off, but not the workers. In reality, the reduction of output in the United States is the occasion for layoffs, and the leisure of the unemployed is mostly involuntary. Workers do not face a perfectly competitive labor market in which they are free to choose the number of hours they work. Nor are the unemployed compensated by extra dividends on shares of U.S. Widget stock they don't own. The total gain for Americans is the same as in the original model, 150 widgets, but the stockholders who enjoy a 230-widget net gain (250 widgets from India less 20 widgets of profit lost because production is curtailed in the United States) have little to do with the 10 workers who lose 80 widgets of wages along with their jobs.

What should workers do when they lose their jobs? Stay put, and the only work available may be flipping hamburgers at the neighborhood McDonalds. How about following the money, moving from a declining region to a boom area? Isn't mobility the name of the game?

Mobility may work for young, unattached men and women, but it's quite another story for the middle aged, certainly for middle-aged parents with school-aged children. Some years ago, the *Washington Post* op-ed columnist Dana Milbank, then a reporter for the *Wall Street Journal*, related one family's journey following the money (Milbank 1992). A sad tale indeed: lower and lower wages; growing mistrust of employers and an accompanying decrease in commitment at the workplace; a growing difficulty in connecting to new people and places—"After you move, you harden at each place. You don't want to get too attached, because saying goodbye gets more emotional"; growing psychological stress, culminating in a heart attack for one parent and a drinking problem for the other and problems in school for the kids. When the family moves for the fourth time, there is no room for the dog—Dad takes him out in the back yard and shoots him.

Economists may talk about winners compensating losers, but actual compensation is something else. Even if it were politically feasible to transfer some of the owners' gains to workers displaced by outsourcing, I've never heard a convincing story about how families are to be compensated when a parent loses his or her job. Even if people avoid the extreme of moving several times, even if they don't end up shooting the dog, how do you compensate a couple who have lived in one place for 45 years, whose two teenagers have attended local schools from kindergarten on, who have all along expected to retire and grow old with the respect and affection of neighbors and kin?

This leaves the Indian. Can we at least say that Bharat gains unequivocally? No doubt the Indian worker gains in material terms: for the same effort, Bharat now enjoys 2.5 times as much widget consumption. But how much better off is he? Working for U.S. Widget brings with it both the disruption of community and the substitution of forced-march Westernization for a more gradual evolution of Indian culture as it confronts globalization. Anyone who sympathizes with the view that Mexican peasants had to be dragged into the twenty-first century, kicking and screaming if necessary, will view forced-march Westernization as a plus (see Chapter 1); those who sympathize with the critique of development and globalization in Chapter 13 will see it as a minus. Plus or minus, such considerations do not fit easily into a critique of economics based on the structural assumptions alone: we are led as if by an invisible hand to consider the foundational assumptions as well. (On the effects of outsourcing on Indian culture and community, see Slater 2004 and Rai 2004.)

To summarize: The wine–cloth model reflects a world in which English and Portuguese yeomen find trade mutually attractive on the basis of comparative advantage rooted in different endowments of natural resources. In Ricardo's world of wine and wool, technologies are immobile because one cannot move the Portuguese sun and the Portuguese soil to England, nor can one move the lush pastures of rainy and temperate England to hot and dry Portugal. By contrast, the widget model captures a world in which technology (and the capital necessary to use the technology) is mobile and natural resources matter little. Today technology moves almost as easily across borders as within a single country.[3] In addition to ignoring the possibility of technology transfer, the standard textbook, with its yeomen who are at the same time owners and workers, producers and consumers, obscures the reality of class divisions. In today's world—contrary to the rhetoric that there are millions and millions of American stockholders—middle- and lower-class wage earners are just that, wage earners, for whom the extra profits associated with moving jobs overseas are cold comfort. Moreover, in today's world labor markets are a long way from the competitive model.

John Maynard Keynes began *The General Theory of Employment, Interest and Money* by arguing that it is even more difficult to unlearn the theories of the past than to construct relevant theories for the present:

> The composition of this book has been for the author a long struggle of escape, and so must the reading of it be for most readers if the author's assault upon them is to be successful,—a struggle of escape from habitual modes of thought and expression. The ideas which are here expressed so laboriously are extremely simple and should be obvious. The difficulty lies, not in the new ideas, but in escaping from the old ones, which ramify, for those brought up as most of us have been, into every corner of our minds. (Keynes 1936, viii)

Keynes concludes the book by stressing that he is not concerned with ideas for ideas' sake:

> The ideas of economists and political philosophers, both when they are right and when they are wrong, are more powerful than is commonly understood.

Indeed, the world is ruled by little else. Practical men, who believe themselves to be quite exempt from any intellectual influences, are usually the
slaves of some defunct economist. Madmen in authority, who hear voices in
the air, are distilling their frenzy from some academic scribbler of a few years
back. I am sure the power of vested interest is vastly exaggerated compared
with the gradual encroachment of ideas. (Keynes 1936, 383)

The practical men and women who are responsible for trade policy today
are equally the slaves of not one but legions of defunct (and functioning)
economists. If you doubt the model, it just shows that you are not used to
thinking like an economist, to making the necessary abstractions that re-
veal the glory of comparative advantage. Class divisions and imperfect
labor markets are for the economist simply details that get in the way of
understanding.

Complete Markets, Externalities, and Public Goods

Even if all markets were perfectly competitive in the textbook sense of the
term, economics would not be problem free. Perfect competition is just one
of the conditions that together guarantee a market system will fulfill the
promise of the first and second welfare theorems. One of the more important additional assumptions is the assumption that markets are complete,
that all economic interaction between people is mediated through markets.
There is a market for every conceivable good, present and future, and every
conceivable circumstance, such as a market for umbrellas available on June
4, 2009, if it is raining, and another market for umbrellas on that date if it is
not raining. (Insurance is the prototype of such *contingent commodities*, to use
the economist's terminology: I pay $200 as a fire-insurance premium on my
barn, and I get two "goods" everyday of the ensuing year, $60,000 if my
barn burns down, $0 if my barn does not burn down. The problem with this
example is a problem endemic to the competitive model: after the first example of such a market, there is a long silence. Once we have exhausted the
list of the relatively few items on which we can purchase insurance, there
are not many markets for contingent commodities.)

The idea of complete markets also rules out what economists call *externalities*, effects of one agent on another, which are not mediated through
markets. Consider an archetypal example: the effects of beekeeping on
apple growing. Bees have a beneficial effect on apples because they help to

pollinate the fruit. If there is a perfectly competitive market in which the owner of the bees sells "pollination services" to the orchard owner, all is well and good. But if the pollination is simply an uncompensated by-product of the beekeeper's honey-making operation, then the effect is "external" to the beekeeper.

Why does this matter? It matters because in the presence of externalities, it is generally possible to improve on the operation of a market system even within the limited criterion of Pareto optimality: some people could be made better off without making anybody worse off. In the present example, starting from a competitive market equilibrium, it would be possible to improve the lot of both the beekeeper and the apple grower by keeping the bees in the orchard longer and letting the beekeeper take a few of the extra apples that result from more intensive pollination. Assuming that only the beekeeper and the apple grower are affected by this transaction, it represents a Pareto improvement: both are made better off by this departure from competitive equilibrium.

Externalities cut both ways. A textbook example of a negative externality is the pollution caused by carbon-based fuels. The combustion of oil to produce electricity and the combustion of gasoline to move automobiles and trucks also produce oxides that are notorious health hazards and contribute to global warming. Pollution is not a commodity; our acquiescence to pollution is not purchased in a perfectly competitive market or, for that matter, in any market at all. Absent these markets, neither producers nor consumers will take account of pollution when making decisions as to how much electricity should be provided, or how much driving we should be doing.

Economists recognize the problems posed by externalities for the two welfare theorems, and they have a standard response: fight fire with fire, which is to say create private property and markets to overcome the effects of nonmarket interactions. Or at the very least, simulate the market mechanism. In the case of honeybees, create a market in "pollination services." Or combine honey and apple production into a single enterprise so that none of the benefits of pollination are external to the beekeeping enterprise. In the case of pollution, create private property rights and a market.

There are situations in which appropriate markets can be created. But the costs (including the externalities) of creating markets may defeat the purpose of making people better off, and so we may simply have to live with externalities. This raises a central question: Are externalities an occasional nuisance or anomaly, rightly treated in the fine print that we need hardly bother to read? Or are externalities everywhere, something we rarely escape?

It obviously makes a huge difference. In the first case, externalities can be treated as relatively minor, second-order effects—effects that can be put to one side for purposes of assessing the welfare properties of the competitive model. In the second case, externalities are central to the discussion and are ignored at the peril of making the discussion irrelevant to the world we actually inhabit. In this regard, maverick economists Kenneth Boulding and Herman Daly have emphasized the difference between "empty world economics" and "full world economics" (Boulding 1966; Daly and Cobb 1989). Once upon a time when the world was sparsely inhabited, once upon a time when we used relatively few resources, it might have been acceptable to relegate externalities to the realm of occasional nuisance and anomaly. But now that we live and work at close quarters to one another, our non-market interactions are much more part of the fabric of our lives, and externalities are of central concern. Pollution, once again, is a case in point. When people lived in small communities with a lot of space between settlements and produced and consumed at relatively modest levels, air and water pollution were relatively minor problems. They become major problems only with the advent of cities and the accompanying growth in population density.

The takeaway is that externalities, Pareto optimality, and individualistic behavior are not mutually compatible. Nobel Laureate Amartya Sen's well-known article, "The Impossibility of a Paretian Liberal," explores the contradiction between Pareto optimality and individualism in the context of externalities: in his example, a negative externality between your consumption and my well-being when your taste in reading matter offends my sense of decency. Libertarians, for whom the individual is sacred, must be prepared to sacrifice Pareto optimality, heresy to mainstream economists for whom Pareto optimality is the closest thing to the Holy Grail.

There is a close cousin of externalities that deserves particular attention. As pointed out in Chapter 1, economists distinguish between ordinary goods, so-called private goods, like a loaf of bread, which have the property that more for you means less for me, and public goods, which have the property that my consumption does not diminish the availability of the good to you. A classical example (going back to Adam Smith) is a lighthouse: up to the capacity of the shipping channel, light for one ship does not mean less light for another. The relationship between public goods and externalities is clear. Providing a lighthouse for one ship provides the same light for another, just as generating electricity from carbon-based fuels adds to pollution.

There are large numbers of goods that are purely or partially "public" in nature—public not in the sense that they are necessarily provided by the public sector but in the sense that they admit of simultaneous consumption by additional people without any diminution in the availability to the existing consumers. The music files that kids (of all ages) download from the Internet, a highway—until it becomes congested—have the property that another person can consume without limiting the consumption of people who are already downloading music or traveling on the road.

Nonrivalry is how economists express this characteristic of public goods. Much ink has been spilled over the issue of whether in addition to nonrivalry it matters whether an individual can be excluded from consumption. Take the example of television signals. Evidently your consumption and mine are nonrivalrous. But does the assumption of excludability apply? Does it matter?

For our purposes, television signals are no less a public good if it is possible to exclude potential consumers, if it is possible for the sender to scramble the signals so that only people equipped with an unscrambler (for which the sender holds the patent) can receive the signals. As with any definition, the appropriate definition depends on the purpose. If the point were to demarcate commodities for which it is possible to have markets from those for which it is impossible, then excludability would certainly be relevant: if it is impossible to exclude people from receiving television signals, then it is hard to see why economic man would pay for the right to receive signals. But the existence of markets is not the issue here. Rather our focus is on the efficiency of markets, as summarized in the two theorems about the Pareto optimality of a system of competitive markets. For this purpose, excludability is irrelevant. Even if television signals could be costlessly scrambled and costlessly unscrambled, so that a market in television signals was feasible, Pareto optimality could not be achieved through a market system. As long as there was one individual who derived even the most minimal benefit from watching television, it would not be Pareto optimal to exclude this individual—as charging any market price higher than he is willing to pay inevitably would.

Why is it nonoptimal to exclude an individual whose willingness to pay is below the market price? Isn't this what markets are about in the first place, to make sure that goods go to their highest valued uses? To be sure, but the assumption behind this idea is that all goods are private goods, so that excluding lower valued uses makes more of the good available for higher valued uses. The case of public goods is different: one person's television viewing does not—by assumption—diminish the availability of the signal to other people, so it cannot be Pareto optimal to deprive anyone of the viewing opportunity.

The existence of public goods does not imply that these goods should be produced and distributed publicly, and certainly not that public goods should be given away. On the one hand, private enterprise has discovered many ingenious ways to structure markets when goods are partially public and partially private. Airline travel is a case in point. The airlines segment the travel market in a variety of ways to charge different fares to different people on the basis of their assumed willingness to pay—exactly what is required for an optimal allocation of airplane seats because of the public-good aspect of air travel. Seniors and youth receive discounts, and personal travel is cheaper than business travel: airlines have figured out that retirees and kids, or indeed anybody traveling for personal reasons, are more flexible than business travelers, so Saturday night stay-overs and advance purchase are often conditions of reduced fares. These are remedies, albeit imperfect ones, to the problems posed by public goods for markets to work efficiently. But they do so by forsaking the competitive market that is the basis of the two welfare theorems; they do so by taking to heart the restrictive conditions under which competitive markets work optimally.

But even where it is difficult or impossible to break up markets into different segments—the term of art is *price discrimination*—public goods do not automatically sound a death knell for the market. One might recognize full well the inefficiency involved in denying a penniless teenager internet access to music files, but defend a market solution on the grounds that property rights in music and the accompanying royalties are a necessary incentive to the production of new music, that the wellspring of musical creativity is the dollar sign. I don't intend to get into the merits of this argument beyond pointing out that just by entertaining it, we have long since left the grounds on which the welfare claims of competitive markets are argued through the two welfare theorems. One can claim quite a bit for markets as stimuli to invention and innovation, but it is not credible to base these claims on a model of perfectly competitive, price-taking agents such as the two welfare theorems envision. Innovation by definition deals with change and novelty, and innovation is shrouded in a mist of uncertainty through which it is im-possible to see sufficiently clearly for there to be markets and prices, much less competitive markets and prices. In consequence, economists have no credible theorems about what regime of intellectual property rights pro-vides the optimal rate of innovation—as if the concept of an "optimal rate of innovation" had any meaning at all.

Uncertainty

We have touched on another reason for market failure, or rather two closely related reasons. The first is radical uncertainty, by which I intend something more than simply a lack of certain knowledge: the emphasis is on the adjective *radical*. By radical uncertainty I mean uncertainty so pro-found as to be intractable by means of a probabilistic analysis. The distinc-tion is between the uncertainty about whether it will rain on Commence-ment Day at Harvard University, for which there is sufficient knowledge to treat the question probabilistically, and the uncertainty about the prospects for the exchange rate between the dollar and the euro in 2050, about which we have (at the time these words are being written) no basis for a proba-bilistic treatment. In principle, where there is sufficient probabilistic knowl-edge, there can be willing buyers and sellers for contingent commodities that resemble insurance policies in the way they compensate people if one state of affairs rather than another turns out to hold sway. So, in principle, this kind of uncertainty—what, following Frank Knight (1940 [1921]), I refer to in Chapter 7 as *risk*—presents no problem for a system of markets, or for the welfare theorems on which the economist's formal defense of the market rests.

We have explored uncertainty at some length in Chapters 7, 8, and 9; it is at the core of my critique of how economics treats knowledge. But it is not clear how radical uncertainty fits into the internal, structural critique. As I pointed out in Chapter 1, behavioral economics, which explores the limits of rational calculation, offers the possibility of a trenchant critique from the inside, but this critique has so far been self-limiting in relation to the nor-mative claims for the market.[4] Behavioral economists do not appear very eager to follow through on the logic of their own critique, instead providing one band-aid after another for the wounds they inflict on mainstream theory—the papers in Camerer et al. (2004) cover a range of wounds and band-aids. For behavioral economics to become more subversive, it would have to pay more attention to how radical uncertainty undermines rational calculation.

The fact is that contemporary economics, including behavioral economics, has pretty much abandoned the distinction between radical uncertainty and risk. All probability is considered to be subjective in nature, and the probability distribution one holds over rainfall in Cambridge, Massachusetts, on the particular Thursday, June 4, on which commencement will take place in 2009 is no different in kind from the probability distribution one holds over the dollar–euro exchange rate in 2050.

That would be a fine resolution of the problem if the markets that the theory posits really existed, namely, different markets for commodities under different circumstances at different times—for example, one market, with its particular price, for umbrellas on Commencement Day in the year 2009 under the assumption of heavy rainfall, and another market, presumably with a lower price, for the same umbrellas at the same time under the assumption of dry weather. In principle, all uncertainty may be equally amenable to a subjective probability calculus. But the very absence of most of these contingent markets speaks volumes about the usefulness of this theory for any other purpose than to clarify the stringent assumptions underlying the two welfare theorems.

My position is that radical uncertainty and risk are sufficiently different that the ways people actually behave in the two situations are dramatically different. One can easily imagine Harvard University, if not the typical proud parent of a graduate, insuring against the prospect of a heavy rainfall on Commencement Day, but there is no futures market for dollars against euros beyond a very short time horizon. Decisions that depend on the dollar–euro exchange rate in 2050 will have to be made on the basis of hunch and intuition, rather than on the basis of market prices. In short, radical uncertainty means that markets are incomplete, a basic violation of the assumptions of the two welfare theorems.

Well-Informed Agents

Textbooks typically highlight another assumption that must be made in order to sustain the claim that the market maximizes the size of the pie, namely, that agents are well informed about the goods and services that pass through the market. This assumption, too, is necessary for a complete set of markets to exist.

"Well informed" is suitably vague, but it can be given more precise content. For one thing, people must know what is going on in the marketplace, whether or not someone down the street is selling Number 2 Winter Wheat at a discount from the price on the Kansas City Board of Trade. (If such sales are taking place, it is a sure sign that the market is not perfectly competitive—why would anyone pay full price for the identical commodity that one can just as easily buy at a lower price?)

But there are more subtle information requirements. It is not necessary that everyone know everything about a commodity, but it is important that there be no systematic biases in information. Consider the market in health insurance. To dramatize the information problem, imagine for the moment that it is impossible to screen or examine applicants.[5] There are "strong" people who are unlikely to become ill and "weak" people who are illness prone, but nobody—apart from the individuals themselves—knows who is strong and who is weak. In this world, the equilibrium price of insurance is unlikely to produce a Pareto optimal amount of health insurance. If the probability of a weak person becoming ill is known, as is the (lower) probability of a strong person becoming ill, and we know the relative numbers of weak and strong people, then we can calculate the insurance premiums needed to cover claims: the individual insurance premium has to be equal to the average probability of illness multiplied by the cost of treatment. As a strong person, I pay a price that exceeds the cost to society of my insurance: the true cost of my insurance is my—lower than average—probability of illness multiplied by the cost of treatment. Conversely, as a weak person, I pay less than the social cost of my insurance, my—higher than average—probability of illness multiplied by the cost of treatment. So strong people buy too little insurance, "too little" in comparison with what they would buy if they paid the real cost of their insurance. By the same token, weak people buy too much. Both groups could be made better off if the prices reflected the true costs of their insurance and they received a sufficient portion of the overall gains from bringing prices into line with costs. Because both groups need receive only a fraction of the total gains of bifurcating the insurance market to make themselves as well-off as with a unified market, there is clearly something left over to distribute across the board. It is this last point—namely, that there is something left over for general distribution after prices are adjusted—which ensures that the move from a single price to separate prices will make everybody better off, the condition of Pareto improvement. That it is possible to improve on the original outcome shows that the original allocation was not Pareto optimal.[6] Even if the original result emerged from a system of perfectly competitive markets.

The informational problem in this example is that we each know about our own health, but no one, including the insurance companies, knows about the health of other people. As a result, two commodities—insurance for strong people and insurance for weak people—are necessarily conflated into a single commodity: insurance pure and simple. The problem of asymmetric information thus fits under the rubric of incomplete markets: if markets were complete, there would be separate markets for the two categories of people. Terminology aside, asymmetric information is sufficiently important that it is generally treated as a problem in its own right, especially because of the important work done by three leading twentieth-century economists, George Akerlof, Michael Spence, and Joseph Stiglitz, on various aspects and complications of asymmetric information, work that led to Nobel Prizes for the three of them in 2001.

Stability and Instability

There is another set of issues that get virtually no attention in the typical elementary text and only cursory attention in advanced texts. These are issues surrounding the so-called stability of equilibrium. The term *stability* is used because economics, imitating physics, sees equilibrium as the norm and asks what happens when equilibrium is disturbed by a shock to the system—for example, an unexpectedly good harvest of apples that leads to a glut in the apple market. Does the system find its way to a new equilibrium? Are there self-correcting forces at work? In other words, is equilibrium stable? Or are there forces that lead the system further away from equilibrium—is the equilibrium unstable?

The issue of stability is important because stability is the guarantee that—assuming only one equilibrium exists—a market system will settle at this equilibrium.[7] Economists once again appeal to prices: just as equilibrium prices imply, fine print aside, that people's actions will dovetail and that the result will satisfy the conditions of Pareto optimality, so does the adjustment of prices ensure that equilibrium will be achieved. In the words of Mankiw, "The price of any good adjusts to bring the quantity supplied and quantity demanded into balance" (Mankiw 2004, 77).

Observe that these claims about prices are very different in kind: the first says that an equilibrium set of prices exists; the second is an assertion not about existence, but about mechanism, namely, that the price mechanism leads the economy to equilibrium. This is much bolder and far-reaching than asserting the mere existence of equilibrium. It is an assertion that the driving force of the economy is prices. When the quantity of pizzas demanded exceeds the quantity producers would like to supply, the price of pizza will rise. When the quantity demanded is less than what suppliers have in mind, the price will fall. And eventually the market will come to rest at a price at which consumers and producers are content with things as they are.

Maybe so. But the case is not ironclad even when we limit our attention to a single market. Nobody has ever made a convincing case that the labor market operates this way. And the case is even less compelling when we look at many markets functioning at the same time, when we look at a system of markets. With a multiplicity of markets, there are many other variables that might operate more powerfully than prices: the level of overall output and income, for example, or even the distribution of income.

The long and the short of it is that absent some very strong simplifying assumptions that no one pretends reflect the real world, the assertion of stability is just that: an assertion, a declaration of faith in the market. Here I should perhaps note an important difference between the typical elementary text and the typical advanced text. Whereas most books on the principles of economics leave things with a recital of the economist's creed à la Mankiw ("The price of any good adjusts . . ."), graduate texts are more circumspect. Graduate texts confess the paucity of theory supporting the claim for the price mechanism as guarantor that things will gravitate toward equilibrium. However, having made what must be regarded as a very serious admission about the limits of markets to deliver even the very limited kind of optimality enshrined in the two welfare theorems, these texts typically move on to other issues. In one leading graduate text I have examined, less than 10 pages out of 1,000 are devoted to the issue of stability (Mas-Colell et al. 1995).

Is Economics Really about the Virtues of Markets?

Economists may respond to the foregoing by denying that welfare economics, the attribution of good (or bad) to market outcomes, is a large part of the enterprise of economics. Economics is really about description, not evaluation. I dispute this. In my judgment, economics has from the outset had a normative and constructive agenda, whether it be to celebrate markets, as in the case of the mainstream from Adam Smith on, or to condemn markets, as in the case of dissenters like Karl Marx. This agenda, I would submit, is inextricably bound up with description. Indeed, at the risk of overrepetition, I reiterate that much of the apparatus of mainstream economics is totally unnecessary if all we are interested in is describing the world. Take, for instance, most of the apparatus of consumer choice. We don't need to inquire how a hungry and thirsty student chooses between one combination of pizza and cola and another, and we certainly don't need to posit any kind of utility maximization. We can start with demand curves and leave the genesis of the demand curve in the black box of the human psyche for someone else to sort out. But if we are to argue that these choices have something to do with human well-being, the apparatus of consumer choice becomes a necessary part of the argument. Nor do we need to assume given preferences if all we are interested in is description. It is difficult but hardly impossible to model changing preferences—a search in the database EconLit on the keywords *endogenous preferences* turned up over 50 items published within the last 20 years. (See Bowles 1998 for a revue of the journal literature.) The problem is that it is difficult to invest individual choices with welfare content if preferences are changing.[8] In short, if the normative agenda were absent, I believe economics would be very different from what it actually is.

If welfare economics is central to the mainstream enterprise, this appendix adds up to quite an indictment—remember that this is a critique from within economics, as distinct from the critique this book emphasizes. Kenneth Arrow, among the great economists of the twentieth century, was recognized with one of the very first Nobel Prizes given in economics for his work on, among other things, general equilibrium theory. Arrow once said to me that the chief virtue of deep study of the theory of general equilibrium was that it revealed how stringent are the requirements for market outcomes to be socially desirable. If we must assume away markets with few sellers, if we must assume away any and all advantages to large-scale production, if we must assume away externalities, public goods, and asymmetries of information—if, in short, we must assume a price-taking market for every conceivable commodity, is there anything worth salvaging of the claim that market outcomes cannot be improved upon by social planning?

Apparently quite a bit, at least as the economist typically sees matters. Consider the issue of price-taking behavior. After explaining carefully to his neophyte readers various forms of market organization ranging from the many sellers of the perfectly competitive case through to the monopoly of a single seller, with stops along the way for the mixed cases of oligopoly (few sellers) and monopolistic competition (more than a few sellers, but not enough to lead to price-taking behavior), Mankiw takes stock: "In the end, monopoly power is a matter of degree. It is true that many firms have some monopoly power. It is also true that their monopoly is usually limited. In these cases, we will not go far wrong assuming that firms operate in competitive markets, even if that is not precisely the case" (Mankiw 2004, 340). In other words, the world is quite messy, so we can assume that one end of the spectrum—the perfectly competitive end—is typical. This may satisfy the instructor of Economics 101, but it would not get a passing grade in Logic 101.

One could take a very different tack, namely, that economics is not really about description or evaluation, that perfect competition and Pareto optimality and the rest are simply devices to teach the real message: the logic of constrained maximization. This was, as pointed out in Chapter 10, Lionel Robbins's view in his pathbreaking *Essay on the Nature and Significance of Economic Science*. In this view, economics is about decision making with complicated goals that partially (at least) conflict—whence the maximization, which is to say maximization of a mathematical index or function that reflects these goals—and limited means to achieve these goals—whence the constraints. In this view, the logic of constrained maximization then contains all the insights of economics: trade-offs, opportunity costs, thinking at the margin, and so forth. We are not supposed to take the competitive model either as a description of the world beyond the ivory tower or as the basis for claims about the virtues of markets.

This would get economics off the hook, in the sense that it would no longer be seen as defending claims about the social desirability of markets. But it would do so at the cost of reducing economics to a set of formalisms without content.

And in any case, the defense of economics as decision theory simply won't wash. Economics may be reduced to a formal logic of constrained maximization—Paul Samuelson, another early Nobel Laureate in economics, made his name by, among other things, demonstrating the formal similarity, as avatars of constrained maximization, of problems with very different substantive properties. But along with the formalization there is always a story, so we can legitimately ask which stories economists pick,

and why these and not other stories. When we look at the stories economists tell, it becomes clear that economics teaches more than the logic of
constrained maximization. Economics teaches a way of seeing the world, a
way of seeing the world that extols the virtues of markets and relegates the
problems to the fine print.

Consider the results of a survey conducted more than fifteen years ago
that solicited the views of economists on a number of market-related issues
(Alston et al. 1992). Because they deal with issues on which the average
noneconomist is unlikely to have an opinion, many of the questions and
answers shed little light on the question of whether there is an economic
way of seeing the world. But some of the questions and answers are more
revealing: For example, only 6.5 percent of respondents disagreed with the
proposition "Tariffs and import quotas usually reduce general economic
welfare."

Such a broad consensus cuts across the distinction between conservative
and liberal. Greg Mankiw, besides being the author of the leading *Principles*
text, served a stint as George W. Bush's chair of the Council of Economic
Advisers (CEA), so I suppose his conservative credentials are not in doubt.
But Mankiw has no shortage of allies across the aisle. During his time as
chair of the CEA, he got involved in a political controversy when his faith in
comparative advantage led him to a position that appeared to many politicians, Democrats and Republicans alike, perilously close to condoning the
outsourcing of American jobs in the larger interest of freer trade. Mankiw
was forced to beat a strategic retreat, apologizing in a letter to the (Republican) Speaker of the House for a " 'lack of clarity' " that " 'left the wrong im-
pression that I praised the loss of U.S. jobs.' " (Bumiller 2004). The economics
profession rallied to their beleaguered colleague. According to *Wall Street
Journal* reporter Alan Murray, the flap "exposed one of the great rifts in the
current U.S. political debate. It isn't Republicans vs. Democrats; it's economists vs. everybody else . . . Democrats of the economic persuasion such
as Clinton Labor Secretary Robert Reich and former Council of Economic
Advisers Chairwoman Janet Yellen were quick to come to his defense"
(Murray 2004).

Free trade is not the only issue on which the economics profession coa-
lesces: cash transfers versus payments in kind are another litmus test. Just
over 15 percent disagreed with the statement "Cash payments increase the
welfare of recipients to a greater degree than do transfers-in-kind of equal
cash value." (Given this consensus on the virtues of cash over payments-

in-kind, it is not surprising that only 19 percent disagreed with the proposition "The government should restructure the welfare system along the lines of a 'negative income tax.'")

In another survey, only 29 percent of the economic theorists polled by a leading health economist, Victor Fuchs (1996), agreed with the idea that "insurance companies should be required to cover all applicants . . . and *not* allowed to charge sicker individuals higher premiums" (emphasis added). In contrast, almost 70 percent of practicing physicians agreed with the statement. Clearly, the economists had absorbed the lessons of asymmetric information better than the doctors and were more concerned with Pareto optimality.

High on the economist's enemies list, right after restrictions on international trade, is rent control. In his textbook, Mankiw quotes approvingly an anonymous economist's view of rent control as "the best way to destroy a city, other than bombing" (2004, 117).[9] Paul Krugman, a leading liberal economist, as well as columnist for the *New York Times*, could not agree more:

> The analysis of rent control is among the best-understood issues in all of economics—among economists, anyway—one of the least controversial. In 1992 a poll of the American Economic Association [cited above— actually the poll included some economists who might not have been AEA members (see Alston et al. 1992, 203)] found 93 percent of its members agreeing that "a ceiling on rents reduces the quality and quantity of housing." Almost every freshman-level textbook contains a case study on rent control, using its known adverse side effects to illustrate the principles of supply and demand. Sky-high rents on uncontrolled apartments, because desperate renters have nowhere to go—and the absence of new apartment construction despite those high rents, because landlords fear that controls will be extended? Predictable. Bitter relations between tenants and landlords, with an arms race between ever-more ingenious strategies to force tenants out—what yesterday's article [about the rental-housing market in San Francisco] oddly described as "free market horror stories"—and constantly proliferating regulations designed to block those strategies? Predictable. (Krugman 2000, originally published in *The New York Times*)

Those who believe that economics is nothing but the logic of constrained maximization have to explain the consistency of the stories economists attach to this logic, or, to put it slightly differently, why economists choose some maximization problems and ignore others. It would not, for example, be difficult to set up a maximization problem for which the outcome is that no deterioration in the quality and quantity of housing results from the imposition of rent control. In fact, it's been done (Arnott 1996). But this is not the story economists generally choose. Instead, as Krugman suggests, "Almost every freshman-level textbook contains a case study on rent control, using its known adverse side effects to illustrate the principles of supply and demand."

So economics does have a story to tell, the story that markets are by and large good for people. This appendix has argued that we don't have to go off the reservation to find holes in the story big enough to drive a truck through. Why, then, this book? Without taking anything away from a critique of economics based on its structural assumptions, I believe there is a deeper critique to be made, a critique that focuses on the foundations of economics in individualism, self-interest, unlimited wants, rationality, and the nation-state.

The structural critique leads to endless wrangling about how well, when all is said and done, the assumption of complete perfectly competitive markets approximates real, existing markets. It may be as Mankiw argues, that the world is not perfectly competitive, but close enough that the competitive model serves as a good first approximation. No amount of evidence will settle whether the model and the world are "close enough," any more than evidence can settle whether a glass is half full or half empty. A foundational critique in effect opens up a second front: let's grant everything that the economist might wish about structure; let's assume that there are no externalities and that everybody possesses the same information; let's assume, in short, complete, price-taking markets. Even if such an idealized world were the world we actually inhabit, this book argues that there would be good reasons to be skeptical of the foundational assumptions of economics. Sufficient reasons to be wary of the claims economists make for markets even if—especially if—you judge the structural critique to be relatively unimpressive on balance.

Externalities, Distribution, and Community

Commercial logging in tropical forests may help to clarify how a critique of economics based on its structural assumptions misses the mark. Logging brings up various externalities: for instance, the value of biodiversity both to the indigenous people for whom it is essential to their way of life and to a wider world that may value biodiversity for reasons ranging from the intrinsic value of a more diverse ecology to specific contributions like medicines derived from tropical plants. Logging also brings up distributional issues in the form of questions about who benefits from the sale of logs and other forest products to a world with an insatiable appetite for these commodities.

The economist's solution is to create separate ownership rights in the forest, to give each individual forest dweller a stake in the benefits of logging and to allow each person to determine whether to allow logging on his or her land, and if so, what kind of logging and how much. For the economist, privatization of the land—enclosure—kills two birds with one stone. It addresses the distributional problem by giving members of the local community a claim on the benefits of logging and allows each individual to internalize the externalities in his or her calculations of the relative benefits of different courses of action. Ownership in severalty takes account of the first welfare theorem in addressing externalities, and the second welfare theorem in redistributing resources so that markets work more equitably.

The problem is that tropical forests are not only resources for the global economy, but places in which indigenous peoples live. These people live in and by forests that they have no wish to own—the idea of owning the forest would appear to them as ludicrous as the idea of owning the air we breathe. And for much the same reason: there is plenty to go around for everybody, and besides, how do you own the source of life itself? But maybe the equation changes when modernity presents itself both in the form of commodities that, for good reasons and bad, fascinate and enthrall indigenous peoples and—more insidiously—in the form of contractors with licenses to cut down the commercially valuable timber.

In practice, when separate ownership rights were proposed to a representative of a forest community in Thailand, the reaction was decidedly negative (see Chapter 13). The forest, as this villager knows and lives it, depends on the community, and privatization would destroy the community. There is no way of incorporating his understanding into the economic approach to externalities and distribution: the very foundations of economics assume the individualism to which the villager objects. The economist's solution will not satisfy people for whom community is important in itself and who see the management of externalities as central to community bonding.

Readers will react to this appendix very differently, according to what they bring to it. Professional economists will have found themselves in familiar territory—perhaps for the first and only time in this book. Readers with some economics under their belt will, I hope, have found this a useful review of material they encountered in undergraduate economics courses— and perhaps have forgotten. If you've never studied economics at all, this appendix will have been hard going; it has presented in very condensed form what it takes hundreds of pages to explain in elementary economics texts and myriad equations to formalize in advanced texts.

The purpose of this appendix is to clear the decks for the main action of this book, which is to lay out a very different critique from the internal one that economists themselves have developed. There is a secondary point: to emphasize that, taken seriously, the internal critique is itself a powerful indictment of the idea that markets are good for people.

The Distributional Roots
of the Enclosure Movement

Chapter 5 argued that distribution, not efficiency, was the driving force of the reorganization of agriculture that we know as the "enclosure movement." To understand enclosure as a move in a game about the distribution of the economic pie, we have to go back in time and follow the evolution of the relationships between the players.

Before the modern era, one was born not only to a physical place, but to a social place as well. This is not to suggest there was no social mobility in earlier times but to assert the greater importance in those days of the condition to which one was born. It was with good reason that the thirteenth-century English jurist Henry de Bracton saw the difference between freedom and serfdom as the most fundamental distinction among people.[1] Serfdom, at least in England, was based on birth: Jack and Jill were serfs if their parents were serfs. A free man (or woman) might temporarily accept the conditions of servitude by taking up a servile tenancy on the land, but in this case servile status lapsed as soon as the tenancy was relinquished. A serf, by contrast, did not cease to be a serf no matter how many free tenancies he held. Nor did—common misperception—"town air make one free." In England, flight conferred freedom only if the lord failed to file a claim for return of the fugitive serf within a year and a day.

It was noted in Chapter 5 that modern concepts of ownership are anachronistic when applied to premodern European agriculture. The same is true of other categories: if lords were not owners in the modern sense, neither were serfs slaves in the modern sense. In England at the time of the Conquest, slaves existed and were duly noted in Domesday, the inventory that William the Conqueror carried out in 1086 of all royal prerogatives—so minute and detailed that it appeared to contemporaries of a piece with the Final Judgment. But though the terminology of slavery survives—serf comes from the Latin for slave, *servus*—it ceases to be the common terminology for describing the condition of unfree people or their tenurial arrangements. The law books of medieval England, surviving court records, and other documents generally speak of *nativi* or *villani*. Indeed, the modern word *slave* and its cognates in other Western European languages derive not from the Latin *servus,* but from the word *Slav*. The etymology reflects the large number of men, women, and children brought west as captives with no rights at all as the Germanic frontier moved eastward in the Middle Ages.

Whatever the terminology, when we examine medieval serfdom we are not dealing with the chattel slavery of the American plantation or the Roman estate. Villeins possessed certain rights and were not subject to the arbitrary power of their lords and masters. The English villein had no recourse against his lord in the royal court, but this did not mean he was without any defense at all. He was part of a community, and the community, if not the individual, was able to resist attempts of the lords to reduce villeins to chattel slaves. Chattel slavery remained for the most part a project of the lords rather than a fact on the ground. Indeed, the facts moved in the other direction: although a sizeable percentage of the population of England at the time of Domesday were counted as slaves (as distinct from villeins), slavery in the sense of people without any rights had all but disappeared three centuries later.

The manor brought lord and peasant together in the common enterprise of agricultural production. Manor refers both to the great house of the lord and to the whole complex of institutional arrangements that governed the exploitation of land and people, arrangements at once economic, political, and judicial. Typically, villein tenants owed labor service in return for their occupancy rights—they plowed, harrowed, weeded, and harvested the lord's *demesne* (the holdings in the open field cultivated directly for the lord's account) as well as their own holdings. There was wage labor, and it played an increasingly important role in the cultivation of the manor as the Middle Ages wore on, but the heart of the manorial system was labor service owed by unfree tenants.[2]

We can get some understanding of the manor as a community by looking at the manorial court, the institution for regulating what we would call civil disputes as well as petty crime. As public institutions decayed in Western Europe after the reign of Charlemagne, the manorial court took over many of the functions that had been exercised by the public courts. The right to hold a court was a symbol of lordship, but also a source of revenue: most offenses were punished by fines, and succession or other transfer of occupancy rights also required the payment of a fine. The "profits of justice" could be an important part of manorial revenue. The Norman Conquest in 1066 brought this system to England.

The lord's project and the reality of the manorial court were at odds. The lord no doubt wished for an administrative tribunal under his thumb or that of his bailiff. The reality was a court whose judgments were to some extent independent of and distinct from the lord's will.

The elusive nature of the manorial court is intimately related to the elusive nature of serfdom. The tenancy formula was itself contradictory. Typically, the villein held land "at the will of the lord according to the custom of the manor."[3] It is not impossible to reconcile the lord's will with manorial custom, but there remains the question of which trumps the other when the two are in conflict.

There is not much doubt about the lord's interest and intent: men who, according to the lord's theory, possessed nothing but what was in their bellies were naturally seen by the lord as possessing no rights within the manorial court. And only exceptionally could the lord be sued in his own court. Like the king in the royal court, the lord enjoyed sovereign immunity.[4] But in practice, the tenants nevertheless had a say, sometimes *the* say, in determining the custom of the manor, and no matter how unappetizing for the lord, the court's judgment was customarily based on the custom of the manor.

In fact, for a large part of the business of the court, it mattered little to the lord what the custom of the manor was. Suppose I brought you before the court because your pig had trespassed on my garden, and your counterclaim was that it was my responsibility to fence my garden well enough to keep out stray animals. What was the lord's interest in the outcome of the case? His concern was that our dispute not interfere with the smooth functioning of the larger agricultural enterprise. In this, as in many of the cases that came before the court, the lord could thus be content with whatever custom happened to be. If custom dictated that it was my problem to fence my garden, so be it. If custom dictated that it was your problem to control your pig, so be it. Either way, the lord would pocket the profits of justice, and passions would—or so the lord might hope—be calmed. Everybody could get back to the business of agricultural production.

The problem for the lord was that it proved difficult to impose a double standard, to demarcate the set of cases where his interest went beyond the fines that might be collected from one party or another, and where he might wish the lord's will to override manorial custom. When you and I together claimed that the custom of the manor was that our labor service did not include extra days of work to bring in a particularly bountiful harvest— we would need whatever labor we could muster to bring in our own crops—we were directly challenging the lord's interest, and in his view his prerogative as well. Here the custom of the manor, if it was in the peasants' power to declare it, was in direct opposition to the lord's will. The lord would surely wish for his will to override manorial custom.

In theory, there was no question. One of the major disabilities of villeinage was that there was no appeal beyond the manorial court. But still a question remains. The lord needed the peasants more than the peasants needed the lord, and he was thus dependent on their good will and respect as well as on their fear. He needed the peasants not only for labor service in the fields, but also to carry on the day-to-day administration of the manor, and this was hard to do without ceding considerable sway to custom.

In order to limit the power of the peasants, English lords made significant innovations in legal procedure. Over time they introduced the new-fangled system of the royal courts, in which there was a strict separation between fact and law. Previously, there had been no such division of labor. The judge had merely been the presiding officer; fact-finding and law-finding had both been firmly in the hands of the jury (a body of men sworn—*juré* in modern French—to the truth). In the new system, the jury (the whole body of peasants in the manorial court) declared the facts of the case, while the prerogative of declaring the law was reserved to the judge (the lord himself on smaller manors, his steward on the larger manors). Insofar as custom was determining, it would be in the power of the lord or his agent, as the judge, to declare what the custom was.[5]

But even when custom was set down at the lord's behest in a manorial "extent" so that the lord would have a fixed list of services to which to hold the peasants, custom might work in the peasants' favor. If the existence of a well-defined list made it hard for the peasants to do less than was on the list, it was by the same token difficult for the lord to impose more on the peasants than the extent called for. In short, the custom of the manor, if not acting as a trump card, was a strong suit in the hands of the peasantry.

The fifteenth century saw the end of the manorial economy based on labor service. The conventional historical wisdom attributes this to the decline in population that followed the Black Death, which had ravaged England in the middle of the previous century, but a purely demographic story is at best incomplete. Changing power relations between lord and peasant must be part of the story, and these changes cannot be explained by demographics alone.

The breakup of the manor transformed social relations beyond recognition. The demesne, the lord's strips in the open fields cultivated by means of labor service owed by villeins, was leased out to "farmers" (as taxes were leased to tax farmers and, in our own day, baseball players are leased out to farm teams). And lords of manors, previously active in the management of their estates (indirectly through their bailiffs if not personally providing direction and leadership), became landlords, recipients of dues paid by villeins in commutation of labor service—"coupon clippers of the soil," in the pithy phrase of the translator of French historian Marc Bloch's overview of feudalism in Western Europe (Bloch 1961 [1939–1940]). As villein obligations above and beyond money dues dwindled away, these dues came increasingly to resemble modern-day rents. Villeins became copyholders, so called because the evidence of the copyholder's rights to the land was a copy of the portion of the manorial court's records that pertained to his tenancy. The manorial court became increasingly a real-estate regulatory commission, losing the powers over petty crime, marriage, and so forth that it had exercised during the Middle Ages. The categories of freeman and serf, separating those who had recourse to the system of royal courts beyond the manor from those who did not, lost their significance, except for matters having to do with real estate. Copyholders were as free in their persons as anybody else, but they lacked recourse to the regular royal courts to press their land claims, recourse guaranteed freeholders by longstanding precedent.

Enclosure is an anodyne name for the protracted struggle in which English copyholders lost their rights to the land. To be sure, in the landlords' theory, there was nothing to struggle about since the copyholder, as the lineal descendent of the villein, had no rights against his lord. But in practice, the copyholder could appeal to custom, with even more hope of success than his villein ancestor had enjoyed, for the copyholder had the backing of the state, which saw clearly the twin advantages—fiscal and military—of a strong peasantry. From the time of Henry VII (reigned 1485–1509) to the Glorious Revolution in 1688, the English state generally weighed in on the side of the copyholder.[6] Francis Bacon summed up the royal perspective in his *History of the Reign of King Henry the Seventh:*

[Enclosures] bred a decay of people, and (by consequence) a decay of towns, churches, tithes, and the like. The King likewise knew full well, and in no wise forgot, that there ensued withhal upon this a decay and dimunition of subsidies [aids or assistance levied with the consent of Parliament] and taxes; for the more gentlemen, ever the lower books of subsidies. . . . This did wonderfully concern the might and mannerhood of the kingdom, to have farms as it were of a standard, sufficient to maintain an able body out of penury, and did in effect amortise a great part of the lands of the kingdom unto the hold and occupation of the yeomanry or middle people, of a condition between gentlemen and cottagers or peasants. Now how much this did advance the militar power of the kingdom, is apparent by the true principles of war and the examples of other kingdoms. For it hath been held by the general opinion of men of best judgment in the wars . . . that the principal strength of an army consisteth in the infantry or foot. And to make good infantry, it requireth men bred not in a servile or indigent fashion, but in some free and plentiful manner. Therefore if a state run most to noblemen and gentlemen, and that the husbandmen and ploughmen be but as their workfolks and labourers, ore else mere cottagers (which are but housed beggars), you may have a good cavalry, but never good stable bands of foot. (Bacon 1972 [1622], 123–124)

I suggested in Chapter 5 that the word *enclosure* mistakes the form for the substance of the conflict between lords and peasants. Enclosing the land (by hedgerows or other physical markers) was only the last act of a long process of inventing, constructing, and—finally—imposing modern concepts of land ownership and at the same time doing away with the complex of coexisting and overlapping claims, duties, and rights over the land that had characterized the open field system. This was Plan B, I suggested, a response to the frustrations the landlords encountered in trying to implement a Plan A of simply raising peasant dues. Plan B was to get rid of the tenants altogether.

From the fifteenth century to the present, commentators have observed that enclosure was often accompanied by the conversion of arable to pasture. The standard view of enclosure sees this, as it sees organizational and technological change more generally, in terms of efficiency: raising sheep was a more efficient use of resources than raising grain. Enclosure was necessary for an efficient response to changes in relative prices that made sheep raising more rewarding than grain production.[7]

In the distributional view, cause and effect are reversed: the desirability of moving from arable to pasture is the result of enclosure, a way of making the dispossessed go away and preempting legal and political challenges to landlord power. Observe that this difference in perspective has no implications for the proposition that sheep were more profitable for the lord than grain. Whichever standpoint we adopt, the efficiency view or the distributional view, sheep farming would have had to be more profitable for lords to make the change. But greater profitability does not necessarily mean greater efficiency. Sheep farming was more efficient only if the peasants' claims to life and livelihood on the land need not be honored, and this, of course, was the nub of the dispute.[8]

Just as copyholders resisted Plan A, they did not accept Plan B without a fight. Indeed, the sixteenth century saw a temporary cessation and even a rollback of enclosure: no doubt the coincidence of copyholders' resistance with the state's interest in a strong peasantry, as set out by Francis Bacon, helped to stem the tide. (Even before the end of the fifteenth century, Parliament had enacted laws forbidding enclosure that depopulated the countryside, but these early enclosures are now seen by historians as the consequence of depopulation rather than its cause [Wrightson 2000, 102–104].)

To be sure, the legal authorities of the day were divided on the degree to which the copyholder's claims might qualify for legal protection in one court or another.[9] As early as 1481, in *Tenores Novelli*, Sir Thomas Littleton had a hand at reconciling the conflict between "the will of the lord" and "the custom of the manor," coming down firmly on the side of the copyholder: "the lord cannot break the custom which is reasonable" (quoted in Kerridge 1969, 139). A later, sixteenth-century edition of *Tenores Novelli* goes even further:

> But *Brian* Chief Justice said, that his opinion hath always been and ever shall be, that if such tenant by custom paying his services be ejected by the lord, he shall have an action of trespass against him. *H.21 Ed. 4* [1482]. And so was the opinion of *Danby* Chief Justice in *7 Ed. 4* [1468]. For he saith that tenant by the custom is as well inheritor to have his land according to the custom as he which hath a freehold at the common law. (quoted in Kerridge 1969, 139n)

This did not provide copyholders with the same protection that freeholders had. Unlike freehold, copyhold was tainted by the legacy of villein status: copyholders could not sue their lords in the royal courts in respect of their claims to the land. But they were increasingly able, in the sixteenth century, to proceed with claims of personal injury. The great seventeenth-century jurist Edward Coke summed up the legal situation this way in *The Compleate Copyholder* (1641):

> A copyholder cannot in any action real, or that savoureth of the realty, implead or be impleaded in any other court but in actions that merely personal he may sue or be sued at the common law.... If a copyholder be ousted by his lord, he cannot maintain an assize at the common law, because he wanteth a franktenement [freehold]; but he may have an action of trespass against him at the common law; for it is against reason that the lord should be judge where he himself is the party. (quoted in Kerridge 1969, 71)

Protection was limited by the custom of the manor. If, for example, a particular manor's custom was that copyholds were inheritable on payment of fixed entry fines, a copyholder would have many of the rights we associate with ownership. He and his heirs would be legally protected in their use of the land upon payment of entry fines and other dues established by custom. Inheritance would be governed by the custom of the manor. The copyholder might or might not be able to sell his right to the land—according to the custom of the manor—but his land could not be seized by his lord on an arbitrary pretext. Nor could entry fines or other dues be set arbitrarily. By contrast, the most a copyholder "for life" could expect by way of legal protection was that the lord respect occupancy rights until the copyholder's death. Coke pushed the envelope even further, arguing that protection might go beyond custom if the custom of the manor was unreasonable—for example, if entry fines were excessive (*Institutes of the Lawes of England,* 1628, chap. 9, sec. 74, quoted in Kerridge 1969, 147; and chap. 10, sec. 80, in ibid., 151).

Whatever the limitations on copyholders, they were in a better position than ever before—and indeed than they would be later, when the balance of power shifted once again in favor of enclosing landlords. The sixteenth and seventeenth centuries were the age of the yeoman farmer, whom Robert Allen (1992) credits with the bulk of the productivity growth of the early modern period—according to Allen some two-thirds of English land was in the hands of smallholders (copyholders and freeholders), and 90 percent of the productivity growth over the period 1500–1800 was the result of what he calls the "yeomen's revolution," to contrast it with the "landlords' revolution" of engrossment and enclosure.

With the Glorious Revolution of 1688, the landlords consolidated their power, so that it was less necessary to create "new facts on the ground," as transforming arable into pasture had done in an earlier era. Indeed, after 1750, most enclosures took place in the context of parliamentary acts, with the power of the state behind the enclosers, the opposite of how state power had been deployed in the sixteenth and seventeenth centuries. Parliamentary enclosures allowed the owners of four-fifths of the land to impose enclosure on a whole village. A small minority of landholders, even a single landholder, could impose their will on the majority if they owned sufficient land. Needless to say, parliamentary enclosure presupposed that the central issue of the earlier struggle over enclosure—namely, who owned the land— had already been decided in favor of the landlord.

As Deirdre McCloskey has written, "The English case [of the open field system] has long been disproportionately important because it has provided a rich set of myths" (McCloskey 1987, 709). I agree with McCloskey, but I dare say we differ about just which part of the story is myth. For my money, the most pervasive myth is the idea that efficiency is the lodestar of institutional change. But then, taking distribution seriously would challenge the basic normative message of economics. It is no wonder that this is yet another instance of the road not taken.

Notes

1. Economics, the Market, and Community

1. Which it might or might not be—see Chapter 3.

2. From the point of view of professional advancement, there are good reasons for diffidence. The editor's preface to *Advances in Behavioral Economics* notes the obstacles that pioneering authors encountered in the early years of behavioral economics: "The general attitude was one of hostility and skepticism . . . it was not uncommon to get a paper returned from a journal . . . with a three sentence referee report saying 'this isn't economics'" (Camerer et al. 2004, xxi).

3. "When you can measure what you are speaking about, and express it in numbers, you know something about it; but when you cannot measure it, when you cannot express it in numbers, your knowledge is of a meagre and unsatisfactory kind" (Lecture to the Institution of Civil Engineers, May 3, 1883, Thomson [Baron Kelvin] 1889, 73).

4. Give Oscar Mayer the benefit of the doubt, and there is still a problem. How do you get local industries to shape up to the quality standards that prevail in the United States? Competition? Maybe, but government regulation has been an important part of the U.S. story: meatpacking was a scandal in the early part of the twentieth century, a scandal that was instrumental in the creation of the Food and Drug Administration. In a replay of U.S. history, one might expect public pressure on the Mexican government to improve quality and health standards in their own meatpacking industry, but pressure comes only from those with a political voice. If the rich and the middle class have the option of buying imported ham—I doubt that many poor people pay the Oscar Mayer premium—this source of pressure will be vastly reduced if not altogether eliminated. The basic point was made over three decades ago by Albert Hirschman (1970). His title, *Exit, Voice, and Loyalty*, encapsulates the theme of this note, namely, that the possibility of *exit* undermines the exercise of *voice*.

5. Mirabeau's pronouncement on insurance is reproduced with a vague attribution to the "French Revolution" in Pierre Richard's *Histoire des Institutions d'Assurance en France* (1956, 37). Michèle Ruffat (2003, 189) attributes the quotation to

Mirabeau, citing as her source L. Gallix, *Il Était une Fois l'Assurance* (Paris: L'Argus, 1985, 265).

6. The idea was not exactly original with Robertson. Adam Smith was drawing on a long line of thinking about how self-interest might be mobilized to serve the common good when he argued that it was to the interests of baker, brewer, and butcher, not their benevolence, that we appeal through the market (Smith 1937 [1776], 14). By channeling economic dependence through the market, we economize on our limited stock of benevolence. To what end? Presumably the same end as for Robertson: to have more benevolence available for ends not served by self-interest, ends such as maintaining community.

7. Lawrence Summers, former president of Harvard University, is the latest avatar of the line of Smith and Robertson: "One of the things that most bothers many people of faith about market mechanisms is the idea that there is something wrong with a system where we are able to buy bread only because of the greed or profit motive of the people who make the bread. Here I would be very cautious. We all have only so much altruism in us. Economists like me think of altruism as a valuable and rare good that needs conserving. Far better to conserve it by designing a system in which people's wants will be satisfied by individuals being selfish, and saving that altruism for our families, our friends, and the many social problems in this world that markets cannot solve" (Summers 2003).

Albert Hirschman takes a middle position. His essay "Against Parsimony" argues that love has characteristics of both a scarce resource used up in the using and a skill improved by practice. "Love, benevolence, and civic spirit . . . atrophy when not adequately practiced . . . yet will . . . make themselves scarce when practiced and relied on to excess" (Hirschman 1984, 94).

2. What Is Community? And Is It Worth the Cost?

1. The terms *exit* and *voice* are Albert Hirschman's (1970).
2. I am indebted to Julius Lester for this reference.
3. Association and community are best thought of as ideal types in the sense of Max Weber. Real groups of real people lie somewhere on a spectrum in terms of commitment and identity, and the spectrum itself shifts over time. In the Middle Ages or the early modern period, membership in a guild or a religious confraternity meant something different from what allegiance to a trade union, manufacturers' association, or devotional society meant in the nineteenth century, not to mention how different are the commitments and identities involved in these associations today.
4. It helps that the Amish have a religious sanction for *Rumspringa*: a central religious tenet of the Amish faith is that baptism is meaningful only for adults who can responsibly choose to be baptized and accept the commitment that it entails. This idea is, of course, not unique to the Amish: it is the distinguishing belief of Baptists worldwide; the Baptist World Alliance includes some 100 million members, divided into 100 or so conventions.

5. More accurately, the U.S. divorce rate is half the marriage rate (Munson and Sutton 2005, 1).

6. The counterclaim of religious fundamentalists—that the religious community is the sole legitimate community—is arguably equally modern in its rejection of context and pluralism.

7. A century ago, the U.S. government took a much harder line when particular religious practices contravened conventional morality. The Mormons were obliged to abandon polygamy as a condition of Utah's entry into the Union.

8. There is a prior question of agency—the very ability to make meaningful decisions—which I am bracketing. Evidently the infant child lacks agency, but it is not a foregone conclusion that the parents are the appropriate surrogates. Who has the moral authority to act on behalf of the child? And on what basis does the appropriate surrogate act appropriately?

   Even if we put these questions aside, there remains another issue: whether the parents "freely" choose the death of their child, or are coerced into this choice by the community. Within the individualistic framework, this last question is critical, but the question comes out of the individualistic framework itself; in a holistic perspective, the binary opposition between free choice and coercion dissolves into the web of relationships between the parents and other members of the community. (Chapter 4 examines the difference between the individualistic and the holistic perspectives.)

3. The Cutting Edge of Modernity

1. Compare Ferdinand Tönnies (2001 [1887], 168), in his classic account of the differences between *Gemeinschaft* (community) and *Gesellschaft* (modern society): "The Community, as far as possible, turns all disagreeable work into an art form in tune with its own nature, giving it style, dignity and charm, and a particular status within its social structure, in the form of a 'calling' and honourable estate."

2. This definition goes back to Lionel Robbins (1948 [1932]), who sought both to expand and to limit the subject matter of economics: *expand* in the sense that economics is no longer limited to the study of material well-being, but becomes a universal science of how people deal with the universal of scarcity; *limit* in the sense that economics is divorced from any value judgments, which Robbins thought inevitably subjective and therefore inherently unscientific. (See Chapter 10 for more on Robbins.)

3. If Marxists have doubts on self-interest, these doubts are muted: it is the self-interest of the bourgeoisie that produced capitalism and the self-interest of the working class that will produce socialist revolution. There is a problem with going from the self-interest of the individual capitalist or worker to the *class-interest* of the bourgeoisie or proletariat. And vice versa. Marx and his early followers had surprisingly little to say on this subject, but latter-day scholars have been keenly aware of the problem. See, for example, Jon Elster (1985, 344–371).

4. But not for the standard efficiency reasons laid out in Appendix A—the Pareto optimal properties of markets. Markets promote production for reasons quite alien to standard economics—namely, markets mobilize kinds of knowledge that economics denies even exist (Chapter 9) and channel competition for status and position into the economic sphere (Chapter 11).

5. Folks who do not believe in the market consensus, who continue to believe in resource depletion, would do well to buy and hold natural resources. If they are right about the future, they will profit from the gap between their estimates of the appropriate prices and existing prices, for as the world gradually comes to see the correctness of their views, existing prices will move to the much higher prices that depletion would mandate.

6. Robert Balling Jr., a climatologist at Arizona State University, is quoted in a 2004 *Business Week* story on global warming as the quintessential optimist: "I'm convinced there will be engineering schemes that will allow our children's children to have whatever climate they want" (Carey 2004, 66). Moreover, economic growth makes more resources available to find and implement the next fix—and the next, and the next—another argument in favor of growth.

The pessimists might answer that even seemingly solved ecological problems have a way of recurring. The latest news on the ozone front is a case in point: the ozone hole grew more in 2006 than in any previous year, almost to the peak reached in 2001. The cause is not clear. One suspect is the dramatic growth in air-conditioning in India and China; the other suspect is the unusually cold winter in the Antarctic in 2006, which may be linked to global warming. Air-conditioning has added to the pressure on the ozone layer despite the lower harmfulness per pound of the new generation of coolants relative to the chlorofluorocarbons that were the main target of the original negotiations leading to the Montreal Protocol of 1987. See Bradsher (2007).

4. Individualism

1. As Stephen Holmes notes in his spirited defense of liberalism, "the original antonym of 'I will do what I want' was 'I will do what my master or my social rank demands'" (1989, 251). But being one's own person is sometimes hard to tell apart from doing one's own thing.

2. This draws heavily on Steven Lukes (1973).

3. The property of some agents may be limited to their physical and mental capacity to labor, their labor power in Marxian terms, their human capital in the contemporary mainstream formulation.

4. More precisely, property that can be freely bought and sold.

5. As laid out in Appendix A, the first welfare theorem is that under certain assumptions, market outcomes are Pareto optimal. The second welfare theorem is that any Pareto optimal outcome can be reached through the market provided the starting point is suitably adjusted. The second theorem tells us not to worry if one market outcome is objectionable because it concentrates income in a few

hands; we can change the distributional outcome without sacrificing the efficiency encapsulated in the idea of Pareto optimality.

6. Observe that the normative and descriptive, the "should" and the "is," are logically separate. I can believe that as society is presently constructed, the individual takes precedence, but that he or she ought not. Or I can believe that whatever the actual state of affairs, all effects of public policy should be reduced to their effects on individuals. I imagine, however, that most people who believe that atomism provides a good description will also accept the normative view that social arrangements ought to serve the well-being of individuals, however well-being is conceived. The converse is not so clear. Many who hold to atomism for normative purposes would not subscribe to atomism as a description.

7. Efficiency and liberty are not the only possible reasons for liking markets: Friedrich Hayek has defended the market on the grounds that, in contrast with a simulated market of the kind that Oskar Lange and others proposed for resource allocation under socialism, the market facilitates, indeed forces, agents to utilize knowledge that cannot be articulated in a precise manner. This idea is explored in Chapter 9. Like Milton Friedman's libertarian argument, this argument—however compelling—is not the argument that standard economics makes in defense of the market.

8. John Locke put the matter thus in ¶54 of the *Second Treatise of Government:* "Though I have said above, Chap. II, *That all Men by Nature are equal,* I cannot be supposed to understand all sorts of *Equality: Age* or *Virtue* may give Men a just Precedency: *Excellency of Parts and Merit* may place others above the Common Level: *Birth* may subject some, and *Alliance* or *Benefits* others, to pay an Observance to those whom Nature, Gratitude or other Respects may have made it due; and yet all this consists with the *Equality,* which all Men are in, in respect of Jurisdiction or Dominion one over another, which was the *Equality* I there spoke of, as proper to the Business in hand, being that *equal Right* that every Man hath *to his Natural Freedom,* without being subjected to the Will or Authority of any other Man" (Locke 1988 [1690], 304).

9. Put to one side issues of whether calculation and deliberation are as feasible as this all-encompassing notion of self-interest suggests, a topic to which we shall return in Chapters 7, 8, and 9.

10. James Gardner (2007) distinguishes between elections as deliberation and elections as tabulation. He concludes that, although American ideology favors deliberation, the logic of the electoral system presupposes that tabulation is the actual end of elections in the United States.

11. In part, oppression is the result of a lack of mutuality in interdependence. Lords and serfs were interdependent in medieval times—the lord depended on the serf for food, and the serf depended on the lord for protection. But the dependence was asymmetrical: the protection offered by the lord, if it was not against his own depredations, was against the depredations of his fellow lords. The interdependence required the political disenfranchisement of the peasants

to sustain itself. Similar arguments can be made about patriarchy, with the addition that economic disenfranchisement reinforced and finally replaced political disenfranchisement in order to create an artificial dependence of women on men.

12. Case in point: before the veil was banned in French public schools, did those Muslim girls who wore the veil choose to do so? Or were they coerced? It may be difficult to answer in an individualistic context, but at least the question makes sense. In the context of community, the question itself is incoherent.

13. Or was it? Sartre does not go there, but a Freudian disposed to examine Ibbieta's unconscious might have a field day.

14. Amartya Sen makes a distinction similar to my distinction between externalities in a utility calculus and obligation. He opposes sympathy to commitment and cites a George Bernard Shaw play, *The Devil's Disciple*, with a character facing a choice much like Ibbieta's, to illustrate the difference. But Sen draws a very different lesson: for him the import of the distinction between sympathy and commitment lies in the problem of eliciting people's true preferences in situations of collective choice where, absent a moral commitment (either to other people's well-being, or simply to truth telling), people generally have an incentive to misrepresent their preferences in order to "free ride" (Sen 1977, 326–335).

15. This is Dumont's conception (1977, 4–14). It is also the story told by Ferdinand Tönnies (2001 [1887]), who, as noted in Chapter 3 (note 1), contrasted premodern Europe based on holistic community (*Gemeinschaft*) with modern Europe based on individualistic society (*Gesellschaft*). Even though, as we shall see later in this chapter, Tönnies believed that community is not altogether absent from the modern world, in his view it survives only in the interstices of a society whose public face is the individualistic.

16. The memo was leaked by a staffer who presumably shared the indignation of many noneconomists to the application of a cost–benefit calculus to issues of human health (*Economist* 1992, 66).

17. "Full knowledge" turns out to be more ambiguous than it appears. In Chapters 7, 8, and 9, I argue that theoretical knowledge—what I call "algorithmic" knowledge—is necessarily incomplete. The missing component is the knowledge of experience. This distinction provides another ground for questioning trade in radioactive wastes, about which one of the contracting parties (maybe both) can plausibly be assumed to lack experiential knowledge.

Another point: in this example, I suppose trade is between individuals to make the case for trade as strong as possible. Supposing governments rather than individuals are the contracting parties would weaken the case for trade in hazardous wastes to the point that even mainstream economists might have difficulties with the idea. The reason is simple: if the government of the Republican Democracy of A contracts with Waste Disposal Inc., chances are that the $200 side payment would end up in the purse of some government official or another, and the radioactive waste would end up in the backyard of poor, powerless folk.

18. Adam Smith famously criticized the division of labor for its stultifying effect on the mind (1937 [1776], 734):

    The understandings of the greater part of men are necessarily formed by their ordinary employments. The man whose whole life is spent in performing a few simple operations, of which the effects too are, perhaps, always the same, or very nearly the same, has no occasion to exert his understanding, or to exercise his invention in finding out expedients for removing difficulties which never occur.

    He naturally loses, therefore the habit of such exertion, and generally becomes as stupid and ignorant as it is possible for a human creature to become.

19. Thomas Hobson, who kept a livery stable in early modern Cambridge, England, allowed customers to choose any horse—as long as it was the horse nearest the stable door (*American Heritage Dictionary* 1991, 615).

20. The bracketed words are absent in the original memo as well as in the *Economist* story.

5. Some History

1. There is a "new institutional economics," which, although squarely within the camp of mainstream economics, takes a much more nuanced view of the evolution of economic institutions than one based purely on efficiency. One of the pioneers of the new institutional economics, Nobel Laureate Douglass North, is also the author of a relatively extreme statement of the view that the transformation of the manorial economy, which culminated in the enclosure movement, was driven by efficiency considerations (North and Thomas 1971).

2. In France, royal protection of peasant communities continued until the end of the ancien régime. The Revolution, in the name of individualism, undid community prerogatives and powers (Root 1987).

3. In this context, subsidies were taxes levied with the consent of Parliament.

4. As Allen (1992) points out, engrossing not only could, but did, take place apart from enclosing the land.

5. The author of this account was one Thomas Walsingham, a monk of St. Albans Abbey, whose *Historia Anglicana* is the basis of our knowledge of Ball's speech as well as the basis of much of our knowledge of the Peasants' Revolt. Walsingham, it is clear, could hardly contain his horror at Ball's seditious preaching. In the twentieth century, I suppose, Ball would have been called a worker priest.

    Observe that Ball provides an unusual twist on the relationship between liberty and equality: in his formulation, equality is the precondition of liberty, not its enemy. Compare this with the libertarian view exemplified by Milton Friedman (1962), Friedrich Hayek (1944), and Robert Nozick (1974).

6. Almost two centuries after Luther and three centuries after the Great Peasant Uprising of 1381, John Locke's *Second Treatise of Government* argues, with John Ball, that the natural state of mankind is individual equality: "Nothing [is] more

evident, than that Creatures of the same species and rank promiscuously born to all the same advantages of Nature, and the use of the same faculties, should also be equal one amongst another without Subordination or Subjection, unless the Lord and Master of them all, should by any manifest Declaration of his Will set one above another and confer on him by an evident and clear appointment an undoubted Right to dominion and Sovereignty" (1988 [1690], ¶4, 269). John Ball's "When Adam delved and Eve span, Who was then the Gentleman?" is more pithy, but Ball and Locke are both expressing the same idea. Did Locke reinvent the wheel, or did the idea of equality persist in the interstices of polite society from Ball's time to Locke's, at which point it had ceased to be seditious?

7. *Sati* is perhaps the wrong analogy: Huxley supposes the victim was inspired by the biblical account of the Akedah, Abraham's almost-sacrifice of Isaac. God, alas, did not provide a substitute offering for the unfortunate brother.

8. A century and a half later, the English politician and statesman Edmund Burke put Elizabeth's point even more succinctly in his first work, *A Vindication of Natural Society:* "The same Engines which were employed for the Destruction of Religion, might be employed with equal Success for the Subversion of Government" (1982 [1756], 6).

9. For example:

> If we now wish to consider the same subject [whether the three estates, clergy, nobles, and commoners, should vote separately or in a single body, by "orders" or by "heads"] according to principles which are made to illuminate it, that is to say, according to [the principles] of social science, we shall see the question take on a new form. (Sieyès 1989 [1789], chap. 3, ¶3, 49)

Or:

> [There is] enough here to demonstrate the obligation of the third estate to form by itself a national assembly and to authorize, on the basis of reason and equity, the claim of this order to deliberate and vote on behalf of the entire nation without exception.
>
> I know that such principles will not be to the taste even of the members of the third [estate] who are the most adept at defending their interests. So be it: provided that it is agreed that I have started from true principles and that I proceed only with the support of good logic. (Sieyès 1989 [1789], chap. 6, 83)

10. Marxists might claim an exemption from this indictment on the grounds that they have consistently criticized capitalism and the economics they regard as apologetics for capitalism. In reality, the Marxian critique of capitalism is not the exception that proves the rule, but instead parallels mainstream practice. Chapter 3 suggested that Marx shared the assumptions of economics and modernity to a greater extent than either disciples or opponents would generally admit, differing chiefly on the question of how good capitalism is as a means to the end of individual development.

6. From Vice to Virtue in a Century

1. The "invisible hand" is the most enduring phrase in Smith's entire work. It is also the most misunderstood. Economists have taken this passage to be the first step in the cumulative effort of mainstream economics to prove that a competitive economy provides the largest possible economic pie (the so-called first welfare theorem, which demonstrates the Pareto optimality of a competitive regime). But Smith, it is evident from the context, was making a much narrower argument, namely, that the interests of businessmen in the security of their capital would lead them to invest in the domestic economy even at the sacrifice of somewhat higher returns that might be obtainable from foreign investment. This selfish concern serves the national interest by building up the national capital stock at a faster rate than would be the case if domestic investors were guided solely by relative returns.

   David Ricardo, the preeminent British economist of the next generation, echoed Smith: "If capital freely flowed towards those countries where it could be most profitably employed, there could be no difference in the rate of profit. . . . Experience, however, shews that the fancied or real insecurity of capital, when not under the immediate control of its owner, together with the natural disinclination which every man has to quit the country of his birth and connexions, and intrust himself, with all his habits fixed, to a strange government and new laws, check the emigration of capital. These feelings, which I should be sorry to see weakened, induce most men of property to be satisfied with a low rate of profits in their own country, rather than seek a more advantageous employment for their wealth in foreign nations" (Ricardo 1951 [1817], 136–137).

   Smith's argument is at best incomplete, for it leaves out the role of foreigners' investment in the domestic economy. It would have to be shown that the gain to the British capital stock from the preference of British investors for Britain is greater than the loss to Britain from the preference of Dutch investors for the Netherlands and French investors for France.

   William Grampp (2000) maintains that Smith's argument was even more limited: for Grampp, defense rather than capital accumulation was the national interest promoted by the invisible hand. In this argument, only domestic capital is available to promote defense, so nothing is lost to Britain on account of Dutch preferences for home investment.

   Emma Rothschild (2001, chap. 5) suggests that Smith's invisible hand is an exercise in irony, which would remove it even further from its modern economic usage.

2. Or in Tocqueville's account of the new United States, "self interest rightly understood" (1969 [1835–1840, vol. 2, part 2, chap. 8], 525–528).

3. Mainstream economists interpret this as the result of a higher demand for labor confronting a fixed supply. Those of a Keynesian or Marxian bent can reach the same result via a different route, in the Keynesian case because a smaller volume

of labor is required to meet any given aggregate demand, and in the Marxian case because "subsistence" grows apace with productivity (S. Marglin 1984a).

4. For example, in *The Republic* Plato has Socrates say to Glaucon: "It will be the business of reason to rule with wisdom and forethought on behalf of the entire soul; while the spirited element ought to act as its subordinate and ally" (441 E, 407).

5. Mandeville goes even further than Hobbes in denigrating rationality, an essential step to establishing the negative pole of the vice–virtue paradox. Where Hobbes merely hints at the accommodation of reason to passion (Hobbes 1968 [1651], 111–112), Mandeville finds no other role for reason whatsoever. Not only is rationality incapable of discovering truth; it is but a fig leaf: "All Human Creatures are sway'd and wholly govern'd by their Passions, whatever fine Notions we may flatter our Selves with; even those who act suitably to their Knowledge, and strictly follow the Dictates of their Reason, are not less compell'd so to do by some Passion or other, that sets them to Work, than others, who bid Defiance and act contrary to Both, and whom we call Slaves to their Passions" (Mandeville, *An Enquiry into the Origin of Honour, and the Usefulness of Christianity in War*, 31, quoted in Mandeville 1988 [1714], lxxix).

6. Professor Hirschman differs on Smith, who, in his view, does not distinguish between interests and passions. I am unconvinced by both the argument he offers and the passage he cites from *The Wealth of Nations* in which Smith uses the two terms without contrasting them (Hirschman 1977, 110–113).

7. It has become fashionable in recent years to downplay Keynes's achievement. David Laidler (1999) is a good example of the trend, the distinguishing feature of which is the inability to see the forest for the trees. Laidler may be right in arguing that anticipation by others of individual elements of *The General Theory* is the rule rather than the exception, but nobody before Keynes put these elements together in a framework that made sense of unemployment as something other than frictional adjustment.

8. Full disclosure: I freely acknowledge my allegiance to the Keynesian fundamentalists.

9. I wrote the first draft of this chapter before the buildup to the second Iraq War. On the last day of 2002, Representative Charles Rangel argued forcefully in the *New York Times* that if the United States was going to war, the risks of death and dismemberment should be borne more equally (Rangel 2002).

7. How Do We Know When We Do Not Know?

1. *Discounted present value* is the value today of a stream of earnings expected over the future. "Discounted" refers to the lower weight placed on future earnings relative to present earnings.

2. He was later persuaded otherwise, apparently by Ramsey.

3. This view of human knowledge makes me skeptical of the possibility that artificial intelligence is close to imitating the human mind. Until we understand more

about how human beings are able to integrate experiential and algorithmic knowledge, we can hardly hope to do so in a machine.

4. This is, of course, the question that plagued the Reformation: some Protestants thought to build an algorithmic Christianity on the basis of self-evident first principles, but the principles were continually contested, sometimes violently. (See Chapter 5 for a particularly bizarre example of a young man who thought God had commanded him to sacrifice his brother.) Even Euclid's axioms have turned out with the passage of time to be less self-evident than had once been supposed—we now have a variety of geometries, each with its own axiomatic basis.

5. Modern, post-Baconian science may be thought of as a systematic procedure for structuring the interaction between algorithm and experience, deduction and induction, in order to arrive at better and better first principles. We work out the consequences of a particular set of first principles—and revise them little by little to the extent that observational data are not consistent with the implications of these principles.

   There is an issue of what constitutes "better and better" first principles. Positivism argues that the proof of the pudding can only be in the eating: better first principles are those that are consistent with the known evidence. Thomas Kuhn, the revisionist historian of science, more or less accepts this as a characterization of "normal science," but distinguishes paradigm shifts as abrupt revisions of first principles in which intuition, hunch, and educated guesswork team up with observation (Kuhn 1970 [1962]).

6. There are exceptions; the law and business faculties of my own university have since their inception given pride of place to the "case method" of instruction, which attempts to condense the experience of the law office or the executive suite into a form accessible to students, and to allow learning to take place in a simulated environment in which mistakes are not too costly. But even these exceptions are coming increasingly under fire from an algorithmic academic establishment.

7. The attacks of Peter Abelard on the doctrinal authority of popes and saints presupposed that in the West even religious knowledge had, by the year 1100 CE, begun to be regarded as algorithmic in nature.

8. Feminists are divided over whether to fight this assumption while accepting the modern ideology of knowledge that prioritizes algorithmic over experiential knowledge, or to fight the ideology itself. Carol Gilligan's well-known work, *In a Different Voice*, can be interpreted as a defense of (feminine) experience against (masculine) algorithm.

8. Sources of the Modern Ideology of Knowledge

1. " 'When *I* use a word,' Humpty Dumpty said, in a rather scornful tone, 'it means just what I choose it to mean—neither more nor less.'

   'The question is,' said Alice, 'whether you *can* make words mean so many different things.'

'The question is,' said Humpty Dumpty, 'which is to be master—that's all.' " (L. Carroll 1992 [1871], 163)

2. In *Gorgias* (465 A, 319), Plato has Socrates say with respect to cooking: "It is not an art [techne], but a habitude [empeiria], since it has no account to give of the real nature of the things it applies, and so cannot tell the cause of any of them. I refuse to give the name of art to anything that is irrational." In *Philebus* (55 D–E, 359), Socrates asks his interlocutor to "consider whether in the manual arts [cheirotechnikai] one part is more allied to knowledge [episteme], and the other less, and the one should be regarded as purest, the other as less pure." For Socrates, "If arithmetic and the sciences of measurement and weighing were taken away from all arts, what was left of any of them would be, so to speak, pretty worthless."

3. In keeping with Plato's blurring of the line between episteme and techne, at issue is a difference not between episteme and techne but between episteme and techne on the one hand and ortha doxa (right opinion) on the other.

4. But it is for "experts in the science of mensuration to elect a land surveyor and for experts in navigation to choose a pilot" (*Politics,* 1282 a 9–10, 227).

5. In the limit, we don't have to throw out anything. Even in the face of repeated confounding of a cherished hypothesis by data, we can hold onto our beliefs—and just wait for more clever technique or interpretation to confirm our faith. In an interview with the undergraduate economics journal of Harvard University, a distinguished colleague and former president of the Economic History Association was asked whether international trade is determined by the relative abundance of different kinds of inputs (the so-called Heckscher–Ohlin model). This colleague responded: "Anybody who has had any exposure to international economics . . . will realize that there hasn't been much modern evidence to support the Heckscher–Ohlin model. How is it possible that 50 years of empirical evidence seems to shoot down this model, yet it still flies high, almost as durable as it always was? The answer is that the model is so plausible and so useful in thinking about trade problems that no economist would think about throwing it away simply because the evidence is inconsistent with it. I know this statement sounds dreadfully anti-scientific, but a number of theorists believe that we just haven't been clever enough to figure out how to map the complexities of . . . today's real world onto our models, that is figuring out ways to retain Heckscher–Ohlin thinking, but in a different guise" (*Harvard College Economist* 2002, 6).

   Now we see through a glass, darkly; but then face to face (1 Corinthians 13:12).

6. In this same book, Luria writes: "At the beginning of this century the German scholar Max Verworn suggested that scientists can be divided into two distinct groups according to their basic orientation toward science: classical and romantic" (Luria 1979, 174). Luria, presumably paraphrasing Verworn, then goes on to characterize classical and romantic in terms strikingly like Pirsig's (1976) and mine. So far, I have been unable to track down any essay by Verworn that makes such a distinction, but I have not given up.

7. Full disclosure: I still can't figure out Luria's principle for excluding one of the

four: Is it the material of which the objects are made? Out with the saucepan, made of metal rather than glass! Or is it their use? Out with the spectacles, which do not hold water!

9. Taking Experience Seriously

1. Or perhaps by God. See Genesis 11:1–9.
2. These assumptions may or may not accurately describe eighteenth-century pin making, but, as indicated, they reasonably characterize at least one important industry of the era—woolen cloth manufacture.
3. If we leave the static context, in which the issue is the distribution of available knowledge, and look instead at the generation of new knowledge, an argument can be made on incentive grounds for allowing the discoverers of new knowledge some control over its distribution. Golden eggs of knowledge may be public goods, but the geese who lay them may not be.
4. The point I am making here has, I believe, much broader application. Paul Romer started a veritable growth industry in 1986 with his idea that knowledge does not conform to the usual assumptions of diminishing returns but instead exhibits increasing returns (Romer 1986). In short, knowledge is a public good that producers can use without diminishing its availability to others.

   This is a theory with radical import: the economy is no longer limited à la Solow (1956) by a "natural rate of growth" dictated by the exogenous rate of growth of the labor force. But this result depends critically on the character of knowledge. To the extent that knowledge is algorithmic and is costless to transmit, diffuse, and replicate, then it is appropriate to treat knowledge as a public good, and therefore to challenge the convexity assumptions of the neoclassical model. But the public-good character of knowledge depends critically on the absence, or at least on the minimal importance, of experiential knowledge in the production process. Romer's warrant for this assumption seems to me no better founded than my own in the research on work organization I have just examined.

   In my preferred alternative to the neoclassical growth framework, labor-force growth is endogenous, so growth is determined by the rate of capital accumulation, even without the introduction of knowledge as a public good. In this view of growth, the import of Romer's argument is much less revolutionary. (See S. Marglin 1984a, chaps. 3–5, 20.)
5. No relation, so far as I know, to Frederick Winslow Taylor.
6. Lange states the rules differently and, indeed, somewhat ambiguously. Lange's first rule is to "impose on each production plant the choice of the combination of factors of production and the scale of output which minimises the average cost of production" (Lange 1936, 62). The ambiguity lies in *whose* average cost is being minimized, the plant's or the industry's. Clearly the goal ought to be to minimize the industry's average cost, which, as Lange correctly notes in the same paragraph, will lead to "the scale of output of a plant being such as to equalize

marginal cost and the price of the product." But this is the same thing as maximizing profits—at least so long as marginal cost is rising with output. (When marginal cost is falling, the rule of equating price to marginal cost will lead to maximizing rather than minimizing total industry costs.)

Lange's second rule is to adjust prices so that price equals average cost (Lange 1936, 62). This is equivalent to adjusting prices in accordance with excess demands and supplies as long as long-run average cost is constant—think of adjustment of supply as taking place through the construction and decommissioning of relatively small identical plants, each operating at the minimum point on its average cost curve. With constant average cost, Lange's second rule insures that, in addition to minimizing cost by appropriately distributing total production among the various plants, the optimal scale of production is achieved.

7. The two issues, independence versus accountability and rules versus discretion, should not be conflated, but they are related. The issue of rules versus discretion can arise only if the prior question of independence versus accountability has been resolved in favor of independence, for political accountability doesn't make much sense in the absence of discretion. Discretion can take the form of experience opposed to algorithm, but it need not. Even within an algorithmic model, there remains the (discretionary) question of setting the parameters that reflect how much emphasis is to be placed on greater price stability relative to the emphasis on greater output.

8. This is the rate of interest at which banks borrow and lend among themselves on an overnight basis, in order to make use of excess reserves or to make sure their reserves meet the minimum requirements of the Federal Reserve. Short-term interest rates on Treasury obligations closely track the federal funds rate.

10. Welfare Economics and the Nation-State

1. A thoroughgoing libertarian has little use for the state, nation-state or no. The logic of libertarian individualism (see Chapter 4) leads to no more than a Hobbesian state, one based on a calculation of the benefits of disarming one's fellows as against the costs of losing some part of one's own freedom of action. In this view, the state has no legitimate role other than to ensure that the players follow the rules of the game; whatever the consequences, the outcomes are legitimate if the rules have been followed. By contrast, for the economist the individual's liberty of action is supposed to serve society—even as society is reducible to the individuals who comprise it.

2. There is another problem with the notion of potential Pareto improvement. In 1939, Nicholas Kaldor proposed the so-called compensation criterion, which relies on potential Pareto improvement. Two years later, Tibor Scitovsky (1941) pointed out the possibility that a move from situation A to situation B could constitute a potential Pareto improvement while the move from B to A could also be potentially Pareto improving. This paradox is possibly of great interest to eco-

nomic theorists and potential theorists but probably of limited interest to everybody else.

3. See Chapter 7.

4. In its first, English, incarnation, nationalism was bound up with individualism as well as with equality and democracy, but on the Continent, individualism was muted, in Greenfeld's view, by the baleful influence of Jean-Jacques Rousseau, not to mention various Germans, for whom "democracy . . . meant nothing but the total submersion of the individual within the collectivity" (Greenfeld 1992, 369).

5. According to the U.S. Census of 1860, 504 men lived in this town (Kennedy 1864, 204); using the age distribution of the county population (Kennedy 1864, 198–199), 35 percent of the men, or 176, would have been between the ages of 17 and 40, presumptive cutoffs for the pool of potential soldiers. The number of men who volunteered for service at the beginning of the war was thus 48 percent, 84 out of 176.

6. What happens to marginal productivity in this classically inspired theory of wages? Does the theory mean that producers don't equate the marginal product of labor to the wage, a condition of maximizing profits? Does it mean that businesses don't try to maximize profits? Even though there are important ambiguities in the very notion of profit maximization once we leave the world of algorithmic knowledge (see Chapter 8), for purposes of the present discussion we have no need to abandon the idea that businesses are systematic profit maximizers. Without the assumption of full employment, profit maximization may produce some of the results associated with the mainstream theory of wages, in particular, the result that the marginal productivity of labor is equal to the wage. But unlike mainstream theory, in which there is an additional assumption of full employment, so that causality runs from the size of the labor force (and the size of the capital stock) to the wage rate, here the conventionally determined wage and the capital stock combine to determine the level of employment. The labor supply adjusts endogenously to demand. In a word, instead of marginal productivity determining wages, as in the mainstream story, wages determine marginal productivity. See S. Marglin (1984a) for the details of this argument.

7. This is the approximate dollar equivalent of the Mexican minimum wage, which varies between 45.81 and 48.67 pesos per day depending on geographic location, at the rate of exchange prevailing in September 2006.

8. According to Arthur Hertzberg, the good count upped the ante considerably: "Jews who refused to surrender the things that kept them apart should be shipped off to Palestine" (Hertzberg 1993, 139).

9. According to the General Accounting Office's most recent report on the effects of sugar import quotas and price supports, the program cost users almost $2 billion in 1998 while putting almost $1 billion in the hands of producers (General Accounting Office 1998, 5–6). The difference between the users' losses and the producers' gains is a measure of the inefficiency of the program, what economists

call a *deadweight loss.* Appendix A argues that the term is tendentious, but perhaps not in this case.

11. Why Is Enough Never Enough?

1. A follow-up *New York Times* story reported a decline for the Clines. In 2002, Dr. Cline's income fell to $250,000, and the family had to economize: they sold the house they bought in 1998 for a $150,000 profit and bought a cheaper one in a less posh neighborhood, without a pool but with one more bedroom. Mrs. Cline had to give up her nanny (Kilborn 2003). The Clines are still in the top 2 percent of the income distribution: approximately 98 percent of American families make do on less.

2. There is a body of work in experimental economics trying to elicit people's attitudes toward fairness in the distribution of the economic pie. Typically, the question is posed as whether one would give up something to prevent another individual from gaining even more. And typically, the answer is that people would indeed go without to prevent other folks from having more. It is hard to distinguish fairness from other reasons (like spite) for sacrificing one's own gain to prevent someone else from improving his lot even more.

3. See, for example, U.S. Bureau of Labor Statistics, *Survey of Consumer Expenditure: Interview Survey, 1984, Bulletin 2267* (quoted in Lebergott 1993, 71).

4. C. Christian von Weizsäcker, a pioneer in the field of modeling endogenous preferences, presents an elegant model for welfare comparisons with changing preferences (von Weizsäcker 2002). It is unclear how restrictive is his assumption ruling out what he calls the Hans-in-Luck phenomenon (after the Grimm Brothers fairy tale), but it seems to me myopic to ignore, as Weizsäcker does, the cumulative effects on present utility of past consumption.

5. The actual ratio in 1998 was 13.6:1. See Jones and Weinberg (2000, 5, table 3): the cutoff for the ninety-fifth percentile was $132,900, and the cutoff for the tenth percentile was $9,700.

6. In "A Short View of Russia," written after a trip to the young Soviet Union in the mid-1920s, Keynes exclaims: "How can I accept a doctrine [communism] which sets up as its bible, above and beyond criticism, an obsolete economic textbook [Marx's *Capital*] which I know to be not only scientifically erroneous but without interest or application for the modern world?" (Keynes 1972 [1925], vol. 9, 258).

7. Relative needs and absolute needs are better thought of as categories for organizing our thinking than as categories etched in stone: many goods have aspects of both. Cigarette smoking nicely illustrates the difficulty of separating actual goods into two hard and fast categories. If, for the teenaged and preteen neophyte, cigarette smoking is mostly about emulation, the craving for tobacco becomes an absolute need once the kid becomes addicted. But that is not the end of the matter: the addict has considerable choice about which container his dose of nicotine comes in, so the relativity of needs reasserts itself. The youngster

becomes open to persuasion: Marlboros will make him a real man, Gitanes a café intellectual; Virginia Slims will make her a modern woman.

8. The thought that relative needs were an important driver of aggregate demand was clearly in the air a generation before Mandeville. Nicholas Barbon, John Houghton, and Dalby Thomas all expressed the same idea before the end of the seventeenth century (Appleby 1977, 170–171). Barbon argued that it "is not Necessity that causeth the Consumption, Nature may be Satisfied with little; but it is the wants of the Mind, Fashion, and desire of Novelties, and Things scarce, that causeth Trade" (quoted in Appleby 1977, 171).

9. These negative externalities have been in the forefront of the critique of consumerism since Thorstein Veblen (1967 [1899]). As if led by an invisible clock, economists have revisited Veblen at intervals of precisely half a century. James Duesenberry (1949) and Robert Frank (1999) have observed that, in a static model, if increases in your consumption make everybody else want more, then increasing your consumption may reduce social welfare. These negative externalities have important policy consequences, consequences that are certainly counterintuitive. For example, taxes may make people better off if consumption is relative. A proportional income tax leaves everybody in exactly the same relative place as before, at least to a first approximation. And the resources raised by taxation can be spent to provide "public goods," which are inherently nonrivalrous (see Appendix A). In addition, if people are induced by the tax to work less, as mainstream economics suggests, people will benefit from greater leisure—assuming leisure is an absolute rather than a relative good. Bringing everybody's consumption down a notch is like making the crowd at a football game sit down. We see as well as when we are all standing, and with less effort. Neither Duesenberry nor Frank (nor for that matter Veblen) addressed the dynamic issue of the impact of rivalry on effort, accumulation, productivity, and living standards.

10. Relative needs are more varied than Keynes's definition suggests, more complex than simply having more than the next guy. One reader of an early version of this chapter pointed out that his preteen didn't want more Nikes than his friends; rather, he had to have his pair of Nikes as the ticket of admission to his peer group. There is an extensive literature on various forms of relativity in consumption. A pioneering paper is by Harvey Leibenstein (1950).

11. I remember traveling to the erstwhile Soviet Union in the 1980s and thinking how much easier it was to read an individual's social class from his or her dress there than under capitalism.

12. These fourteenth-century laws were a compromise: merchants could dress like gentry, but only if they were five times as rich (Thrupp 1989 [1948], 148).

13. Across the Channel from England, a compatriot of the author of *Le Bourgeois Gentilhomme* complained of imposters "who dress like a gentleman . . . corrupting our ancient discipline." Antoine de Montchretien, *Traicte de l'Oeconomie Politique* (1889 [1615]) 60; quoted in Lebergott 1993, 4. Monsieur Jourdain, Molière's bourgeois gentilhomme, had only one question with regard to his

consumption choices: were these the goods and services that "quality people" would consume?

14. A point I am willing to stipulate, as the lawyers say, but not to concede.

15. A very informative account of want creation in the half century from 1880 to 1930 is *Land of Desire* by William Leach.

16. There is surely some irony in the denouement of Goethe's version: the moment when Faust can say "stay a while, you are so beautiful" comes as he contemplates the success of a vast project of economic development, a project that creates a space for millions to live in freedom. The irony is that Faust's transcendent moment comes in contemplating rather than experiencing the success of his development project.

17. Over the last forty years, spending on health care in the United States has grown from less than 7 to more than 17 percent of personal consumption expenditure. This growth is expected to continue over the foreseeable future. The federal government alone spent (through Medicaid and Medicare) an amount equal to 3.5 percent of GDP on health care at the beginning of this century; in 2001 *BusinessWeek* forecast that on the basis of existing programs, federal government spending on health care will more than quadruple as a share of total output by 2075, to 14.5 percent of GDP. And that was before the government added a prescription-drug benefit to Medicare. (For historical data, see Bureau of Economic Analysis 2007, table 2.3.5. For forecasts, see Gleckman 2001, 81.)

18. To be sure, health care is not purely absolute. You or I might feel the need for cosmetic surgery because Mr. Jones has just had a hair transplant or Mrs. Jones a face-lift. Friends in India tell me that when bypass surgery came to Delhi, it became for a time the thing to do to keep up with the Singhs.

19. For instance, an operation for early-stage cancer may lower momentary utility during convalescence, but the expectation is that the operation will pay off in terms of higher momentary utility down the road while also lengthening the road.

20. This is a simplification but not a caricature. See, among others, Michael Grossman (1972, 1998), Walter Ried (1998), and Martin Forster (2001).

21. Health economists polled by Victor Fuchs a few years ago overwhelmingly agreed with the view that "The primary reason for the increase in the health sector's share of GDP over the past 30 years is technological change in medicine." Others polled—economic theorists and practicing physicians—were not so sure (Fuchs 1996, 8).

22. Even if we add in those who produce the fertilizers, pesticides, equipment, fuel, and other off-farm purchases that go into agricultural production, as we should, it is still a very small fraction of the labor force that feeds the rest of us.

23. Benjamin Friedman (2005) argues that not only does growth become a plausible basis for social cohesion; growth also fosters social values of tolerance, openness, generosity, and democracy. Growth, in Friedman's view, generates positive moral externalities and is thus to be valued beyond its material dimension.

12. The Economics of Tragic Choices

1. Against this, one can argue that poorly informed young women don't go into garment factories with their eyes wide open, and that once there, the pressures of making good in their new lives trap them into an existence they would not have freely chosen if they knew what they were getting into. Economists can counter that as sweatshops become more widespread and ever more people enter the ranks of sweatshop workers, it becomes harder to sustain the charge that these workers are in effect duped or seduced. There is surely some truth in this response; yet, just as surely, there remain exceptions to the argument that people know what they are getting into—in the case of agricultural workers, the health effects may be rare enough that it takes a long time to understand the association between pesticide use and cancer or birth defects, so that the "eyes wide open" case is less convincing.

2. According to Charles Segal (1981, 205, quoted in Nussbaum 2001, 176–177n), "Through its choral song, the *polis* arrives at self-awareness of the tensions between which it exists. Embodying these tensions in art, it can confront them and work towards their mediation, even though mediation is not permitted to the tragic heroes within the spectacle itself. The play in its social and ritual contexts achieves for society what it refuses to the actors within its fiction."

3. Nike's share of the footwear market in the United States fell from about one-half in 1999 to just under one-third in 2002. Recently, Bloomberg reported that Nike's share of the market in running shoes was again close to one-half in 2006 (see Business Wire 2000 for information on Nike's market share in 1999 and 2000; Just-style.com 2003 for information for 2002; and Cheng 2007 for information for 2006).

4. Arabica is the type of coffee normally used to make premium roasted coffee—as distinct from instant coffee, which is made from robusta. Lower-priced blends of roasted coffees are often made from mixtures of arabica and robusta. Arabica is less heat tolerant than robusta and therefore more limited by terrain.

5. Albeit the coffee they produce is of lower quality. The reduction in quality matters less than it might have in the past because of technological innovations that have made it possible for the roasters and processors to incorporate lower quality coffees in their blends (Sorby 2002, 2).

6. The seminal article was written by Nobel Laureate Thomas Schelling (1968). Since then the considerable literature ranges from reports of experiments that test whether minimally identifiable individuals are treated with more consideration than anonymous ones (Small and Lowenstein 2003)—they are—to the public policy implications of the distinction between identifiable and statistical individuals (Hammitt and Treich 2007). The Hammitt–Treich article contains a useful bibliography.

7. The term *countervailing power* is John Kenneth Galbraith's, who saw an opposing power bloc as a more effective way to counter entrenched economic power than the traditional remedy of increasing the number of competitors (Galbraith 1952).

Galbraith thought "trust busting" unsuited to the conditions of contemporary capitalism.

8. Disparities in market power may not be of the utmost importance in explaining distribution within the chain of value, but these disparities may be the key to understanding why the returns to Third World producers of coffee and other raw materials fluctuate so drastically over time, while the returns to processors, wholesalers, and retailers in the rich countries are relatively stable.

9. One estimate puts the fraction at 20 percent (Lewin et al. 2004, 101–102).

13. From Imperialism to Globalization, by Way of Development

1. Cultural imperialism is not limited to the West. In India, *Hindutva* represents the attempt to homogenize a tremendously diverse patchwork of cultures into a highly politicized Hinduism. Although defeated in the last general election in 2005, the party espousing Hindutva remains a strong force in Indian politics. The Chinese government has been even more thorough in imposing Han culture on its minorities. At the same time, both India and China routinely decry the cultural imperialism of the West.

2. I am sure there are exceptions, who might claim as their motto Ralph Waldo Emerson's (1940 [1841], 152) dictum: "A foolish consistency is the hobgoblin of little minds."

3. Las Casas became bishop of Chiapas (Mexico) in 1544 but did not last long in Ciudad Real, the seat of his bishopric; his stand on behalf of the indigenous people incurred the wrath of the Spanish colonists. Returning to Spain in 1547, Las Casas never set foot in Mexico again.

4. The text of Kipling's poem can be found on the W. W. Norton Web site, http://www.wwnorton.com/college/history/ralph/workbook/ralprs30b.htm (accessed June 4, 2007).

5. I defer to a common misperception in my use of the term *Luddite*. This was the name given the nineteenth-century English artisans who, under the leadership of the mythical General Lud, demolished machinery that was destroying their trades. Like the Amish, Luddites were not indiscriminately opposed to technology; they distinguished machinery that was compatible with artisanal production from machinery that displaced it. On Luddism and much else of relevance to the breakdown of workers' communities under the onslaught of the market, see Thompson (1963, 521–602).

6. Maimonides offers a second reason for circumcision—maintaining the community:

   Those who believe in the *unity of God* should have a bodily sign uniting them so that one who does not belong to them should not be able to claim that he was one of them, while being a stranger. For he would do this in order to profit by them or to deceive the people who profess this religion. Now a man does not perform this act upon himself or upon a son of his unless it be in consequence of a genuine belief. For it is not like an incision in the leg or a burn in the arm, but is a very, very hard thing.

It is also well known what degree of mutual love and mutual help exists between people who all bear the same sign, which forms for them a sort of covenant and alliance. *Circumcision* is a covenant made by *Abraham our Father* with a view to the belief in the *unity of God*. Thus everyone who is circumcised joins *Abraham's covenant*. . . . This also is a strong reason, as strong as the first, which may be adduced to account for *circumcision;* perhaps it is even stronger than the first. (Maimonides 1963 [1191], 610)

Appendix A

1. At its most extreme, in 1932, measured unemployment in the United States reached one-fourth of the labor force, but this is actually an understatement. At the time of the Depression, some 25 percent of the U.S. labor force was employed in agriculture, which suffered from low prices and underemployment rather than from unemployment. So it would be more informative, certainly in making comparisons with the present, to regard unemployment as having reached one-third of the nonagricultural labor force. Today, with agriculture having shrunk from 25 percent of the economy to practically zero, the labor force and the nonagricultural labor force are virtually the same thing.

2. Of course, I have cooked the books to make sure that my 250 gallons of wine just balances your 50 yards of cloth at the assumed price ratio of 5:1. But the lesson is general; the price ratio itself is supposed to adjust the quantities of the two goods offered on the market.

3. Ricardo himself recognized the importance to the theory of comparative advantage of the assumption that technology and capital as well as labor were immobile. He famously contrasted domestic and foreign trade as differing precisely because of the ease with which productive factors moved internally, as compared with the difficulty for these same factors to move across international borders (Ricardo 1951 [1817], 135–136).

4. An exception to the general diffidence of economists with respect to the normative implications of behavioral economics is Edward Glaeser (2003, 19), who has explicitly acknowledged that "if consumers reason poorly and don't maximize their welfare, then the basis of traditional welfare economics is in shambles." Glaeser is untroubled by this conclusion because he has a substitute defense of the market at hand: the alternative to the market is the state, which is likely to make a worse mess of things than the market ever will. In this, Glaeser echoes the libertarian attack on the state in Adam Smith's paean to the invisible hand quoted at the beginning of Chapter 6. (The published version of Glaeser's paper [2004] omits the shambles but retains the libertarian argument for the market.)

5. Of course, screening and examination of applicants for health insurance is possible, and insurance companies generally either refuse to insure applicants who do not pass their screening or insist on higher premiums. But as long as the applicant

knows something about his or her health that can't be picked up in an exam, the problem of asymmetric information remains, at least in attenuated form.

6. In the absence of compensation for the weak, we might judge that on balance the distributional gains from pooling the risks of the weak and the strong outweigh the efficiency gains of segmenting the markets for the two groups. This involves a value judgment: for example, that on average the weak are likely to be poorer than the strong and therefore more deserving, or that for purposes of health care we are all in it together and that, rich or poor, the strong ought to subsidize the weak.

7. "Global" stability means that wherever the system starts from, it will go toward equilibrium; "local" stability requires that the system begin somewhere in the neighborhood of equilibrium.

8. Herb Gintis pointed this out over three decades ago (1971). More recently, Robert Sugden (2004) has recognized the implications for normative economics of abandoning the assumption of exogenous preferences, but, like Glaeser (see note 4 above), is not troubled by these problems because he has an alternative defense of the market. Against the traditional defense that rests on the outcomes of market choices, Sugden argues for the market on the basis of the opportunities it gives for choice.

9. My thought on reading this was that, instead of going to war in Iraq and elsewhere to bring about "regime change," the U.S. government should have sought U.N. resolutions imposing rent control on recalcitrant dictators. Failing U.N. approval, the U.S. government could have imposed rent control unilaterally.

Appendix B

1. *Omnes homines aut liberi sunt aut servi*—All men are either free[men] or serfs (*De Legibus et Consuetudinibus Angliae* [On the Laws and Customs of England], ca. 1235, quoted in Pollock and Maitland 1968 [1895], 412).

2. Free peasants, too, might owe labor service. The menial nature of the serf's labor distinguished it from the service of the free peasant, whose labor was in general less physically onerous, work such as supervising the villeins. And, as has been noted, free peasants might take up villein tenements, tenements that carried with them menial services. But free peasants, unlike villeins, were legally free to walk away from these tenements.

   Legal theorists took another view of serfdom. Bracton distinguished the unfree from the free by the uncertainty that was the unfree man's lot: the villein did not know in the evening what he would have to do the next morning. This characterization is to be understood figuratively rather than literally. The villein probably knew better than most free people what he would be doing the next day since his life was governed by the agricultural calendar. Bracton's point is that the serf was under the arbitrary power of his lord and was not free to manage his own affairs according to his own judgment.

3. *Ad voluntatem domini secundum consuetudinem manerii.* Here is an example of a manorial court's judgment that invokes the dual formula: "And the said tenements were handed over to the said John Richard *to be held at the will of the lord,* etc. And for this [reason] it is decided that the said John is to have and hold the said tenements *according to the custom of the manor,* etc" [emphasis added]. The original Latin is as follows: *Et sic dimissa fuerunt tenementa predicta predicto Johanni Richard, tenendum sibi ad volutatem domini, etc. Et super hoc consideratum est quod predictus Johnnes habeat et teneat tenementa predicta sibi secundum consuetudinem manerii, etc.* (This judgment is from 1372, in Raftis 1968. The English text, which I have slightly edited, is on p. 35, the Latin on p. 216.)

4. There are cases of a lord appearing (through an attorney) to defend himself against a serf's claim, cases in which the lord did not have sovereign immunity. These cases are problematic, however, because the manors on which they took place were encumbered by a peculiar legal status deriving from their having come to their present lords as gifts of the king. As such, the tenants, free and serf, were protected by royal law from the imposition of more onerous conditions by the new lord than had existed when the manor was in the king's direct possession. Examples are reported in Maitland (1889, 99ff).

5. Maitland's introduction to a collection of cases from the manorial courts lays out this theory of a gradual usurpation by the lords of the tenantry's prerogatives as custodians of law as well as finders of fact (Maitland 1889, lxv–lxxiii).

6. The evolution of agriculture followed a different trajectory in England than on the Continent. In England, the end result was the extinction of the peasant community. In France, the process ended in a strengthening of the peasant community vis-à-vis the lords. In large part, the difference lies in how state power was deployed. As has been noted, state power in England was arrayed on the side of peasant communities until the magnates captured state power in the Glorious Revolution, after which state power served the interests of landlords. Similarly, in France, the monarchy saw the advantages of protecting peasant communities (Root 1987). The difference between the two countries was that the French Revolution came a century later, so the peasantry had that much more time to consolidate its power, and successive post-Revolutionary governments in France were more constrained by the need to finance military expenditures than the British had been after the Revolution of 1688.

   The consequences of the difference between the role of the state in France and England during the eighteenth century lasted until quite recently. Marc Bloch found the imprint of medieval and early modern differences on both the social and the physical geography of France and England well into the twentieth century (Bloch 1967 [1936], 11–15): France remained a country of small family farms, whereas England had long since become a country of large-scale agriculture.

7. Against the argument that it was a rise in the price of wool relative to the price of grain that motivated conversion from arable to pasture, Allen (1992, citing Lloyd 1973) argues that the relative prices of grain and wool did not change that

much. In this view, the relevant price ratio was the price of agricultural products relative to the cost of labor. As the cost of labor rose in the wake of the Black Death of the fourteenth century, the balance was shifted toward wool production, sheep raising being less labor intensive than grain.

8. If sheep farming were unambiguously more efficient, then it might have been expected to replace arable farming whatever the status of the peasant community. But the historical record is silent with respect to shifts from arable and mixed farming to sheep raising where the peasants were able to resist the lords.

It bears repeating that the time-honored term *enclosure* has been used here both in the narrow meaning of the word and for the larger process of "engrossing," by which landholding became concentrated in a relatively small number of hands. Conversion of arable to pasture was not necessary for this larger process to take place. As Allen (1992) has shown for the Midlands, holdings were consolidated into large units without conversion, with significantly greater effects on distribution than on efficiency. Landlords gained two ways: (1) by driving real wages paid to men and women who now were hired hands below the return that proprietor–tenants would have received for their effort and skill; and (2) by being in a position to claim the fruits of increased productivity for themselves.

9. As are latter-day experts on the period. Richard Tawney (1967 [1912]), followed by Charles Gray (1963), argued that protection came relatively late, in the sixteenth century. Eric Kerridge (1969) sees legal protection as coming much earlier, with less division among jurists. Reviewers of Kerridge's book were not persuaded by his argument (Barton 1971; Bean 1971).

References

Alborn, Timothy. 2001. "Senses of Belonging: The Politics of Working-Class Insurance in Britain, 1880–1914." *Journal of Modern History*, 73:561–602.

Allais, Maurice. 1953. "Le Comportement de l'Homme Devant le Risque: Critique des Postulats et Axioms de l'École Américaine" (Human Behavior toward Risk: A Critique of the Postulates and Axioms of the American School). *Econometrica*, 21:503–546.

Allen, Robert. 1992. *Enclosure and the Yeoman*. Oxford: Clarendon Press.

Alston, Richard, J. R. Kearl, and Michael Vaughan. 1992. "Is There a Consensus among Economists in the 1990s?" *American Economic Review*, 82:203–209.

American Heritage Dictionary, 2nd college ed. 1991. Boston: Houghton Mifflin.

American Museum of Natural History. Center for Biodiversity and Conservation. 2007. *Biodiversity in Crisis? An Introduction to the Issues and Comparison of Opinions from Scientists and the Public.* http://research.amnh.org/biodiversity/crisis/ resconpercap.html (accessed June 5, 2007).

Anderson, Benedict. 1983. *Imagined Communities: Reflections on the Origin and Spread of Nationalism.* London: Verso and NLB.

Anderson, Elizabeth. 1993. *Values in Ethics and Economics.* Cambridge, Mass.: Harvard University Press.

Anderson, Robert, and Peter DeTurk. 2002. "United States Life Tables 1999." *National Vital Statistics Reports,* 50, no. 6. Hyattsville, Md.: National Center for Health Statistics.

Apffel-Marglin, Frédérique, and Stephen Marglin, eds. 1990. *Dominating Knowledge: Development, Culture, and Resistance.* Oxford: Clarendon Press.

———. 1996. *Decolonizing Knowledge: From Development to Dialogue.* Oxford: Clarendon Press.

Appleby, Joyce. 1977. *Economic Thought and Ideology in Seventeenth-Century England.* Princeton, N.J.: Princeton University Press.

Aristotle. 1980. *The Nicomachean Ethics,* trans. David Ross, rev. J. L. Ackrill and J. O. Urmson. Oxford: Oxford University Press.

———. 2005. *Politics,* trans. H. Rackham. Cambridge, Mass.: Harvard University Press.

Arnauld, Antoine. 1964. *The Art of Thinking: Port Royal Logic,* trans. J. Dickoff and P. James. New York: Bobbs-Merrill. [Originally published in French in 1662.]

Arndt, H. W. 1987. *Economic Development: The History of an Idea.* Chicago: University of Chicago Press.

Arnott, Richard. 1996. "Time for Revisionism on Rent Control?" *Journal of Economic Perspectives,* 9:99–120.

Arrow, Kenneth. 1963. *Social Choice and Individual Values,* 2nd ed. New York: Wiley. [Originally published in 1951.]

———. 1963–1964. "The Role of Securities in the Optimal Allocation of Risk-Bearing." *Review of Economic Studies,* 31:91–96. [Originally published in French in 1953.]

Arrow, Kenneth, and Gerard Debreu. 1954. "Existence of Equilibrium for a Competitive Economy." *Econometrica,* 22:265–290.

Bacon, Francis. 1972. *The History of the Reign of King Henry the Seventh.* Indianapolis: Bobbs-Merrill. [Originally published in 1622.]

Banuri, Tariq, and Frédérique Apffel-Marglin. 1993. *Who Will Save the Forests? Resistance, Knowledge, and the Environmental Crisis.* London: Zed Books.

Barton, John. 1971. "Agrarian Problems in the Sixteenth Century and After." *English Historical Review,* 86:618–619.

Baumol, William, and Alan Blinder. 2004. *Economics: Principles and Policy,* 9th ed. Mason, Ohio: Thomson/South-Western.

Bean, J. M. W. 1971. "Agrarian Problems in the Sixteenth Century and After." *Renaissance Quarterly,* 24:389–391.

Behlmer, George. 1982. *Child Abuse and Moral Reform in England, 1870–1908.* Stanford: Stanford University Press.

Bellah, Robert, Richard Masden, William Sullivan, Ann Swidler, and Steven Taylor. 1996. *Habits of the Heart: Individualism and Commitment in American Life,* updated ed. Berkeley: University of California Press.

Bellamy, Edward. 1996. *Looking Backward, 2000–1887.* New York: Dover Publications. [Originally published in 1888.]

Belloc, Hillaire. 1923. *The Modern Traveller.* London: Arnold. [Originally published in 1898.]

Bender, Sue. 1989. *Plain and Simple: A Woman's Journey to the Amish.* San Francisco: HarperCollins.

Berman, Marshall. 1988. *All That Is Solid Melts into Air: The Experience of Modernity.* New York: Penguin. [Originally published in 1982.]

Bhagwati, Jagdish. 2004. *In Defense of Globalization.* New York: Oxford University Press.

Black, Christopher. 1989. *Italian Confraternities in the Sixteenth Century.* Cambridge: Cambridge University Press

Bloch, Marc.1961. *Feudal Society,* trans. L. A. Manyon. Chicago: University of Chicago Press. [Originally published in French in 1939–1940.]

———. 1967. *Seigneurie Française et Manoir* Anglaise (French Seigneury and English Manor), 2nd ed. Paris: Armand Colin. [Originally published in 1960, based on lectures delivered at the Sorbonne in 1936.]

Boualili, Halima. 2001. "Des Juifs en 1789 aux Musulmans en 2001" (From the Jews in 1789 to the Muslims in 2001). *Hommes et Libertés,* no. 113–114,

mars–juin. http://www.ldh-france.org/docu_hommeliber3.cfm?idhomme=648&
idpere=613 (accessed June 9, 2007).

Boulding, Kenneth. 1966. "The Economics of the Coming Spaceship Earth." In
H. Jarrett, ed., *Environmental Quality in a Growing Economy*. Baltimore: Johns
Hopkins Press, pp. 3–14.

Bowles, Samuel. 1998. "Endogenous Preferences: The Cultural Consequences of
Markets and Other Economic Institutions." *Journal of Economic Literature*,
36:75–111.

Bradsher, Keith. 2007. "The Price of Keeping Cool in Asia; Use of Air-Conditioning
Refrigerant Is Widening the Hole in the Ozone Layer." *New York Times*, February
23, 2007, p. C-1. http://select.nytimes.com/search/restricted/article?res=
F70E1EFC3B5A0C708EDDAB0894DF404482 (accessed June 22, 2007).

Bruce, John, ed. 1849. *Letters of Queen Elizabeth and King James VI. of Scotland*.
London: Camden Society.

Bruner, Jerome. 1979. *On Knowing: Essays for the Left Hand*. Cambridge, Mass.:
Harvard University Press. [Originally published in 1962.]

Buber, Martin. 1958. *Hasidism and Modern Man*, ed. and trans. Maurice Friedman.
New York: Horizon.

Bumiller, Elisabeth. 2004. "Bush Acts to Ease the Furor over Jobs Shipped Abroad."
New York Times, February 13, p. A-1. http://select.nytimes.com/search/restricted/
article?res=F20A10F93A5E0C708DDDAB0894DC404482 (accessed June 6,
2007).

Bureau of Economic Analysis. 2007. *National Income and Product Accounts*. Washington, D.C.: U.S. Department of Commerce. http://bea.gov/national/nipaweb/
TableView.asp#Mid (accessed June 2, 2007).

Burke, Edmund. 1982. *A Vindication of Natural Society*. Indianapolis: Liberty Fund.
[Originally published in 1756.]

Business Wire. 2000. "Athletic Footwear Market Share Report Announced for First
Quarter of 2000; Nike Holds Commanding Percentage of Footwear Market after
First Quarter." April 7. http://www.findarticles.com/cf_dls/m0EIN/2000_April_
7/61368089/p1/article.jhtml (accessed June 5, 2007).

Calabresi, Guido, and Phillip Bobbitt. 1978. *Tragic Choices: The Conflicts Society Confronts in the Allocation of Tragically Scarce Resources*. New York: Norton.

Cambridge Dictionary of Philosophy, 2nd ed. 1999. E. Audi, ed. Cambridge: Cambridge
University Press.

Camerer, Colin, and George Lowenstein. 2004. "Behavioral Economics: Past, Present,
Future." In Colin Camerer, George Lowenstein, and Mathew Rabin, eds., *Advances
in Behavioral Economics*. Princeton, N.J.: Princeton University Press, pp. 3–51.

Camerer, Colin, George Lowenstein, and Mathew Rabin, eds. 2004. *Advances in
Behavioral Economics*. Princeton, N.J.: Princeton University Press.

Carey, John (with Sarah Shapiro). 2004. "Global Warming." *BusinessWeek*, August
16, p. 60.

Carlyle, Thomas. 1850. "West India Emancipation." *Commercial Review of the South
and West*, n.s., 2:527–538. http://cepa.newschool.edu/het/texts/carlyle/carlodnq

.htm (accessed March 14, 2007). [Originally published anonymously as "Occasional Discourse on the Negro Question," in *Fraser's Magazine for Town and Country*. London, 1849.]

Caro, Robert. 1974. *The Power Broker: Robert Moses and the Fall of New York*. New York: Knopf.

———. 1982. *The Years of Lyndon Johnson*, vol. 1, *The Path to Power*. New York: Knopf.

Carroll, James. 2001. *Constantine's Sword: The Church and the Jews*. Boston: Houghton Mifflin.

Carroll, Lewis. 1992. "Through the Looking-Glass and What Alice Found There." In *Alice in Wonderland*, 2nd ed., ed. Donald J. Gray. New York: Norton, pp. 101–209. ["Through the Looking-Glass and What Alice Found There" was originally published in 1871.]

Cheng, Andria. 2007. "Nike Chief Executive Parker Innovates to Spur Sales (Update1)." Bloomberg.com, posted March 21. http://www.bloomberg.com/apps/news?pid=newsarchive&sid=a5TYtl5egzq0 (accessed June 22, 2007).

Clark, Geoffrey. 1999. *Betting on Lives: The Culture of Life Insurance in England, 1695–1775*. Manchester, UK: Manchester University Press.

Clawson, Mary. 1989. *Constructing Brotherhood: Class, Gender, and Fraternalism*. Princeton, N.J.: Princeton University Press.

Daly, Herman, and John Cobb Jr. 1989. *For the Common Good: Redirecting the Economy toward Community, the Environment, and a Sustainable Future*. Boston: Beacon Press.

Danvila y Collado, Manuel. 1894. *Reinado de Carlos III*, vol. 2, *Historia General de España* (Reign of Charles III, vol. 2, General History of Spain), under the direction of Antonio Cánovas del Castillo. Madrid: El Progreso Editorial.

Debreu, Gerard. 1959. *Theory of Value*. New York: Wiley.

Descartes, René. 1980. *Discourse on Method and Meditations on First Philosophy*, trans. Donald A. Cress. Indianapolis: Hackett Publishing Co. [*Discourse on Method* was originally published in 1637 and *Meditations on First Philosophy* in 1641.]

Diamond, Peter. 1967. "The Role of the Stock Market in a General Equilibrium Model with Technological Uncertainty." *American Economic Review*, 57:759–776.

Dickinson, H. D. 1933. "Price Formation in a Socialist Community." *Economic Journal*, 43:237–250.

Dodds, E. R. 1951. *The Greeks and the Irrational*. Berkeley: University of California Press.

Donne, John. 1975. *Devotions upon Emergent Occasions*, ed. Elizabeth Savage. Salzburg: Institut für Englische Sprache und Literatur, Universität Salzburg. [Originally published in 1624.]

Drake, Donald. 1991a. "A Deadly Illness, a Choice for Amish." *Philadelphia Inquirer*, February 24, p. 1-A.

———. 1991b. "Amish Boy Dies; Had Rare Illness." *Philadelphia Inquirer*, March 20, p. 1-B.

Duesenberry, James. 1949. *Income, Saving and the Theory of Consumer Behavior*. Cambridge, Mass.: Harvard University Press.

Dumont, Louis. 1977. *From Mandeville to Marx: The Genesis and Triumph of Economic Ideology.* Chicago: University of Chicago Press.

Economist. 1992. "Let Them Eat Pollution." February 8, p. 66.

Eliot, T. S. 1934. *The Rock: A Pageant Play Written for Performance at Sadler's Wells Theatre, 28 May–9 June 1934, on Behalf of the Forty-Five Churches Fund of the Diocese of London.* London: Faber & Faber.

Ellsberg, Daniel. 1961. "Risk, Ambiguity, and the Savage Axioms." *Quarterly Journal of Economics,* 75:643–669.

Elster, Jon. 1985. *Making Sense of Marx.* Cambridge: Cambridge University Press; Paris: Editions de la Maison des Sciences de l'Homme.

Emerson, Ralph Waldo. 1940. "Self Reliance." In Brooks Atkinson, ed., *The Complete Essays and Other Writings.* New York: Modern Library, pp. 145–169. ["Self Reliance" was originally published in 1841.]

Feldstein, Martin. 1973. "Tax Incentives, Corporate Saving, and Capital Accumulation in the United States." *Journal of Political Economy,* 82:905–926.

Feldstein, Martin, and George Fane. 1973. "Taxes, Corporate Dividend Policy and Personal Savings: The British Postwar Experience." *Review of Economics and Statistics,* 55:399–411.

Finetti, Bruno de. 1980. "Foresight: Its Logical Laws, Its Subjective Sources." In Henry Kyburg Jr. and Howard Smokker, eds., *Studies in Subjective Probability,* 2nd ed. Huntington, N.Y.: Krieger, pp. 53–118. [Originally published in French in 1937.]

Finkel, Avraham. 1990. *The Responsa Anthology.* Northvale, N.J.: Jason Aronson.

Fletcher, Anthony, and Diarmaid MacCulloch. 2004. *Tudor Rebellions,* 5th ed. Harlow, UK: Pearson Education. [Originally published in 1968 under the sole authorship of Anthony Fletcher.]

Flynn, Maureen. 1989. *Sacred Charity: Confraternities and Social Welfare in Spain, 1400–1700.* Houndmills, UK: Macmillan.

Forster, E. M. 1938. "Living Philosophies—I: Two Cheers for Democracy." *The Nation,* July 16, p. 65.

Forster, Martin. 2001. "The Meaning of Death: Some Simulations of a Model of Healthy and Unhealthy Consumption." *Journal of Health Economics,* 20:613–638.

Foster, George. 1965. "Peasant Society and the Image of Limited Good." *American Anthropologist,* 67:293–315.

Frank, Robert. 1999. *Luxury Fever: Money and Happiness in an Era of Excess.* New York: Free Press

Frank, Robert, Thomas Gilovich, and Dennis Regan. 1993. "Does Studying Economics Inhibit Cooperation?" *Journal of Economic Perspectives,* 7:159–171.

Fraser, Jill. 2001. *White-Collar Sweatshop: The Deterioration of Work and Its Rewards in Corporate America.* New York: Norton.

Friedman, Benjamin. 2005. *The Moral Consequences of Economic Growth.* New York: Knopf.

Friedman, Milton. 1953. "The Methodology of Positive Economics." In *Essays in Positive Economics.* Chicago: University of Chicago Press, pp. 3–43.

———. 1957. *A Theory of the Consumption Function*. Princeton, N.J.: Princeton University Press.

———. 1962. *Capitalism and Freedom*. Chicago: University of Chicago Press.

Friedman, Milton, and Rose Friedman. 1980. *Free to Choose: A Personal Statement*. New York: Harcourt Brace Jovanovich.

Fuchs, Victor. 1996. "Economics, Values, and Health Care Reform." *American Economic Review*, 86:1–24.

Galbraith, John Kenneth. 1952. *American Capitalism*. Boston: Houghton Mifflin.

———. 1958. *The Affluent Society*. Boston: Houghton Mifflin.

———. 1967. *The New Industrial State*. Boston: Houghton Mifflin.

Gandhi, Mohandas Karamchand. 1931. *Young India,* October 15, p. 310. Web site maintained by Bombay Sarvodaya Mandal and Gujarat Vidyapith (Ahemedabad). http://www.mkgandhi.org/momgandhi/chap39.htm (accessed June 26, 2007).

Gardner, James. 2007. "Deliberation or Tabulation? The Self-Undermining Constitutional Architecture of Election Campaigns." *Buffalo Law Review*, 54:1413–1482.

Gellner, Ernest. 1964. *Thought and Change*. London: Weidenfeld and Nicholson.

———. 1983. *Nations and Nationalism*. Ithaca, N.Y.: Cornell University Press.

General Accounting Office. 2000. *Sugar Program: Supporting Sugar Prices Has Increased Users' Costs While Benefiting Producers*. Washington, D.C.: United States General Accounting Office, RCED-00-126.

Georgescu-Roegen, Nicholas. 1971. *The Entropy Law and the Economic Process*. Cambridge, Mass.: Harvard University Press.

Gilligan, Carol. 1982. *In a Different Voice: Psychological Theory and Women's Development*. Cambridge, Mass.: Harvard University Press.

Gintis, Herbert. 1974. "Welfare Criteria with Endogenous Preferences: The Economics of Education." *International Economic Review*, 15:415–430.

Glaeser, Edward. 2003. "Psychology and the Market." Cambridge, Mass.: Harvard Institute of Economic Research Discussion Paper Number 2023, December.

———. 2004. "Psychology and the Market." *American Economic Review*, 94:408–413.

Gleckman, Howard. 2001. "Social Security Isn't the Only Surplus Buster." *Business-Week*, May 21, p. 81.

Goggin, Michael. 2004. *Is It Time for a Change? Science, Policy, and Climate Change*. Senior honors thesis, Harvard College.

Gosden, P. 1973. *Self-Help: Voluntary Associations in the 19th Century*. London: Batsford.

Gray, Charles. 1963. *Copyhold, Equity, and the Common Law*. Cambridge, Mass.: Harvard University Press.

Grampp, William. 2000. "What Did Smith Mean by the Invisible Hand?" *Journal of Political Economy*, 108:441–465.

Greenfeld, Liah. 1992. *Nationalism: Five Roads to Modernity*. Cambridge, Mass.: Harvard University Press.

———. 2001. *The Spirit of Capitalism: Nationalism and Economic Growth*. Cambridge, Mass.: Harvard University Press.

[Gresser, Charis, and Sophia Tickell]. 2002. *Mugged: Poverty in Your Coffee Cup*. Boston: Oxfam America.

Grewal, David. 1998. *Optimality and Evolution in Economics: Darwinism in the Study of Firms and Institutions.* Senior honors thesis, Harvard College.

Grossman, Michael. 1972. "On the Concept of Health Capital and the Demand for Health." *Journal of Political Economy,* 80:223–255.

———. 1998. "On Optimal Length of Life." *Journal of Health Economics,* 17:499–509.

Grossman, Sanford, and Oliver Hart. 1986. "The Costs and Benefits of Ownership: A Theory of Vertical and Lateral Integration." *Journal of Political Economy,* 94:694–719.

Hacking, Ian. 1975. *The Emergence of Probability: A Philosophical Study of Early Ideas about Probability, Induction and Statistical Inference.* Cambridge: Cambridge University Press.

Hammitt, James, and Nicolas Treich. 2007. "Statistical vs. Identified Lives in Benefit-Cost Analysis." *Journal of Risk and Uncertainty,* in press.

Hardin, Garrett. 1968. "The Tragedy of the Commons." *Science,* 162:1243–1248.

Harlow, Jules. 1989. *Siddur Sim Shalom: A Prayerbook for Shabbat, Festivals, and Weekdays,* personal size edition. New York: The United Synagogue of Conservative Judaism.

Harrod, Roy. 1948. *Towards a Dynamic Economics: Some Recent Developments of Economic Theory and Their Application to Policy.* London: Macmillan.

Hart, Oliver. 1995. *Firms, Contracts, and Financial Structure.* Oxford: Clarendon Press.

Hart, Oliver, and John Moore. 1988. "Incomplete Contracts and Renegotiation." *Econometrica,* 56:755–786.

Harvard College Economist. 2002. "An Interview with Professor Jeffrey G. Williamson," Vol. 2, no. 1:5–11.

Hayek, Friedrich. 1940. "Socialist Calculation: The Competitive 'Solution.'" *Economica,* 7:125–149.

———. 1944. *The Road to Serfdom.* Chicago: University of Chicago Press.

———. 1945. "The Use of Knowledge in Society." *American Economic Review,* 35:519–530.

Hertzberg, Arthur. 1993. "The Enlightenment and Western Religion." In Eugene Fisher, ed., *Interwoven Destinies: Jews and Christians through the Ages.* New York: Paulist Press, pp. 134–142.

Hirschman, Albert. 1970. *Exit, Voice, and Loyalty: Responses to Decline in Firms, Organizations, and States.* Cambridge, Mass.: Harvard University Press.

———. 1977. *The Passions and the Interests: Political Arguments for Capitalism before Its Triumph.* Princeton, N.J.: Princeton University Press.

———. 1984. "Against Parsimony: Three Easy Ways of Complicating Some Categories of Economic Discourse." *American Economic Review,* 74:89–96.

Historical Statistics of the United States, Colonial Times to 1970, Part 1. 1975. Washington, D.C.: Bureau of the Census.

Hobbes, Thomas. 1968. *Leviathan.* Harmondsworth, UK: Penguin Books. [Originally published in 1651.]

Holmes, Stephen. 1989. "The Permanent Structure of Anti-Liberal Thought." In N. Rosenblum, ed., *Liberalism and the Moral Life.* Cambridge, Mass.: Harvard University Press, pp. 227–253.

Huxley, Aldous. 1952. *The Devils of Loudun*. New York: Harper & Brothers.

Jacobs, Jane. 1961. *The Death and Life of Great American Cities*. New York: Random House.

Jones, Donald H., and Daniel Weinberg. 2000. "The Changing Shape of Income Distribution." *Current Population Reports*, P60-204. Washington, D.C.: U.S. Census Bureau.

Just-style.com. 2003. "US Athletic Footwear Market Stumbles towards 2007." July 22. http://www.just-style.com/features_detail.asp?art=664 (accessed June 9, 2007).

Kahneman, Daniel, and Amos Tversky. 1979. "Prospect Theory: An Analysis of Decision under Risk." *Econometrica*, 47:263–291.

Kaldor, Nicholas. 1939. "Welfare Propositions of Economics and Interpersonal Comparisons of Utility." *Economic Journal*, 49:549–552.

Kennedy, Joseph. 1864. *Population of the United States in 1860; Compiled from the Original Returns of the Eighth Census*. Washington D.C.: Government Printing Office. Bureau of the Census Web site, http://www2.census.gov/prod2/decennial/documents/1860a-07.pdf (accessed March 5, 2007).

Kerridge, Eric. 1969. *Agrarian Problems in the Sixteenth Century and After*. London: George Allen and Unwin.

Keynes, John Maynard. 1921. *A Treatise on Probability*. London: Macmillan.

———. 1931. "Economic Possibilities for Our Grandchildren." In *Essays in Persuasion*. London: Macmillan, pp. 358–373. [Originally published in *The Nation and Athenaeum*, October 11 and 18, 1930.]

———. 1936. *The General Theory of Employment, Interest and Money*. London: Macmillan.

———. 1937. "The General Theory of Employment." *Quarterly Journal of Economics*, 51:209–223.

———. 1972. "A Short View of Russia." In *The Collected Writings of John Maynard Keynes*, vol. 9. London: Macmillan, pp. 253–271. [Originally published in *The Nation and Athenaeum*, October 10, 17, and 25, 1925. Abridged in *Essays in Persuasion*. London: Macmillan.]

Keynes, John Neville. 1917. *The Scope and Method of Political Economy*, 4th ed. London: Macmillan. [Originally published in 1890.]

Kilborn, Peter. 2003. "Judging the Tax Plan: Four Families Shrug." *New York Times*, January 13, p. A-11.

Klosko, George. 1986. *The Development of Plato's Political Theory*. New York: Methuen.

Knight, Frank. 1940. *Risk, Uncertainty and Profit*. Boston: Houghton Mifflin. [Originally published in 1921.]

Kristof, Nicholas, and Sheryl WuDunn. 2000. "Two Cheers for Sweatshops." *New York Times Sunday Magazine*, September 24, p. 70.

Krugman, Paul. 2000. "A Rent Affair." *New York Times*, June 7, p. A-31.

Krugman, Paul, and Maurice Obstfeld. 2000. *International Economics: Theory and Practice*, 5th ed. Reading, Mass.: Addison-Wesley.

Krugman, Paul, and Robin Wells. 2005. *Microeconomics*. New York: Worth.

Kuhn, Thomas. 1970. *The Structure of Scientific Revolutions,* 2nd ed. International Encyclopedia of Unified Science, vol. 2, no. 2. Chicago: University of Chicago Press. [Originally published in 1962.]

Kushner, Lawrence. 2000. *Honey from the Rock: An Introduction to Jewish Mysticism—Special Anniversary Edition.* Woodstock, Vt.: Jewish Lights Publishing. [Originally published in 1977.]

Laidler, David. 1999. *Fabricating the Keynesian Revolution.* Cambridge: Cambridge University Press.

Lakatos, Imre. 1970. "Falsification and the Methodology of Scientific Research Programmes." In Imre Lakatos and Alan Musgrave, eds., *Criticism and the Growth of Knowledge.* Cambridge: Cambridge University Press, pp. 91–195.

Lange, Oskar. 1936. "On the Economic Theory of Socialism: Part One." *Review of Economic Studies,* 4:53–71.

Lazonick, William. 1974. "Karl Marx and Enclosure in England." *Review of Radical Political Economics,* 6:1–59.

Leach, William. 1993. *Land of Desire: Merchants, Power, and the Rise of a New American Culture.* New York: Pantheon.

Lebergott, Stanley. 1993. *Pursuing Happiness: American Consumers in the Twentieth Century.* Princeton, N.J.: Princeton University Press.

Leibenstein, Harvey. 1950. "Bandwagon, Snob, and Veblen Effects in the Theory of Consumers' Demand." *Quarterly Journal of Economics,* 64:183–207.

Lennon, Carole (chairperson), Ann Bailey, et al. [American Academy of Pediatrics Task Force on Circumcision]. 1999. "Circumcision Policy Statement." *Pediatrics,* 103:686–693.

Leopold, Aldo. 1968. *A Sand County Almanac.* Oxford: Oxford University Press. [Originally published in 1949.]

Levy, David. 2001. "How the Dismal Science Got Its Name: Debating Racial Quackery." *Journal of the History of Economic Thought,* 23:5–35.

Lewin, Bryan, Daniele Giovannucci, and Panos Varangis. 2004. "Coffee Markets: New Paradigms in Global Supply and Demand." Agriculture and Rural Development Discussion Paper 3. Washington, D.C.: International Bank for Reconstruction and Development, World Bank.

Lewis, W. Arthur. 1955. *The Theory of Economic Growth.* London: Allen & Unwin.

Lindsey, Brink. 2003. "Grounds for Complaint? 'Fair Trade' and the Coffee Crisis." Trade Briefing Paper No. 16, Center for Trade Policy Studies. Washington, D.C.: Cato Institute.

Locke, John. 1980. *Second Treatise of Government,* ed. C. Macpherson. Indianapolis: Hackett Publishing Co. [As the title indicates, this is the second of the two treatises originally published in 1690.]

———. 1988. *Two Treatises of Government,* ed. P. Laslett. Cambridge: Cambridge University Press. [Originally published in 1690.]

Lohmann, Larry, Thomas Wallgren, and Witoon Permpongsacharoen. 1994. "Intercultural Politics: The Coevolution of a Forestry Master Plan and Its Critiques." Unpublished paper presented to the conference *People's Economy,*

People's Ecology, held at the Rockefeller Foundation Conference Center in Bellagio, Italy, August.

Lowenstein, Roger. 2000. *When Genius Failed: The Rise and Fall of Long-Term Capital Management.* New York: Random House.

Lukes, Steven. 1973. *Individualism.* Oxford: Blackwell.

Luria, Alexander. 1976. *Cognitive Development: Its Cultural and Social Foundations,* ed. Michael Cole, trans. M. Lopez-Morillas and L. Solotaroff. Cambridge, Mass.: Harvard University Press. [Originally published in Russian in 1974.]

————. 1979. *The Making of Mind: A Personal Account of Soviet Psychology,* ed. Michael Cole and Sheila Cole. Cambridge, Mass.: Harvard University Press.

Lyons, John. 1969. *Structural Semantics: An Analysis of Part of the Vocabulary of Plato.* Oxford: Basil Blackwell.

Macaulay, Thomas. 1920. "Minute on Education." In H. Sharp, ed., *Selections from Educational Records, Part I. 1781–1839.* Calcutta: Superintendent Government Printing, pp. 107–117. Reprinted by National Archives of India, Delhi, 1965. [The "Minute on Education" was written in 1835.]

Macpherson, C. B. 1987. "Individualism." In J. Eatwell, M. Milgate, and P. Newman, eds., *The New Palgrave: A Dictionary of Economics,* vol. 2. London: Macmillan, pp. 790–793.

Maimonides [Moses ben Maimon]. 1963. *Guide of the Perplexed,* trans. S. Pines. Chicago: University of Chicago Press. [Originally published in 1191.]

Maitland, F. 1889. *Selected Pleas in Manorial and Other Seignorial Courts,* vol. 1, *Reigns of Henry III and Edward I,* edited for the Selden Society. London: Bernard Quaritch.

Malinvaud, Edmond. 1986. "Pure Profits as Forced Saving." *Scandinavian Journal of Economics,* 88:109–130.

Mandeville, Bernard. 1988. *The Fable of the Bees, or Private Vices, Publick Benefits,* vol. 1, ed. F. Kaye. Indianapolis: Liberty Classics. [*The Fable of the Bees* was originally published in 1714, and the Kaye edition was originally published in 1924.]

Mankiw, N. Gregory. 2001. "The Case against the Living Wage." *Harvard Magazine,* November–December, p. 70.

————. 2004. *Principles of Economics,* 3rd ed. Mason, Ohio: Thomson/South-Western.

Marglin, Jessica. 2006. *Jews into Frenchmen? The Alliance Israélite Universelle and French Pre-Colonial Policy in Morocco, 1862–1912.* Senior honors thesis, Harvard College.

Marglin, Stephen. 1969. "Information in Price and Command Systems of Planning." In J. Margolis and H. Guitton, eds., *Public Economics: An Analysis of Public Production and Consumption and Their Relations to the Private Sectors.* New York: St. Martin's, pp. 54–77.

————. 1974. "What Do Bosses Do? The Origins and Functions of Hierarchy in Capitalist Production, Part I." *Review of Radical Political Economics,* 6:60–112.

————. 1975. "What Do Bosses Do? The Origins and Functions of Hierarchy in Capitalist Production, Part II." *Review of Radical Political Economics,* 7:20–37.

————. 1979. "Catching Flies with Honey: An Inquiry into Management Initiatives to Humanize Work." *Economic Analysis and Workers' Management,* 13:473–487.

———. 1984a. *Growth, Distribution, and Prices*. Cambridge, Mass.: Harvard University Press.

———. 1984b. "Knowledge and Power." In F. Stephen, ed., *Firms, Organization and Labour*. London: Macmillan, pp. 146–164.

———. 1990. "Losing Touch: The Cultural Conditions of Worker Accommodation and Resistance." In F. Apffel-Marglin and S. Marglin, eds., *Dominating Knowledge: Development, Culture, and Resistance*. Oxford: Clarendon Press, pp. 217–282.

———. 1991. "Understanding Capitalism: Control vs. Efficiency." In B. Gustaffsson, ed., *Power and Economic Institutions: Reinterpretations in Economic History*. Aldershot, UK: Edward Elgar, pp. 225–252.

———. 1996. "Farmers, Seedsmen, and Scientists: Systems of Agriculture and Systems of Knowledge." In F. Apffel-Marglin and S. Marglin, eds., *Decolonizing Knowledge: From Development to Dialogue*. Oxford: Clarendon Press, pp. 185–248.

Marketplace Morning Report. 2003. Broadcast December 8. http://www.lexis-nexis.com (accessed June 5, 2007).

Martin, Marie-Madeleine. 1951. *The Making of France: The Origins and Development of the Idea of National Unity*, trans. B. North and R. North. London: Eyre and Spottiswoode. [Originally published in French in 1949.]

Marwell, Gerald, and Ruth Ames. 1981. "Economists Free Ride, Does Anyone Else? Experiments on the Provision of Public Goods, IV." *Journal of Public Economics*, 15:295–310.

Marx, Anthony. 2003. *Faith in Nation: Exclusionary Origins of Nationalism*. New York: Oxford University Press.

Marx, Karl. 1959. *Capital*, vol. 1, *A Critical Analysis of Capitalist Production*. Moscow: Foreign Languages Publishing House. [Originally published in German in 1867.]

———. 1970. *A Contribution to the Critique of Political Economy*, ed. M. Dobb, trans. S. Ryazanskaya. New York: International Publishers. [Originally published in German in 1859.]

Marx, Karl, and Friedrich Engels. 1955. *The Communist Manifesto*, ed. S. Beer. New York: Appleton-Century-Crofts. [Originally published in German in 1848.]

———. 1959. "The German Ideology." In L. Feuer, ed., *Marx & Engels: Basic Writings on Politics and Philosophy*. Garden City, N.Y.: Doubleday, pp. 246–261. ["The German Ideology" was written in 1845.]

Mas-Colell, Andreu, Michael D. Whinston, and Jerry R. Green. 1995. *Microeconomic Theory*. New York: Oxford University Press.

McCloskey, Deirdre [Donald]. 1985. *The Rhetoric of Economics*. Madison: University of Wisconsin Press.

———. 1987. "Open Field System." In J. Eatwell, M. Milgate, and P. Newman, eds., *The New Palgrave: A Dictionary of Economics*, vol. 3. London: Macmillan, pp. 709–711.

McCullough, David. 2001. *John Adams*. New York: Simon & Schuster.

McMillan, John. 2002. *Reinventing the Bazaar: A Natural History of Markets*. New York: Norton.

Meacham, Bradley. 2002. "How Fair Is Fair Trade Coffee? Larger Growers Excluded Despite Good Records." *Seattle Times,* September 11, p. E-1.

Milbank, Dana. 1992. "The Modern Okies: Industrial Migrants Scour U.S. for Work, with Dwindling Luck." *Wall Street Journal,* March 2, p. A1.

Mill, John Stuart. 1850. "The Negro Question." *Littell's Living Age,* 24:465–469. http://cepa.newschool.edu/het/texts/carlyle/millnegro.htm (accessed March 14, 2007). [Originally published anonymously as a letter to the editor in *Fraser's Magazine for Town and Country,* London, 1850.]

———. 1947. *On Liberty,* ed. A. Castell. New York: Appleton-Century-Crofts. [Originally published in 1859.]

Miniño, Arialdi, Elizabeth Arias, Kenneth Kochanek, Sherry Murphy, and Betty Smith. 2001. "Deaths: Final Data for 2000." *National Vital Statistics Reports,* 50, no. 15. Hyattsville, Md.: National Center for Health Statistics.

Mobil Corporation. 1993. "Hands off the Fed." Paid advertisement. *New York Times,* December 2, p. A-27.

Modigliani, Franco, and Richard Blumberg. 1954. "Utility Analysis and the Consumption Function: An Interpretation of Cross-Section Data." In Kenneth Kurihara, ed., *Post-Keynesian Economics.* New Brunswick, N.J.: Rutgers University Press, pp. 388–436.

Montaigne, Michel de. 1965. *The Complete Essays of Montaigne,* trans. Donald Frame. Stanford: Stanford University Press.

Morris, Frederic. 1972. *From Cottage to Factory.* Senior honors thesis, Harvard College.

Munson, Martha, and Paul Sutton. 2005. "Births, Marriages, Divorces, and Deaths: Provisional Data for 2004." *National Vital Statistics Reports,* 53, no. 21. Hyattsville, Md.: National Center for Health Statistics. Data updated electronically on February 15, 2006, at www.cdc.gov/nchs/data/nvsr/nvsr53/nvsr53_21.pdf (accessed June 6, 2007).

Murray, Alan. 2004. "Despite the Outcry, Mankiw Was Right about Outsourcing." *Wall Street Journal,* February 17, p. A4.

Myers, A. 1969. *English Historical Documents, 1327–1485.* London: Eyre & Spottiswoode.

Nehru, Jawaharlal. 1946. *The Discovery of India.* Calcutta: Signet Press.

———. 1958. *Speeches,* vol. 1, 2nd ed. New Delhi: Government of India.

Nike, Inc. 2001. "Labor Practices." *Nike's Fiscal Year 2001 Corporate Responsibility Report.* http://www.nikebiz.com (accessed March 22, 2004).

Nisbet, Robert. 1990. *The Quest for Community: A Study in the Ethics of Order and Freedom.* San Francisco: ICS Press. [Originally published in 1953.]

North, Douglass, and Robert Thomas. 1971. "The Rise and Fall of the Manorial System: A Theoretical Model." *Journal of Economic History,* 31:777–803.

Nozick, Robert. 1974. *Anarchy, State, and Utopia.* New York: Basic Books.

Nussbaum, Martha. 1986. *The Fragility of Goodness: Luck and Ethics in Greek Tragedy and Philosophy.* Cambridge: Cambridge University Press.

———. 2001. "The Costs of Tragedy: Some Moral Limits of Cost:Benefit Analysis." In M. D. Adler and E. A. Posner, eds., *Cost-Benefit Analysis: Legal, Economic, and Philosophical Perspectives.* Chicago: University of Chicago Press, pp. 169–200.

Nussbaum, Martha, and Amartya Sen. 1989. "Internal Criticism and Indian Rationalist Traditions." In Michael Krausz, ed., *Relativism: Interpretation and Confrontation*. Notre Dame, Ind.: Notre Dame University Press, pp. 299–325.

Oakeshott, Michael. 1991. *Rationalism in Politics and Other Essays*. Indianapolis: Liberty Press.

Overton, Mark. 1996. *Agricultural Revolution in England: The Transformation of the Agrarian Economy, 1500–1850*. Cambridge: Cambridge University Press.

Persky, Joseph. 1990. "Retrospectives: A Dismal Romantic." *Journal of Economic Perspectives,* 4:165–172.

Pigou, Arthur C. 1952. *The Economics of Welfare*. London: Macmillan. [Originally published in 1920.]

Pirsig, Robert. 1976. *Zen and the Art of Motorcycle Maintenance: An Inquiry into Values*. London: Transworld.

Plato. 1925a. "Gorgias." In *Lysis, Symposium, and Gorgias,* trans. W. R. M. Lamb. Cambridge, Mass.: Harvard University Press, pp. 247–533.

———. 1925b. "Philebus." In *Statesman, Philebus, and Ion,* trans. Harold N. Fowler and W. R. M. Lamb. Cambridge, Mass.: Harvard University Press, pp. 1–195.

———. 1945. *The Republic of Plato,* trans. Francis Cornford. New York: Oxford University Press.

PNC Advisors. 2005. "Many Wealthy Americans Have Done Nothing to Protect Assets and Are Worried about Financial Security, Family Values, According to Largest Study of Its Kind Released Today." January 10. http://www.pncadvisors .com/print/pdf/1,1218,,00.html?PDF=/files/section/pdf/WealthandValueSurvey _1634.pdf (accessed February 23, 2005).

Polanyi, Karl. 1944. *The Great Transformation: The Political and Economic Origins of Our Time*. New York: Rinehart.

Polanyi, Michael. 1962. *Personal Knowledge: Towards a Post-Critical Philosophy*. Chicago: University of Chicago Press. [Corrected edition. Originally published in 1958.]

Pollin, Robert, and Stephanie Luce. 1998. *The Living Wage: Building a Fair Economy*. New York: New Press.

Pollock, Frederick, and Frederic Maitland. 1968. *The History of English Law,* vol. 1, *Before the Time of Edward I*. Cambridge: Cambridge University Press. [Originally published in 1895.]

Popkin, Richard. 1979. *The History of Skepticism from Erasmus to Spinoza*. Berkeley: University of California Press.

Popper, Karl. 1968. *The Logic of Scientific Discovery*. New York: Harper & Row. [Originally published in German in 1935.]

Poterba, James. 1987. "Tax Policy and Corporate Saving." *Brookings Papers on Economic Activity,* 1987:455–503.

Putnam, Hilary. 1974. "The 'Corroboration' of Scientific Theories." In P. Schilpp, ed., *The Philosophy of Karl Popper,* Book 1. La Salle, Ill.: Open Court, pp. 221–240.

———. 2002. *The Collapse of the Fact/Value Dichotomy and Other Essays*. Cambridge, Mass.: Harvard University Press.

Quintanilla, Carl. 1999. "The Hog Farmers' Losses Put a Butcher Shop on Knife-Edge." *Wall Street Journal,* March 24, p. A1.

Raftis, J. Ambrose. 1964. *Tenure and Mobility: Studies in the Social History of the Medieval English Village.* Toronto: Pontifical Institute of Medieval Studies.

Rai, Saritha. 2004. "U. S. Payrolls Change Lives in Bangalore." *New York Times,* February 22, p. A-6.

Ramsey, Frank. 1980. "Truth and Probability." In Henry Kyburg Jr. and Howard Smokker, eds., *Studies in Subjective Probability,* 2nd ed. Huntington, N.Y.: Krieger, pp. 23–52. [Originally published in 1926.]

Rangel, Charles. 2002. "Bring Back the Draft." *New York Times,* December 31, p. A-19.

[Raworth, Kate]. 2004. *Trading Away Our Rights: Women Working in Global Supply Chains.* Oxford: Oxfam International.

Ricardo, David. 1951. *On the Principles of Political Economy and Taxation,* vol. 1 of *The Works and Correspondence of David Ricardo,* ed. Piero Sraffa with the collaboration of M. H. Dobb. Cambridge: Cambridge University Press. [*On the Principles of Political Economy and Taxation* was originally published in 1817.]

Richard, P. 1956. *Histoire des Institutions d'Assurance en France* (History of Insurance in France). Paris: L'Argus.

Ried, Walter. 1998. "Comparative Dynamic Analysis of the Full Grossman Model." *Journal of Health Economics,* 17:383–425.

Robbins, Lionel. 1948. *An Essay on the Nature and Significance of Economic Science,* 2nd ed. London: Macmillan. [Originally published in 1932.]

Robertson, Dennis. 1956. *Economic Commentaries.* London: Staples.

Robinson, Joan. 1956. *The Accumulation of Capital.* London: Macmillan.

———. 1962. *Essays in the Theory of Economic Growth.* London: Macmillan.

Romer, Paul. 1986. "Increasing Returns and Long Run Growth." *Journal of Political Economy,* 94:1002–1037.

Root, Hilton. 1987. *Peasants and King in Burgundy: Agrarian Foundations of French Absolutism.* Berkeley: University of California Press.

Rosenberg, Tina. 2003. "Why Mexico's Small Corn Farmers Go Hungry." *New York Times,* March 3, p. A-22.

Rothschild, Emma. 2001. *Economic Sentiments: Adam Smith, Condorcet, and the Enlightenment.* Cambridge, Mass.: Harvard University Press.

Ruffat, Michèle. 2003. "French Insurance from the *Ancien Régime* to 1946: Shifting Frontiers between State and Market." *Financial History Review,* 10:185–200.

Sacks, Oliver. 1985. *The Man Who Mistook His Wife for a Hat and Other Clinical Tales.* New York: Summit Books.

Said, Edward. 1978. *Orientalism.* New York: Random House.

Samuelson, Paul. 1954. "The Pure Theory of Public Expenditure." *Review of Economics and Statistics,* 36:387–389.

———. 1955. "Diagrammatic Exposition of a Theory of Public Expenditure." *Review of Economics and Statistics,* 37:350–356.

Sandel, Michael. 1996. *Democracy's Discontent: America in Search of a Public Philosophy.* Cambridge, Mass.: Harvard University Press.

———. 1998. *Liberalism and the Limits of Justice,* 2nd ed. Cambridge: Cambridge University Press. [Originally published in 1982.]

Sartre, Jean-Paul. 1971. *Le Mur* (The Wall). Paris: Editions Gallimard, Livre de Poche. [Originally published in 1939.]

Savage, Leonard J. 1954. *The Foundations of Statistics.* New York: Wiley.

Schelling, Thomas. 1968. "The Life You Save May Be Your Own." In S. Chase Jr., ed., *Problems in Public Expenditure Analysis.* Washington, D.C.: Brookings, pp. 127–162.

Schor, Juliet. 1991. *The Overworked American: The Unexpected Decline of Leisure.* New York: Basic Books.

Schumpeter, Joseph. 1934. *The Theory of Economic Development: An Inquiry into Profits, Capital, Credit, Interest, and the Business Cycle,* trans. R. Opie. Cambridge, Mass.: Harvard University Press. [Originally published in German in 1911.]

———. 1954. *History of Economic Analysis.* New York: Oxford University Press.

Scitovsky [de Scitovszky], T. 1941. "A Note on Welfare Propositions in Economics." *Review of Economic Studies,* 9:77–88.

Segal, Charles. 1981. *Tragedy and Civilization: An Interpretation of Sophocles.* Cambridge, Mass.: Harvard University Press.

Sen, Amartya. 1970. "The Impossibility of a Paretian Liberal." *Journal of Political Economy,* 78:152–157.

———. 1977. "Rational Fools: A Critique of the Behavioral Foundations of Economic Theory." *Philosophy and Public Affairs,* 6:317–344.

———. 1999. *Development as Freedom.* New York: Knopf.

———. 2005. *Identity and Violence: The Illusion of Destiny.* New York: Norton.

Shipton, Parker. 1989. *Bitter Money: Cultural Economy and Some African Meanings of Forbidden Commodities.* Washington, D.C.: American Anthropological Association.

Sieyès, Emmanuel. 1989. *Qu'est-ce Que le Tiers Etat?* (What Is the Third Estate?) Paris: Presses Universitaires de France. [Originally published in 1789.]

Simon, Herbert. 1955. "A Behavioral Model of Rational Choice." *Quarterly Journal of Economics,* 69:99–118.

———. 1956. "Rational Choice and the Structure of the Environment." *Psychological Review,* 63:129–138.

Slater, Joanna. 2004. "For India's Youth, New Money Fuels a Revolution." *Wall Street Journal,* January 27, p. A1.

Small, Deborah, and George Lowenstein. 2003. "Helping *a* Victim or Helping *the* Victim." *Journal of Risk and Uncertainty,* 26:5–16.

Smith, Adam. 1937. *The Wealth of Nations,* ed. E. Cannan. New York: Modern Library. [Originally published in 1776.]

———. 1982. *The Theory of Moral Sentiments,* ed. D. Raphael and A. Macfie. Indianapolis: Liberty Classics. [Originally published in 1759.]

Smith, Geri, and Cristina Linblad. 2003. "Mexico: Was NAFTA Worth It? A Tale of What Free Trade Can and Cannot Do." *BusinessWeek International Editions,* December 23, p. 34.

Solow, Robert. 1956. "A Contribution to the Theory of Economic Growth." *Quarterly Journal of Economics*, 70:65–94.

Sorby, Kristina. 2002. "Coffee Market Trends." Background paper to World Bank Agricultural Technology Note 30, "Toward More Sustainable Coffee." Washington, D.C.: International Bank for Reconstruction and Development, World Bank.

Stack, Carol. 1975. *All Our Kin: Strategies for Survival in a Black Community*. New York: Harper Colophon.

Stiglitz, Joseph. 1994. *Whither Socialism?* Cambridge, Mass.: MIT Press.

Sugden, Robert. 2004. "The Opportunity Criterion: Consumer Sovereignty without the Assumption of Coherent Preferences." *American Economic Review*, 94:1014–1033.

Summers, Lawrence. 2003. "Morning Prayers, Appleton Chapel, Memorial Church, Harvard University." September 15. http://www.president.harvard.edu/speeches/2003/prayer.html (accessed September 19, 2003).

Swart, Koenraad. 1962. " 'Individualism' in the Mid-Nineteenth Century, 1826–1860." *Journal of the History of Ideas*, 23:77–90.

Taussig, Michael. 1980. *The Devil and Commodity Fetishism in South America*. Chapel Hill: University of North Carolina Press.

Tawney, R. H. 1938. *Religion and the Rise of Capitalism*. London: Penguin. [Originally published in 1926.]

———. 1967. *The Agrarian Problem in the Sixteenth Century*. New York: Harper and Row. [Originally published in 1912.]

Taylor, Fred. 1929. "The Guidance of Production in a Socialist State." *American Economic Review*, 19:1–8.

Taylor, Frederick Winslow. 1967. *The Principles of Scientific Management*. New York: Norton. [Originally published in 1911.]

Taylor, John. 1993. "Discretion vs. Policy Rules in Practice." *Carnegie-Rochester Conference Series on Public Policy*, 39:195–214.

———. 1998. "An Historical Analysis of Monetary Policy Rules." Cambridge, Mass.: National Bureau of Economic Research Working Paper 6768.

Thompson, E. P. 1963. *The Making of the English Working Class*. New York: Random House.

Thomson, William [Baron Kelvin]. 1889. *Popular Lectures and Addresses*, vol. 1. London: Macmillan.

Thrupp, Sylvia. 1989. *The Merchant Class of Medieval London, 1300–1500*. Ann Arbor: University of Michigan Press. [Originally published in 1948.]

Tocqueville, Alexis de. 1969. *Democracy in America*, ed. J. Mayer, trans. G. Lawrence. New York: Doubleday. [Originally published in French, 1835–1840.]

Todorov, Tzvetan. 1984. *The Conquest of America: The Question of the Other*, trans. Richard Howard. New York: Harper & Row. [Originally published in French in 1982.]

Tomsho, Robert. 2000. "Dirt Poor: Colorado Farmers Find Their Water Is Worth More Than Their Crops." *Wall Street Journal*, April 25, p. A1.

Tönnies, Ferdinand. 2001. *Community and Civil Society*, ed. Jose Harris, trans. Jose Harris and Margaret Hollis. Cambridge: Cambridge University Press. [Originally published in German in 1887.]

Toulmin, Stephen. 1990. *Cosmopolis: The Hidden Agenda of Modernity*. New York: Free Press.

Tversky, Amos, and Daniel Kahneman. 1981. "The Framing of Decisions." *Science*, 211:453–458.

Ulrich, Laurel. 1991. *A Midwife's Tale: The Life of Martha Ballard, Based on Her Diary, 1785–1812*. New York: Vintage.

United Nations Development Programme. 2002. *Human Development Report 2002*. New York: Oxford University Press.

Valladolid Rivera, Julio. 1998. "Andean Peasant Agriculture: Nurturing a Diversity of Life in the *Chacra*." In Frédérique Apffel-Marglin with PRATEC, eds., *The Spirit of Regeneration: Andean Culture Confronting Western Notions of Development*. London: Zed Books, pp. 51–88.

Van Kley, Dale. 1996. *The Religious Origins of the French Revolution: From Calvin to the Civil Constitution, 1560–1791*. New Haven, Conn.: Yale University Press.

Varney, Pamela, ed. 1998. *The Sweatshop Quandary: Corporate Responsibility on the Global Frontier*. Washington, D.C.: Investor Responsibility Research Center.

Veblen, Thorstein. 1967. *The Theory of the Leisure Class*. New York: Viking. [Originally published in 1899.]

———. 1990. "The Evolution of the Scientific Point of View." In *The Place of Science in Modern Civilization and Other Essays*. New Brunswick, N.J.: Transaction, pp. 32–55. [Originally published in 1908.]

Vernant, Jean-Pierre. 1982. *Mythe et Pensée chez les Grecs: Études de Psychologie Historique* (Greek Myth and Thought: Studies in Historical Psychology), vol. 2. Paris: Francois Maspero. [Originally published in 1965.]

Vidal-Naquet, Pierre. 1983. *Le Chasseur Noir: Formes de Pensée et Formes de Société dans le Monde Grec* (The Black Hunter: Forms of Thought and Forms of Society in the Greek World). Paris: La Decouverte/Maspero.

von Mises, Ludwig. 1935. "Economic Calculation in the Socialist Commonwealth." In F. Hayek, ed., *Collectivist Economic Planning*. London: Routledge, pp. 87–130. [Originally published in German in 1920.]

von Neumann, John, and Oskar Morgenstern. 1944. *The Theory of Games and Economic Behavior*. Princeton, N.J.: Princeton University Press.

von Weizsäcker, C. Christian. 2002. "Welfare Economics bei Endogenen Präferenzen: Thünen-Vorlesung 2001" (Welfare Economics with Endogenous Preferences: The Thünen Lecture 2001). *Perspektiven der Wirtschaftspolitik*, 3:425–446.

Wall Street Journal. 2004. " 'Benedict Arnold' CEOs." February 12, p. A12.

Walzer, Michael. 1983. *Spheres of Justice: A Defense of Pluralism and Equality*. New York: Basic Books.

Warren, Elizabeth, and Amelia Tyagi. 2003. *The Two-Income Trap: Why Middle-Class Mothers and Fathers Are Going Broke*. New York: Basic Books.

Washington Post. 2002. "Curriculum Guide: Sneaker Supply and Demand." *Inside the Washington Post,* 1, no. 17. http://washpost.com/nielessonplans.nsf/0/ 9F52FEC2D8EDA1DB85256BBF004DEC33/$File/01–137Shoesb.pdf (accessed April 25, 2004).

Watt, Ian. 1996. *Myths of Modern Individualism: Faust, Don Quixote, Don Juan, Robinson Crusoe.* Cambridge: Cambridge University Press.

Weber, Max. 1958. *The Protestant Ethic and the Spirit of Capitalism.* New York: Scribner. [Originally published in German in 1904–1905.]

Weiner, Tim. 2003. "Free Trade Accord at Age 10: The Growing Pains Are Clear." *New York Times,* December 27, p. A-1.

West, Rethel. 1923. *History of Milo, 1802–1923.* Dover-Foxcroft, Maine: Fred Barrows, Printer.

Winthrop, John. 1838. "A Modell of Christian Charity." *Collections of the Massachusetts Historical Society,* Boston, 3rd series, 7:31–48. [Originally delivered as a sermon aboard the *Arbella,* en route from England to America, 1630.]

World Commission on Environment and Development. 1987. *Our Common Future.* Oxford: Oxford University Press

Wrightson, Keith. 2000. *Earthly Necessities: Economic Lives in Early Modern Britain.* New Haven, Conn.: Yale University Press.

Xenos, Nicholas. 1989. *Scarcity & Modernity.* London: Routledge.

Yardley, Jim. 2001. "Well-Off but Still Pressed, Doctor Could Use Tax Cut." *New York Times,* April 7, p. A-1. http://www.nytimes.com/2001/04/07/politics/07TEXA .html?pagewatned=print (accessed April 7, 2001).

Yezer, Anthony, Robert Goldfarb, and Paul Poppen. 1996. "Does Studying Economics Discourage Cooperation? Watch What We Do, Not What We Say or How We Play." *Journal of Economic Perspectives,* 10:177–186.

Zeckhauser, Richard. 1986. "Comments: Behavioral vs. Rational Economics: What You See Is What You Conquer." In Robin Hogarth and Melvin Reder, eds., *Rational Choice: The Contrast between Economics and Psychology.* Chicago: University of Chicago Press, pp. 251–265.

Note on Sources and Permissions

Some of the ideas and text of Chapters 1, 2, 3, and 13 appeared in Stephen Marglin, "Development as Poison: Rethinking the Western Model of Modernity," *Harvard International Review* 25, no. 1 (Spring 2003).

Parts of Chapters 4 and 10 appeared in Stephen Marglin, "Individualism and Scarcity," in *Globalization, Culture, and the Limits of the Market: Essays in Economics and Philosophy*, edited by Stephen Cullenberg and Prasanta Pattanaik (New Delhi: Oxford University Press, 2004). This essay also appeared in French translation as "Individualisme et Rareté," translated by Jean-Pierre Berlan, in *Ordre et Désordres dans l'Économie-Monde*, edited by Pierre Dockès (Paris: Presses Universitaires de France, 2002).

Parts of Chapters 7 and 8 appeared in Stephen Marglin, "Losing Touch: The Cultural Conditions of Worker Accommodation and Resistance," in *Dominating Knowledge: Development, Culture, and Resistance*, edited by Frédérique Apffel Marglin and Stephen Marglin (Oxford: Clarendon Press, 1990), and in Stephen Marglin, "Farmers, Seedsmen, Scientists: Systems of Agriculture and Systems of Knowledge," in *Decolonizing Knowledge: From Development to Dialogue*, edited by Frédérique Apffel-Marglin and Stephen Marglin (Oxford: Clarendon Press, 1996). These essays also appeared in Spanish translation as "Perdiendo el Contacto: Las Condiciones Culturales de la Adaptación y la Resistencia Obreras," and "Agricultores, Semilleristas, y Científicos," in Stephen A. Marglin, *Perdiendo el Contacto: Hacia la Descolonización de la Economía*, translated by Carmen Camacho, Hugo Pereyra, and Jorge Ishizawa (Cochabamba, Bolivia, and Lima, Peru: CAI PACHA and PRATEC, 2000).

Part of Chapter 10 appeared in Stephen Marglin, "How the Economy Is Constructed: On Scarcity and Desire," in *Social Inequality: Values, Growth, and the State*, edited by Andrés Solimano (Ann Arbor: University of Michigan Press, 1998).

Part of Appendix A was originally published under the title "Outsourcing Common Sense" in the *Los Angeles Times*, April 25, 2004.

Permissions: In addition to the permissions listed on the copyright page, I acknowledge permission to quote from the following: John Maynard Keynes, "The General Theory of Employment," *The Quarterly Journal of Economics*, 51:2 (February, © 1937 by the President and Fellows of Harvard College and the Massachusetts Institute of Technology); Paul Krugman, "A Rent Affair," June 7, 2000, and Tim Weiner, "Free Trade Accord at Age 10: Growing Pains Are Clear," December 27, 2003, both originally published in *The New York Times; Honey from the Rock: An Introduction to Jewish Mysticism—Special Anniversary Edition* © 2000 by Lawrence Kushner (Woodstock, VT: Jewish Lights Publishing), p. 70, permission granted by Jewish Lights Publishing, P.O. Box 237, Woodstock, VT 05091, www.jewishlights.com; and Geri Smith and Cristina Lindblad, "Mexico: Was NAFTA Worth It?" *BusinessWeek*, international edition, December 22, 2003. The quotation from Friedrich Hayek is from "The Use of Knowledge in Society," *American Economic Review* 35 (1945): 519–530.

Index